MORE PRAISE FOR
THE FIGHT FOR FIFTEEN

"David Rolf has helped put low-wage workers in Seattle at the forefront of a national movement for a $15 minimum wage; his forward thinking helped paved the way for some of the greatest progress toward addressing our nation's growing income inequality that we've seen in decades."
—Saru Jayaraman, author of *Behind the Kitchen Door* and co-founder of Restaurant Opportunity Centers United

"David Rolf shows that raising the minimum wage to $15 is both just and necessary, lest the American dream of middle-class prosperity turn into a nightmare of enduring poverty for millions of workers in the bottom half of wage earners."
—David Cay Johnston, Pulitzer Prize–winning author of *The Fine Print* and *Free Lunch*

"David Rolf has become the most successful advocate for raising wages in the twenty-first century. Where others talk, David leads, and his book is an inside look at a campaign that has the potential to make work pay again."
—Andy Stern, senior fellow at Columbia University's Richard Paul Richman Center for Business, Law, and Public Policy and former president of the 2.2-million-member SEIU

"David Rolf's first book is a call to action, reminding us that we define what's possible in politics, and that the future of the economy is at stake. If you're interested in what can actually be done about inequality, read this book."
—Ai-jen Poo, director of the National Domestic Workers Alliance and author of *The Age of Dignity: Preparing for the Elder Boom in a Changing America*

David Rolf is the president of SEIU 775 and an international vice president of SEIU. He has led some of the largest organizing efforts since the 1930s, including the successful organization of 74,000 home care aides in Los Angeles and the campaigns to win $15 wages in SeaTac and Seattle. He lives in Seattle.

The Fight
for Fifteen

The Fight for Fifteen

The Right Wage for a Working America

David Rolf

assisted by Corrie Watterson Bryant

THE NEW PRESS

NEW YORK
LONDON

Requests for permission to reproduce selections from this book
should be mailed to: Permissions Department, The New Press,
120 Wall Street, 31st floor, New York, NY 10005.

Published in the United States by The New Press, New York, 2016
Distributed by Perseus Distribution

ISBN 978-1-62097-113-0 (pbk.)
ISBN 978-1-62097-114-7 (e-book)
CIP data available

The New Press publishes books that promote and enrich public discussion and understanding of the issues vital to our democracy and to a more equitable world. These books are made possible by the enthusiasm of our readers; the support of a committed group of donors, large and small; the collaboration of our many partners in the independent media and the not-for-profit sector; booksellers, who often hand-sell New Press books; librarians; and above all by our authors.

www.thenewpress.com

Composition by dix!
This book was set in Electra

Printed in the United States of America

2 4 6 8 10 9 7 5 3 1

There would be no Fight for $15 in America without the courage and leadership of the fast-food workers, airport workers, home care workers, child care workers, and retail workers who have had the courage to walk off the job to protest poverty wages and demand a union. This book is for them.

Contents

Acknowledgments

Thanks, first, to Corrie Watterson Bryant, who took a leave of absence from her job as an SEIU 775 research analyst to do the difficult work of assisting and collaborating with me in all aspects of researching and writing this book; to my editor Marc Favreau, whose idea this book was; to my agent Rafe Sagalyn; and to the great teams at The New Press, ICM/Sagalyn, and SEIU, all of whom supported me through the writing, editing, and publishing process.

SEIU National elected leaders Mary Kay Henry and Mike Fishman, and staff leader Scott Courtney, have provided the nation's most critical leadership in the Fight for $15. SEIU staffers Judy Scott and Inga Skippings generously offered to read and review this book's manuscript and offer suggestions. John Sweeney and Andy Stern passed along a great, growing, and innovative union to today's leaders of SEIU.

SEIU 775 officers Adam Glickman and Sterling Harders were Fight for $15 leaders in their own right in SeaTac and Seattle. Together with the rest of the SEIU 775 executive board and staff, they also allowed me to spend the time necessary to complete this book, even when it meant juggling more responsibilities themselves.

Many public officials helped achieve $15 in SeaTac and in Seattle. In SeaTac this includes Congressman Adam Smith, King County executive Dow Constantine, King County council members Julia Patterson and Dave Upthegrove, State Senator Karen Kaiser, and State Representative Mia Gregerson. In Seattle, this includes Mayor Ed Murray, Seattle City Council members Sally Bagshaw, Tim Burgess, Sally Clark, Jean Godden, Bruce Harrell, Nick Licata, Mike O'Brien, Tom Rasmussen, and Kshama Sawant. Seattle's Income Inequality

Advisory Committee members included co-chair Howard Wright, Janet Ali, Sarah Cherin, Maud Daudon, Craig Dawson, Bob Donegan, David Freiboth, Joe Fugere, Audrey Haberman, Nick Hanauer, Pramila Jayapal, Nicole Vallestero Keenan, Eric Liu, Gordon McHenry, Dave Meinert, Craig Schafer, Diane Sosne, David Watkins, Michael Wells, and Ron Wilkowski. City of Seattle staff and advisers who worked on the $15 wage policy included Brian Surratt, Robert Feldstein, Chris Gregorich, Carlo Caldirola-Davis, and John Howell.

In addition to those already listed, the following low-wage worker activists, leaders, organizers, and campaign advisers each played an important role in fighting for $15 in Seattle and/or SeaTac: Imam Ahmed M. Abdulkadir, Abdirahman Abdullahi, Samatar Abdullahi, Mahad Aden, Ubah Aden, Yusur Aden, Habiba Ali, Tim Allen, Andrew Beane, Sabe Belucnew, Rachel Biru, Reverend Jan Bolerjack, Socrates Bravo, Malcolm Cooper-Suggs, Cary Davis, Caroline Durocher, Eric Frank, Gerald Hankerson, Halimo Harsi, Jason Harvey, Reverend John Helmiere, Carlos Hernandez, Zachary Heim, Alex Hoopes, Dmitri Iglitzin, Sandeep Kaushik, Dan Kully, Sylvia Liang, Don Liberty, Philip Locker, Coulson Loptmann, Lisa McLean, Joe Mizrahi, Abdi Mohamed, Abdirahman H. Mohamed, Molly Moon, Stefan Moritz, Phillip Neel, Nick Norman, Artie Nosrati, Tracy Newman, Binah Palmer, Claudia Paras, Sejal Parikh, Ben Patinkin, Brittany Phelps, Martina Phelps, Memo Rivera, Jonathan Rosenblum, Sergio Salinas, Dave Schmitz, Zach Silk, Christian Sinderman, Leonard Smith, Jess Spear, Ian Stewart, Rich Stolz, Andrew Thibault, Brianna Thomas, Crystal Thompson, Tracey Thompson, Emma Tupper, Erik Van Rossum, Heather Weiner, Hosea Wilcox, Sage Wilson, Liam Wright, and Amirah Ziada.

My friends Nick Hanauer, Denny Heck, Eric Liu, Ai-Jen Poo, and Andy Stern provided the advice and peer pressure necessary to convince me to become an author and to make me not want to give up. My parents, Margo Rolf and Don Rolf, taught me not just to read and write, but to love history and learning. The most important thanks go, with love, to my wife, Kylie.

Introduction

This book is about why Americans should organize to demand a $15-per-hour basic wage. Workers in SeaTac, Seattle, San Francisco, Los Angeles, and other cities have already won $15, while fast-food, home care, child care, retail, airport, and many other workers all around the country are still fighting for a livable wage.

But this is also a book about the larger story of work and workers in America, and how we can save the American Dream.

The United States was hardly a nation born into perfection. At the dawn of the republic, we had slavery, smallpox, short life expectancy, and suffrage restricted to property-owning white males.

But we also had a dream—a dream of liberty and justice for all. And for two hundred years, we passed along more liberty and more justice, always through struggle, to more and more Americans with each passing generation.

There was a time—not long ago—when American workers could expect to join the middle class if they worked hard and to retire after decades of hard work to a modest but secure life. There was a time—not long ago—when Americans could honestly look their kids in the eye and promise that they would enjoy a better life then their parents had had.

That was the essence of the American Dream, now receding into memory for many and at its moment of greatest peril.

FROM POVERTY TO PROSPERITY

I like to think about the story of my maternal grandfather. Rohey Lon "Roy" Hawks was born in 1912 in Virginia, into a family of poor Appalachian farmers and laborers. He had ten siblings. Traveling by buggy and train, the family migrated to Kentucky. His mother died when he was in sixth grade and he dropped out of school to take care of his younger siblings. Roy entered the workforce as a teenager, going to work at a sawmill, earning $1 for a ten-hour shift. As a young adult he worked on his small farm in Barnett's Creek, Kentucky, and earned extra money by sharecropping, training mules, and doing day labor. When work was scarce during the Great Depression he rode boxcars around the country looking for work anywhere he could get hired.

When a steel mill in Cincinnati was hiring, Roy moved the family there, then later went back to rural Kentucky to run a general store. So it went for the 1930s and 1940s. Then, in 1950, he got a job working as an industrial carpenter at a General Motors (GM) automobile plant in Evendale, Ohio. He joined the United Automobile Workers union (UAW). He went on strike three times over the years, walking the union picket line on his assigned shifts and earning pocket money painting his neighbors' houses until the strike ended.

My grandfather saw his pay rise and gained employer-paid health care benefits and a pension. He bought a small home with enough of a yard to plant a garden. GM even paid for a lawyer to write his will, thanks to a provision in the UAW contract that required the company to contribute to a legal service plan for employees.

His two sons served in Korea and Vietnam and then went on to work in factories like their father. His two daughters built careers as a hotel manager and a classroom teacher. He retired from GM after twenty-five years with the company and fifty years in the workforce, but he didn't like being idle. So when his youngest son borrowed enough money to buy a small manufacturing business processing sand and gravel for pet aquariums, Roy went to work there, designing and building industrial equipment until he turned eighty. In his quasi-retirement, he also spent a lot of time at church, with his children and grandchildren, and he stayed active in his union retiree chapter.

Roy died of a heart attack at age eighty-three one morning while he was rototilling his garden. The house and the car were paid for. Between his pension check, Social Security, and the money he and his wife Phinie Mae had saved, there was enough to allow her to continue living at their home until she needed nursing home care, and then to pay for the cost of the nursing home without having to go on Medicaid. After she passed away there was a modest inheritance for their children. All of this was possible on the earnings of a man who had been born into poverty and who spent most of his life as a factory worker.

Roy Hawks was a winner in the American economy, but not because he was well educated, a great innovator, a company founder, an athlete or a performer, or a lottery winner. He worked hard. He was honest, sober, and thrifty. He also worked much of his career with a strong union at a time when the nation was committed to building a strong middle class. And those things made all the difference.

FROM PROSPERITY TO UNCERTAINTY

Today's working class is no less hardworking than Roy Hawks and the tens of millions of other Americans who joined the middle class for the first time in the mid-twentieth century. But today's workers have a lot less going for them. Unions are smaller and weaker than at any time in the past century. Government policy has turned increasingly against working people and in favor of corporations. American corporations themselves have abandoned the mid-twentieth-century ethos of "all boats rise together" in favor of a philosophy of "shareholder value above all," turning against their own employees in their quest for ever-higher share prices and executive compensation.

During Seattle's fight for a $15 minimum wage in 2014, the *Seattle Times* profiled five low-wage workers who were active in supporting the higher minimum wage.[1]

William Thielen, fifty-three, worked two jobs as a housecleaner and a grocery clerk for a combined $27,000 a year. He told the *Times* that he had to declare bankruptcy when he was temporarily laid off during the recession and that he hadn't been able to afford a trip back home to Montana to attend his father's funeral.

Cynthia Vaughn, fifty-eight, was a home care worker who had seen her wages rise from $7.18 to $12.05 under her union contract, but whose own health problems made her physically demanding job of caring for the elderly and disabled particularly challenging. Vaughn couldn't pay all her bills at once, so she would negotiate payment plans she had to save up for the $220 she needed for orthopedic shoes by putting aside a few dollars each month.

Crystal Thompson, thirty-three, made the state minimum wage of $9.32 at Domino's Pizza and shared a one-bedroom apartment with her seven-year old son, who slept on the living room couch. With unpredictable work hours, Thompson said she couldn't afford to give her son money to buy books at the school book fair or send him to summer camp. She couldn't afford a car. She was reluctant to let her son play outside in her high-crime neighborhood.

Sarah Evanson-Isaac, thirty-seven, was a deli clerk and cook making $12.70 an hour. She had spent time in homeless shelters after divorcing and taking on $200,000 in student loan debt from the law degree she could almost afford to finish. Evanson-Isaac shared a bunk bed with her nine-year-old daughter and for a while lived in a shared basement apartment where the heat never climbed above fifty-five degrees.

Carlos Trujillo, forty-four, a janitor at Amazon.com earning $12.60 an hour, was unable to afford an apartment of his own for himself and his two children, instead sharing a small house with his sister and her daughter. Trujillo rationed gas money $10 at a time and couldn't pay for after-school care for his daughter or repairs for his truck, much less save for his daughter's college education.[2]

William, Cynthia, Crystal, Sarah, and Carlos are just like thousands of other workers I've met during nearly a quarter century of work as a union organizer and labor leader. They are just as good-natured, hardworking, and honest as the blue-collar workers of my grandfather's generation. But they were born at the wrong time, when both the employment contract and the social contract that helped create the middle class are eroding.

Fifteen years into the new millennium, our nation has reached a strategic inflection point. Most Americans are no longer getting ahead. Jobs are changing for the worse. Inequality—the percentage difference in income and wealth between the wealthiest and the rest of us—is approaching Third World levels. This vast inequality distorts the decisions our nation makes, tilting the playing field ever more toward the very rich. A solid middle class can build a civic life, participate in politics, and think about the future. A nation of struggling poor people cannot. By every measure we are not a poor nation—we are the richest in the world. And yet our middle class is shrinking, our wages are flat, and more and more of our nation's families are falling behind rather than getting ahead.

LOOKING AHEAD

We can begin to build a different future for our nation by starting in the easiest place: raising the minimum wage to a livable level. No other mechanism is as effective or as fast. Deep change requires generations of effort, and we should commit ourselves to those changes—tackling embedded racial and gender inequity, rebuilding our neglected infrastructure, revitalizing our educational system, building new forms of worker bargaining power. But we can't let a generation of American prosperity slip by while we wait.

This book is also about not being able to wait for basic economic opportunity, to pay the rent, to get off food stamps, to pay an unexpected doctor's bill, to have dinner with our families at night, or for the next generation to have a shot at the American Dream.

This book will cover:

- How Americans fought for and created the world's biggest middle class, but then fell victim to a war on American workers during the past forty years;
- How current trends point to an emerging future of work that is even less secure than the fissured employment relationship we are experiencing today;
- How American workers have been organizing and fighting back over the past two decades;
- How the little city of SeaTac, Washington, pioneered a $15 wage for airport, transportation, and hospitality workers by popular vote in 2013;
- How Seattle workers won the nation's first true $15 minimum wage in 2014;

- Why $15 is the right wage for a working America;
- Why opponents of minimum wage increases misunderstand how the economy works and how trickle-down economics has failed America;
- What, in addition to minimum-wage increases, we need to do as a nation to rebuild a strong middle class for the twenty-first century.

We were born a nation with high ideals of justice, freedom, opportunity, and yes—happiness. We have chased the American Dream across the generations, over the oceans, to the West, onto farms, into factories, through the Civil War, on union picket lines, in struggles for voting rights, and now into the technological future. Today we are experiencing one of the most profound and in many ways exciting moments of social and economic transformation in human history. But it is one in which the economics and politics of our nation have tilted away from "justice for all" and toward the enrichment of a powerful few at the expense of the productive many.

This is the moment we can't miss, the chance to link the vast gains from technology, a globally connected economy, and an ever more highly educated workforce to a more shared and inclusive prosperity, one that will support economic innovation and social stability far into the future.

Building a more inclusive prosperity won't be easy, but there are already signs that we can succeed. Workers eager for change have sparked new movements and new ways of organizing, showing that it's possible for ordinary people to improve their wages, their work, and their workplaces, even as the old model of labor unionism fades. And in the void left by a conflicted and ineffective federal government, cities and states all over the country are taking up the gauntlet and legislating the will of the American people: higher wages.

American workers do not *deserve* to make low wages, and a disappearing middle class is not inevitable. It is a choice, and we should make a different one.

The Fight
for Fifteen

1

America at 200

The American Dream Versus
the War on the Middle Class

Imagine an alternative history of the 1976 presidential election. America is celebrating its bicentennial with fireworks, and two men— a Republican from Michigan and a Democrat from Georgia—are campaigning to be president. What if one of them had given a speech that predicted the future?

> My fellow Americans, this difficult decade will soon come to an end. The national hangover from Vietnam and Watergate will slowly fade. There will be no more lines for gasoline, no more stagflation. In fact, soon the Berlin Wall will crumble, the Cold War will end, the nuclear threat will recede, and there will be no more foreign military threats to our soil. The last of the formal legal barriers to full economic participation for women and people of color will fall. China, Korea, Brazil, India, and South Africa will join the global economic community and lift hundreds of millions of people out of life-threatening poverty.
>
> Americans will invent or reinvent industries that will create more wealth than has been created in the history of human kind. Technology will dramatically improve the lives of almost all Americans and most people around the globe. And America will continue to be the world's wealthiest nation with the most productive workers.

That would have been an incredible, truly astounding, set of predictions, all of which, as it turns out, would have come true. But imagine that the speech continued:

Of all of the new wealth our country produces, 95 percent will go to the top 1 percent of income earners. A few hundred wealthy families will amass more wealth than the bottom 50 percent of households combined. The bottom 80–90 percent won't see a penny of increased income, and in fact the bottom 50 percent will have to take a pay cut. We are going to export manufacturing, import Third-World wages, divest from our infrastructure, de-tax, deregulate, globalize, and privatize.

We are going to break the unions, bankrupt our pension system, shred the funding for rural and urban public education, and make debt-free college a thing of the past. We will turn our backs on the middle class and replace old Jim Crow laws with a new economic apartheid for black and brown Americans. The net economic impact of women doubling their workforce participation from 1977–2012 will be zero dollars in take-home pay for the bottom 90 percent of income-earning families. So the same family that can live a reasonably comfortable middle-class life on a single person's income today will need two or even three incomes to live the same life a generation from now.

Obviously, giving such a speech would have doomed anyone's presidential candidacy. His party probably would have been out of power for years. No one in America would have voted for such a vision. And yet, just like the optimistic first part, that second part of our fictional presidential campaign speech would also turn out to be true. And it became true not because of some historical accident, but because our economic system was intentionally rigged to favor large corporations and wealthy Americans over everyone else. "Trickle-down economics" was woven into the national consciousness as if it were written into the founding documents of our country. Two hundred years of struggle and progress have been intentionally reversed over the course of the past forty years. If a foreign power had announced that was its plan for America, we would have gone to war.

WHERE WE STOOD AT AGE 200: WORLD'S LARGEST MIDDLE CLASS AND AN INCREASINGLY ACCESSIBLE AMERICAN DREAM

By America's two hundredth birthday, we had created a nation in which workers shared the benefits of a growing economy. For much of the twentieth century, the United States experienced high levels of growth *and* rising levels of equality, a combination that "confounded historical precedent and the theories of conservative economists."[1] Incomes grew rapidly and at roughly the same rate up and down the income ladder, doubling between the late 1940s and early 1970s.[2] The poorest fifth of households, in fact, saw faster growth than other groups—while the top 5 percent saw the slowest.[3]

As worker productivity increased, so did wages: a worker in 1973 was almost twice as productive as in 1948 and earned nearly twice as much.[4] The result was that the bottom 90 percent of families reaped more than two-thirds of the gains during this period, up from only 16 percent in the early 1930s.

Driven by strong labor, civil rights, and antipoverty movements, and by constant pressure to show that American capitalism functioned better than Soviet communism, politicians of the time kept expanding economically inclusive policies. During his 1960 presidential campaign, John F. Kennedy said he would accelerate economic growth by increasing government spending and cutting taxes. He advocated for medical help for the aged, aid for inner cities, and increased funding for education. Congress enacted much of his policy agenda after his death in 1963.

Kennedy's successor Lyndon Johnson sought to build a "Great Society" by expanding the benefits of America's thriving economy to more citizens. Federal spending increased dramatically, as the government launched such new programs as Medicare, food stamps for the poor, and a host of initiatives to increase the quality of education and make college more affordable.

Here is a picture of America at the peak of our prosperity:

- In 1980, Americans at every level (except the 5th percentile) had the highest incomes in the world.[5]

- The share of total income going to the top 1 percent of earners fell to a historic low of 8 percent in the 1960s and 1970s, with income inequality hitting its low point in 1968.[6]
- In the late 1960s, more than half of households were squarely middle class by income, earning $35,000 to $100,000 a year in today's dollars.[7]
- In 1970 two-thirds of families lived in middle-income neighborhoods.[8]
- By the 1950s, nearly 85 percent of American teenagers were attending high school full-time, compared to less than 20 percent of teenagers in most European nations.[9]
- Black poverty declined dramatically through the 1960s, falling from a rate of 55 percent in 1959 to 32 percent ten years later.[10]
- By 1973, the share of all Americans living in poverty bottomed out at a historic low of 11 percent, having been cut in half in just fifteen years.

Our tax policy supported these widely shared gains; a report by the International Labour Organization and World Trade Organization found that the inequality prevalent before World War II did not rebound afterward due to the introduction of progressive taxation and estate taxes.[11]

The heads of many corporations believed that their workers mattered, and that they had a responsibility to treat them fairly. "Maximizing employee security is a prime company goal," said General Electric's manager of employee benefits in 1962.[12] Whether such sentiments were heartfelt or merely a reflection of the social and cultural norms of the times, they helped.

We were beginning to see success in the civil rights and feminist movements, as African Americans and women demanded and won real progress in labor force participation, wages, and job opportunities.

We arrived at this moment with a great American Dream unfolding, and not because it was handed to us—generations of workers had fought hard for shared prosperity, and both companies and politicians had responded. Most Americans held the view that we had the best economic system in the world, and the eventual collapse of the Soviet Union seemed to prove it. We were number one.

THE WAR ON THE MIDDLE CLASS: 1976–PRESENT

And then the dream began to unravel. At the same time the War on Poverty was beginning to give people a shot at the middle class, a new War on the Middle Class began, which would eventually pull the rug out from under American families. Even while civil rights and women's movements were establishing new expectations of equality, a radical new strain of laissez-faire capitalism was establishing its dominance in economics, business, and politics.

Most people were first exposed to these ideas when Ronald Reagan became president, when they were told that what they had long believed was the road to prosperity—good wages, strong unions, sensible regulations, and a reasonable safety net—was actually the road to ruin. They were told that prosperity instead "trickled down" to workers from the "job creators" in big business, and that they should be grateful to these powerful and beneficent institutions for their jobs, opportunities, and middle-class lifestyles. The American public, feeling burned by high inflation and unemployment, began to accept this narrative and the antigovernment, pro–big business agenda that came with it. Many working-class Americans—often white, male, older, or southern—also responded with discomfort to increasing racial and gender equality by voting against their own pocketbook interests for politicians who appealed overtly or more subtly to racism and sexism.

So, beginning in the 1980s, financiers and corporate leaders began to achieve their long-sought goal of returning to the "opportunity" of the Gilded Age, freed from unions and government regulation. Americans were told that wealth would trickle down to regular families, with everyone sharing a bigger piece of a bigger pie. As part of the new "market fundamentalism," we were told that markets were basically infallible, and government tinkering could only distort the economy and impede economic growth. The unregulated market began to be seen as fundamentally beneficent and government as the enemy of growth.

As the financial sector soared in the 1980s, these beliefs crystallized into a cultural sensation. One of the more memorable movie moments of the decade was a monologue by *Wall Street*'s Gordon Gekko: "Greed . . . is good. Greed is right. Greed works. . . . And greed—you

mark my words—will not only save [this company], but that other mal-
functioning corporation called the USA!"

The speech, which director Oliver Stone intended as satire of what
he saw as ruling-class selfishness in the Reagan era, instead frequently
drew raucous cheers from movie audiences. Big business lobbying
groups and public relations campaigns had convinced many Americans that the principle of considered self-interest could, indeed, empower individuals, liberate companies, and restore the faded luster of
the United States. "Greed is good" became a kind of de facto motto
for 1980s America.

According to the new zeitgeist, the wolves of Wall Street weren't
dangerous. They had sharp teeth, but we would all benefit from their
kills. Plus if you worked hard, you too could be a wolf. Americans
began to believe these new stories and glorify extreme wealth with a
fervor that was shared by everyone from conservative preachers to the
president, from *Wall Street* to Madonna as the Material Girl, throwing
money in the air.

It is now thirty years later, and we have seen a savings and loan
crisis, wild interest rate spikes, a couple of housing busts, a few major bubbles, two recessions and a third that was more like a depression. It is obvious that—though the belief that greed is good may have
mellowed—those stories are still driving our basic economic agreements as a society. And it has begun to destroy us.

The American economy no longer works for most people in the
United States. We know this from a raft of economic data showing the
trends: a small percentage of the population reaps the lion's share of
economic growth while most workers face weak job prospects, stagnant wages, and increasing financial strain as the cost of education,
housing, and health care grow ever more expensive.

America has long been a beacon of economic opportunity to the
world, a place where anyone can achieve success through hard work.
But today the United States lags behind most other developed nations
in levels of inequality and economic mobility. Deeply rooted structural discrimination continues to hold down women and people of
color, and more than one-fifth of all American children now live in
poverty.

So how could so many important people be so wrong about how

the economy fundamentally works? Perhaps because the storytellers behind the curtain had an incredible incentive for selling their theories to all of us, doing with rhetoric what could not be done with force. The point of foisting trickle-down economics, deregulation, and union busting on the American public was never to share the gains with regular workers. It was to turn the economy into a wealth-generating machine for the people who already had the most.

The rosy stories of trickle-down economics were mostly make-believe, but one part was real: the wolf of Wall Street, which by the Great Recession was emboldened enough to come for our middle-class jobs, our homes, and our retirement savings. Over the past thirty-five years, America's policy choices have been grounded in false assumptions. But inequality is not inevitable: it is a choice we make that follows from how we structure our economy. The rise of a strong middle class in the United States was not an accident, and its decline was not an accident either.

Working Americans built the middle class by shaping the political process to produce shared prosperity and economic security, by building unions and bargaining collectively with their employers, by pressing for better wages, better working conditions, and better benefits. And when the clout of the middle class and labor unions declined, starting in earnest in the late 1970s as business mobilized on a scale never before seen and money became more and more important in politics—the middle-class share of national income declined as well.

The current moment is one of reckoning, of acknowledging that we are casualties in a multi-decade war on American workers. Of realizing that we've been had.

THE WIDEST WEALTH GAP ON RECORD

The wealth gap is one of the starkest measures of this war's twisted success. Wealth is not merely income, but also includes a household's savings, home equity, investments, and debts. As pointed out by economists Emmanuel Saez and Gabriel Zucman, U.S. wealth concentration has followed a "U-shaped" evolution over the past hundred years: high in the beginning of the twentieth century, falling from 1929 to 1978, and increasing continuously since then.

The share of wealth owned by the middle class followed the inverse pattern: increasing from the early 1930s to the 1980s, peaking in the mid-1980s, and declining since then.[13] Saez and Zucman find that:

- The top 1 percent—1.6 million families with net assets above $4 million—now control 42 percent of total household wealth.
- The next 9 percent of families, each with a net worth between $660,000 and $4 million, hold 35 percent of total household wealth.
- The bottom 90 percent of families now hold an average of $84,000 in wealth, representing only 23 percent of total American household wealth.

The last time our nation saw wealth concentration like this, we were headed into the Great Depression.

But post-Depression financial regulation sharply limited the Gilded Age model of the fabulously wealthy financial-industrial baron. New Deal legislation stabilized the economy and reduced wealth concentration for more than fifty years. As these policies were reversed from the 1970s through the 2000s, the average wealth of the top 1 percent began to grow again, at an average rate of 8 percent per year.[14] By 2012, the wealth share of the top 0.1 percent was close to the 1916 and 1929 peaks, and three times higher than in the late 1970s.

These trends accelerated markedly during the Great Recession of 2007–9, as the gains from the recovery flowed almost exclusively to the richest Americans. From 2009 to 2011 alone, the mean wealth of the top 8 million households rose 22 percent, while the remaining households actually saw a *reduction* in household wealth. Eight million households now control more than $3 million in wealth per household, while the rest hold about $140,000 each. The top households gained $5.6 trillion in two years, while the bottom 90 percent lost $600 billion.[15] The trend of wealth flowing to the top holds even as we zoom in on the earnings of the 1 percent—the lion's share of gains have gone to the top tenth of one percent. Fewer than 200,000 families now control 22 percent of all American household wealth, enjoying estates ranging from $20 million and rising into the billions.

The aftermath of the Great Depression featured New Deal programs that aimed to correct the issues that had caused the crash and to mitigate its effects—including financial sector regulation, programs to directly create jobs, and new policies to distribute wealth more evenly. But the Great Recession sputtered out with only a single major progressive legislative accomplishment (health care reform) while the government bailed out Wall Street, insurance companies, banks, and automobile manufacturers. In the wake of the recession, the bottom 90 percent found their home equity lost or devalued and a weak labor market that didn't allow them to fully recover to even their mediocre prerecession baseline. Research shows that one of the primary drivers behind the decline of the bottom 90 percent has been the evisceration of home equity, formerly the bastion of middle-class security along with pensions, which have also been slashed.[16]

At the same time, the stock and bond markets rallied, and because affluent households typically have their assets concentrated in stocks and other financial holdings, the wealthiest households walked away much richer while the rest were left behind. And, in fact, less affluent households even saw a reduction in their stock investments—fewer directly owned stocks and mutual fund shares in 2011 (13 percent) than in 2009 (16 percent), meaning a smaller share enjoyed the fruits of the stock market rally.[17]

Saez and Zucman also found that the wealthy are saving far more than other earners, while their investments are producing high returns that further drive a wedge between them and other workers: "Income inequality has a snowballing effect on the wealth distribution," they said. Top earners invest a lot of their money, which drives up their wealth, which leads to more capital investment, contributing more to their incomes in the form of capital gains. "Our core finding," Saez said, "is that this snowballing effect has been sufficiently powerful to dramatically affect the shape of the US wealth distribution over the last 30 years." More proof? Wealth today is ten times more concentrated than income, owing to the snowball effect of investment and capital gains.[18]

Most Americans have no idea how wealthy "the other half" really is. As economist Thomas Piketty suggests, "wealth is so concentrated that a large segment of society is virtually unaware of its existence, so that some people imagine that it belongs to surreal or mysterious entities."[19] Yet four hundred families really do have more wealth than half of all Americans combined, and these are not people that you will ever meet or even see on television. They also pay less than 17 percent of their adjusted gross income in taxes—far below the rate for middle-class earners. Why? Because much of their income comes in the form of capital gains from investment, which are taxed at much lower rates than wage income.[20]

GIANT AND GROWING INCOME GAP

And then we have income inequality, the buzzword of our modern economic discontent. Piketty, famous for his groundbreaking work on inequality, *Capital in the Twenty-First Century*, said that the current level of income inequality in the United States "is probably higher than in any other society at any time in the past, anywhere in the world, including societies in which skill disparities were extremely large."[21]

The by now well-established spike of wealth at the top is due not only to capital gains by stock market investors but also to a surge in top incomes. Since 1980, the average income of the 1 percent has shot up more than 175 percent, and the 1 percent has captured virtually all postrecession income gains. As Piketty and Emmanuel Saez report, 95 percent of all income growth between 2009 and 2012 went to the top 1 percent.[22] As with wealth, the majority of the income gains went to the extreme upper-end earners, the 0.1 percent and corporate executives in particular.[23]

Extraordinary executive pay increases have been a major driver in doubling the income shares of the 1 percent and 0.1 percent over the past thirty years.[24] From 1978 to 2013, CEO compensation increased an astonishing 937 percent, a rise more than double the stock market growth over the same period.[25] The skyrocketing pay received by CEOs of large firms has also pulled up the pay of other one-percenters—including their fellow executives and managers.

The "labor share," or how much of the economic pie goes to all workers, has declined, while the owners of capital are getting a bigger share of gross domestic product (GDP) than they were before. A particularly jarring example: it would take a million hours of work for the typical McDonald's crew member to earn what the company's CEO took home last year—a gap that has doubled in the past decade.

Figure 1.1: Most income gains have gone to extreme upper-end earners

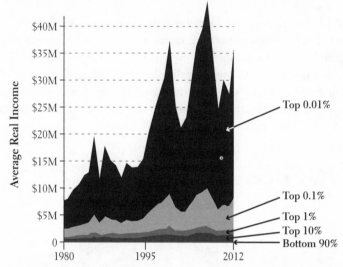

Source: Dave Gilson, "Chart: It's Never Been a Better Time to Be Rich," *Mother Jones*, September 25, 2014.

Since 1980, total compensation has fallen as a share of national income by 6 percent, while corporate profits are up by 5 percent. Corporate profits in 2013 comprised the highest share of national income ever, while *employee compensation as a share of national income is at its lowest point since 1951.*[26]

Zooming in on compensation paints an even bleaker picture. The Levy Economics Institute at Bard College found that the top 1 percent is taking a much bigger piece of the income pie as "financial and top incomes grew tremendously at the expense of labor compensation."[27] And the gains diverted from the 99 percent to the 1 percent? $1.8 trillion of net national income in 2012 alone.[28] The trend is similar in Europe and Japan.

Robert H. Frank, an economist at Cornell University and the

author of *The Winner-Take-All Society*, explains that across most white-collar professions—whether dentists or sales supervisors—a very small group at the top is doing spectacularly well even as the great majority is mostly plugging along. "No matter who you are, whatever group you define yourself in terms of, you're poorer now in relative terms than you were earlier," he said.[29]

Black Americans have been hit particularly hard by these trends and, as Joseph Stiglitz observed, racial disparities drive a particularly deep and intractable wedge between the haves and the have-nots: "Racial discrimination—through legalized segregation in the nineteenth and first half of the twentieth century and through the de facto segregation and discrimination that persist today—is a clear driver of economic inequality in the United States."[30]

Figure 1.2: For the first time in 100 years, the top 10% are earning more than half of the nation's income

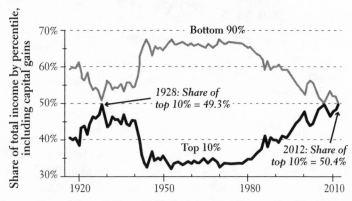

Source: Dave Gilson, "Chart: Half of All Income Goes to the Top 10 Percent," *Mother Jones*, September 30, 2014.

At the same time that top incomes have been soaring, the proportion of total income held by low- and middle-income people has declined by more than a percentage point each year between 1979 and 2011.[31] That's a seriously unhealthy trend. But what if the middle class were doing as well as the 1 percent? What if our household incomes had grown at the same rate? The Economic Policy Institute found that the answer was a healthy income of $156,318 per household. Instead, the average household between the 20th and 80th income percentiles makes less than half that: $72,036, up only 17 percent from 1979.[32]

The net result of increases at the top and stagnation for the rest? Income inequality is reaching the most extreme levels in American history. Against a backdrop of fairly steady economic growth, the richest Americans have raced ahead while the rest are stalled. For the first time in a hundred years, the top 10 percent are earning more than half the nation's income—due to rise to 60 percent if current trends continue.

Not encouragingly, the share of income earned by the 1 percent now most resembles the period just before the Great Depression.[33]

Figure 1.3: Share of income earned by the 1 percent

1774	7% (includes slaves)
1860	10% (includes slaves)
1929	22%
1960	10%
2012	22%

Inequality has impacts that reach far beyond the bank account— high levels of inequality are correlated with a multitude of social problems, from poor mental and physical health to diminished class mobility, reduced participation in civic and democratic life, and eroding social cohesion. Inequality also threatens economic growth. Even financial institutions such as Standard & Poor's (occasionally) get it:

"Inequality may heighten the susceptibility of an economy to booms and busts" and "may also spur political instability—thus discouraging investment. The affluent may exercise disproportionate influence on the political process, or the needs of the less affluent may grow so severe as to make additional cuts to fiscal stabilizers that operate automatically in a downturn politically unviable."[34]

Other advanced nations are not experiencing the income inequality at the levels we are. As Joseph Stiglitz said, "America now lags behind any country in the old, ossified Europe that President George W. Bush used to deride. Among our closest counterparts are Russia with its oligarchs and Iran."[35] And while rising economies like China and Brazil have been investing in raising up their poorest citizens, we have not taken similarly aggressive steps.

Though most people are comfortable with *some* level of income inequality, and believe that entrepreneurial risk taking and innovation should be rewarded, almost nobody thinks these levels of income inequality are ideal. A Harvard Business School study showed that when asked to choose their ideal distribution of wealth, 92 percent of those surveyed chose a distribution that was *more equitable* than our current condition.[36] The same study showed that Americans generally think the income distribution is far more balanced than it actually is.[37]

Even some conservative Republicans are starting to understand that income inequality is bad for our country. Alan Greenspan, an ardent advocate of free markets, has recognized inequality as a fundamental threat to our economic system and admits that, "You cannot have the benefits of capitalist market growth without the support of a significant proportion, and indeed, virtually all of the people; and if you have an increasing sense that the rewards of capitalism are being distributed unjustly the system will not stand."[38]

STAGNANT INCOME AND WAGES FOR THE BOTTOM 90 PERCENT

While wealth accumulation at the top is being driven by lavish executive pay and capital gains, families at the middle and bottom are experiencing stagnant wages and disappearing middle-wage jobs. Wage growth has flatlined for a generation—hourly wages for most workers increased a mere 0.1 percent per year on average since 1980, and between 2000 and 2013 the median family income actually *decreased* by 7 percent despite a 65 percent increase in worker productivity over the same period.[39]

Thirty years of wage stagnation was not inevitable, especially during periods of soaring economic growth. It means that someone else took the money that could have gone to the middle class. Middle-income workers earn no more now than they did in the late 1970s, while those in the lower-wage cohort have lost ground, a trend that has accelerated since the Great Recession. Overall, private sector workers have seen their compensation *fall* since 2010.[40] Even arch-conservative U.S. senator Ted Cruz acknowledged this reality: "You want to talk about what's making life hard for working men and women, [it's] wage stagnation," he said.[41]

The downward wage pressure on middle-wage workers is worsened by changes in the economy that tilt the share of jobs away from middle-wage jobs and toward lower-paying ones. During the Great Recession, high- and middle-wage jobs were the hardest hit, while the recovery brought back jobs—but a disproportionately high number of them were low-wage.[42] Americans aren't less skilled or less educated than in 2009, but they are now all too often forced to accept jobs that are more poorly paid. Things haven't been as bad in other developed nations, most of which have seen slow income growth over the past decades. The United States is at the bottom of international rankings of income growth.[43]

The value of the minimum wage has also eroded. The minimum wage is a big factor not just for those who earn it, but for U.S. wage growth as a whole because it sets a salary floor. In order to maintain a ladder of different wage levels inside a company, the firm will raise other, higher-paid workers' salaries when the minimum wage increases. Congress hasn't raised the minimum wage enough to compensate for inflation, let alone the increased cost of living. So the purchasing power of the minimum wage has declined over time.

The eroding minimum wage contributes to a growing gap between wage earners at the bottom and those in the middle—a gap that grew by 18 percent from 1979 to 2011 and explains much of the wage gap between low and middle earners.[44] In other words, there are two gaps opening up—the one between the very top earners and everyone else, and the one between the lowest earners and the middle earners.

Low-wage earners are actually being paid less now than they were before in 2009; the wages of the lowest-paid workers have declined by 6 percent.[45] It is also becoming increasingly difficult to put together a full-time schedule at many low-wage jobs, particularly in fast food and retail. While many middle-class workers are finding that their job obligations are creeping into free time and family time, low-wage workers have seen hours cut due to a weak job market, causing underemployment (employment below the level that an employee's skills and education would qualify her for, if employers had to compete for employees). Taken together, the unemployed and the underemployed total a depressing 11 percent of the workforce, or 17.5 million workers. The total un- and underemployment rate is much higher in many states—at or above 15 percent in Arizona, California, and Nevada.[46]

Low-wage families with children are facing particular hardship. Since 1975, the poorest third of children have experienced a *decline* in family income. The top third of children, on the other hand, live in families whose incomes have risen from 25 to more than 100 percent during the same period. Income inequality doesn't just affect workers—it begins in the cradle.[47]

Adding to the difficulty, three in five American workers are paid by the hour, a situation made more precarious by the advent of new technology that allows employers to micro-adjust workers' schedules to match the ebb and flow of customer demand. Workers are often sent home without pay if there isn't enough work, or required to be on call 24/7 but scheduled for only fifteen or twenty hours per week—few enough to keep employees under the level that would require paid overtime or qualify them for an employer-paid health care plan.[48]

Slow household-income growth is especially disturbing when we consider that households are working far more hours than they were thirty years ago, mostly because more women are now in the workforce. The share of American mothers who work full-time, year-round, rose from 27 to 46 percent over the past thirty-five years. In addition, the median annual hours worked by women rose by 739 hours per year—the equivalent of eighteen additional forty-hour workweeks per person.

THE SHRINKING MIDDLE CLASS

All of these trends are conspiring to shrink the middle class, as workers increasingly fall into two categories: low income versus high income, unpredictably scheduled hourly versus full-time, positions protected by employment law versus those that are not. The share of Americans that count as middle income has been shrinking for several decades.

In the final decades of the twentieth century, the middle class (households making between $35,000 and $100,000 a year) shrank a bit as more Americans moved up the economic ladder. But since 2000, the middle class has been dwindling for a more alarming reason: the great twenty-first-century wage slowdown has shrunk family incomes, and middle earners are now falling into the lower tier rather than climbing up.[49] This is historic.[50]

Even many middle-income earners have been losing ground and are functionally no longer middle class. A middle-earning American family makes slightly less than such a family did fifteen years ago. If the median household income had kept pace with the productivity of the economy since 1970, it would now be nearly $92,000, not $50,000.[51] As Rakesh Kochhar of Pew Charitable Trusts said of declining median wages, "Middle income is not necessarily the same thing as middle class"[52]

The American Dream has always included the idea that if we work hard, we can do better than our parents did, and the next generation better than us. But younger households, headed by people thirty through forty-four years old, are more likely to be lower income today than in 2000.[53] And young adults under thirty-five actually earn less today than their parents did in 1980.[54] That's why for young adults the contrast with their parents' and grandparents' generation can be hard to stomach—it's not just flat wages that are the problem, it's losing their grip on progress.

Even higher education is no longer a near-guarantee of middle-class security: college graduates are less likely to be middle or high income than they were in 2000. And a high school diploma in the 1970s meant that you would at least have a good shot at making a middle income— but the decline of high-paying blue-collar jobs has changed all that.[55] Many of the cities with the biggest declines in median income, like Detroit, Cleveland, Flint, and Toledo, were industrial hubs that were crushed by the demise of manufacturing employment.

The gap between whites and blacks and Hispanics has also widened over the past fifteen years. Half of black households and 43 percent of Hispanic households were already lower income in 2000, and 5 percent more black and Hispanic households have fallen out of the middle class today.

UNIONS IN DECLINE

Unions were instrumental in creating the American middle class, and today they continue to empower millions of Americans to bargain for wages and benefits that are capable of sustaining a middle-class standard of living. Among workers in similar jobs, unionized employees are significantly more likely to earn middle-class wages and to have sick, family, and vacation leave policies, health care, and retirement plans. Unions also improve wages and job quality even for those who are not members; in areas and industries with a high degree of union representation, unions exert upward pressure on industry standards across the board.

Collective bargaining is an important contributor to inclusiveness in advanced economies. According to the Center for American Progress, "in the United States, it plays a significant role in reducing wage inequality." As the number of unionized Americans went up, so did wages, as well as health benefits, pensions, and vacation time.

The wage premium earned by union members can be substantial and tends to be higher for low- and middle-income workers. Even today, despite the weakness of organized labor, median weekly earnings for unionized workers are about $200—or 27 percent—more than for nonunion workers.[56] Among workers who have never graduated high school or hold only a high school degree, employees with the protection of collective bargaining agreements earn 30 percent more than employees without them.[57] Unionized workers are also 28 percent more likely to be covered by employer-provided health insurance and 54 percent more likely to have employer-provided pensions. For people of color, unions provide an even more significant benefit than for whites, helping to close racial wage gaps; Hispanic and black men secure the highest wage advantages from unionism, followed by Hispanic and black women.[58]

Unions help workers earn more money, and they know it. Surveys show that 53 percent of nonmanagerial, nonunion workers say they would likely vote for a union in their workplace. Yet worker power declined steadily throughout the second half of the twentieth century, and continues to drop year after year. The data seem to indicate that there is a tipping point for unionization to exert a big influence on wages and working conditions—and beginning in the 1980s, we tipped over to the wrong side.

Though unionization rates initially began to drop in the 1950s, by the 1970s the union membership rate (or "union density") was still more than 25 percent of all workers and the number of union members was at its highest point in history. [59] In 1983, union density had dropped to 20 percent, with about 18 million union workers. By 2014, it was just 11 percent, with 15 million union members.

Union density is much higher in the public sector (36 percent) than the private sector, where it's less than 7 percent—the lowest rate in modern history and approximately what it was prior to any modern labor laws and before the birth of most of today's largest unions. The absolute number of private sector workers in unions is now half of what it was in the late 1970s.[60] While other advanced nations have also seen declines in unionization, few have been as dramatic as ours. Among OECD nations, union density averages 28 percent, compared to 11 percent here.

A watershed moment came in 1978, when the U.S. Chamber of Commerce blocked labor law reform legislation that had the personal support of President Jimmy Carter. Business historian Kim McQuaid called 1978 the "Waterloo" for unions. There began labor's noticeable decline in power and the soon-to-be-noticeable decline in the power of American workers to demand their share of the nation's wealth.

As Kevin Drum of *Mother Jones* said of this legislative defeat, "Organized labor, already in trouble thanks to stagflation, globalization, and the decay of manufacturing, now went into a death spiral. That decline led to a decline in the power of the Democratic Party, which in turn led to fewer protections for unions. Rinse and repeat. By the time both sides realized what had happened, it was too late—union density had slumped below the point of no return."[61]

Unions have gone into serious decline because the world in which today's unions grew and thrived has largely disappeared. And, for a variety of legal, cultural, and political reasons, today's unions have been unable to innovate or adapt. There are now many more workers who have *no legal right* at all to form a union than there are workers with a union. This includes everyone from low-wage "supervisors" at fast-food chains to registered nurses in many nursing homes, to millions of workers with no fixed employment relationship (contract, contingent, temporary, freelance, and guest workers), to public sector workers in the South and Southwest, and farmworkers in forty-nine states. And this doesn't even include the workers for whom organizing is a practical, if not legal, impossibility—those who work for small businesses, those who live in the greater part of the country where unions are no longer organizing at all, or those who work in industries with no established union.

In cases where workers are eligible to organize labor unions, the rules governing union elections have been so narrowed and tilted in favor of employers that companies have strong incentives to engage in antiunion activity. The union avoidance industry helps businesses keep unions out of their workforce, while hundreds of right-wing publications and media outlets promote viscerally antiunion views. Antiunion think tanks and legal foundations exist in nearly every state, and thousands of national, state, and local business associations lobby against any pro-worker legislation and policies. When unions have tried to pass stronger laws protecting workers' right to organize, they have been defeated again and again. By 2004, the situation had deteriorated so much that a global human rights investigatory group, Human Rights Watch, reported that "freedom of association is a right under severe, often buckling pressure when workers in the United States try to exercise it."[62]

In the strategic arms race between big business and labor, labor has been left in the dust. The reality is that for all intents and purposes, the twentieth century's model of American labor relations is gone. Although individual unions in specific industries and in an ever-shrinking number of states and cities may survive for years to come, it will generally be with dwindling memberships, with declining economic power, and on defensive political footing. When big business got its way and began to aggressively bust existing unions, block union drives, refuse to bargain reasonable contracts, and defeat labor law reform, American workers began to lose ground economically.[63]

The decline of unions has affected middle-wage men more than any other group, and explains about three-fourths of the expanded wage gap between white- and blue-collar men.[64] And as middle-class workers got less, the upper echelon of earners got more.

Without unions or any other similarly powerful force to fight for workers, the middle class is dwindling. As Kevin Drum said in *Mother Jones*, "It was unions that made the American economy work for the middle class, and it was their later decline that turned the economy upside-down and made it into a playground for the business and financial classes."[65]

IT DOESN'T HAVE TO BE THIS WAY

Through hundreds of years of struggle and progress, we arrived in an era in which workers shared the benefits of a growing economy. Through the 1970s, the United States experienced high levels of growth *and* rising levels of equality, a combination that was previously thought impossible. And then we took it apart. The American Dream and the American middle class are under assault like never before, the result of four decades of trickle-down economics and an assault sweeping in its scope and stunning in its results.

Beginning in the 1980s, right-wing politicians, financiers, and corporate leaders began to achieve their long-sought ambition of pushing up profits by pushing down worker compensation and deregulating the economy. But to get there, they had to break the unions and disempower our governing institutions. Done, and done.

So now we've returned to levels of income inequality not seen since the pre-Depression era, experienced decades of flat wages, are watching our middle class unravel, and don't exactly see a light at the end of the tunnel.

Will America continue to be the world's wealthiest nation with the world's most productive workers? Or will the great twenty-first-century wage slowdown become the new normal, with each generation of children doing more poorly than their parents? The answer isn't immediately obvious, especially considering the profound changes in the modern economy that are transforming the employment relationship and, to some extent, even the nature of work itself.

2

The New Work

Fissured, Flexible, Insecure

Cyberpunk author and futurist William Gibson famously said "the future is already here, it's just not evenly distributed." The same could be said about the future of work. Even while most American workers still work something like a full-time job, the paradigm of employment in the United States has been shifting for some time. A growing number of Americans now not only experience lower real wages, less spending power, higher poverty rates, lower mobility, fewer benefits, and less job security than their parents (as we saw in chapter 1) but also are increasingly experiencing a change in the *structure of employment itself.*

It used to be you either had a job or you didn't. If you were a working adult, you almost certainly had an employer (or owned your own business), worked full-time, and received benefits like vacation time and health care at your job. Today, the businesses that individuals work for are increasingly not the ones they are employed by. For the past two decades, the linkages between work and employment have become increasingly "fissured," particularly in fast-growing service industries. Instead of being employed full-time by the company they actually work for, people instead experience an often tenuous connection to a subcontractor, a temp agency, an erratically scheduled part-time job, a contract, or a gig. Borrowed from the music industry, the word "gig" has been applied to all kinds of independent, impermanent, often task-based work. The "gig economy" encompasses everything from driving for Uber and temping to doing micro-jobs for an online platform such as Amazon's Mechanical Turk.

Though full-time employment has been falling for years, it has been estimated that half of the jobs added after the Great Recession are outside the bounds of traditional full-time employment, leaving about 40 percent of American workers in some kind of alternative work arrangement—including contingent, independent, and part-time.[1] This number is up from about 30 percent in the late 1990s and early 2000s.[2] Most of the growth is in contingent work, which includes anyone who doesn't have a contract for ongoing employment, such as independent contractors, temps, day laborers, and more. A recent survey by the Freelancers Union estimated that about a third of American workers are now contingent.[3]

THE FISSURED WORKPLACE

For workers in the fissured world, the basic elements of employment—hiring, evaluation, pay, supervision, training, coordination—are now performed by multiple companies, one of which may or may not be called an employer. Responsibility for working conditions has become blurred. And this is intentional. Employers fissure the employment relationship to reduce the costs of paying permanent full-time employees and shield themselves from the responsibility of upholding labor laws and protections.

The Department of Labor has said that fissuring has increased the number of vulnerable workers with reduced protections under labor law and that these business practices are associated with a high incidence of wage and hour violations, particularly in the highly fissured industries, which include construction, hospitality, and janitorial services.[4] Department of Labor Wage and Hour director David Weil has said, "Traditional approaches to enforcing [labor] laws ignore the myriad new relationships that lie below the surface of the workplace. As a result, the laws crafted to safeguard basic standards, to reduce health and safety risks, and to cushion displacement from injury or economic downturn often fail to do so."[5]

SUBCONTRACTING AND OUTSOURCING

Even for workers who have an employer, it is increasingly one in name only, who acts more like a temp agency, "employing" a high-turnover labor pool and providing minimal benefits, training, or job security.

This is the new world of subcontracting. Here the paternalistic but generous company of the 1950s gives way to an employer who is controlling but not caring, where labor is not an asset to be cultivated but something that looks more like exploitation.

Subcontracting used to be about acquiring specialized services when a certain task was too far outside of your company's core expertise. Subcontracting was often found in industries such as construction or women's clothing manufacturing that required lots of complex pieces to come together in just the right way. It doesn't make sense for a construction company to specialize in each of the hundreds or thousands of tasks needed to raise a skyscraper or build a bridge. Pouring concrete five hundred feet up in the air or underwater welding are jobs best left to the experts, who can do it better, cheaper, and more safely. But in the past two decades, we have seen a new kind of subcontracting, one that contracts out core activities of a company to subcontractors—for the sole purpose of minimizing costs. In this model, building management companies contract out to janitorial firms, coal companies contract out coal mining, cell phone companies contract out the construction and maintenance of cell towers.

The contracting company often sets rigid requirements for its contractors but gives work to the lowest bidder. This squeeze forces contractors to cut corners of one kind or another to win contracts. And while the company sets standards for completed work, it usually has nothing to say about how employees are treated. Maybe subcontractors will pay their employees fair wages or comply with required safety rules—or maybe they won't. If the subcontractor is found in violation of wage or safety laws, after all, it's not the larger company's reputation or finances on the line. As a coal industry spokesperson said, "Look around in corporate America at what people are doing to avoid healthcare and other payments. They're contracting out work. That's the whole point of using contractors."[6]

A 2014 report by the National Employment Law Project (NELP) profiled industries in which domestic outsourcing is prevalent, such as retail, hospitality, janitorial services, home health care, and the public sector. The authors observed that jobs in industries with high levels of outsourcing are characterized by lower pay, greater uncertainty in hours and schedules, and, according to the report, higher rates of violations of workplace laws. All of this leads to economic distress for families and communities.

Domestic outsourcing can change an employee's formal status or create a tenuous status within standard employment; while some of these workers may be identified as contingent in data sources, others may be counted as standard full-time workers even though they face increased employment instability. There are limits to what workers can do about it within traditional labor law. As companies use subcontractors to distance themselves from responsibility for the workers they once directly employed, workers face enormous obstacles to organizing against labor abuse. Previous models of organizing depended on workers' ability to build power by aggregating their numbers and making collective demands on their employers. But layers of subcontracting distance workers from their "real boss": the corporation at the top of the chain.

PART-TIME WORK

The nature of part-time work, like subcontracting, has shifted in the new economy. Part-time workers are different from the general working population. More than two-thirds are women. They are more likely to be black or Latino than their full-time coworkers. They earn lower wages and are more likely to be poor.[7] Many part-timers are working fewer than thirty-five hours a week because that's what fits for them. Whether they are going to school while working or have child or eldercare responsibilities, these workers don't want to or can't have a full-time job. But for a quarter of part-timers this isn't a choice at all—they are involuntarily part-time because they can't find more work.[8]

During the Great Recession, there was a steep increase in the number of people working involuntarily part-time, as employers cut back on full-time positions and workers scrambled to get whatever work was available. Today, the share of people unwillingly underemployed at part-time jobs is still almost double what it was in 2007: about 7 million are trying to get by on too few hours, wanting more work but unable to get it.[9]

This isn't just a matter of not enough jobs to go around, this is also a deliberate move on the part of some employers to duck the extra benefits that full-time workers earn. Part-time workers don't get paid overtime, often don't qualify for an employer's health care or retirement plans, don't get (unpaid) leave under the Family and Medical Leave Act, and may not be able to claim unemployment benefits. Just 21 percent of part-time employees, for example, are in employer-backed retirement plans, compared with 65 percent of full-timers.[10]

Since 2006, the retail and wholesale sector has cut one million full-time jobs while adding 500,000 part-time jobs. Over the past two decades, many major retailers went from 70 to 80 percent full-time to at least 70 percent part-time, according to one retail industry consultant.[11] This trend has frustrated millions of Americans who want to work full-time and not have their pay and benefits reduced. The widening use of part-timers has been a bane to many workers, pushing them into poverty and forcing some onto food stamps and Medicaid.

Working an hourly schedule has become an especially precarious proposition in low-wage sectors such as retail, restaurants, and health care. In the past, part-timers might work the same schedule of four- or five-hour shifts every week. But workers' schedules have become far less predictable and stable. As employers require ever more flexibility, part-time workers are often given short notice of their schedules. This practice is enabled by what experts call "predictive scheduling." Many retailers now use sophisticated software that tracks the flow of customers or production, allowing managers to assign just enough employees to handle the anticipated demand. "Many employers now schedule shifts as short as two or three hours, while historically they may have scheduled eight-hour shifts," said David Ossip, founder of the scheduling software company Dayforce.[12]

Some employers ask workers to come in at the last minute or go home once they arrive if there isn't enough demand at that moment. Workers risk losing their jobs or being assigned fewer hours in the future if they are unavailable. Micro-adjusting workers' schedules allows employers to match customer demand and, equally carefully, to avoid allowing workers to work full-time schedules and get the benefits that come along with it. Even while they are expected to be available whenever business is in operation, many workers are now scheduled for fewer and fewer hours.

Workers subject to predictive scheduling are suffering a loss not just of overtime, health care coverage, and unemployment benefits, but of control over their lives. University of Chicago researchers Carrie Gleason and Susan Lambert found that employers dictated the work schedules for about half of young adults, without their input. For part-time workers, their hours worked per week during the previous month fluctuated an astonishing 87 percent.[13] Not only are work hours unstable, they are also unpredictable: almost half of part-time workers don't know their schedule from one week to the next.[14] Part-time workers live with the constant anxiety of whether enough hours will be doled out at the right times; when they'll get their schedule and if it will change; and, for working parents, who will take care of the kids when the desperately needed on-call shift pans out.

Why is this happening? Cutthroat corporate pressure to cut costs. "Frontline managers face pressure to keep costs down, but they really don't have much control over wages or benefits," explained Lambert. "What they have control over," she said, "is employee hours."[15] This is especially true at franchises, where the corporate parent sets the terms of many or most aspects of doing business—including prices, menus, suppliers, and advertising budgets—but not fair wages or hours for employees. In 1950, the United Auto Workers and General Motors reached an historic agreement, "The Treaty of Detroit," which provided annual cost-of-living increases to base pay and established employer contributions to health insurance, unemployment insurance, and a retirement plan. This norm spread to Ford and Chrysler, then to steel and other major industries, giving both workers and corporations stability and predictability. But some weren't content to give workers their share. It was only four years later that blender salesman Ray Kroc acquired marketing rights from his largest customer, the McDonald brothers, and borrowed a business model from the sewing-machine industry—franchising—that centralized profit and distributed risk, avoiding employer responsibility for livable wages and benefits. The company would get rich, successful franchisees could live an upper-middle-class lifestyle, and workers would remain poor and unbenefited no matter how long they worked for the restaurant chain.

Franchisees are required to invest their own money into purchasing or leasing the business; the fast-food parent corporations are guaranteed a large share of the store's revenue (and usually set prices and menus as well). The individual franchisees carry almost all of the risk, including the employment relationship with their workers. But because the parent company carefully controls so many aspects of the business and extracts a large portion of the franchisees' revenue, the only route to profitability for most fast-food restaurants is to keep labor costs as low as legally possible—or even lower: a Department of Labor investigation found that fast-food outlets owned by franchisees were less likely to comply with labor laws than other fast-food outlets, because the "franchisees' incentive [was] to keep costs low." [16] Josh Sanburn wrote in *Time*, "While often responsible for determining employee wages, franchise owners are still held on a tight leash by the companies themselves in terms of what they can pay." [17]

Managers squeeze in the place they can squeeze, profits flow to the corporation, and the risk of doing business is effectively shifted onto frontline workers, "who pay in hours, stress and insecurity," according to Gleason and Lambert. With ever-changing hours and schedules, "work is omnipresent, yet completely uncertain." [18] Unpredictable part-time schedules also fuel underemployment, as a worker subject to this kind of scheduling can't easily take another part-time job to fill in the gap—they're expected to be on call (available to work shifts for which they might or might not be needed). Even if they manage to hold down more than one job, it still takes a toll in commuting between multiple workplaces, none of which is likely to offer full-time benefits.

TEMPORARY WORK

Temping has been a visible part of the American world of work since the 1960s, when it was framed as a way for middle-class housewives to earn a bit of extra money, according to sociologist Erin Hatton, author of *The Temp Economy: From Kelly Girls to Permatemps in Postwar America*. Kelly Girl Services advertised its infamous "Never-Never Girl," who "never takes a vacation or a holiday. Never asks for a raise. Never costs you a dime of slack time. (When the workload drops, you drop her.) Never has a cold, slipped disc, or loose tooth. (Not on your time anyway!) Never costs you for unemployment taxes and social security payments. Never costs you for fringe benefits. Never fails to please." [19]

Temp agencies like Kelly were able to gain a foothold in a

union-dominated labor market because married women weren't thought of as breadwinners who needed full-time hours and benefits to support their families. "That's how [temp agencies] gained entry into the labor market," says Hatton, "but once they gained legitimacy, they were able to spread out." She says that from the beginning temp agencies employed men in manual labor and manufacturing, but deliberately marketed temp work as for the "girls" in part to avoid conflicts with powerful unions. (Kelly Girl Services changed its name to Kelly Services and began marketing more directly to men in the late 1960s.)[20]

The advertising has grown subtler in subsequent decades, but the point of using temps is absolutely the same: either to employ someone for a short time for a truly temporary assignment such as covering the duties of an employee out on leave or, all too commonly, to skirt the traditional benefits afforded to permanent full-time workers by hiring temporary, staffing, or leasing firms to payroll their existing staff, who then become the employees of the staffing firm.

Temporary workers are those with "a single employer, client, job, or contract project where their employment status is temporary," according to the Freelancers Union.[21] Temp workers are classified differently than independent contractors, who are working on a project-to-project basis for a variety of clients. Temporary employment is a diverse umbrella of work types; some workers are employed by temporary employment agencies, others are hired directly by companies, some are on-call workers, others are day laborers hired off the street or at day laborer agencies.

The Freelancers Union and the Government Accountability Office (GAO) estimate that the number of temps is now between about 5.5 and 6.3 million.[22] The government's General Social Survey estimates that up to 5 percent of workers could now be considered temps.[23] The number of workers employed through temp agencies has climbed to a new high—almost 3 million, according to the Bureau of Labor Statistics, representing a record 2 percent share of the nation's workforce. The share of temporary workers has increased every year since 2009, indicating that the rise in temp employment during the Great Recession perhaps was not solely tied to the downturn; the recession seems to have marked yet another unfortunate turning point for workers seeking permanent full-time jobs with benefits.[24] Walmart and temp firm Kelly Services were the second- and third-largest employers in 2014, surpassed only by the U.S. government.[25]

The typical temp is also doing different kinds of work than a few decades ago. Office and administrative workers—the prototypical "Kelly girl"—were once the majority of temps, but by 2001 blue-collar workers in light industry or warehouses were the majority.[26] These of course were once good jobs, often unionized, now farmed out to blue-collar temp agencies.[27]

The perma-temp status of so many workers is not an accident but has become a way of doing business for many companies. The share of workers in temporary positions usually tracks closely with the ups and downs in the overall economy. In an exaggerated way, however, temps are disproportionately thrown out of work when there is a slowdown; when the economy starts to pick up, however, businesses are still wary of committing to making permanent hires and disproportionately hire temps. More than five years into a recession recovery marked by halting growth, many businesses are still adding temp jobs rather than permanent ones.[28]

But are those temp jobs really temporary? In a bald-faced attempt to circumvent labor law and even internal corporate policies, many temporary workers now work side by side with regular employees and do the same work for long periods of time—but don't receive the benefits of regular employment. This often unnoticed workforce of perma-temps numbers about 3.3 million, and includes long-term workers misclassified as temps, contract workers, and independent contractors.[29] In 2005, the government found that 27 percent of temporary help agency workers, 50 percent of direct-hire temporaries, and 55 percent of contract workers reported that they had worked at their current job assignment for one year or more.[30]

Firms say they hire temps to minimize the risks of hiring full-time employees. But the risk has just been shifted—to the workers. Contingent workers, including temps, make about 11 percent less per hour than regular workers for the same work.[31] A 2012 UC Berkeley Labor Center study found that temporary workers in California were twice as likely as non-temps to live in poverty, receive lower wages, and face less job security. Median hourly wages for temp workers were about

$14 compared to over $19 for non-temps.[32] The Berkeley study concluded that temporary and outsourced arrangements erode wages and working conditions for workers in those positions. For temporary workers employed in manual occupations in particular, it may also mean being subject to unsafe working conditions and other abuses as host companies and temp agencies each blame the other for health and safety violations.

Temping may also hurt long-term earnings prospects. For example, a study of welfare-to-work participants in Detroit found that temporary workers experienced lower earnings over the long run than direct hires in comparable jobs because the assignments were short-lived by their very nature.[33] Unsurprisingly, the job benefits are worse for contingent workers—that is, if they receive benefits at all. Many receive no benefits, not even sick days or paid holidays. Temps are about two-thirds less likely than standard workers to have a work-provided retirement plan and less than half as likely to have employer-based health insurance, a Government Accountability Office study found.[34] A typical temporary employment agency contributes $100 per year to an employee's 401(k) plan, according to the Center for a Changing Workforce, and the health coverage offered tends to be minimal plans with high deductibles and lots of exclusions.[35] In addition, temp workers face penalties when they are not working because of arbitrary restrictions in state unemployment insurance programs that effectively exclude them from coverage. One study estimates that temporary workers are 28 percent less likely than all other workers to receive jobless benefits despite the often-erratic nature of their work assignments.[36] The workers that need unemployment support the most, in other words, are the least likely to get it.

For many Americans, temping isn't a stopgap—it's a job. But because it doesn't generally include the pay, security, or benefits of a traditional job, staffing work is unfortunately, as the National Employment Law Project observed, "one part of a larger story about the declining middle class in our country."[37]

THE NEW FACE OF FREELANCING

We traditionally think of freelance contractors as graphic designers, journeyman carpenters, home computer repair technicians, and other skilled workers who have what it takes to earn a living on their own—finding their own (often short-term) gigs, frequently managing their own work, paying their own Social Security and Medicare taxes, and buying their own health care.

Businesses and individuals hire freelancers because it's a cost-effective way to complete short-term or specially skilled projects without having to hire a full-time employee. Many freelancers—particularly those under thirty-five—also enjoy the flexibility and control they have over their work, choosing where and when they want to work and what types of projects they want to take on. A national survey by the Freelancers Union found that while the most common motivation for freelancing was to earn extra money, the second most compelling reason was "to have more flexibility in my schedule." Slightly more than half of those surveyed said they began freelancing by choice, not necessity.[38]

Twenty-three million people are now working as independent contractors, according to the Freelancers Union. A few million of those workers own their own freelance companies and employ a couple of other people, but the majority are simply on their own.[39] More than any other type of contingent work, independent contracting is growing, with the number of independent contractors approximately doubling in the past ten years. These numbers are expected to keep rising. Freelance staffing firm MBO Partners predicts that self-employed workers will outnumber traditional full-time workers within the next decade. In New York City alone, the self-employed accounted for nearly two-thirds of job growth since 1975.[40]

While many freelancers continue to find work through traditional contracting arrangements, a growing number are using online outsourcing marketplaces such as Upwork (formerly Elance-oDesk) and Freelancer.com to connect with firms seeking to fill their business needs through contract work.

The new health care marketplaces created by the Affordable Care Act may also add to the freelance boom by allowing workers, even those with preexisting conditions, to enroll in health insurance when they change jobs. The Robert Wood Johnson Foundation predicts 1.5 million more people will become self-employed now that they can find affordable health insurance through the new health insurance marketplaces.

But this is the rosy side of freelancing. Despite their significant contributions to the economy, independent workers lack the job protections guaranteed to traditional employees under the old twentieth-century model of work. They do not qualify for unemployment insurance, are excluded from wage protections, and lack access to group-rate benefits, all because they don't get a W-2. They also don't tend to make very much—an internal Freelancers Union survey found that most of the group's members earn less than $50,000 a year from freelancing, and about a third earn less than $25,000. It's no surprise, then, that the Great Recession hit these workers harder than most. In 2009, 81 percent of independent workers surveyed by the Freelancers Union did not have enough work, and half experienced periods without any work. The survey also found that 12 percent of independent workers, many of them college graduates in their thirties and forties, received food stamps during the recession. Even if they do have work, freelancers still have to get paid—but 40 percent of survey respondents had trouble getting paid their owed wages in the previous year, with the average survey respondent unable to collect nearly $6,000.[41]

Freelancing has some upsides for workers, but often it's not what workers would choose if they had better alternatives. There are freelance graphic designers, programmers, and scientists who choose the flexibility and high hourly pay of independent work, but they are what Saket Soni of the National Guestworkers Alliance calls the "free agents," contrasting them with the much larger group of "unfree free agents" who freelance because they don't have better alternatives. As workers without stability or many legal protections, freelancers are in a sense the canary in the coal mine for the larger workforce. Freelancers Union president Sara Horowitz said in an interview, "In today's economy, there's a huge chunk of the middle class that's being pushed down into the working class and working poor, and freelancers are the first group that's happening to."[42]

THE RETURN OF VIRTUAL SERVITUDE

The workers who are most vulnerable to exploitation are those who have the least bargaining power: low-paid, part-time workers in the fast-food industry, immigrants with limited English skills, seasonal agricultural workers isolated in the fields. These workers have always faced an uphill battle to secure even the most basic protections that many workers used to take for granted: to take a day off to be with a sick child, to have a schedule that allows you to get eight hours of sleep between shifts, to simply get paid for the hours you've worked. But these "rights" are not guaranteed for many modern workers, and in fact some abuses have become more extreme as hypercompetitive corporate practices have taken root and labor's power has declined over the past few decades.

Slave to the Schedule: Clopening and Predictive Scheduling

Low-wage workers are not only forced to take more hours (if they can get them) to make ends meet but also working increasingly erratic and punishing schedules with last-minute work assignments, impromptu cancellations of work shifts without pay, or the chaos of being on call. One extreme example is the growing practice of managers scheduling the same workers who close up at night to open the store the next morning. The practice has even has earned its own name: "clopening."

Steven Greenhouse in the *New York Times* told the story of Shetara Brown of Tampa, Florida, who makes $8.10 an hour working about twenty-five hours a week as a cashier at a Taco Bell. "On the nights when she has just seven hours between shifts, Brown drops off her three young children with her mother. After work, she catches a bus to her apartment, takes a shower to wash off the grease and sleeps three and a half hours before getting back on the bus to return to her job." When she has clopening shifts, her children hardly see her for days. Brown says she stops by her mother's for an hour or two to see her children, and then heads home to sleep. "My kids say, 'Mommy, I miss you,'" she told Greenhouse. "I get so tired it's hard to function. I feel so exhausted. I don't want my kids suffering not seeing me. I try to push to go see them."[43] But Brown doesn't turn down the clopening shifts she's offered. She needs the hours.

Brown is not an anomaly in the modern economy: 44 percent of working Americans are unable to arrange their work schedules to meet their responsibilities at home. In addition to wages and scheduling issues, wage-earning parents are crunched by other stingy workplace policies—only 15 percent of minimum-wage earners have paid sick time, and 11 percent have access to paid parental leave (for high-paid workers, it's 80 and 66 percent, respectively).[44] The United States is the only industrialized nation that does not guarantee working mothers paid time off to care for a new child, and the only developed country that doesn't guarantee paid sick leave.

Jason Hughes, a McDonald's worker in Fremont, California, told Greenhouse that sometimes he was ordered to punch out soon after starting work and to wait around the store—unpaid. "I'd have to be ready to punch in as soon as the store gets busy," he said. "When the store is understaffed, our management would tell us we can't take our breaks."[45] In several lawsuits, workers have contended that they were told to clock out after business slowed down but remain in the restaurant or parking lot so they could be on hand to clock back in when hourly sales picked back up. At McDonald's, franchisees have used software that calculates employee-to-sales ratios and instructs restaurants to reduce staffing when sales drop below a certain level in any given hour. As a result, some McDonald's workers have been ordered, upon reporting to work, not to clock in for an hour or two and instead wait until more customers arrived.[46]

Law as Employer Advantage: Noncompetes

Employers have become increasingly creative in restricting workers' compensation and bargaining power. One recent "trick" is the use of noncompete clauses in employment contracts for low-wage employees. The heads of large companies, top scientists, and engineers have traditionally signed noncompete agreements that prevent them from jumping ship to a competitor for a reasonable period of time and taking "trade secrets" with them. Because top knowledge workers hold their companies' most valuable assets essentially between their ears, noncompete agreements may make sense for these employees.

But what about a sandwich maker at a Jimmy John's chain restaurant? Is an employer entitled to tell what you can and can't do for two years after working a wage job with no benefits? The *Huffington Post* covered this new way to squeeze low-wage workers in an article absurdly titled "When the Guy Making Your Sandwich Has a Noncompete Clause," saying the Jimmy John's agreement is "quite shocking in its scope." Under the Jimmy John's Confidentiality and

Non-Competition Agreement, employees agree not to work for another shop that makes sandwiches within three miles of *any* Jimmy John's store for *two years* after departing. As the *Huffington Post* reports, there are so many Jimmy Johns's in the United States that the agreement effectively blacks out an area of six thousand square miles in forty-four states. In other words, you really can't leave and go to another, vaguely similar shop for the next two years.[47]

So in 2014, assistant store managers Emily Brunner and Caitlin Turowski filed a class action lawsuit against Jimmy John's and a franchisee, claiming they were shorted on pay and asking the judge to bar Jimmy John's from maintaining the noncompete agreement, arguing that the agreement is overly broad and "oppressive."[48] But a federal judge in Illinois declined to grant an injunction that would have overturned them, leaving employees and former employees bound by the agreements.

And it's not just Jimmy John's. This new strategy is being used in other low-wage industries, including personal care and services (where 12 percent of employees have signed a noncompete agreement) and installation and repair services (11 percent). According to a *New York Times* exposé, a Massachusetts man whose job involved spraying pesticides on lawns had to sign a two-year noncompete agreement. A recent graduate was required to sign a one-year noncompete with a marketing firm for an entry-level social media job. And even interns aren't immune—a college student on a summer internship signed a one-year agreement at an electronics firm. "There has been a definite, significant rise in the use of noncompetes, and not only for high tech, not only for high-skilled knowledge positions," according to Orly Lobel, a law professor and the author of a book on noncompetes, *Talent Wants to Be Free*. Noncompetes, he said, have "become pervasive and standard in many service industries."[49]

This isn't really about trade secrets (in a sandwich shop!) or the ability of companies to protect their intellectual property. As the *Huffington Post* said, what it's really about is that "a company in this position may feel there's little to lose by inserting such language into an agreement. Even if the clause failed to hold up in court, the very possibility of limited employment opportunities could dissuade certain workers from rocking the boat."[50]

Legal Loopholes: Guest Workers

We have seen how employers are increasingly relying on layers of contractors to shield themselves from their moral and legal obligations
and how this distancing has hurt the average worker. While it is legal
to use contract labor, some of these distancing practices fall into an
even grayer legal zone, relying on what amount to legal loopholes in
U.S. immigration law to employ foreign guest workers.

Saket Soni of the National Guestworker Alliance said, "Guestworkers help us see what all work will look like one day as employers relentlessly replace what were once stable, living-wage jobs with ever more
precarious, poorly-paid temporary jobs. In the process, employers have
treated guestworkers as the ultimate exploitable workforce and the ultimate tool for undercutting local workers."[51]

International workers can work under a diverse array of visas, each
with its own maze of regulations. The J-1 "cultural exchange" program came under particular scrutiny after a blow-up with exploited
student workers at a Hershey chocolate factory in Palmyra, Pennsylvania, during the summer of 2011. The J-1 program allows students to
travel to the United States for short-term employment that will expose
them to daily life in America, while allowing them to earn income to
travel and see the country. Private companies bring in J-1 workers to
labor in a wide range of jobs, from low-wage work in fishing, farming,
landscaping, and child care to middle-wage fields like teaching and
nursing. There are about 170,000 J-1 workers in the United States at
any given time.[52] Employers like the J-1 because it allows them to hire
temporary foreign workers without paying payroll taxes or, in some
cases, compensating them at all.

By the summer of 2011, Hershey had subcontracted its entire logistics operation, bringing in global subcontracting corporation DHL,
which in turn contracted the work out to logistics corporation Exxcel,
which contracted it out to temp agency SHS, which contracted out to
a recruiter that, through the J-1 visa program, brought approximately
four hundred foreign students from around the world to Pennsylvania.[53]

Students from China, Turkey, Ukraine, Moldova, Mongolia, Roma-
nia, Ghana, Thailand, and other countries had contracted with agencies in their home countries to work for Hershey, packing chocolates.
The students came eager to work and to participate in the educational

and cultural exchange they had been promised. But according to an investigative report by a team of law professors on human rights, the students found that "the living and working conditions that they faced in Hershey fell far short of the program's promise" and that "the students described being employed in a packing factory, working at punishing speeds under abusive supervision in physically grueling work, that—after deductions were taken for housing and other employment-related costs—netted them a first week's salary as low as $20 for the week."[54]

Other guest workers have not received as much attention as the Hershey's J-1 students but are subject to even worse treatment. In 2012, the Guestworker Alliance uncovered appalling abuses at a Walmart seafood supplier in Louisiana, CJ's Seafood, as well as at a dozen other Walmart suppliers. For years, C.J.'s Seafood had been replacing U.S. workers with H-2B guest workers, who came here legally under visas for low-skilled seasonal workers in industries that supposedly cannot find enough Americans to do the job. The *New York Times* reported that "the program has been dogged by charges of wage abuses, fraud and involuntary servitude, including in investigations by the Government Accountability Office."[55] At C.J.'s Seafood, these abuses took the form of forced labor, shifts of up to twenty-four hours without overtime pay (or inadequate hours followed by threats if a worker tried to find work elsewhere), and discrimination. As the National Guestworker Alliance summarized, "Walmart, while claiming to hold its suppliers to the highest standards—profited from the guestworkers' captivity."[56]

Writing for *Dissent*, reporter Josh Eidelson investigated the H-2B situation, interviewing Laura Sanchez (not her real name), a guest worker at Viet Foods in Louisiana. Eidelson reported that Sanchez "lives in a small room in a small building adjacent to the plant. There's barbed wire over the fence." Sanchez said that her first season as a guest worker had been a "horrible disappointment." She was immediately forced to borrow money from her new boss for basic necessities for her supposedly free housing. She was injured constantly. According to Eidelson "when workers asked about getting hours at another job, the boss threatened to report them to immigration."[57]

These are just a few cases representing a much larger set of problems for guest workers, foreign workers brought to our country by private companies who are working under many different visa types with limited governmental oversight. As labor historian Nelson Lichtenstein said, "employers for a century have been trying to import workers who have something less than full citizenship. . . . From a management perspective, they're the perfect workers."[58]

The New York Times published an editorial about the H-2B program after the seafood abuses were uncovered, serving as a call to arms to end this system: "It is time to banish the idea that forced labor and sweatshop exploitation are problems of bygone eras or distant countries. These conditions exist within America's borders."[59]

Legal Violations: Forced Labor

The labor violations faced by other groups of workers in the modern workplace go even beyond abuse, and into forced labor and even slavery. As an example, in August 1995, the California Department of Labor discovered seventy-two Thai immigrants working under slave-like conditions in a garment sweatshop in El Monte, east of Los Angeles. The immigrants worked for 69 cents an hour, locked in a two-story, seven-unit apartment complex ringed with razor wire and fences spiked with inward-facing bars. The windows had been covered with cardboard, and the interior converted into a maze of crowded living areas and sewing workspaces. One man told the Department of Labor's agents that he had been recruited in Bangkok, then was made to surrender his passport to his employer once he reached Los Angeles. He spent four years working in the El Monte facility, and had never been allowed to leave the building or contact his family. A woman imprisoned for seven years said that "she long ago lost all hope of ever winning freedom." The investigation found that workers were threatened with rape and murder if they stopped working. After the raid, then-labor secretary Robert Reich launched a nationwide crusade against sweatshops.[60]

Nail salons are another hotbed for extreme labor violations—because again, the workers are vulnerable immigrants who are often unaware of their rights or relatively powerless to change their situation. Sarah Maslin Nir of the New York Times conducted a major investigation of local nail salons in 2015, interviewing more than 150 nail salon workers and owners in four languages. She found that "a vast majority of workers are paid below minimum wage; sometimes they are not even paid. Workers endure all manner of humiliation, including having their tips docked as punishment for minor transgressions, constant video monitoring by owners, even physical abuse," and that "employers are rarely punished for labor and other violations." The *Times* reported that beginning manicurists often work without wages until their bosses decide to pay them—a condition found in almost every New York area salon. One typical story was found at a salon in Manhattan's West Village, where new employees are required to *pay their employer* $100 per week to work, then work without pay for weeks before finally receiving "regular" paychecks of as low as $30 for a day's work, well below New York's minimum wage.[61]

A world away from Manhattan, in the tomato fields of Florida, agricultural workers pick about 90 percent of the U.S.-grown fresh tomatoes harvested between December and May each year. These same tomato-growing operations were described by Florida U.S. attorney Douglas Molloy in 2009 as "ground zero for modern slavery" in a 2009 *Gourmet* magazine exposé by Barry Estabrook. Instead of protections, Florida tomato workers all too often receive abusive treatment. Mexican immigrant Mariano Lucas Domingo, along with several other men, was held as a slave in a box truck for years in the early 2000s. According to Lucas, his "employer" cashed $55,000 of his paychecks, only randomly doling out small amounts of pocket money. "Taking a day off was not an option," reported Estabrook. "If Lucas became ill or was too exhausted to work, he was kicked in the head, beaten, and locked in the back of the truck. Other members of [the] dozen-man crew were slashed with knives, tied to posts, and shackled in chains." Lucas finally escaped in 2007 by punching a hole in the roof of the truck where he was imprisoned.[62]

These were not isolated incidents: in one tomato operation that was prosecuted for slavery, the grower held more than four hundred people in debt bondage, forcing them to work long hours under the constant watch of armed guards. Since 1997, investigations have resulted in the freeing of more than a thousand men and women held in slavery. "Unlike victims of other crimes, slaves don't report themselves," said prosecutor Molloy. The slaves "hide from us in plain sight." Former picker and workers' rights activist Gerardo Reyes said that the victims of this system come to Florida for one reason—to send money to their families back home. "But when they get here," said Reyes, "it's all they can do to keep themselves alive with rent, transportation, food. Poverty and misery are the perfect recipe for slavery." According to the *Gourmet* exposé, "when asked if it is reasonable to assume that an American who has eaten a fresh tomato from a grocery store or food-service company . . . has eaten fruit picked by the hand of a slave, Molloy said, 'It is not an assumption. It is a fact.' "[63]

Working on Demand
In addition to the more typical routes to contingent work—through temp agencies, part-time jobs, freelance projects—middle-class refugees and new immigrants alike have found a new kind of work as independent contractors in the "on demand" economy.[64] This is the emerging economy in which smartphone apps disrupt old industries and put immense power and flexibility in the hands of consumers, who can now order an ever-increasing number of goods and services on their computers and smartphones for nearly immediate use or consumption.

Some of the new faces of freelancing are workers in this on-demand economy: Uber and Lyft drivers, Postmates, Instacart, and Caviar delivery people, and workers for hundreds of other companies that use online platforms to connect consumers directly with services. According to the platform companies, the workers are technically not employees but independent contractors operating tens of thousands of single-person companies. The on-demand economy is delivering these services through online platforms including transportation leaders Uber and Lyft, home-renting platform Airbnb, the personal assistant and day labor app TaskRabbit, and business services such as Amazon's Mechanical Turk and Upwork, which connect businesses directly to gig workers. One leading venture capitalist, Fred Wilson, believes that in the not-so-distant future, nearly all business will be conducted on a "radically decentralized peer-to-peer level." "Think about gambling without a casino," he said. "Think about stock trading without an exchange. Think about real-estate transactions without deeds. Think about transactions without clearinghouses. That is a world we are heading into."[65]

Is the radically decentralized world we're heading into also one without jobs? Workers for these applications show up (sometimes only virtually), perform a task, get paid, and may never interact with the customer or end-user again. An on-demand economy worker might have twelve gigs in a month, a week, or a day. Almost uniformly, those workers are treated as independent contractors rather than salaried employees. In the on-demand economy, work is even more piecemeal than in traditional freelancing and temping, and even the language we use to describe it is in flux—1099, on-demand, task-based, free-lance, gig, temp, sharing, peer-to-peer, independent.

The largely Silicon Valley–based, venture-capital-backed innova-tors, developers, and coders who develop and operate these platforms stand to win handsomely. But while the workers in the on-demand economy gain flexibility and much greater control over their time, they lack even the most basic safety net that most American workers expect.

We've come a long way from the mid-twentieth-century American economy in which many workers could expect to turn a single skill, craft, or credential into lifelong employment within a single industry, sector, or profession, or even with a single employer. Many workers are now experiencing total freedom and total risk colliding in a work environment that is the most atomized possible and largely low-wage. For all that's good and exciting about the emergence of work-distribu-tion platforms and micro-task employment, these workers are truly on their own.

Uber and On-Demand Transportation

Only one on-demand company is famous enough to have spawned a verb that serves as a stand-in for the entire phenomena: Uber. Uber was the company that first brought the on-demand economy and gig work to national attention, and today the smartphone-powered trans-portation platform has been so wildly successful that companies now want to "Uberize" anything that a customer with more money than time might want. There are now on-demand apps for everything from flower delivery to dog walking to health care in your home.

Founded in San Francisco in 2009 and today operating in fifty-three countries, Uber pairs its smartphone app with a seemingly endless supply of freelance drivers to supply a luxury that was once reserved for the wealthy: a private chauffeur at your beck and call. Uber provides an application that allows consumers to order a ride via smartphone, track their driver's location, and automatically pay their driver without ever getting out their wallet. There is also a ratings system for the driver and passenger to evaluate one another.

Uber had sales of more than $1 billion in 2014—not bad for a five-year-old company. With sales already growing 400 percent per year, Uber is now planning to spend more than $1 billion to expand its operations into China.[66] Its incredible growth mirrors the ambition and regulator-may-care attitude of the Valley from which it was born. Uber didn't ask for permission to operate a new kind of transportation in a regulatory gray space—it just "hired" drivers and put out an app. Wherever Uber gets a foothold, the service is defended by die-hard Uber customers from calls for greater regulation (which are often spearheaded by the highly protected and regulated taxi industry).[67] The other major on-demand transportation companies, Lyft and Sidecar, have a substantially similar business model. Lyft, while still far behind Uber in sales, saw sales growth of 487 percent in 2014 and has raised $333 million from venture capitalists.[68]

Like other fissured workplace strategies, the on-demand economy offloads the business risk, including the bulk of the expense of doing business, onto other parties while taking a hefty cut of every transaction. Uber is the perfect example: it is a transportation company that doesn't own any cars or employ any drivers but has a customer following with "cult-like devotion" to its service.[69] If Uber had employees, though, it would be a major employer—it has more than 200,000 active drivers, roughly double the delivery workforce at UPS. The number of drivers has been doubling every six months.[70]

Uber also promises big things for its drivers—plenty of work, good money, flexible hours, even discounts on vehicles. The one thing that is not promised when someone becomes a driver is the legal consideration of being an Uber employee. Uber drivers are deemed independent contractors and receive a 1099 form, not a W-2, for their tax returns. Drivers foot the bill for everything from the cost of their cars (which must be less than five years old and are subject to regular inspection by Uber), to gas, insurance, maintenance, and repairs.

Under the current arrangement, Uber claims that its only contribution to its business model is providing a smartphone application—the driver and rider contract for the ride. Yet drivers are required to maintain their cars and personal appearance in a particular way, are not allowed to refuse rides if the app assigns them, are not permitted to take tips from passengers, and are subject to many other requirements and restrictions. The company sets the terms of work without acting as an employer required to pay minimum wage, Social Security, or Medicare taxes, much less vacation, sick days, or health care.

Drivers' expenses add up, with ride-service drivers spending an average of $965 a month on their car, gas, and insurance. On-demand services like Uber require all drivers to carry car insurance and verify that it is current, but obviously the checks aren't comprehensive: a survey of on-demand drivers found that 8 percent of drivers said that they didn't have insurance.[71] This is a legal gray zone for drivers, passengers, and Uber—one of many.

Being in the gray zone has risks for the business as well as its workers. In 2015, the California Labor Commission potentially changed the on-demand game by ruling that Uber driver Barbara Ann Berwick was actually an employee, not an independent contractor as Uber claimed. Berwick had sued Uber for compensation of driving-related expenses including mileage and tolls. The commission ruled that Uber is an employer because it is "involved in every aspect of the operation." Uber responded that it is "nothing more than a neutral technology platform."[72] The commission called out Uber's control over its workers, including the fares drivers charge; the technology tools they use; the model of cars they drive; what portion of fares go to Uber versus to the driver; its monitoring of their approval ratings and termination of access to their system if ratings fall below a near-perfect score; and, to some extent, how often drivers work. Though the ruling applies only to a single worker, it's the first shot across the bow at the on-demand model of nonemployment.

The National Labor Relations Board issued a ruling later in 2015 that was potentially even more significant. Saying that the old standard is "increasingly out of step with changing economic circumstances," the board ruled that companies can be held responsible for labor violations committed by their contractors.[73] The Browning-Ferris decision stated that two or more companies are "joint employers" if they share the ability to govern the terms and conditions of a worker's employ-ment. If a company has the right to govern a worker's employment but chooses not to exercise that right, now they can still be held liable for the other employer's misdeeds. No more hiding behind layers of subcontractors, temp or guest worker agencies, or on-demand tech-nology platforms—now the government will be asking not who pays an employee but who holds the ultimate authority over that worker's terms of employment.

THE FUTURE: ROBOTICS AND ARTIFICIAL INTELLIGENCE TRANSFORM WORK?

Like the other changes discussed in this chapter, technology is contrib-uting to the insecurity of the modern worker, altering both the kinds of jobs available and the nature of the work, and perhaps even determin-ing whether there is work for humans to do at all.

Machines are undoubtedly replacing humans in some kinds of work, while other kinds are becoming hybridized, with humans and machines *interacting* to produce work. A growing number of futurists, technologists, entrepreneurs, scholars, economists, and other thought leaders are pointing to a real possibility of mass technological unem-ployment—that is, a world where much of the work now done by peo-ple will be done by machines, robots, and artificial intelligence. This isn't exactly a new story: think about buggy drivers, steam engine me-chanics, tollbooth workers, switchboard operators, and checkout clerks.

But the increasing *speed* of technological acceleration may soon outpace the economy's ability to replace obsolete jobs with new ones. And some workers who even today seem irreplaceable by technology—from oncologists to journalists to accountants and bus drivers—could find themselves competing with intelligent machines. Other changes include increases in the pace of work (enabled by robots and other computerized technology) and new types of work that couldn't exist without computers. The net effect of these changes is still not known, because most experts agree that we are still early in the "third indus-trial revolution," and that—just as for steam engines and electricity—the ultimate effects of breakthrough new technologies take many decades to show themselves.

What we do know is that over the past three decades, technology has radically altered how some types of work are done, including production work and routine transaction work, among many others. Robots are substituted for assembly-line workers in production work, and ATMs and PayPal are substituted for bank tellers. Until the past decade, the dominant view among economists was that technological change favored skilled workers, a theory dubbed "skill-biased techno-logical change." They believed that professions requiring more educa-tion and skills were less likely to be automated and that to the victor would go the spoils: skilled workers would receive higher wages be-cause technology increased their productivity and therefore the de-mand for their labor.

This consensus may be changing. According to a 2013 study by University of Oxford economists Carl Benedikt Frey and Michael Os-borne, 47 percent of jobs in the United States are believed to be at risk of automation within the next few decades.[74] That 47 percent isn't only manufacturing and routine service jobs—it also includes skilled, white-collar desk jobs like accounting, law, and technical writing. If even half of Frey and Osborne's prediction is closer to the mark, many workers are in for a rude awakening sometime before what they as-sumed would be the end of their careers. As the *Financial Times* wrote, "Almost any job that involves sitting in front of a screen and manipu-lating information is threatened."[75] And work traditionally considered creative is not necessarily off the chopping block: *Wired* quotes a tech-nology expert who predicts that within about a decade 90 percent of news articles will be computer-generated.[76]

But we don't need predictions to get a sense of how serious the threat of widespread technological unemployment is—the threat has been named, and those names are Baxter, Amelia, and Watson.

Baxter is a factory robot that can be programmed by grabbing its arms and guiding it through the motions necessary to do a sequence of manual labor. Its creator, Rethink Robotics, sells the robot for only $25,000, which works out to about $4 an hour over its lifetime. Baxter can, of course, operate 24/7 without breaks (unless it breaks). In an interesting twist, because Baxter is cost-competitive with even Chi-nese labor, Rethink Robotics hopes that Baxter will ultimately "enable domestic firms to competitively insource manufacturing jobs and thus improve efficiency."[77]

Amelia, a virtual service-desk assistant from IPsoft, helps with employee training at Shell Oil. Amelia can learn from natural language interactions to solve customer problems. "More than a typical chat bot," says *TechWorld*, "cognitive computing software Amelia can learn from experiences with customers, which will mean less intervention from human agents—and software developers." The software works "like how you would teach a human."[78]

Watson, the IBM artificial intelligence supercomputer, can, like Amelia, understand questions posed in natural language and answer them. But Watson has a far greater command of human language than any prior artificial intelligence computer and has the assembled data of the Internet at its disposal. It is now the world *Jeopardy!* champion, beating out Ken Jennings, who holds the record for the longest winning streak in the show's history. "I had a great time and I would do it again in a heartbeat," said Jennings. "It's not about the results; this is about being part of the future." He's a better loser than Dutch chess grandmaster Jan Hein Donner, who was asked how he would prepare for a chess match against an artificial intelligence computer like IBM's famous Deep Blue. Donner replied, "I would bring a hammer."[79] But more profoundly, Watson may even be what MIT futurist Andrew McAfee calls "the world's best diagnostician"—an artificially intelligent doctor. "Watson basically went to med school after it won *Jeopardy!*" he said.[80] Watson now assists doctors in diagnosing patients and suggesting treatments.

Most potentially job-displacing technology isn't as sophisticated as Watson, but taken together it still could make a mark in the next few decades.

As this book goes to publication, Google is about to put hundreds of self-driving cars on the road; transportation could be fully automated within a decade. Rio Tinto's "mine of the future" in Western Australia has fifty-three autonomous trucks moving iron ore.[81]

Work Fusion's software automates big office projects, which isn't very revolutionary—until it divides the job up into micro-tasks, automates any repetitive elements, and bids out any work that requires human thought through crowdsourcing platforms. Martin Ford, author of the 2005 book *Rise of the Robots*, notes that the software takes the automation of office work even one step further: it monitors what the micro-task workers are doing and learns from them so that, over time, it can automate more and more: "As the freelance workers do their jobs they are, in effect, training the system to replace them. That's a pretty good preview of what the future looks like," says Ford.[82]

Facebook's Cyborg program puts even computer systems administrators out of work—it manages the company's vast farm of data servers, requiring only one human technician for every twenty thousand computers. Martin Ford quotes the co-founder of a start-up dedicated to the automation of gourmet hamburger production: "Our device isn't meant to make employees more efficient. It's meant to completely obviate them."[83] Many futurists believe that 3-D printing is poised to revolutionize manufacturing as we knew it.

North America is becoming an international hub for industrial robotics. Statistics from the Robotic Industries Association show that North American companies bought $1.48 billion worth of robots in 2012 alone, exceeding previous sales records and bringing the total number of robots used in U.S. factories to 225,000 (we are now second only to Japan in the number of industrial robots in our factories).[84]

In contrast to earlier disruptions, which affected particular sectors of the economy such as transportation or garment manufacturing, the effects of today's robotics and artificial intelligence revolution are also "general purpose." In other words, no jobs will necessarily be spared. Even the high-flying, high-paying financial services sector has not been spared—in 2000 the sector employed 150,000 people in New York; by 2013 that number had dropped to 100,000. It has been estimated that up to 70 percent of equity trades are now done by algorithms.

The United States has already experienced measurable technological unemployment for about the past fifteen years, when a divergence began between labor productivity (up) and employment and median income (stagnated or dropped). Erik Brynjolfsson and Andrew McAfee call this phenomena "the great decoupling," stating that "it is a different pattern than what we have seen during the preceding 200 years, [and] the biggest single explanation is that technology has been affecting far more middle-skilled jobs."[85]

But while many observers of the middle-class jobs crisis have focused on offshoring as the core ill of American workers, Brynjolfsson and McAfee argue that automation is the real point of efficiency-focused and cost-cutting modern business practices. As they say, "Offshoring is often only a way station on the road to automation."[86] And without any changes in how the gains of technological advancement are distributed, the computers aren't just coming for our jobs—they're coming for the entire consumer economy. Ford notes that by skewing the gains of the new economy to a few, robots "weaken the chief engine of growth—middle-class demand."[87]

Other technology and labor experts have a somewhat more moderate view of the impact of technological change on employment. Researchers David Autor, Frank Levy, and Richard Murnane have argued that technology can replace human labor in routine tasks— tasks that can be expressed in step-by-step procedures or rules—but (as yet) cannot replace human labor in nonroutine tasks.[88] Because most job growth in mature economies involves and will continue to involve complex interactions, not routine production or transaction work, these thinkers don't foresee large unemployment effects in the foreseeable future from technological advancement.[89]

David Autor, an MIT economist, believes that while it is highly likely that the majority of jobs will be reconfigured in some way due to automation and robotics, accounts of technological displacement are widely overstated. He is quoted in the *Wall Street Journal* saying that his is "the non-alarmist view."[90] Autor reminds us that there aren't many train firemen (who shoveled the coal into steam locomotives), typists, or elevator operators left, but that these changes have not reduced overall employment or lowered earnings compared to the early part of the century. "It has done the opposite," as *The Guardian* reported, "raising productivity on average and [leading] to more interesting, more cognitively challenging, better paid and less dangerous jobs."[91]

Other skeptics of technological unemployment point out that it can't really be happening—or be all that bad—because there's no statistical relationship between the change in factory employment and robot use. Mark Muro of the Brookings Institution found that some countries that have adopted robots much faster than the United States, including Germany and South Korea, saw far smaller losses in jobs between 1996 and 2012. Meanwhile, both Britain and Australia have lagged on introducing robots, yet suffered deeper job losses.[92]

Lawrence Mishel of the Economic Policy Institute agrees with this assessment. "Robots are everywhere in the news but they do not seem to leave a footprint in the data," he says. "The data on investments and productivity cast doubt on any accelerated robot activity," because "the growth of labor productivity, capital investment and, particularly, investment in information equipment and software has strongly *decelerated* in the 2000s."[93]

Autor does agree that automation has hurt employment—but in a targeted way, because it is still difficult for machines to perform tasks that require adaptability, common sense, or creativity. He also doesn't see the automation wave killing a wide array of jobs as fast as other experts predict. What journalists and futurists overstate, he says, is the extent of machine substitution for human labor, while they ignore the strong complementarities between humans and machines.[94]

Perhaps we are also worrying so much about technological unemployment right now because the overall economy is weak. Mishel directly rebuts McAfee and Brynjolfsson's claim that automation is responsible for wage inequality and slow job growth, stating that it is due not to robots but to slow economic growth resulting from "the collapse of two asset bubbles and inadequate policy responses." He points the finger at an anemic economy, noting that "Job growth occurs when economic growth exceeds productivity."[95] He also argues that McAfee and Brynjolfsson's theories will fuel the mistaken narrative that technology is responsible for our job and wage problems and that we are powerless to obtain more equitable growth."[96]

It may still be too soon to tell whether the growing ranks of observers and experts pointing to the possibility of disruptive, widespread technological unemployment are right or wrong or somewhere in between. Case in point: a 2014 Pew survey found that just under half of technology experts said automation would displace "significant numbers of both blue- and white-collar workers" over the next decade. Some said it would leave "masses of people who are effectively unemployable."

But the other half said it will create more jobs than it destroys.[97] Frey acknowledges that "we speculate about technology that is in only the early stages of development."[98]

While technological unemployment proponents make a strong case, time and data will be the ultimate judges. What is clear is that it's no longer a possibility that we can dismiss out of hand based on the false alarms of the past two centuries. If anyone in the mid-1970s had predicted all of the other trends about work in America that we have reviewed in the previous two chapters, skeptics probably would have been in the majority. And they would have been wrong.

If automation does cast a significant portion of society into unemployment, we have serious policy work to do. As Autor has said, "If we automate all the jobs, we'll be rich—which means we'll have a distribution problem, not an income problem."[99] Economist Jared Bernstein says, "When it comes to the future of work, it's not the robots that worry me. It's the policymakers."[100]

For tens of millions of Americans who still work standard, often full-time jobs for traditional employers, the generation-long trend has been toward lower wages, fewer (if any) benefits, and a massive transfer of risk and costs from employers onto employees. Job security is largely a thing of the past outside of a few privileged professions. Most workers still work traditional jobs, but the jobs have simply *become much worse*.

For tens of millions of additional workers in the new economy, there isn't really such a thing as a "standard" job at all. You might have a "traditional" full-time job but work for a subcontractor whose own relationship to the upstream payer or user of its services is itself dependent and precarious. You might need to piece together multiple part-time and/or temporary jobs, or freelance gigs, into one full-time income. You might find your employer using every technological, legal, or even illegal means to maximize his profit while preventing you from leaving for a better job, holding him accountable for legal or contract violations, gaining access to full-time work or benefits, or even getting paid fairly at all.

Or, like tens of millions more workers, you might spend part of each workday, workweek, or career literally on your own, depending on handheld work-distribution technology to compete locally or globally for micro-jobs, hoping to piece together an income from the gig economy that offers immense freedom and flexibility but equally low pay and no structure, stability, or security.

Or, perhaps, you might find that your whole career plan—a carefully built résumé, a degree or credential, years of experience, and well-developed skills—could suddenly be upended by the next disruptive technological breakthrough—perhaps by a digital platform that enables workers around the world to compete with you for less money, or perhaps even by a software package, robot, or a digital printer.

Add it all up and a clear picture emerges: for many working Americans, work is coming apart. In the next chapter, we will see what some workers are doing about it.

3

It Doesn't Have to Be This Way

Resistance, Unrest, and Innovation

Just as the future isn't equally distributed, it's also not predetermined. Below the radar screens of politicians and the mainstream media, the story of the 1990s and 2000s isn't only about America's politics and its economy turning against working people. It is also a tale of how workers, activists, and leaders have resisted dominant economic theories and planted seeds of agitation and popular unrest along with new forms of worker organization and broad-based efforts to raise wages. There are cracks in the monolithic facade of trickle-down economics, and there is hope, because some people are now starting to see through it and organize new ways for everyday Americans to build power.

The work is happening in Los Angeles and Chicago, Seattle and New York City, over the Internet, and in the Florida tomato fields. It's happening with enterprising activists and fed-up fast-food workers, in think tanks and academic centers, on college campuses and in city councils around the country. It's happening in worker centers agitating for change in immigrant-heavy low-wage sectors of the economy, in new political organizations, and with regular citizens taking to the streets to protest the greatest wealth transfer in U.S. history.

No one has yet found a replacement for the power and reach that labor unions wielded to level the playing field for workers—in fact, many of the new models face the same challenges as unions do. But below the surface of our brutal new economy, the past two decades have seen an encouraging amount of unrest, adaptation, and experimentation in the service of a more equitable economy. As New York University history professor Kim Phillips-Fein notes, "the story of the rise and fall of the labor movement offers unsettling insights, and no assurances, about a revival. Then again, gauzy nostalgia is not what the country needs."[1] Ai-Jen Poo, a leader in the new world of alternative labor organizations, agrees. "Given what we're up against," she says, "it's about any and all tactics."[2]

OLD MODELS, NEW WORKERS

Even as the proportion of unionized Americans has declined over the past three decades, certain groups of workers have still found representation—and raises—with labor unions that developed strategies for organizing the most marginalized workers. Workers with no previous platform for unionization—including janitorial workers for low-cost contractors and home care workers for the disabled and elderly—found a voice in innovative campaigns that adapted the old clunky collective bargaining machinery of the twentieth century for decidedly postmodern workforces, in challenging circumstances that did not allow for traditional industrial organizing.

Labor Goes on the Offensive in the 1990s: Justice for Janitors
The Service Employees International Union (SEIU) is responsible for the Justice for Janitors campaign, one of the most successful labor organizing efforts of the past twenty-five years. Since 1990, Justice for Janitors (J4J) has won dozens of contracts with commercial cleaning contractors and organized over 225,000 janitors throughout the United States and Canada. In more than a dozen cities, including Los Angeles, Denver, Miami, Houston, Boston, Minneapolis, and Washington, D.C, J4J has re-unionized the commercial cleaning sector and won better wages, working conditions, hours, and health care for janitors.

The fight began in the late 1980s after janitors were hit by a steady decline in wages, benefits, and union job opportunities. In the early 1980s the average janitor earned more than $7.00 an hour plus health insurance, but by 1986 wages had dropped to $4.50 and health care had been cut.[3] The janitorial industry pushed down wages and working conditions and broke unions, replacing largely working-class African American labor with more easily exploited undocumented immigrants.

The J4J campaign followed the money upstream from a host of

janitorial contractors to the ultimate decision makers: the building owners. The campaign also fought for and won master contracts, which cover all union janitors in an industry or region regardless of whether a particular janitor's company was party to the original deal. Early campaign successes, particularly in Denver, San Jose, and Los Angeles, paved the way for other major metropolitan areas to secure similar bargains.

The architects of the campaign, SEIU's Stephen Lerner and Jono Shaffer, wrote in 2015 that: "The Justice for Janitors campaign succeeded because it relentlessly went after the building owners and financiers at the top of the real estate industry—the people who truly had power over the janitors' livelihood—not the cleaning companies who were powerless subcontractors. The campaign also exposed an economy that was increasingly using subcontracting and other schemes to separate and isolate workers from the corporations and companies that were actually in control of their wages, benefits and overall working conditions."[4] J4J inspired hundreds of thousands of janitors to organize in more than thirty cities in North America through the Justice for Janitors campaigns.[5] The strategy and tactics that made these wins possible were varied—from scrappy street protests to sophisticated political and research efforts:

- "In your face" protests drew public attention and support, and embarrassed key individuals in the janitorial industry.
- J4J pressured government agencies while they built relationships with politicians, learning that "it didn't take a contract to redefine the relationship with the company," according to a case study by Roger Waldinger et al.[6]
- The campaign also developed and backed pro-worker candidates. Thousands of union activists, drawn disproportionately from immigrant-heavy locals, became politically engaged and walked precincts in Latino and African American neighborhoods at election time.
- J4J also brought a business-oriented understanding of the industry to the fight: the labor organizers knew more about the industry than the business owners did.
- Though J4J is widely seen as a bottom-up campaign, it had a crucial top-down component. Union leaders like Andy

Stern, then the president of SEIU, and John Sweeney, then the president of the AFL-CIO, emphasized organizing above all else and were willing to spend on campaigns like J4J, which the case study described as "not cheap by any stretch of the imagination."[7]

- The J4J campaign also required perseverance—after the first two years of organizing in Los Angeles, for instance, the results were not very promising.

Another reason J4J was so exciting was that it was a symbolic moment of strength and hope for the labor movement. "Part of the reason the whole labor movement rallied around this strike is that it was a taste of what labor can and will look like as it rejuvenates itself," Lerner told the *Los Angeles Times*. "Many of our battles over the last 10 years have been defensive battles. This was 100% offensive."[8]

For Lerner and Shaffer, though, "the key lesson is that there is no silver bullet. There isn't one thing, one strategy, one action, or one tactic that magically beats billionaires or creates the space for a movement to develop." Yet they note that J4J did provide some unquestionable top-level lessons for future "alt labor" campaigns: "We have to look up the economic food chain and target the real culprits. We have to bring as many stakeholders to the fight as possible, and creatively and aggressively organize to disrupt business as usual for those in control—that can mean strikes, civil disobedience, engaging shareholders, or directly challenging other business, social, and political interests and their exploitative practices and schemes."[9]

But despite the dramatic success of J4J campaigns in many individual cities, U.S. janitors today earn less on average than they did in the early 1980s, after adjusting for inflation. Most janitors today are still poor and not protected by a union. In thirteen of the twenty fastest-growing cities, there is no janitor's union at all, so the work tends to be minimum wage and unbenefited.

Los Angeles Home Care Organizing

Home care has historically been a "hidden workforce" conflated legally and in the public mind with homemakers and domestic servants. But, in the words of the Economic Policy Institute, home care workers are "critical to the U.S. economy" because they "free the time and attention of other workers. They are professional health care workers but tend to work in the shadows, socially isolated and often without employment contracts, leaving them with little job security and vulnerable to exploitation." Home care workers are disproportionately middle-aged women of color or immigrants, though the exact mix of race, ethnicity, and citizenship status depends on the region of the country.[10]

Home care workers care for elderly and disabled people in their homes, allowing their clients to live independently and saving the government enormous amounts of money compared to nursing home care. A home care worker's duties include all tasks needed for daily living, ranging from bathing their clients to preparing meals, organizing their schedule, and administering medications. Home care work is often difficult and stressful, requiring a range of skills from heavy lifting to coping with end of life issues. As the Department of Labor stated in a 2015 ruling that brought home care workers under the protection of the Fair Labor Standards Act, "As more individuals receive services at home rather than in nursing homes or other institutions, workers who provide home care services . . . perform increasingly skilled duties. Today, direct care workers are for the most part not the elder sitters that Congress envisioned when it enacted the companionship services exemption in 1974, but are instead professional caregivers."[11]

Home care workers provide essential services for our most vulnerable citizens and their families, yet their pay is lower than almost any other job in health care. The average wage for home care workers nationally was $9.70 an hour in 2010, according to the Bureau of Labor Statistics.[12] And an ever-growing number of workers are subject to these low wages: since the 1980s, home care has been one of the fastest growing sectors of the health care industry—and of the entire economy. The Economic Policy Institute estimates that the number of home care workers needed in the workforce will double from 1.1 million in 2010 to 2.1 million in 2020, with the total number of Americans in need of long-term care rising 100 percent, from 13 million in 2000 to 27 million in 2050.[13]

In its 2015 ruling, the Department of Labor stressed that home care workers needed better wages—not just for themselves and their families, but for their clients as well: "The earnings of these workers remain among the lowest in the service industry, impeding efforts to improve both jobs and care," it said. "The Department of Labor believes that the lack of Fair Labor Standards protections harms direct care workers, who depend on wages for their livelihood and that of their families, as well as the individuals receiving services and their families, who depend on a professional, trained workforce to provide high-quality services." [14]

Despite the critical nature of the work they do, many home care workers fall into an employment-law limbo, like so many workers in the "1099 economy" who lack a clear employer to bargain with. The key to unionization for Medicaid-reimbursed home care aides, as *The Nation* wrote, "has been using political pressure to change the laws or win executive orders to render the state or some new public entity the employer for purposes of bargaining." [15] And that is what SEIU did with home care workers in California and Illinois and then across the country.

The fight to improve wages and working conditions in California began in the 1980s and continued for the next twenty years. Los Angeles caregiver Verdia Daniels, who would spend twelve years fighting for union recognition, recalled speaking to organizer Kirk Adams for the first time in 1987 and realizing that there were tens of thousands of other minimum-wage home care workers like her in Los Angeles County alone—in other words, that there were enough workers to have power if they united together. [16]

Initially relying on traditional union organizing tactics alone, we found that the big wins for workers weren't happening, though. Once we shifted our organizing, policy, and coalition-building focus to making the State of California the employer of record, we began to make real progress. California SEIU locals employed three interrelated strategies: (1) grassroots organizing by workers to build political power, (2) changing policy at the state and county levels, and (3) working in coalition with groups of seniors and disabled care recipients. [17]

In February 1999, 74,000 home care workers in Los Angeles County voted to join SEIU, in the biggest organizing victory for the U.S. labor movement since workers at Ford's River Rouge plant joined the United Auto Workers in 1941. It was a campaign that SEIU organizer Kirk

Adams had started in 1987 and that I had the privilege to lead from 1995 until the victory in 1999. Realizing success took twelve years of organizing among a low-wage, diverse, and isolated workforce scattered around the more than four thousand square miles of Los Angeles County.

"It's something big for us," said home care worker Maria Alvarez at the time. She reported that after fourteen years on the job, she still earned only $5.75 an hour. "I'm so happy about the union I feel like flying," she said. "They'll help us win benefits, like health insurance and vacations. Right now, we don't have nothing." [18]

Similar organizing efforts in other California counties, and the growth of home care overall in the years since, have brought the total number of union-represented California home care workers to more than 280,000. In addition, campaigns by both SEIU and AFSCME adapted the California model in other states, including Connecticut, Illinois, Maine, Maryland, Massachusetts, Michigan, Minnesota, Missouri, Ohio, Oregon, Pennsylvania, Vermont, and Washington. Other home care workers in Illinois, Indiana, Montana, Nevada, New York, and Washington won union representation under more traditional labor laws in the private sector.

By 2015, over 600,000 home care workers had won union representation. In most states, wages for workers increased by 100 percent, and workers won health insurance and workers' compensation insurance for the first time. In some states the new unions negotiated longevity-based pay scales, employer-paid training, mileage reimbursement, dental and vision insurance, paid time off, and overtime protection. In an era of overall union decline, the rise of the home care workers movement is the most salient counterexample of how even low-wage, invisible workers can adapt collective bargaining to achieve power and a substantially better life.

A note about the leadership required to achieve these victories: under the leadership of Andy Stern, first as SEIU's organizing director (1984–96) and then as SEIU president (1996–2010), the national union invested tens of millions of dollars in organizing new workers and innovating within the existing collective bargaining model. Stern was the most forward-thinking labor leader of his generation, leading SEIU to invest in adapting old-model collective bargaining to a decidedly postmodern workforce, through campaigns including Justice for Janitors and state-by-state home care organizing efforts.

THE LIMITS OF THE OLD MODEL

Justice for Janitors and the home care campaigns were both enormous successes that have raised wages and benefits and improved working conditions for hundreds of thousands of low-wage and often-marginalized Americans. However, these efforts to extend the model of traditional unionization are limited by a number of factors. It is incredibly time-consuming and expensive to organize a campaign like Justice for Janitors. And the legal gray area that allowed Medicaid-paid home care workers to pass state and local bargaining laws is not found in many other sectors. The SEIU-created home care model of organizing, however impressive its wins, is also limited by antilabor governors, right-to-work laws, and antilabor court decisions (such as the 2014 Supreme Court ruling in *Harris v. Quinn*, which allowed home care workers employed by the State of Illinois to opt out of paying union dues—even while SEIU was still representing them).[19]

The state-level home care victories depended on government policy that valued workers and the collective bargaining process; our efforts were ultimately rebuffed in the Midwest (Ohio, Michigan, and Wisconsin eliminated bargaining rights for home care workers only a few years after they had been implemented) and never took hold in the South. Even the most ambitious and successful attempts to extend the life of the old collective bargaining model—such as SEIU's historic J4J and home care campaigns—seem to be swimming against an increasingly strong current.

GIVING GRIDLOCK THE RUNAROUND: USING LOCAL POLITICS TO LIFT WORKER STANDARDS

With the federal government's power often arrayed against working people and increasing gridlock and partisanship preventing federal action, the worker advocates of the 1990s and 2000s have increasingly turned to municipal government to win campaigns that advance workers' issues. At the core of this strategic vision is the conviction that cities—not the national government—are the arenas where progressive initiatives have the best prospects for enduring success.

Public Dollars for Public Benefit: The Living-Wage Movement

One of the first major victories of this locally based economic justice movement began in the early 1990s in Baltimore, where a community-labor coalition won the nation's first "living wage" law. Living-wage laws require companies that receive municipal contracts or subsidies to pay their workers fair wages. The basic tenets of the living-wage movement are that people who work full-time shouldn't live in poverty, and that taxpayer dollars shouldn't subsidize poverty-wage jobs. As Article 23 of the United Nations Universal Declaration of Human Rights states, "Everyone who works has the right to just and favourable remuneration ensuring for himself and for his family an existence worthy of human dignity." [20]

Living-wage laws typically cover only businesses that receive state assistance or have contracts with the government. Companies that do business with the government have to pay workers at least a specified minimum hourly rate, usually a few dollars above the state minimum wage. These contractors may range from janitorial companies to day care providers, from garbage haulers to airport companies and landscapers. With wage rates ranging from $9 to $14 per hour and higher, living-wage laws raise the wage for public contractors closer to a level that allows low-income workers to meet their families' basic needs. Most living-wage laws also provide wage credits for employers to provide health care.[21] Some living-wage laws require a higher pay rate for employers that don't provide employee health benefits. Other provisions may mandate sick leave, whistleblower protections, family and medical leave, or other worker protections.

The living-wage movement has grown into one of the most prominent ways to use government to rebalance the economic scales for workers: public contracts for procurement of goods, works, and services alone are worth approximately $9.5 trillion per year.[22] These laws have spread rapidly over the last two decades, typically mandating a wage floor significantly above the state and federal minimum wage—high enough so a full-time worker can support a family above the federal poverty level.

However, a growing number of living-wage ordinances have a broader reach and apply to most or all businesses in an area. Taken together, living-wage laws have arisen as "one of the nation's strongest grass-roots political reactions to more than a quarter-century of rising economic inequality," in the words of journalist David Moburg. At the heart of these laws is the conviction that as a major player in the economy, government should use its buying power to support local families instead of driving down wages. "If taxpayers are ultimately paying the wages of contract employees anyway," as Moburg says, "why not simply pay the employees a living wage directly?"[23] This is a fiscal argument as well a moral one, because when businesses pay workers low wages, local taxpayers end up subsidizing these companies through unreimbursed medical care, tax credits, food stamps, and the social costs of poverty and inequality.

Since the first living-wage victory in Baltimore in 1994, the idea has captured the imagination of activists across the country. Starting with a few laws passed around the country in the 1990s, by 2008 there were more than 140 jurisdictions with some kind of living-wage ordinance, including Boston, San Francsico, and St. Louis, as well as the State of Maryland.[24] "The living-wage campaign has developed a whole consciousness about the status of low-wage workers that hadn't existed before," says union organizer and activist Vivian Rothstein.[25]

Living-wage law campaigns don't necessarily lead to the creation of self-sustaining organizations—the organizations behind the living-wage movement continue to depend on funding from unions and foundations. These wins are also much harder to pull off in localities that aren't bright-blue Democratic, lack a strong labor movement, or don't have the ability to run a ballot initiative. And despite the energy unleashed across the country by the living-wage idea, the movement has so far directly benefited only a tiny portion of the low-wage workforce. However, the movement does continue to show promise in reshaping political debates, electing local candidates, influencing local economic development strategies, fostering unionization where it's feasible, and transforming local politics. As a result of the movement, "no candidate, national or local, can avoid talking about living wages or living-wage jobs," says Chicago SEIU leader Keith Kelleher. "It's changed the political vernacular."[26]

Third Party Power: New York's Working Families Party

Another way to change the political vernacular is by going directly into the belly of the beast—forming a new political party directly focused on workers' issues. In American political history, third parties have rarely managed to emerge as one of the major parties by "knocking an existing one off its roost," as history website ThisNation.com puts it. Rather, they have used their voice to boost specific issues onto the national stage.[27]

Veteran organizer Dan Cantor aimed to accomplish something different with the Working Families Party. "I didn't believe," he said, "that the excitement of a presidential campaign was transferrable to the slow grind of building the kind of institutional trust and relations you need to contest for power."[28] So he built something that could.

The core ballot strategy of the Working Families Party (WFP) relies on "fusion voting" or cross-endorsement laws, which allow two or more political parties to list the same candidate on the ballot, pooling the votes for that candidate. New Yorkers voted for Bill de Blasio, for example, on either the Democratic or the WFP ballot line. Fusion laws allow third parties to pool enough votes to automatically qualify for the ballot in the next election and build name recognition and influence over time without acting as a potential spoiler.[29] WFP has achieved more than any other modern third party in reaching these goals. Some of the party's most prominent endorsed candidates include U.S. senators Chris Murphy (CT) and Jeff Merkley (OR), New York City mayor Bill de Blasio, New York governor Andrew Cuomo, and Connecticut governor Dan Malloy As Sarah Jaffe wrote in *In These Times*, "the party's 15 years of clout has given it enough leverage in the states where it works to demand politicians take a position. Elected officials who have had or want the WFP's backing—which means on-the-ground support come election time as well as a stamp of progressive approval—have an incentive to back its policies."[30]

There are now active WFP chapters in New York, Connecticut, Maryland, New Jersey, Oregon, Pennsylvania, and Washington, D.C., along with offshoots in other states. The party is beginning to rack up a list of impressive wins. That includes the WFP cross-endorsed candidate Bill de Blasio as mayor of New York City in 2013, when he swept to victory along with a slate of other progressive WFP candidates, including twelve new progressive city council members.[31] In Connecticut in February 2015, the party elected Ed Gomes to the Connecticut State Senate as the first candidate elected solely on the WFP line, and as its first candidate elected to a state legislature anywhere in America.[32] In 2014, WFP helped persuade the Oregon legislature to enact a proposal that would drastically reduce student debt.

Around the country, there are other noises about independence from the Democratic Party—perhaps the loudest coming from Chicago, where the Chicago Teachers Union is joining other labor and community groups to form an independent political organization. WFP leader Bertha Lewis knows perhaps better than anyone else how hard those fights can be. But she thinks they're worth it: "Sometimes, in years past, you couldn't tell a Democrat from a Republican. No one wanted to talk about race; no one wanted to talk poverty. This whole conversation that we're having nationally about inequality is because [groups like WFP] kept to our principles and our ideas and kept saying, 'There is inequality, there is inequality, there is inequality.'"[33]

"We found our muscle," Lewis concluded. But despite its strong start, the WFP hasn't built many wins other than fusion ballot access, and depends on strong unions to be its largest contributors and its governing coalition. Cantor's organization has shown it has the stuff to win local, as well as win big—but can it grow meaningful power, becoming independent of union and philanthropic funders and of the party-line Democrats they wish to influence or unseat?

A New Model for Old Labor: The Los Angeles Alliance for a New Economy

As labor unions have dwindled in numbers and influence, more than two hundred nonunion worker advocacy groups have sprouted across the nation, struggling to find new ways to lift wages and improve working conditions. These groups, collectively called alt-labor, have shown that community organizing, labor partnerships, and politics can be good bedfellows—and often accomplish more than "big L" labor can on its own.

Established in 1993, the Los Angeles Alliance for a New Economy (LAANE) was originally born out of labor leaders' frustration with traditional union strategy and tactics, and it has grown into one of the most successful alt-labor groups in the country. Madeline Janis, LAANE's first director, said that LAANE was founded because "the old way of labor's doing politics—donating money to candidates—wasn't working." In partnership with the Los Angeles County Federation of Labor, LAANE created a new model: "LAANE would formulate a progressive vision and agenda, and labor would hold elected officials accountable to that vision," said the late Miguel Contreras, one of its founders.[34]

The group first came to public notice in 1997 when it spearheaded a living-wage ordinance for employees of companies with city contracts. LAANE targeted contractors who worked on properties that received public money. Addressing the issue of insecure employment because of an ever-shifting set of low-bid contractors, LAANE won worker-retention ordinances and living-wage ordinances for jobs funded by the city. Worker-retention ordinances guarantee workers the right to stay on the job when they get a new employer; living-wage ordinances guarantee workers a higher-than-minimum-wage rate and health benefits. LAANE persuaded the Los Angeles City Council to enact one of the nation's first living-wage laws—the current version requires pay of $12.28 an hour for workers employed by city contractors or companies receiving city tax breaks.[35] Soon after that, LAANE also set the bar for community benefit agreements: local governments had often compelled developers to pay their construction workers a living wage, but these agreements actually made government assistance conditional on future tenants paying their employees a living wage even after the projects were completed.[36]

By organizing around particular development projects, LAANE had raised wages for many workers—but had not enabled many to join a union and enjoy the security and benefits that membership brings. "We wanted to link our policy work to the industries that unions could organize and that are the core of the L.A. economy," says Roxana Tynan, now LAANE's director.[37]

In 2014, LAANE scored a big win with its new focus. About two years prior, LAANE's organizers hatched plans for a $15.37 minimum wage for hotel workers. LAANE decided to focus on the hotel industry because such a high percentage of its workers live in poverty. Steven Greenhouse reported in the *New York Times*, "With the Chamber of Commerce denouncing the proposal, LAANE supporters knocked on the doors of thousands of small businesses to seek their support and to show that not all businesses were against the plan."[38]

As urban policy professor Peter Dreier notes, LAANE is unique in that it "saw that in a city of immigrants you don't have to vote to get involved in politics. You can make phone calls and knock on doors." [39] Seven hundred and fifty small-business owners signed a petition backing the higher wage, with hundreds placing "Raise L.A." stickers in their windows. The city council ultimately approved the legislation.

These successes have marked LAANE as "the policy shop for the entire L.A. progressive movement" including environmental and immigrant groups, according to Janis. "The unions didn't have the capacity to think about the entire regional economy and where their industries fit into it, much less come up with way to transform those industries," says Janis. "So we did." [40]

But LAANE is still funded primarily by philanthropists and by unions in Los Angeles. Without a self-sustaining revenue source, the model is inherently dependent on the largesse and vision of other organizations, some of them far external to its own work—and, in the case of the unions, with a declining revenue base.

CREATIVE ADAPTATION: THE FREELANCERS UNION AND THE GIG ECONOMY

As we saw in the previous chapter, employment is increasingly fissured and contingent. Many of the largest employers in the United States are now primarily hiring temporary workers, and it has been estimated that half of the jobs added after the Great Recession are contingent. [41] All of the trends taken together have brought us to a moment when more than a third of the American workforce is freelance, temp, or part-time (up from about 30 percent in the late 1990s and early 2000s). [42] But new kinds of initiatives have begun springing up to support these nontraditional workers—initiatives that are even further afield from traditional labor organizations and techniques than the organizations discussed in the previous section.

Alt-Labor Finds a Service Niche: The Freelancers Union

One of the most inspiring reactions to the gig economy has been the Freelancers Union, founded by Sara Horowitz twenty years ago in New York City. Soon after landing a job at a Manhattan law firm at the beginning of her career, Horowitz was shocked to discover that it planned to treat her not as an employee but as an independent contractor. "I saw right away that something wasn't kosher," she recalled in an article published in the *New York Times*. Horowitz realized that she was part of a cost-cutting trend that was affecting a growing swath of the American workforce and that she could do something about it. She and two other lawyers who were also hired as independent contractors formed what they jokingly referred to as the "Transient Workers Union," with the motto "The union makes us not so weak." [43]

Though the Freelancers Union is an alt-labor organization and doesn't bargain with employers like a regular union, it does address gig workers' top concern: affordable health insurance, which Horowitz calls workers' "major pain point." [44] In 2001, the Freelancers launched a new model of affordable group rate health coverage for independent workers and formed a full health insurance company in 2008. More than 25,000 New York workers are now covered by the plan, which brings in over $100 million in revenue every year and boasts an astonishing 95 percent re-enrollment rate. The Obama administration was sufficiently impressed and awarded the Freelancers $340 million in low-interest loans to establish cooperatives in New York, New Jersey, and Oregon to provide health coverage to nontraditional workers. [45]

The Freelancers also count 300,000 members among their ranks nationwide, which include what the *New York Times* called "a motley collection of workers in the fast-evolving freelance economy—whether lawyers, software developers, graphic artists, accountants, consultants, nannies, writers, editors, Web site designers or sellers on Etsy." [46] The Freelancers don't just provide services to their members, they're also active in changing policy—persuading New York City, for example, to eliminate the unincorporated business tax for independent workers who earn less than $100,000 a year, a move that saves a freelancer up to $3,400 annually. "The social unionism of the 1920s had it right," Horowitz reflects. "They said, 'We serve workers 360 degrees. It's not just about their work, it's about their whole life.' We view things the same way." [47]

Horowitz's untraditional, entrepreneurial ideas have gained traction beyond what Greenhouse calls "the usual worker-advocacy crowd." Among other recognition, Horowitz was recently appointed to the board of the Federal Reserve Bank of New York. She "saw that labor unions basically haven't innovated for several generations, and in the meantime the world has changed and there were tremendous needs that weren't being met," says Bill Drayton, the founder of Ashoka, a nonprofit foundation that invests in social entrepreneurs.

Perhaps more than any of the other alt-labor organizations, the Freelancers Union has succeeded in building something approximating scale (with hundreds of thousands of members), and in achieving a revenue stream that's not nearly as fragile as that of organizations that rely exclusively on philanthropy and unions for their funding. The question remains, however, whether it can build the economic and political power required to truly transform the lives of workers in the gig economy through increasing pay, benefits, and income security, not just the provision of services to workers in a world where the upstream economic actors ultimately call all the shots.

Power Through Transparency? Rating, Review, and Petition Platforms for Workers

Figuring out how to support and empower workers in the new economy isn't simple. One promising avenue is the growth of online reputation and review sites, which use the tools of the Internet to help workers choose better employers—and to push employers to become better ones.

While many rating and review systems, like Yelp and Amazon, help consumers make better-informed purchasing decisions, a few like Glassdoor are beginning to help people make an even more important decision: where to work. Nearly half of all job hunters now consult Glassdoor, which encourages workers to post reviews of their employer.[48] The site provides a platform that has been lacking, for workers to give *anonymous* feedback about their employers. And they have done so, by the millions. The business magazine *Inc.* calls Glassdoor "an anonymous forum for employees to dish on companies, bosses, and salaries, and distill scores down to an easy, five-star system."[49]

A more purely grassroots reputation and review effort is Turkopticon, which works inside the Mechanical Turk service run by Amazon.com. Mechanical Turk, named after a famous eighteenth-century chess-playing robot that turned out to conceal an elf-sized grand master, has excited technology watchers who like the idea that crowd-sourcing can become crowd-working. Instead of hiring employees or negotiating freelance contracts, anyone can post a job that can be done on a computer, such as transcribing an audio recording or writing ad copy, to the Mechanical Turk website and instantly pick from a host of willing (or desperate) workers. The "requester" posts a job, known as a HIT—a human intelligence task—to Mechnical Turk, naming their price and how quickly they want the hit done. The person taking the job is said (ironically?) to "take a HIT." Known as Turkers, these workers sometimes take jobs for just pennies per task.

Amazon is coy about their numbers, but it's estimated that between $10 million and $150 million in transactions go through Mechanical Turk each year, with Amazon taking between 10 and 20 percent.[50] There are now more than 500,000 Turkers in 190 countries. But even the best and most recommended workers have no minimum-wage protections, benefits, or security—nothing but a few dollars or cents in their Amazon account. The median hourly wage for tasks performed on Turk is a mere $1.38.[51] And Turkers get paid only if their requester is satisfied with the work they've done—there is no appeal process available for Turkers who have been exploited or scammed. "Effectively, the system allows any hirer to live the free market dream," said Julian Dobson of the *Huffington Post*, by "bypassing all labor regulation and achieving a complete separation between the commissioning of work and the welfare of the worker."[52]

Enter Turkopticon, a small piece of software that helps workers track which employers are worth their effort—and which to avoid. Written by Lilly Irani, a technology specialist at the University of California, Turkopticon is a browser plugin that gives Turkers a reliable way to check the reputation of requesters. As a worker browses HITs, Turkopticon places a button next to each requester and highlights requesters for whom there are reviews from other workers. Turkopticon's site says that it "lets you report and avoid shady employers," and that it "helps the people in the 'crowd' of crowdsourcing watch out for each other—because nobody else seems to be."[53] Dobson notes, "Far from the market regulating itself, it was down to an independent academic and groups of workers sharing their experiences to bring some order to it."[54]

In 2012, former union staffer Michelle Miller began to notice a pattern of "spikes in attention" around new economy worker issues, like issues of exploitation faced by the Turkers. "A group would form around an issue for a couple of weeks," she says. "There would be some excitement, some media coverage of the issue the workers were talking about, and then it would either be resolved or it wouldn't be, and everything would sort of dissipate back to the way it was."[55] Her answer was a platform, Coworker.org, that allows workers to post petitions—directed at their employer or other upstream decision maker—to agitate for change in their working conditions. Coworker describes itself as "a global platform for engaging in workplace advocacy." It's different from existing petition sites such as Avaaz.org and Change.org in that it builds communities not around one-off issues, but around workplaces, whether virtual or physical—though most of the petitions have been created by non–gig economy workers with a physical workplace. Once someone self-identifies as associated with a workplace, Coworker keeps them updated about new campaigns relevant to that workplace.

For workers, gig economy and otherwise, these platforms are important tools for navigating a virtual workplace where employers can be distant and unaccountable. But they go only so far in providing a sustained support structure for the growing number of workers in the freelance economy. And none of these organizations is building permanent worker institutions that replicate the power and reach of traditional unions. In a loose labor market, bad employers still hold the advantage when workers stand up for themselves.

On-Demand Advocacy: Peers.org and Online Platforms
The on-demand economy is built around the short-term leasing of human and physical resources—usually through an online platform. Sometimes referred to by supporters as "the sharing economy," Kevin Roose in *New York Magazine* describes the label as a "a Silicon Valley–invented term used to describe the basket of start-ups (Uber, Lyft, Airbnb, et al.) that allow users to rent their labor and belongings to strangers," while Natalie Foster, a leader in the on-demand economy, defines it as "people coming together person-to-person and exchanging goods, time, money, homes, skills, and doing it in a way that is inspiring."[56] Jason Tanz attributes the success of these start-ups to the invention of a "set of digital tools that enable and encourage us to trust our fellow human beings."[57]

Peers.org, started in 2013 by many of the leading on-demand platforms to help advocate for the on-demand economy, has stepped into this gray space, providing both services to on-demand companies and a unified political base against unwanted regulation. Founded by veteran organizer Foster, Peers' work has three main prongs: "grow, mainstream and protect."[58] Peers seeks to improve workers lives in the on-demand economy without generating conflicts with their employers: the online platforms. Peers skirts these conflicts because it's a grassroots partner with the platforms, united in their desire to carve out a space for these services to thrive, particularly by ensuring that local city councils don't regulate them out of business.

Foster and the Peers crew began their work by talking to people all over the country about the on-demand economy, including on-demand companies as well as the people who work on their platforms. Foster found that while "people have had positive experiences with everything from Etsy to Uber to local tool sharing," according to Nancy Scola on NextCity.org, "those people didn't necessarily see themselves as participating in anything more meaningful than one-off transactions." So, Foster said, "we decided to create that container."[59]

Peers has filled that container with offerings similar to the Freelancers Union's, with two types of insurance for sharing the risk in the on-demand economy. Airbnb hosts and ride-hailing drivers can now opt in to an insurance program protecting against damages or losses due to unexpected disruptions in employment. Peers' Homesharing Liability Insurance is an inexpensive personal liability plan that covers accommodations shared through any platform (with Airbnb being by far the biggest, though HomeAway.com and VacationRentals.com are also players). Smartly, the insurance allows hosts to opt in to the insurance for only the months that they need it.

Peers' other insurance offering is their Keep Driving insurance, which provides access to a working car in the event that a ride-hailing driver's car is damaged in an accident, while the Keep Driving program is available for delivery drivers not employed by a ride-hailing company like Uber, Lyft, or Sidecar. Though ride-hailing companies don't allow drivers to use other people's cars, Peers has also worked out a deal that lets drivers rent cars through the hybrid rental company Breeze. As Peers' executive director, Shelby Clark, said when announcing the new insurance programs, "When the solutions don't exist, we will build them ourselves."[60] Foster is highly optimistic that Peers has a place in the new economy because work distribution platforms, in her words, "will be the defining economic story of the 21st century."[61]

The uprisings and worker-empowering tech platforms of the new economy are an encouraging sign. But although millions of workers are now engaged in what is still the newest part of our economy, there have been no true home runs that have yet succeeded in doing the thing that workers need most: lifting their wages to a livable level for the twenty-first century.

ALT-LABOR RISES FROM IMMIGRANT WORKER CENTERS

If the on-demand economy consists largely of jobs that were once full-time and permanent, the "excluded economy" largely consists of jobs that never had protections at all or have been systematically stripped of protections even prior to the advent of the technologically enabled gig era. Agricultural and domestic workers were never included in the major labor legislation that brought us a defined workweek, overtime pay requirements, and so on. Restaurant workers are usually paid a specially designated "subminimum" wage and left to make up the difference in tips. Guest workers in the United States on visas are by definition tied to a particular employer and what few rights they have under the law are hard to enforce in practice.

Even in the "old" economy, race, gender, and immigration status tracked strongly with a lack of formal job protection. Tipped workers are highly likely to be female, most hourly and piece-rate agricultural and guest workers are immigrants, and domestic workers are often both female and people of color. They were all excluded from the labor laws meant to protect white males. Excluding domestic workers and agricultural workers from both the National and Fair Labor Standards Acts was part of a key compromise to secure the votes of Southern Democrats in Congress during the New Deal. Southern Democrats were concerned that these predominately black workers would gain economic and political power if they were able to unionize or secure higher wages. One of the original demands of the 1963 March on Washington was a "broadened Fair Labor Standards Act to include all areas of employment which are presently excluded."[62]

As the American economy shifts toward low-wage service and gig work, more and more workers are left out of the legally mandated basic labor contract between employers and employees, lacking the legal option to collectively bargain—assuming they even had the power to overcome the steep hurdles currently required for winning a union representation election. Many corners of the service sector are virtually union-free—even where, as in restaurants, workers have the legal right to organize.

In the past twenty years, however, another answer has appeared for these excluded workers. Known as worker centers, these organizations fight for worker justice among nonunion workers, often those excluded legally or in practice from formal labor markets and labor laws. Worker center expert Janice Fine of Rutgers University defines them as "community based mediating institutions that provide support to low-wage workers."[63]

Servitude in Modern America: Coalition of Immokalee Workers

The Coalition of Immokalee Workers (CIW) was founded in 1996 by former migrant farmworker Lucas Benitez and lawyer Greg Asbed in Immokalee, Florida. CIW identifies as a worker-based human rights organization and focuses on improving the working conditions and pay of agricultural workers as well as ending the modern-day slavery once prevalent in the Florida tomato fields. Benitez's involvement in the work of CIW and its predecessor (Southwest Florida Farmworker Project) dates to 1993, when he helped organize a boycott against a field supervisor accused of abusing a worker. He has been called the "Cesar Chavez of the new millennium."

"Slavery has a modern form: it's called debt bondage, and you can find it in the Florida citrus industry," one labor publication asserted in 2002 after CIW uncovered and investigated three Florida-based growers for conspiracy to hold workers in involuntary servitude, winning federal criminal convictions against the companies (for servitude as well as extortion and use of a firearm during a crime of violence).[64] CIW's community participation in slavery investigations has been cited across the nation as a model for antislavery work; it pursued a half dozen slavery cases that helped free more than a thousand workers.

The CIW has used a combination of community organizing,

protests, marches, boycotts, online advocacy, and hunger strikes to pressure the largest sellers of tomatoes—quick service restaurants and supermarket chains—to join its Fair Food Program. The program has directly targeted the companies' brands by raising consumer awareness of conditions in the fields, encouraging consumers to sign petitions, as well as boycott companies who will not sign on to the program. By traveling up the supply chain to find recognizable brands—those with the most to lose from prolonged negative publicity—CIW has won fifteen major restaurant, grocery, and food-service agreements. Showing CIW's incredible persistence, some corporate campaigns have gone on for more six years before achieving success. Brands signed to date include:

Yum! Brands (Taco Bell)—2005
McDonald's—2007
Burger King, Subway, and Whole Foods—2008
Compass and Bon Appétit Management Company—2009
Aramark and Sodexo—2010
Trader Joe's—2012
Chipotle Mexican Grille—2012
Walmart—2014
Stop and Shop, Giant, and the Fresh Market—2015

In 2010, after more than a decade of boycotts and legal wrangling, CIW finalized a landmark agreement with local tomato growers and buyers to pay the pickers a higher rate for the fruit they harvest.[65]

The heart of CIW's program, though, is not the additional wages—it's the education. The Fair Food Program is implemented, monitored, and enforced by the related Fair Food Standards Council. Worker leaders and staff run daily sessions in the fields on labor rights. Working together, CIW and the pickers now ensure that all workers in this high-turnover industry know what they're owed under the terms of the Fair Food Program as well as through traditional labor law.

One historic measure of the coalition's victory comes from CIW co-founder and former tomato worker Lucas Benitez. At a congressional hearing, he recalled how during a 1997 worker hunger strike a grower said that they would never meet the workers' single demand for dialogue. "Let me put it to you like this: The tractor doesn't tell the farmer how to run a farm," the grower said. "That's how they've always seen us," Benitez added. "Just another tool and nothing more. But we aren't alone anymore. Today there are millions of consumers with us willing to use their buying power to eliminate the exploitation behind the food they buy. And a new dawn for social responsibility in the agriculture industry is on its way."[66]

Eric Schlosser, the author of *Fast Food Nation*, also noted the enormous significance in the win:

> This may be the most important victory for American farmworkers since passage of California's Agricultural Labor Relations Act in 1975. That bill heralded a golden age for farm workers. But the state government apparatus it created, the Agricultural Labor Relations Board, got taken over by the growers in the 1980s and watered down the reforms.
>
> In Florida, the Coalition has chosen a different path, avoiding government and putting pressure on the corporations at the top of nation's food chain. The strategy clearly works and can be emulated by other workers in other states. In the absence of a government that cares about the people at the bottom, here's a way to achieve change.[67]

The CIW and the worker leaders have achieved enormous improvements in the Florida tomato-growing industry. But their successes have been long in coming and require an ongoing, deep commitment to community organizing with the Immokalee workers, raising a question as to whether this model is scalable to other parts of agriculture or to the larger economy. Other possible limitations include the industry-wide low-wage floor in agriculture—could CIW's efforts ever help lift these workers, who do backbreaking labor that cannot reasonably be continued past the age of fifty, out of poverty-level jobs?

Strikes Without Unions: New York Taxis
In New York City in the late 1990s, another alt-labor campaign made the public take notice, but it used very different tactics than did the workers in Immokalee. In a move that presaged the "new economy"

restructuring to come, in 1979 the city's Taxi and Limousine Commission severed taxi drivers from traditional employment with the cab companies and converted them into independent contractors. The lucky owners of taxi medallions—the astronomically expensive permits to operate NYC cabs—leased them out in twelve-hour shifts to drivers, who now had to pay medallion owners for the privilege of driving cabs. Drivers were stripped of health benefits—and the right to unionize (one-sixth of the drivers had previously been unionized).

But the taxi drivers fought back. Led by twenty-three-year-old Indian immigrant Bhairavi Desai, a group of allied workers called the New York Taxi Workers Alliance began aggressively organizing. By 1998, the Taxi Workers had enough momentum to launch a strike that shut down most of New York City's cab service. Drivers were pushing back against Mayor Rudy Giuliani's proposed new rules that included more expensive insurance requirements and faster suspensions for drivers with violations. One day in May, drivers stepped out of their cars and onto the streets to distribute thousands of leaflets to the public. Giuliani dismissed the strike as "a theater of the absurd," but the *New York Times* reported that "city officials were stunned" by its success.[68] The drivers didn't stop Giuliani's new rules, but the drivers now knew what they could do.

In 2004, the Taxi Workers were able to leverage a fare increase with the Taxi and Limousine Commission—the first real raise for drivers in many years (before that, when there was a fare increase fleet owners would just raise the lease rates). And in 2007, the drivers won an even bigger set of concessions after holding a two-day work stoppage: the Taxi and Limousine Commission passed a suite of pro-driver measures which raised fares, created a health-care and disability fund, and capped the fees drivers paid to leasing companies for their cabs.

The organization has now grown to 15,000 members, an impressive *half* of the city's active licensed drivers. They pay $100 a year to fund the bulk of the organization's $600,000 budget. But the drivers' raises in 2007 only brought their wages back to where they were following their last raise in 2004. Taxi Workers' coordinator Victor Salazar says the group must expand its membership to effect more meaningful change, building on its model of workplace activism and political mobilization.[69] Whether or not that is possible, the question remains whether the Taxi Drivers' model could be effective in other cities, which are generally far less dependent on taxi service than New York (where more than half of all households own no cars). Despite its successes, nothing approaching the group's power has appeared elsewhere. Furthermore, in an Uber-ized (and ultimately driverless) economy, will it even be worth trying?

Isolated But Not Alone: Domestic Workers United and the National Domestic Workers Alliance

Domestic workers, much like home health care workers, work long hours doing manual and emotional labor with few legal protections. The domestic workforce—those who clean or care for children in the home—is also almost exclusively female and disproportionately minority, and was also excluded from the National Labor Relations Act. The National Domestic Workers Alliance reports that 23 percent of domestic workers are paid below the state minimum wage, and 70 percent make less than $13 an hour. The median wage of live-in domestic workers is $6.15 an hour—with no overtime.[70]

Unlike home care workers, no segment of the domestic industry has been unionized, or even represented by a strong advocacy organization. "Women's work in the home has never been recognized as work," according to the Association for Women's Rights. "It is seen as 'help,' and thus, by extension, women working in others' homes as wage labor have never been recognized as real workers."[71] Domestic workers do not have traditional workplaces, and private individuals are not traditional employers. Isolation, a lack of free time and paid leave, and, for immigrants, fear of deportation have all stood in the way of domestic workers finding a collective voice.

The past decade, however, has seen an unlikely surge of organizing by American domestic workers. Ai-jen Poo is the most well known American advocate for domestic workers' rights. Along with South Asian domestic workers who had previously worked in Hong Kong as domestics before arriving in New York, Poo co-founded the alt-labor group Domestic Workers United (DWU) in 2000. They knew that they deserved more than what they found in the United States, because the domestic workers in Hong Kong all work under a standard contract and have a powerful history of organizing.

Through the 2000s, organizers built relationships one conversation at a time, and word spread about DWU among networks of immigrant workers, through churches, and around the playgrounds frequented by nannies. In 2003, DWU members celebrated its first major win, the passage of legislation in New York City compelling employment agencies that place domestic workers to play a role in protecting the rights of domestic workers, as well as a resolution calling on all domestic employers to follow the guidelines in DWU's standard contract. DWU has also raised the visibility of domestic workers in New York by exposing cases of exploitation and organizing grassroots campaigns for power, respect, and fair labor standards. Since 2000, DWU has won over $400,000 in unpaid wages for exploited domestic workers in the state.

But the effort for which DWU is primarily known is the New York Domestic Workers Bill of Rights. A DWU convention resulted in the drafting of the first Domestic Workers Bill of Rights, and by 2010 the organization was formidable enough to pressure the New York State legislature into passing it. The bill, passed with union and grassroots support, gave protections to domestic workers, including a living wage, overtime, a weekly day of rest, a minimum of three paid days off a year, and legal protection from harassment and discrimination. The bill is the most comprehensive law protecting domestic workers in the history of the United States.

Poo also established a related umbrella organization, the National Domestic Workers Alliance (NDWA), in 2007 to consolidate the voice and power of domestic workers as a workforce. NDWA has grown into an alliance of thirty-five local, grassroots, membership-based affiliate organizations like DWU, uniting thousands of nannies, housecleaners, and caregivers in eighteen cities and twelve states around the country.[72]

While DWU and NDWA have achieved some notable organizing successes with a morally compelling and media-savvy movement, domestic workers still face a number of serious hurdles. There is no sustainable revenue model, outside of philanthropic grants, to carry on this work. And the DWU's flagship legislation, the Bill of Rights, is very difficult to enforce. A 2012 study commissioned by the Ford Foundation found that in spite of the Bill of Rights, the wages and working conditions of domestic workers in New York hadn't improved.[73]

As Ai-Jen Poo says, "Care jobs are the jobs of the future. The question is: will they be good jobs with paths to opportunity, or will they be 21st-century sweatshops?"[74]

NDWA has captured the imagination of many progressives with its early organizing and its Bill of Rights campaigns. The challenges they face, however, are similar to those of other alt-labor organizations: how to exercise power to change workers' lives for the better, how to impact the majority of U.S. domestic workers (not merely a tiny handful), and how to build a revenue stream that insulates the organization from the fickleness of philanthropic grant cycles.

From 9/11 to Organizing the 99%: The Restaurant Opportunities Center

The Restaurant Opportunities Center (ROC) was initially formed to assist surviving restaurant workers who were displaced by the attacks of September 11, 2001. Formed by UNITE HERE and other unions as the Immigrant Workers Assistance Alliance project, it ran a temporary relief center for the 350 workers at Windows on the World, the restaurant atop the North Tower of the World Trade Center. The Alliance found that demand for assistance remained high after 9/11, leading immigration attorney Saru Jayaraman and former Windows on the World waiter Fekkak Mamdouh to found the Restaurant Opportunities Center of New York (ROC-NY) as a permanent restaurant workers' organization.

Jayaraman describes ROC as a "place to begin to organize the 99 percent of the industry that doesn't have a union," and journalist Josh Eidelson calls ROC "an all-purpose resource for food-sector employees." ROC educates workers about their rights and provides instruction in restaurant and English-language skills; advises and publicizes "high road" employers; and engages in grassroots action to raise public and customer awareness, such as street protests at restaurants.[75]

The ROC also lobbies state and local lawmakers and helps workers take legal action to enforce their rights, which it says are violated more often than in any other industry.[76] "I have worked in all sorts of restaurants—Italian, French, and American—and they all violated my rights," says ROC New York (ROC-NY) volunteer organizer Juan Martín Reyes Varela. "In particular, I experienced racial insults because of the color of my hair, the color of my skin, and my accent."[77] In New York, over 90 percent of restaurant workers are unorganized, and 67 percent are immigrants, many of them undocumented. To organize these workers, ROC-NY activists begin by talking to them about their rights. Reyes Varela worked at the Famous Pizza Restaurant on Ann Street, which went out of business after 9/11. "ROC-NY gave me classes and advised me," he said. "They explained that even though a worker may be illegal, he or she still has rights as a worker, such as the right to overtime. Now that I know my rights, I feel more secure."[78]

In 2009, ROC expanded nationally and now maintains staffed chapters in ten cities and has an operational presence in another thirty cities, providing fund-raising, training, and technical assistance to each chapter with the goal of helping each grow into a self-sustaining affiliate within a few years. ROC has pursued lawsuits against restaurants in New York, Detroit, New Orleans, and elsewhere for wage theft, working off the clock, discrimination in promotion, and other issues. Nationally, the center has won settlements against thirteen employers, winning about $6.5 million in back wages and penalties, since its inception in 2001.

ROC initially made its mark by targeting high-profile restaurateurs in Manhattan, including Daniel Boulud of Daniel, Alan Stillman of Smith & Wollensky, and, most recently, celebrity chef Mario Batali's restaurants. Employees complained of overtime violations and racial discrimination at Del Posto, Batali's Italian restaurant in Manhattan, and following a two-year fight Batali settled. Del Posto will become one of the "high road" employers collaborating with the center to implement improved benefits. In a statement to the *New York Times*, Batali maintained his company's innocence but said he looked forward to working with the center.[79]

ROC also operates two model restaurants in New York and Detroit to train workers in the restaurant business; they pay living wages and benefits and are substantially led by employees. The founding members of the Colors restaurants included a number of former Windows on the World workers.

While worker centers are effective in helping to curb legal abuses, they are less influential in changing policy or the overall economic terrain in a way that significantly improves workers' lives. Centers are also primarily dependent on philanthropy; even the Taxi Workers Alliance, one of the standout centers in terms of independent revenue, receives dues from fewer than a quarter of its members. The National Domestic Workers Alliance receives dues from none of its members.[80] The core challenge, as Rutgers labor professor Janice Fine says, is that as worker centers "struggle to identify tactics and strategies that will be effective for workers who have very little economic and political power," they "have not yet figured out how to formalize membership and many may never do so." She noted that "it is not yet clear whether immigrant worker centers will follow a trajectory toward social movement organization, labor market institution, or a new organizational form altogether."[81]

POPULAR UPRISINGS, LARGE AND SMALL

Some experiments that have built power for working people are not institutional organizing efforts, but rather sparks that turned into flames, however briefly. The protests against the World Trade Organization's trade agreement in 1999, protests against Wisconsin governor Scott Walker's law to de-unionize public sector workers in 2011, and, most significantly, the Occupy movement of 2011 were all genuine social movements for a moment in time. They were inspiring, at times they were frustrating, and they were real. They weren't part of any group's annual plan and budget, but rather spontaneous and viral responses by masses of people that changed the national conversation, despite not having a lasting organizational presence or, ultimately, winning any clear demands.

The Battle in Seattle, 1999

In addition to the struggles of the historically marginalized, low-wage, and disproportionately immigrant home care workers, janitors, and agricultural and restaurant workers that we have examined so far, the 1990s also saw the first surge of resistance around the loss of traditionally blue-collar middle-class jobs—particularly in manufacturing. Throughout the 1980s and 1990s, trade agreements and domestic policy had supported the shift of manufacturing jobs to countries with fewer environmental protections, lower wages, and fewer rights.

In the United States, the North American Free Trade Agreement

(NAFTA) was the most (in)famous of these agreements. Signed by President Bill Clinton in 1993, NAFTA is a free trade and investment agreement that caused the displacement of more than 879,000 U.S. jobs, mostly in high-wage manufacturing industries. NAFTA provided investors with a unique set of guarantees designed to stimulate foreign investment and the movement of factories within the hemisphere, especially from the United States to Canada and Mexico. No labor or environmental protections were contained in the core agreement. As a result, according to the Economic Policy Institute, "NAFTA tilted the economic playing field in favor of investors, and against workers and the environment, resulting in a hemispheric 'race to the bottom' in wages and environmental quality." [82]

By the late 1990s, there was a significant amount of public anger over the effects of NAFTA and other global trade agreements. A loose coalition with varying motivations (pro-labor, anticapitalist, antiglobalization, pro-environment) and equally varied tactics came together for the 1999 World Trade Organization meeting. These protesters formed what Howard Zinn called "a remarkable set of alliances—steelworkers rallied with environmentalists, and machinists joined animal rights activists." The summit meeting of the WTO was shaken by the severity of the protests that ensued, and the talks eventually collapsed. Prior to the "Battle of Seattle," there was almost no mention of antiglobalization in the U.S. media, but the WTO protests forced the media to report on why so many people were so angry about the WTO. It represented a shift in the opinion climate: the moment when the unchallenged dominance of twenty years of right-wing economics began to unravel. [83]

Though the movement didn't survive in a form that brought singular change to the balance of globalized corporate power, the Battle in Seattle was significant. As Zinn put it, "probably the most dramatic attempt to bring to the American people and to the world the facts of corporate domination over the lives of ordinary people was [seen at] the great gathering of demonstrators in Seattle in the last months of 1999." [84]

Wisconsin, 2011

A very different kind of uprising took place more than a decade after the WTO uprising in Seattle. Wisconsin was the first state in the

United States to provide collective bargaining rights to public employees. But in 2010, Wisconsin elected Scott Walker to the governor's mansion. Immediately after his inauguration, Walker introduced a "budget repair plan" that limited collective bargaining powers for most of Wisconsin's public employees under the auspices of balancing the state budget. Without a union contract, public workers' wages and benefits could be more easily cut. Walker threatened that thousands of state workers would have to be laid off unless public employees were stripped of their collective bargaining rights.

A firestorm of controversy immediately ignited. But Walker knew what he was getting into: he called on the Wisconsin National Guard and other state agencies to "prevent disruptions in state service" (in the form of public workers walking off the job). Calling on the Guard underscored "just how accompli he considered his fait," said Harold Meyerson in the *Washington Post*.[85]

Activists started organizing. Demonstrators came to the state capitol in Madison in February 2011 and began a dizzying and dramatic week of protesting the budget "repair" bill. On February 15, tens of thousands of protesters demonstrated in and around the capitol building, chanting, "Kill the Bill." Union members, students, and citizens testified before the Wisconsin legislature during public hearings that lasted seventeen hours (the majority opposed the bill).[86] A few days later, in one of the most impressive Hail Mary passes in American political history, senate minority leader Mark Miller led all fourteen senate Democrats in fleeing to Illinois to prevent the quorum necessary for a vote. The missing legislators pledged that they wouldn't return to Wisconsin unless Walker agreed to remove the limitations on collective bargaining from the bill. The total number of protesters reached one hundred thousand.[87]

But in the end, the Wisconsin Assembly found a way to pass the bill, stripping public workers of their collective bargaining rights. Protesters and assembly Democrats shouted, "Shame!" as the Republican legislators quickly filed out of the building after the vote.[88] The *Washington Post* wrote that week, "In Egypt, workers are having a revolutionary February. In the United States, by contrast, February is shaping up as the cruelest month workers have known in decades."[89]

Though Walker's death blow to public sector collective bargaining in Wisconsin has had far-reaching consequences—emboldening other Republican-controlled states to enact measures that weaken unions and cut worker benefits—the protesters showed that even with the right-wing power machine arrayed against Wisconsin's workers, a stand by ordinary people could make the nation pay attention to workers' issues. The *American Prospect* reflected during the protests that "the backlash against Walker's successful drive to end collective bargaining for Wisconsin's public employees has been stunning in its scope, intensity, and (ongoing) duration. The big political question," it said, "is how far and how deep that backlash will go."[90]

Four years later, it hasn't, sadly, gone very far. Wisconsin was only the first of several states to adopt anti-worker legislation following the 2010 elections. Walker ultimately succeeded in his repeal of collective bargaining laws and inspired other anti-worker governors to do the same.

Occupy Wall Street, 2011

In the wake of the revolutionary demonstrations and protests of the Arab Spring, a group of organizers gathered in the summer of 2011 to share the lessons of the anti-austerity and pro-democracy uprisings that had been erupting in Egypt, Tunisia, Greece, Spain, and elsewhere. The lessons of protests in Europe, the Mideast, and New York City were woven together and the idea for Occupy Wall Street was born. At the same time, as *Adbusters'* Kalle Lasn and Micah White wrote in June 2011, "America needs its own Tahir" and called for a "Million Man March on Wall Street" (Tahir was the square in Egypt that became synonymous with the Egyptian freedom movement).

Agitation was growing organically and simultaneously among other groups, all reacting to income inequality as well as the Great Recession and subsequent bank bailouts. Several thousand union members and supporters marched on Wall Street; the online hackers collective Anonymous spread information about hacks on prominent financial websites; a New York City activist launched a Tumblr page, "We Are the 99 Percent"; and in August a group of artists were arrested after days of protesting on Wall Street—nude.[91]

Occupy was never conventional or tame. It represented a popular uprising that was not organized along familiar lines. "The traditional left—the unions, the progressive academics, the community organizations—wanted nothing to do with this in the beginning," said filmmaker Marisa Holmes.[92] Many labor leaders sat up and took note of the impact that Occupy had on the national consciousness about income inequality: a movement had galvanized the nation around ordinary people's economic issues—and it wasn't the institutional labor movement. However, SEIU and other unions did send funding and staff to "occupations" occurring in dozens of cities around the country.

The Occupy slogan "We are the 99%" called out the small segment of the population that was benefiting from current policies (the 1 percent) and united those who were not (the 99 percent) under a common banner. During the fall of 2011, tens of thousands of protesters marched in the streets of more than nine hundred cities around the world, occupied the London Stock Exchange, and hacked the website of the New York Stock Exchange.[93] More than any recent movement, Occupy set the stage for the fast-food protests of 2013 and the broad public support that greeted the demand for higher wages.

SYNTHESIZING TACTICS AND TAKING ON BIGGER TARGETS

The economic justice movements, campaigns, and organizations we have covered in this section are now inspiring a new generation of initiatives. They may occur in the context of hope for eventual union recognition, but are open to other outcomes. They adopt strategies and tactics from mass uprisings, union campaigns, worker centers, local political efforts, and other sources, and mix them into what are essentially long-term efforts by workers to make demands on some of the most powerful actors in the economy. Mark Meinster, who has worked to organize Walmart warehouse workers in Illinois, reflected that "the labor movement has tried a range of strategies over the last 20 years—comprehensive campaigns, neutrality agreements, NLRB organizing—and while we've learned a lot through those strategies, none of it has reversed the decline. So now we're at a point where there's openness to new strategies."[94]

The following campaigns, at Walmart and in the fast-food industry, reveal how the right combination of new-labor strategies and tactics—the energy of street protests, the savvy of a well-organized campaign, and the persistence of a community-based advocacy organization—has begun to change the playing field and win big-money gains for workers.

Making Change While Making Low Wages: OUR Walmart

Walmart is the nation's largest retailer and largest private employer, with over 1.4 million associates—Walmart employs nearly one out of every one hundred U.S. workers.[95] It is known for its rock-bottom prices and—thanks to the activism of its employees—the public is also increasingly aware of its rock-bottom wages. The company made $16 billion in profit last year, and the majority-owner Walton family is worth almost $145 billion. Yet the company pays two-thirds of its workforce—825,000 workers—less than $25,000 a year, with similarly stingy benefits.[96] So it's no surprise that Walmart costs taxpayers $6.2 billion annually in public assistance support—between $3,015 and $5,815 per worker.[97]

Walmart has long been the "Holy Grail" of organizing, but unions have had no success with traditional organizing campaigns there. Decades of attempts to unionize Walmart stores in the United States and Canada have been met with firings of union activists, outsourcing, and even store closings.[98] Walmart management has an ironclad no-unions policy: the only Walmart store where workers ever succeeded in unionizing all of its nonmanagement employees, in Quebec, Canada, in 2005, was promptly shuttered by management before contract negotiations could even begin. The Supreme Court of Canada found that Walmart violated labor law when it closed the store. "Once a union has been certified, you have to negotiate," said University of Ottawa labor professor Gilles LeVasseur.[99]

Walmart has been a particularly significant target for worker advocates not just because it stands for low wages, but because the company is so large that it sets wages and prices among suppliers and competitors. As journalist Erica Smiley wrote, "as the largest U.S. employer, Walmart sets the standard not just for the retail and service industries, but for the economy as a whole. Walmart's poor labor practices and standards put pressure on many other businesses to lower wages and benefits in order to compete. The result is a Walmart economy where our jobs, health care and labor standards have all downgraded."[100]

For the past decade, multiple labor groups have tried to organize with Walmart workers. But the most prominent and successful advocacy group has been OUR Walmart (Organization United for Respect at Walmart), initially resourced and spearheaded by the United Food and Commercial Workers Union (UFCW). Headed by veteran Justice for Janitors organizers, OUR Walmart's cleverly named "Making Change at Walmart" campaign began working with Walmart associates in late 2010. Its official launch at Walmart's 2011 annual shareholders meeting featured a rally with dozens of Walmart associates and hundreds of former associates and supporters.

In November 2012, the campaign launched its signature effort— a national Black Friday protest, with five hundred associates in forty-six states walking off the job and rallying at Walmarts across the country.[101] Walmart asked the National Labor Relations Board to block the protests, but the board refused. OUR Walmart Leader Dan Schlademan said, "We had a goal on Black Friday to see if we could get a 1,000 actions in Walmart stores, and actually had 1,200." [102]

Building on this success, OUR Walmart repeated the Black Friday walkouts and protests in 2013 and 2014. Workers in multiple states submitted formal strike notices, and thousands nationwide rallied in front of stores.[103] Workers called on the retail giant to pay them a living wage of $15 an hour, to provide a work schedule with consistent, full-time hours, and to stop retaliating against workers who speak out. Other workers "may want to do a strike as well but are hesitant," said Charles Brown, an OUR Walmart member who unloads trucks in Newport News, Virginia. "They need to know they don't have anything to be afraid of. If we don't stand up, no one else is going to stand up for us." [104] Brown missed three shifts to take part in the demonstrations.

Observers of the strikes were impressed with the scope of their impact. The *Huffington Post* labor reporter Dave Jamieson wrote that the sight of Walmart workers going on strike over the past few years gave "a shot in the arm to the labor movement, [and] even if the numbers aren't large enough to impact sales," the protests "aren't necessarily meant to disrupt the company's operations, but instead to draw attention to the participants' grievances." [105]

Aside from the Black Friday strikes, other current OUR Walmart efforts include rallies at Walmart's annual shareholders meeting; members from all over the nation head to Arkansas in the "Ride for Respect."[106] Hundreds of self-described "Walmart moms" have also held strikes in twenty cities nationwide. In 2014, they protested their low pay and erratic schedules at stores in Orlando, Chicago, Dallas, Pittsburgh, and other cities.

After years of pressure, workers saw a breakthrough success: on February 23, 2015, Walmart announced that it would raise its minimum wage to $10 an hour by February 2016.[107] Observers credited groups like OUR Walmart for the move, which will affect five hundred thousand employees nationwide. "The move comes in the face of pressure from labor groups and allies calling for a 'living wage' at retailers and fast-food companies across the country," Nathan Lane reported for Reuters.[108]

Other major retailers followed suit almost immediately, including Target (the second-largest U.S. retailer) as well as TJ Maxx and Marshall's. All committed to raising wages to $10 an hour (though Target workers would only get from $9 to $10 after six months on the job, starting in 2016). The retailers are in increasingly good company: in 2014, the Gap also decided to increase its minimum wage to $10 an hour to attract better job candidates, and IKEA upped its average pay to $10.76 an hour. Insurance company Aetna announced that it would raise pay at the bottom of its wage scale to $16 an hour to reduce turnover and improve performance.[109]

Another change that appears to have been inspired by workers' activism is Walmart's new program to increase workers' hours and give them some control of their schedules. Walmart's Access to Open Shifts program, which lets workers sift the internal scheduling system for available slots, was brought online nationwide in 2014. Notably, a Coworker.org petition was one of the tactics used by workers to pressure Walmart for more transparency in the scheduling system.[110]

Despite its successes, OUR Walmart faces many of the same issues as other alt-labor organizations. It has grown from a hundred members in 2011 to "thousands" in 2015, but with membership dues of about $5 a month, the group still has to rely on external grants and union support for most of its revenue.[111] Despite its savvy use of social media to connect workers, its reach among Walmart employees is limited compared to a traditional union.

Still, the agitation among Walmart workers and the success of OUR Walmart provides a playbook for workers itching to improve conditions at other antiunion corporations. One way to interpret the raises announced in 2015 is that, though Walmart won't soften on unions, they may follow the public outcry around low wages. As labor historian Nelson Lichtenstein said, this suggests that OUR Walmart may be "the next best thing to a union to survive within one of America's most antiunion corporations."[112]

And hopefully this is just the beginning. "Walmart workers have proved they can move the most powerful retailer in the world to change," said *Time* magazine. "That means they, and others, can do it again."[113]

The Fight for 15 Begins: Fast-Food Strikes

No one could possibly argue that fast-food workers or Walmart employees are winners in the economy. They earn minimum wage or slightly above. Unlike a lot of other restaurant and hospitality industry workers, they don't generally get tips. On paper, they may be eligible for employer-paid health benefits but in practice their bosses schedule them to work few enough hours that they rarely qualify. And if they do, the employee premium share is usually so high that workers can't afford it. Other employment-related benefits range from skinny to nonexistent.

Based on popular mythology and stereotype, these jobs were *supposed* to be "starter jobs" for teenagers or those without other job skills. Yet the vast majority (over 80 percent) of fast-food and similar low-wage service jobs are held by adults. A quarter of them are held by adults over the age of forty. Twenty-three percent of the workers are moms raising kids. If the stereotype was ever true, it's not anymore.

The companies where they work are some of the nation's most profitable and most recognizable brands. Unpleasant and poorly compensated work performed by millions of Americans creates wealth for shareholders, to the tune of tens of billions of dollars in profits each year. This is work that can't be exported to the Third World—but the subsistence wages are as close to Third World levels as you can legally pay in the United States.

Although the Great Recession technically ended in 2010, workers in 2012 were still experiencing what economist Aaron Pacitti called "The Great Stagnation," with poor job prospects and low wages. (In fact, most Americans still feel that the economy is in a recession, according to a poll by NBC News and the *Wall Street Journal*.)[114]

Workers were tired of being underpaid—they were ready to stand up and fight. So in 2012, SEIU International president Mary Kay Henry launched the "Fast Food Forward" and "Fight for 15" campaigns. The idea was simple: demand a living wage and the right to form a union without retaliation. Building upon strategies pioneered in the Justice for Janitors campaign and furthered by the OUR Walmart campaign, the fast-food campaigns brought workers, unions, and community and religious organizations together to create a new movement of the lowest-wage workers in cities around the country.

Pivoting off the Occupy movement, the fast-food campaigns empowered local workers to strike and protest by connecting them with trained, experienced union and community organizers. The inspiring walkouts by fast-food workers for "$15 and a union" have now become the largest single set of mobilizations by low-wage workers in contemporary history.

The first strike, in November 2012, took place in New York City. Working with an organization called New York Communities for Change, SEIU and a host of other community, civil rights, labor, and religious organizations supported some two hundred workers in walking off the job. Two hundred is a tiny number in a city of 8 million people, but still newsworthy because it was the first labor protest by fast-food workers within living memory.

Eight-year KFC veteran Pamela Waldron told the *New York Times*, "I'm protesting for better pay. I have two kids under 6, and I don't earn enough to buy food for them." Waldron earned just $7.75 an hour and was assigned only twenty hours a week, earning her an income of about $8,000 a year.[115]

Mary Kay Henry underlined the importance of the protest to the larger economy. "The reality is that hundreds of thousands of fast-food workers need food stamps and other help from public assistance and private charities just to tread water in this economy. The fast-food companies," she said, "could easily afford to pay their employees more. People who work for the richest corporations in America should be able to afford at least the basic necessities to support their families."[116]

Linking their actions to the worker unrest in other low-wage industries, Henry said, "Fast food workers, like workers at Walmart are taking a brave step forward."[117] Steven Greenhouse in the *New York Times* also tied the fast-food protests to growing unrest during the previous weeks, saying that workers are growing "increasingly frustrated about pay stagnating at $8 or $9 an hour, translating into $16,000 or $18,000 a year for a full-time worker."[118]

Through the following spring of 2013, workers in Chicago, St. Louis, Detroit, Kansas City, and Milwaukee conducted one-day strikes to demand "$15 and a union." By December, workers in more than a hundred cities had coordinated one-day walkouts and marches with a single message: $15 and a union. The movement picked up steam as President Obama renewed a long-neglected pledge to raise the federal minimum wage; by early 2014 he was suggesting $10.10.

New York workers walked out again in April 2013, this time doubling their numbers.[119] The strike on April 4 was timed to coincide with the anniversary of Martin Luther King Jr.'s assassination. When King was shot and killed in 1968, he was visiting Memphis, Tennessee, to rally on behalf of striking sanitation workers. MSNBC reported at the scene of the strike, quoting strike leader and Taco Bell employee Chad Tall as saying that fast-food workers and Memphis sanitation workers have had "similar struggles. The thing that set [the sanitation workers] apart from everyone else is they made a decision to change it."[120]

Soon, workers in Chicago, St. Louis, and Detroit also joined one-day strike actions, each the product of SEIU organizers working with local coalitions to support direct action by fast-food workers. In each case, organizers found workers who were ready to take action, including risking their jobs, to protest the cycle of poverty in which they found themselves trapped. And in each case, the strikes found a supportive audience among religious, civil rights, immigrant, and community organizations.

It was hardly a "normal" union organizing campaign (if there is such a thing). Many in the labor movement were skeptical of SEIU's investment in the fast-food campaign: how would workers end up in the union and paying dues? Josh Sanburn wrote in *Time*, "For decades, fast food employees have essentially been unorganizable in any traditional sense . . . they're going up against a corporate structure that has been able to keep any sorts of unionization efforts from creeping into the workplace for decades."[121] The primary barrier to winning a union at a fast-food restaurant is that most fast-food workers don't work directly for their parent company, such as McDonald's or Subway. Instead, they work for individual franchise owners, ensuring that each individual fast-food outlet would have to organize and win union recognition separately. So there's not one central employer to bargain with (as in a traditional union campaign). Bargaining with the national chains would require them to admit they were "joint employers" under the law, something the franchise model was in many ways a shell game designed to protect them against.

There didn't seem to be a clear answer to the question of how fast-food workers would join a union when SEIU made its first investments in late 2012. And it's increasingly clear that if an answer does emerge, it may look very different than a traditional twentieth-century collective-bargaining-based union.

What Mary Kay Henry was asking the union to do was to make a leap of faith: let's start building a movement of low-wage workers first, organized around a clear and moral set of demands, and worry about the end game later. Maybe the workers would end up having something like traditional union representation, or maybe a not-so-traditional organization. What form victory would take would just have to be figured out as we built the national campaign. As Henry said at the time: "Membership is not our foremost question. Our first concern is winning fifteen dollars and a union."[122]

In some ways, SEIU's investment in the fast-food strikes mirrored earlier eras of labor history, in which hundreds of thousands of workers from different industries would organize together to support one another's interests. In the 1930s, industrial workers began walking picket lines for one another, winning victories for autoworkers, then for steelworkers, then mine and rubber workers. A motto of industrial unionism was "The longer the picket line, the shorter the strike." Championel by John L. Lewis, the leader of the United Mine Workers, this form of "industrial unionism" quickly won collective-bargaining contracts with two of the most powerful antiunion corporations, General Motors and United States Steel, paving the way for the intensive unionization of blue-collar jobs that helped to lift millions into the middle class during the twentieth century.

August 2013 marked the beginning of a new form of "industrial unionism," but this time it was a movement of underpaid workers in one service industry—fast food—receiving support from workers in other service industries through SEIU. On August 29, the first coordinated national fast-food strikes ignited in Seattle, New York, St. Louis, Detroit, Harrisburg, Milwaukee, Chicago, Flint (Michigan), and Kansas City—sixty cities in total around the United States.[123] The strikes coincided with the fiftieth anniversary of the March on Washington, and an editorial in the *New York Times* declared that "the marchers had it right 50 years ago. The fast-food strikers have it right today."[124]

The minimum-wage increases that workers saw that year are directly tied to fast-food workers' highly public and clear demand for higher wages. In 2014 and 2015, they kept up the pressure for meaningful change and broadened their reach. The next round of "Fight for $15" protests covered more than two hundred cities around the globe, uniting fast-food and other low-wage workers.[125]

In the wake of the massive protests over the racially linked police killings in 2014 and 2015, calls for a $15 hourly wage have increasingly linked the struggles for fair pay and civil rights. At an organizing meeting in Atlanta in early 2015, fast-food workers joined with other low-wage workers to plan the next round of public actions. Members of the Black Lives Matters movement joined the session, along with three octogenarians who shared their experiences from the famous 1968 sanitation workers' strike in Memphis, during which Dr. King was assassinated. One speaker told the crowd that the Fight for 15 and the Black Lives Matter movements "are one." Home health aide and fast-food worker Ebony Hughes, who is African American and makes $7.50 an hour at both of her jobs, told the *New York Times* that "I feel like the fight for 15 and the black lives matter movement is connected. Most of the people who are fighting for 15, they look like me." [126]

"The fast-food strike is arguably the most successful public protest movement since Occupy Wall Street, from which it surely draws a ton of inspiration," said journalist David Goldstein in *The Stranger*. "Unlike Occupy, though, the fast-food strike is backing up grassroots fervor with the organizational experience and resources of the SEIU, lending a more focused and disciplined message to the effort." [127] Ultimately though, the workers built the power that transformed the national conversation.

President Obama noticed as well, in his Labor Day speech in 2014: "All across the country right now, there's a national movement going on made up of fast-food workers organizing to lift wages so they can provide for their families with pride and dignity. There is no denying a simple truth: America deserves a raise. Folks are doing very well on Wall Street, they're doing very well in the corporate boardrooms. If I were busting my butt in the service industry and wanted an honest day's pay for an honest day's work, I'd join a union." [128]

The fast-food and Walmart campaigns—both of which are long-term, large-scale, and big-win—have fed grassroots strength into the movement against income inequality. The critical element has been workers stepping into the streets and the public limelight, showing the nation that even some of the most poorly paid and disrespected segments of the American workforce has the strength and self-respect to demand better for themselves and their families. The actions of fast-food and Walmart workers who were fed up has changed the public's perception of who they are and focused public attention on the fact that no one can live with dignity on the minimum wage in the post-recession era.

As Mary Kay Henry said, "this movement is changing our political debate. The movement is changing what employers think they can get away with, and the movement is making cities and states raise minimum wages." [129] Together, low-wage retail and fast food are the backbone of the low-wage service economy and if they can be transformed, it will fundamentally transform the future of American workers.

• • •

Through almost three decades of experiments, adaptations, uprisings, and organizing efforts, a different picture is coming into focus than the one painted on the pages of the *Wall Street Journal*. Unions are still in decline, and many people in the labor movement are rightly depressed about that. Yet amid the difficulties faced by organized labor there has been a flowering of resistance and innovation in an attempt to lift up workers in the twenty-first-century economy. Many of these efforts were victorious to a point, others dramatically failed, while some continue to muddle along with small-scale victories and organizing achievements. Others are newer works in progress. Together these efforts signal the emergence of a new resistance to the impoverishment of work and the exclusion of workers from the social contract. The future of these efforts relies on the creativity of organizers and the support of the public but, more than anything, on the bravery of American workers.

As Josh Eidelson wrote in the *American Prospect*, "the alternative tactics have their limits—particularly in the case of alt-labor groups, which don't get to pair them with collective bargaining. Everything depends on the willingness of workers to stick their necks out, confront their bosses, risk their livelihoods, and assert the rights they win."[130]

But when workers are willing to take a risk, they may also find themselves winning far more than they had thought possible. Which brings us to Seattle, and the minimum-wage fights of 2013 to 2014 that changed the conventional wisdom of what workers can do with the right timing, and the right alliances.

4

The Little City That Could

Winning a $15 Wage in SeaTac

Reverend Jan Bolerjack is a minister at the Riverton Park United Methodist Church in SeaTac, Washington. SeaTac is a small, working-class suburb of Seattle named after its own airport, Seattle-Tacoma International Airport (Sea-Tac for short).

Soon after she began ministering at the church, Reverend Bolerjack noticed that among the people standing in line for the church's weekly food bank were several with aviation company logos sewn onto their jackets. Not giving it much thought at first, she assumed that companies at Sea-Tac Airport must have donated old uniforms to a local thrift store or charity. It was only later that she realized many of those lining up for free bags of canned food, dry goods, and toilet paper in fact worked full-time at the airport—*they were wearing their uniforms.* But despite working for some of the biggest aviation companies in the world, they were still unable to feed their families without assistance from Reverend Bolerjack's food bank.[1]

This story of the passage of the nation's highest living wage in SeaTac in 2013 began as a union organizing tactic and ended with the national spotlight trained on a small, impoverished, heavily immigrant suburban city. The story of SeaTac brought new hope for local economic justice movements—and it also represented a turning point, a signal moment for the minimum-wage movement indicating that something big was afoot.

Welcoming 35 million passengers a year, Seattle-Tacoma International Airport is a regional economic powerhouse. Washington State's major airport, Sea-Tac Airport generates $13 billion in net economic impact, $2 billion in direct earnings, and claims in its publicity materials to be responsible for creating more than 138,000 jobs (90,000 jobs directly). It's also the epicenter of a substantial low-wage economy. While we think of pilots, mechanics, and flight attendants as having comfortable middle-class jobs, there are thousands of other workers in the airport economy living in or near poverty, some forced to hold down as many as three jobs in order to just make ends meet.[2]

It wasn't always this way. In the 1970s, Washington State congressman Adam Smith's father was a baggage handler at Sea-Tac Airport. Ben Smith earned about $6.69 an hour working for United Airlines, or about $61,000 in 2014 dollars.[3] As a member of the Machinists' union, he had employer-paid health benefits and a pension. He was able to buy a home in SeaTac. It was a typical, even boring, American story: hard menial work from nine to five, a dignified life with stability but no real luxuries, a mortgage, and the promise of a better life for his children. His son, Adam, attended local public schools, and went on to college and law school. Congressman Smith said of his upbringing, "It was only because of my father's union, and the benefits he had worked a lifetime to secure, that my family could continue to pay the bills so that I could finish my education. My father's decent wages and benefits enabled me to pursue my hopes and dreams."[4]

Nearly forty years later, in 2013, Alex Hoopes also worked as a baggage handler at Sea-Tac Airport, loading bags onto United Airlines flights.[5] But unlike Congressman Smith's father, Hoopes didn't work for United. He worked for a nonunion contractor, Air Serv, making $9.50 an hour (less than $20,000 per year). He had no employer-paid health plan, and certainly no pension. Unable to afford a car, he commuted to work by bus, twenty-five miles from the distant suburb of Lakewood, where he could rent a room for $150 a month. Owning a home was unimaginable. Just paying for health care costs kept Hoopes one step ahead of debt collectors.[6]

He was not alone.

Hosea Wilcox, a skycap for a Delta contractor, had to apply for food stamps after thirty-one years on the job because his company cut back his hours. Wilcox spoke out publicly about his situation and was subsequently fired.[7]

Socrates Bravo was a ramp agent, slinging hundred-pound bags for the largest contractor at the airport, Menzies Aviation. Bravo was making minimum wage without benefits after more than four years with Menzies and worked sixty to seventy hours per week to try to make ends meet. His schedule meant sacrificing valuable quality time with his two-year-old daughter.

Tatyana Rymabruk, a cabin cleaner for a contractor called DGS, spent her days scrubbing toilets and vacuuming aisleways. She earned barely above Washington State's minimum wage, and the company health plan cost so much to buy into that she realized she'd have to spend 25 percent of her salary to qualify. So instead, when she needed to see a doctor, she'd fly back home—*to the Ukraine.*

Amina Mohamed, a dispatcher, auditor, and cabin cleaner for DGS, reported that after four years with the company, she still earned only $1.50 per hour over the minimum wage. DGS used to offer medical benefits and five days of vacation time, but anyone hired after 2010 had no benefits and no paid time off.

Alex Popescu, a jet fueler for a contractor called Airline Service International Group (ASIG), earned just over the state minimum wage. An honorably discharged U.S. Marine of twelve years who served a total of five combat tours in Kosovo, Afghanistan, and Iraq, Popescu had higher hopes for his post-military career than barely making above the minimum wage.

A generation ago, the jobs performed by Alex, Hosea, Socrates, Tatyana, Amina, and Alex would have paid a living wage, complete with benefits and reasonable job security. What these workers want is simple: to get paid enough to live a dignified and decent life without having to rely on a handout from government or charity. Instead, they find themselves working multiple jobs for low pay, commuting long distances to cheap exurban housing, facing retaliation for speaking out about their working conditions, and even flying to a former Soviet republic to obtain affordable health care.

The story of what happened to the jobs and the workers at Sea-Tac Airport has unique elements due to the nature of airport economics and regulations. But it is also just another chapter in the same sad tale that could be told by millions of American workers today: good jobs outsourced or offshored, union protections stripped, wages and benefits subjected to relentless downward pressure. The decade-long struggle to improve wages and working conditions at Sea-Tac Airport is also part of a story with many similar chapters across the United States: fighting for a better life in our workplaces, in our city halls and state capitols, at the ballot box, and—when we must—in the streets. But the story of SeaTac is also a special one because here in this small, disadvantaged town, workers organized, stood up, fought back, and won: in 2013 they achieved the highest living wage in American history.

OUTSOURCED AT THE AIRPORT: POVERTY JOBS, RECORD PROFITS

Following the Airline Deregulation Act of 1978, U.S. air carriers engaged in a race to find ways to reduce costs without sacrificing market share and found that they could contract out many essential functions to create competition among contractors. Forty years ago, major airlines directly hired and managed employees to run ground services at airports, both inside and outside the terminal. The people who loaded your luggage, cleaned your cabin, and fueled your plane worked for the same company as your pilot and flight attendant. But as airlines faced industry-wide challenges in the 1990s and 2000s, the trend toward outsourcing intensified in an attempt to cut labor costs.[8]

Baggage handlers, skycaps, jet fuelers, cabin cleaners, food preparers, ramp operators, and wheelchair attendants increasingly work not for the major carriers, but for contractors who essentially serve as labor intermediaries. At most major airports, airlines now have several companies to choose from for ground services, and they benefit from fierce competition among the contractors to keep costs low. There are approximately eighteen thousand airport workers employed by companies that provide contracted services to the major airlines at Sea-Tac Airport.[9]

Not only has the absolute number of outsourced jobs increased, but the share of outsourced jobs has also increased substantially, from 16 percent in 1991, to 19 percent in 2001, to 26 percent by 2011.[10] And that does not even take into account the labor that is outsourced to other countries: today 71 percent of all U.S. airline heavy maintenance is now outsourced, double the rate in 2003. In many cases maintenance is outsourced to developing nations.[11] This trend has led to serious concerns about oversight and safety as FAA inspections, data reporting requirements, and industry licensing guidelines have failed to keep up with the new industry structure.[12]

Between 2002 and 2012, outsourcing of baggage handlers more than tripled, to 84 percent, while average hourly real wages across both directly hired and outsourced workers declined by 45 percent, from over $19 an hour to $10.60. Outsourcing of vehicle and equipment cleaning jobs doubled to 84 percent, while wages fell 25 percent from the equivalent of over $15 an hour to $11.40. Today even the highest paid outsourced workers in these ground-based airport jobs earn less in real terms than the average directly hired worker in the same job a decade ago.[13] These contracting companies—an alphabet soup of brands largely unknown to the public—performed work previously done by airline employees holding down family wage jobs.

Under the new model, the work was barely above the minimum wage and the workers often were dependent on food stamps, housing assistance, Medicaid, and other public services. The surprisingly low pay and benefits provided by contractors has created a subclass of poverty-wage workers at the airport, part of a two-tiered system of aviation workers: customer-facing, well-paid, mostly union workers who are employed directly by the airlines (pilots, flight attendants) and mostly invisible, low-wage nonunion workers with few protections. Airlines have kept only the employees that are most visible to the public in-house, which in many cases, not coincidentally, are the higher-paid, more likely to be white, and nonimmigrant workers with strong union protection. The large percentage of poor immigrants in the contracted airport workforce, while essential contributors to the overall business and customer experience, remain virtually invisible to the public, making it even harder for these workers to organize and defend themselves.

Sea-Tac Airport wheelchair attendant and union activist Habiba Ali noted, "A lot of workers come from another country and have never had a union before. You can know the thing if you have it. But most people don't have knowledge of it. If you talk with people about their bills, almost every person is worse than me, but they don't see the process. They don't want to take time off of their jobs. If you say let's go knock doors, they say I can't because I'm working. And they do need to work to survive."[14] Sea-Tac Airport ramp agent Socrates Bravo added, "The immigrants are afraid. When they get a green card, [workers] go to a job fair and Menzies will hire you on the spot. I think they may be more afraid to stand up for themselves because they think they might get deported."[15]

SEIU organizer Abdi Mohamed acknowledged that helping immigrant workers organize can be challenging. "We did a lot of income inequality education with immigrant workers at the airport," he said, "educating them about why the economy is broken and why it's so difficult for them. Some people would tell you that they're not a citizen so they can't sign a petition. We said you can voice your rights in the workplace no matter what." Mohamed added that the organizers needed to explain to the workers "that they were not challenging the United States government, they were challenging a bad boss."[16]

High turnover is another barrier to low-wage workers fighting for better treatment at work. As Bravo noted, "turnover is high, so most [interested workers] come to a meeting or rally but after a couple of months they're not there anymore."[17] These workers are not only paid rock-bottom wages, they are also subject to unusually dangerous working conditions. And if something goes wrong, there's no big-name corporation with its reputation on the line, or any union advocating for workplace protections. The contractors are merely faceless proxies for the airlines who hire them, part of a continually changing landscape of mostly small contractors who are constantly under threat of being replaced by an even more ruthlessly cost-cutting outfit.

In 2012, the average wage of contracted-out Sea-Tac Airport workers was approximately $9.70 an hour.[18] Airport workers, both directly employed and contractors, made an average of just $1,472 per month, or $18,000 per year—below the federal poverty level for a family of three and far below a monthly budget required to makes ends meet in the Puget Sound area.[19] These earnings even fell far below a living wage for a single adult in Washington State—a living wage is defined as one that allows people to meet their basic needs without public assistance and that provides them with some ability to deal with emergencies and plan ahead. That figure was about $15 an hour for full-time work in 2011.[20] Airport contractors also earned far less than other air transportation workers, including Alaska Airlines employees ($73,500), air transportation workers in King County ($68,900), and combined Sea-Tac air and ground workers ($44,700).[21] Some of the contracted-out work was historically low-wage (food prep), but much was not (aircraft fuelers, ramp workers).

While labor costs were being forced down as a result of the airlines' outsourcing model, the public was left picking up part of the tab for impoverishing the workforce. A 2012 study showed that between 2006 and 2010, contract workers at Sea-Tac Airport cost the taxpayers of Washington over a million dollars per year in medical assistance costs alone.

DANGEROUS CUTS: RACE TO THE BOTTOM ON SAFETY

Airplanes and airports are dangerous places. There are machines—big, heavy ones. There are highly combustible fuels and volatile industrial chemicals not suitable for humans to touch or breathe. And there are the normal daily toxins that you'd find in any large public space: urine, feces, and blood in the bathroom, germs carried from every country on earth.

The Federal Aviation Administration (FAA) does a good job of guaranteeing that planes can take off and land safely—otherwise many more lives would be lost in tragedy, customers would have no confidence, and the airline industry would go bankrupt (again). But for ground workers, the real danger isn't an aircraft mechanical malfunction or pilot error. The real danger is that their employers may not do everything needed to keep the workplace safe. Of course it's cheaper not to, and if the employers don't keep costs low they will lose their contracts. So they cut corners not just on worker compensation but also on equipment and training.[22]

In talking with workers at the airport, we heard stories of trucks moving around the tarmac without properly functioning brakes. We also heard about cabin cleaners with as little as ten minutes to clean up after 150 passengers and crew members on a plane, often without enough rubber gloves. Their hands got soaked in cleaning fluid and they breathed the chemical fumes while cleaning the bathroom toilets. In safety and health hazard allegations filed with Washington's workplace safety agency, workers complained of limited or no access to bathrooms while cleaning aircraft cabins and lack of protective equipment such as masks and gloves when using caustic chemicals.[23]

One of the most outrageous experiences we heard about airport workers was the story of jet fuelers like Alex Popescu. Workers filed complaints with Washington State alleging faulty hose connections, resulting in leaks during fueling that cause fuel-soaked uniforms that workers must take home to wash in their own laundry rooms or at laundromats despite the fact that it is dangerous and illegal to do so. To protest, in 2012 the jet fuelers went to the headquarters of the Port of Seattle, which operates Sea-Tac Airport. They showed up at a public meeting of the elected Port Commission, held in the port's sprawling, upscale (and taxpayer-funded) waterfront headquarters—and were told they had to leave because it was against Port policy to allow hazardous substances (i.e., *their uniforms*) in the boardroom.[24]

Airport workers show up to work while sick because many live paycheck to paycheck and have no other choice—no shift means no pay. Nationwide, only one in five (18 percent) low-wage workers in the private sector are provided paid sick days, while a 2008 survey of airport workers in San José revealed that only 4 percent had any paid sick days.[25] Yet many airport workers have higher exposure to infectious disease spread by travelers than in the average workplace, and they in turn can pass the illnesses to travelers. For these workers, though, staying home sick is a luxury they cannot afford.

Another significant safety issue is high employee turnover. Low wages are linked to high turnover rates, and high turnover rates are linked to safety problems. Less experienced workers are more likely to make mistakes, some of which can have safety consequences for themselves, their co-workers, and passengers.

RECORD PROFITS AT THE PORT

Even in the midst of the Great Recession, the Port of Seattle, the public agency that operates Sea-Tac Airport, saw passenger travel rise 5 percent and the Port's net assets increase from $2.6 to $2.8 billion. In 2011, the Port's Aviation Division reported $43 million in revenue after expenses. And the commission that directs the Port was so pleased with the Port's economic performance that it voted to give Port CEO

Tay Yoshitani a 9 percent pay raise, bringing his annual salary to $367,000.[26]

At the same time, Alaska Airlines, the dominant airline operating at Sea-Tac, made a record $244 million in profit in 2011. Alaska and its subsidiary Horizon Air control 55 percent of the gates at Sea-Tac and are the single most powerful economic and political force inside the airport. While airline industry stock values fell an average of 25 percent in 2010, Alaska Air Group stock rose 30 percent in 2011.[27] Alaska Air Group's profit margin of 6.6 percent was the highest margin of any major carrier. Bill Ayer, the retiring CEO of Alaska Air Group, said, "2011 was a stellar year. Record adjusted earnings represent our eighth consecutive annual profit. . . . Working together with determination and perseverance, our people pushed our company to the top in terms of nearly every operational, customer service, and financial measure."[28] Ayer and the other top management at Alaska Air Group were richly rewarded for their performance: Ayer made $3.36 million in 2010, while the top six employees at Alaska Air Group received a total of $11.77 million in compensation.

So the cause of low pay, bad training, and poor working conditions was obviously not profits or stock values. The problem was that corporations such as Alaska Airlines increasingly saw higher labor costs as a competitive disadvantage—a luxury and a relic and a disservice to shareholders. While the airline industry is highly competitive, it is the workers who have paid the price to keep the companies' stock prices rising. Whether the airline is a relative winner or a loser in the game of shareholder value, the workers are losers.

But what could they do about it?

PUSHBACK . . . AND GETTING PUSHED BACK

As early as 1999, workers saw the writing on the wall at Sea-Tac. The airport was still heavily unionized, but extensive deunionization had occurred in the 1980s and 1990s. Some workers began agitating for improved labor standards, with the support of the AFL-CIO and local unions affiliated with the Teamsters and SEIU. Campaigns to raise labor standards at other airports, such as at San Francisco International Airport, had been fairly successful. At SFO, all ground handlers, passenger services workers, and security screeners won workplace improvements that are still in place. The improvements included a guaranteed health insurance for low-wage workers and more training for workers with safety and security functions.[29]

At Sea-Tac, however, a similar campaign in 2000 and 2001 to raise workplace standards didn't end in an agreement. Then the terrorist attacks of 9/11 took place and a recession hit. After that, organizing efforts at Sea-Tac Airport essentially ceased for many years. But corporate efforts to drive down wages at the Port of Seattle didn't.

One of the longest-running and most contentious labor issues in the Seattle region is not at the airport, but involves the same agency that runs Sea-Tac, the Port of Seattle. The Port is a government agency responsible for maritime operations at Seattle's seaport as well as operations at Sea-Tac International Airport. While paying its own CEO very handsomely, the Port has spent the better part of a decade resisting demands by local labor groups to play a more active role in ensuring that jobs at the seaport and the airport were actual living-wage jobs.

Just like the airlines, the Port had taken advantage of transportation deregulation in the late 1970s to contract out essential services and drive down wages—in this case, short-haul trucking between the Port and nearby destinations. Dave Freiboth, the head of the King County Labor Council until 2015 and formerly president of a local maritime union, explained: "In the good old days it was pretty much all union at the Port, it was old-fashioned labor relations. But when the shippers decided to use the deregulation of the trucking industry to get around some of the short-haul trucking costs, that started a certain amount of labor unrest that's been going on for than more 15 years."[30] But while it oversaw the deregulation of services at the Port, its governing commission insisted that it had no legal authority to improve pay or working conditions. This was a classic case of the contracting-out practices we examined in chapter 2, in which employers distance themselves from workers through layers of contractors, squeezing pay and eliminating benefits by claiming that their low-bid contractors are responsible for compensation. When it comes time to improve wages and working conditions, there is no responsible party to be found.

In 2005, another major player entered the outsourcing game: Alaska Airlines fired its ground service workers at Sea-Tac, terminating

almost five hundred baggage handlers and contracting out their services work to Menzies Aviation. At the same time, the company responsible for the airport's food and drink concession operations, HMS
Host, refused to come to an agreement with the union representing
its workers. After contract negotiations deteriorated, the Port broke
up the master concessions lease and allowed nonunion companies
to come in and offer concessions at the airport. This stung for workers who were already earning low wages and it accelerated the labor
unrest at the airport.[31]

In 2011, as the movement against income inequality began to heat
up and Occupy protesters took to the streets, a community group
called Working Washington took to the streets in a different way. The
group was formed by a group of Washington SEIU locals, including
my own, SEIU 775. Working Washington organizers knocked on a
hundred thousand doors in Seattle to talk with the working poor about
their jobs, and found that a lot of people were working low-wage jobs
at the airport. We also heard an overwhelming amount of anger and
unrest around the poor pay and working conditions at those jobs.

The situation at Sea-Tac had reached a breaking point. As the
Teamsters local organizing director, Leonard Smith, noted, "starting
with Occupy, workers in this region just sort of looked around and said,
'I don't have to be underpaid. I can do something better.' "[32]

A coalition of airport workers, community groups, and labor organizations, including Working Washington, the Teamsters, and SEIU,
decided to take on the challenge of poverty jobs at the airport. Our
coalition's demand was for the Port of Seattle to establish a living-wage
policy for airport workers, including minimum wages, health benefits,
and other basic workplace rights. We also wanted the Port and the
large airlines to require their tenants and subcontractors to remain
neutral if workers wanted to organize a union.

Six months later, in February 2012, about four hundred Port
truckers went out on a multiweek strike. The strike received national
attention decrying the drivers' poverty wages and safety hazards and
was called "the most serious effort to date to win back rights that
many truckers had over 30 years ago, before the deregulation of the
industry."[33]

However, there was still no meaningful movement on wages or

working conditions at the Port or at airline subcontractors. Airport workers wanted to put pressure on the Port to do the right thing. With assistance from organizers from Working Washington, SEIU, and the International Brotherhood of Teamsters, they identified Alaska Airlines as the most strategic airline to target. If Alaska would agree to require its subcontractors to improve pay and grant workers a fair union recognition procedure, it would have the impact of setting a new norm for the entire airport.

A new strategy was born: instead of simply targeting one employer to unionize and then another in a piecemeal fashion, the unions and the workers decided to launch a much broader campaign to "Make Every Airport Job a Good Job." It was a larger, publicly facing demand that spoke to the needs and economic aspirations of all workers, regardless of occupation or employer, not just those attempting to organize at a particular company. Workers began to speak up and take action around rampant workplace problems: low wages, discrimination, safety violations, and a lack of respect. Jet fueler Alex Popescu explained why he joined the Good Jobs effort: "Despite my qualifications and ability, I have been reduced to working for just above minimum wage. I feel that after serving and sacrificing for so long, it's appalling that I have to choose between filling my gas tank or feeding my family."[34] Through the rest of 2012, thousands of airport workers marched and picketed; spoke at Port Commission meetings; and rallied with elected officials, faith leaders, and immigrant rights activists.

The Good Jobs effort helped to lay the groundwork for the even bigger campaigns to come, uniting workers and assembling a powerful coalition of allies. Jonathan Rosenblum, who led Working Washington's coalition-building efforts at the airport, reflected, "Community partnership in the organizing was vital from the start. The active, early support of mosque and church leaders, social service agency leaders, business owners and civic leaders was crucial to winning workers to the cause."[35]

January 2013 saw the beginning of a new effort at the airport, building on the successes of the Good Jobs campaign: Sea-Tac workers started signing union cards to unite with SEIU and the Teamsters. It wasn't a long, drawn-out union campaign. Veteran SEIU organizer Memo Rivera, who helped lead the effort, recalled that "the workers were sick and tired of small changes, and they wanted to see a big change. In our organizing committee meetings, in all of them the workers said that their number one issue was RESPECT. So this is when they decided to move to a union cards campaign.

"In February the organizers stayed at the airport twenty-four hours a day for one hundred hours straight. We left just to sleep and shower. We got the cards so quickly because we were living at the airport, talking with every single worker, and because workers were talking with their coworkers, getting cards." [36]

The workers signed enough cards to declare a union. But under the 1926 labor law governing airports, because the workers only represented one airport (Sea-Tac) among their companies' many operations, the employer did not have to recognize the union, nor did the government have to hold a union election. And they didn't.

Leonard Smith of the Teamsters summed up the final, disappointing chapter of this organizing effort, saying: "We got majority and did a mass march on the boss. We got three school buses and loaded them up and demanded recognition [for the union]. It was a lot of fun. Of course the company refused and said thank you very much for your visit. So from my perspective, we were stuck. We had nowhere to go on this campaign." [37] Former King County Labor Council leader Dave Freiboth described the situation leading up to this point: "We went to the airline industry and said we have to deal with these low-wage jobs. And they basically told us to go count sand." [38]

BREAKTHROUGH: TAKING IT TO THE BALLOT WITH PROPOSITION 1

Then, one of the airport organizers hit upon an out-of-the-blue idea. If we can't win a pay raise and a union contract at Sea-Tac the old-fashioned way, why not write the equivalent of a union contract into law? A law that could actually pass, because people were fed up with income inequality.

Up to this point, the effort at Sea-Tac Airport and the Port had been focused on two specific solutions: (1) a living-wage policy that could be passed by the Port and (2) "neutrality" agreements that would make it possible for workers to join a union without retaliation and negotiate a contract. For over a year, they had tried without success to get the attention of Alaska Airlines and the Port. Perhaps there was something to be learned from the growing movement for $15.

Living-wage laws already covered several airports on the West Coast, including San Francisco, Oakland, San Jose, and Los Angeles. Other airports around the country with living-wage laws include Miami, St. Louis, Hartford, and to a limited extent Philadelphia and Syracuse.[39] In some cases, airports have put in place accompanying mandates for benefits, training, worker retention, and labor peace agreements. Many of these laws had by then been on the books for a few years, but somehow there hadn't been a spike in airline ticket prices. Or a decline in the number of contractors willing to bid on airline subcontracts or in vendors willing to operate restaurants or retail establishments. In fact, what resulted was both a higher employee retention rate in these airports and an increase in the number of firms willing to bid on the work.

The SeaTac City Council could be asked to pass a living-wage policy, but a quick look at the political leanings of that body wasn't encouraging. Despite the fact that SeaTac was a diverse and increasingly impoverished city, the city council was almost all white and upper middle class. A coalition of Republicans and conservative Democrats governed the council, and although the mayor was sympathetic, he didn't think he had the council votes to pass an ambitious living-wage ordinance.

But SeaTac, like many cities in Washington State, also allows citizens to place a proposed law on the ballot for voters to approve or reject.[40] In much of the western United States, these ballot measures (variously called initiatives, propositions, measures, or referenda) are a common way of making law. Most famously, California passed Proposition 13 in 1978, permanently limiting the growth of state tax revenue (and, some would say, dooming its ability to effectively budget for decades to come).

Ballot measures have been used to raise wages at both the state and local levels all across the country. In the past ten years, minimum wages have been put on the ballot in thirteen states—and passed in *every single one*.[41] In 2014, four states—Alaska, Arkansas, Nebraska, and South Dakota (not exactly liberal bastions)—approved minimum-wage increases through ballot measures; Illinois voters approved an advisory measure. In 2013, voters in New Jersey effectively overrode Governor Chris Christie's veto of the minimum-wage bill the legislature had passed, approving an increase through a ballot measure.

Karen Keiser, a state senator representing the area around SeaTac, underlined the necessity of this kind of solution: "When you see a community in decline and the associated problems in health care and education, you need to figure out a way to rebuild—or fight back. It obviously wasn't working to go company by company. So that means you need some kind of broad-based standard. Unfortunately, we are at such a divided time in our politics that no broad social policy can get through. But these policies are all very popular with the public."[42]

A plan to craft a living-wage policy slowly took shape in SeaTac. As discussed in chapter 3, the first group of fast-food workers went on strike in New York City in the fall of 2012, gaining national attention. The winter and spring of 2013 saw similar strikes in six Midwestern cities and Seattle. The organizers in Sea-Tac were inspired to push for a similarly ambitious wage.

A team assembled to write the ballot initiative, including organizers from immigrant, faith, and community groups; Working Washington; SEIU; the Teamsters; UFCW (the workers' union that represented some of the retail employs at SeaTac), and UNITE HERE (the union that represented restaurant, food service, and hotel workers at or near the airport).

Ultimately, the policy wasn't just about $15 an hour, although that was its most significant element. The team, now named the SeaTac Committee for Good Jobs, included the following provisions in what would become SeaTac Proposition 1:

- Wages for covered employees in SeaTac would rise from the state minimum of $9.32 to $15 per hour on January 1, 2014, and would adjust upward with inflation every January 1 thereafter.
- Covered employees would earn one hour of sick leave for every forty hours worked (or about five days per year). At that point very few employees had any sick leave at all.

- Employers would not be able to hire new part-time employees until they had offered full-time work to incumbent part-time employees.
- Hotel and restaurant employers would be barred from skimming employees' tips (a common practice in hotels).
- Workers would have job protections if their contractor changed (there were no such protections in place).
- The City of SeaTac would set up enforcement and audit provisions.
- Workers could go to court to enforce the law. The primary enforcement mechanism was private right of action— a lawsuit against the noncompliant company—a much stronger enforcement tool than the customary regulatory processes in living-wage laws.

The initial polling on SeaTac Prop. 1 was encouraging. Every major provision won majority support among registered voters. It wasn't a slam dunk—the standard wisdom in the business of ballot measure campaigns is that you're not safe unless you poll above 60 percent. Prop. 1 was polling in the high 50s. On April 26, 2013, we submitted our initial petition to the SeaTac city clerk, and another version on May 1. On May 9, the city approved the subject matter of the petition.

On June 5, 2013, workers, unions, and community allies delivered boxes of initiative petition signatures to SeaTac city hall to qualify the Good Jobs Initiative for the November ballot. After discounting illegible signatures, signatures from people who weren't registered voters in SeaTac, and duplicates, King County Elections found 1,780 valid signatures.[43] The county clerk approved, and Prop. 1 would be placed on the November 2013 ballot for a vote of the people.

If workers and organizers had been hoping that the imminent threat of an immediate $15 wage would bring Alaska Airlines and the Port to the table, they were soon proven wrong. They were not planning to budge an inch on anything. The first shot across the bow came the next month, on July 2. A coalition of businesses going by the name Common Sense SeaTac (including Alaska Airlines, the Washington Restaurant Association, and Filo Foods) asked the SeaTac City Council to appoint a petition review board to reexamine the signatures. The city agreed, appointing a committee that included SeaTac's mayor, city administrator, and police chief. And on July 8 the business coalition also filed the first of several lawsuits attempting to prevent SeaTac voters from ever voting on Proposition 1. But judges ultimately ruled that the measure had obtained enough valid signatures and belonged on the ballot. At the same time, a spokeswoman for Alaska Airlines ominously said the company was "still considering its legal options."[44]

The campaign against Prop. 1 was predictable: opponents claimed that it would cost jobs, drive business out of SeaTac, and was the "highest minimum wage in the country." The man who ran the local MasterPark franchise publicly claimed that if Prop. 1 passed he would replace all of his employees with automated kiosks.[45]

Scott Ostrander was the general manager of the Cedarbrook Lodge, a luxury hotel, conference center, and restaurant complex sitting beside a lake in one of SeaTac's few upscale neighborhoods. Cedarbrook attracts a steady business of corporate retreats, business travelers on overnight layovers, and diners at the only truly high-end restaurant in SeaTac. Ostrander was one of the leading opponents of Prop. 1. At one meeting of local anti–Prop. 1 businesses, where prime rib and red wine were being served at lunch, he spoke about how afraid he was of Prop. 1 passing. Ostrander said that his employees "all get two meals a day, complimentary," but if the proposition passed, he would no longer be able to afford to feed his employees free meals from the hotel kitchen. And sometimes, he said, "that's the only meal they get."[46] He was basically admitting that his employees were paid so little that they couldn't afford food.

But what was exceptional about the SeaTac living-wage fight was that proponents didn't concede the "job killer" argument. We actually argued the reverse: better wages meant more customers, more customers meant more business, more business meant more jobs, and more jobs would in turn lead to more wages and more customers. There would be a virtuous cycle lifting all economic boats. In the mail, in TV ads, and door to door, the Yes for SeaTac campaign (the official name of the political committee established under Washington's election laws) made the case that raising wages was the right—and the smart—thing to do. The argument was made that it would help workers and help the economy, and that it would help SeaTac's economy come back—a lot of older voters remembered the days when SeaTac was growing and more prosperous.

One of the most compelling voices in the pro–Prop. 1 campaign was Don Liberty. Liberty was the owner of the Bull Pen Bar and Grill, a sports bar located on a busy stretch of International Boulevard south of the airport. It's an area of town occupied by small, down-market hotels, quick-serve restaurants, pay-to-park lots, and, up the street by maybe a quarter mile, Alaska Airlines' corporate headquarters. The Bullpen is a working-class place, with a menu of burgers, pizza, wings, beer on draft, and TVs to watch the ball game of your choice.

As a small business with only a few dozen employees and located off airport property, the Bullpen wouldn't be subject to Proposition 1's wage and employment requirements. The easiest thing for Don Liberty to have done would have been to stay out of this particular fight. Instead, Liberty became one of the leading spokespeople for Prop. 1. As the owner of a neighborhood bar and grill, he recognized something that the CEOs of some of the region's biggest companies apparently didn't—if wages at the town's largest employment center went up, he'd have more customers, and those customers would have more money to spend.

Liberty had always tried to be a good employer. His servers, cooks, and dishwashers earned between $12 and $16 per hour plus tips. Liberty said, "I'm proud that our employees are like family and everyone is paid a fair wage. The big corporations at the airport can be paying fair wages too."[47] He became one of the unlikely spokespeople for Prop. 1, appearing on TV ads and in mailers, and he was interviewed by the local media dozens of times. He said a pay increase for airport workers would be good for his business: "I have owned and operated the Bull Pen Bar and Grill in SeaTac for over 30 years. Many of my customers, as well as others living in our city, tell me they are struggling to make ends meet," said Liberty, whose granddaughter helps manage their family-run business. "I and more than 20 other small business owners in SeaTac believe that Proposition One will help make eating out and shopping a more commonplace affair in our city."[48]

Another leader of the SeaTac campaign was Abdirahman Abdullahi. Abdullahi was a Somali immigrant earning $11.20 an hour after six years as a rental car supervisor at Hertz. He often worked combined seventy-hour weeks at two jobs to help support his family of four. "We want to achieve the American Dream," he said. By 2013, Abdullahi was volunteering virtually full-time on the campaign to pass Prop. 1. He worked first as a signature gatherer and then went door to door and to the nearby mosque, organizing Somali workers in favor of Prop. 1. The way he saw it, it was about people power—everyone in town knew that the airport was thriving and successful, while the neighborhoods around it sank deeper into poverty.[49]

Somali immigrant Habiba Ali also volunteered on the campaign, working up her courage to do things she normally wouldn't do, like public speaking. "I went to the mosque," she said. "There's a lot of Somali guys there and usually I wouldn't want to go, but sometimes I did speak. That was hard to do."[50]

Airport workers also reached out to the press. Chris Smith, who worked at the airport for twenty years and lived in the city of SeaTac, wrote an op-ed for the *Puget Sound Business Journal*, saying:

Reporters ask me, a 49-year-old SeaTac voter and father of three, what difference would $15 an hour make in your life? It means that my family and I would finally have the opportunity to make ends meet. I wouldn't have to work while exhausted or sick. Instead of scrimping just to get by (and often not), we may have money to pay both the electricity and the garbage bills. We would even be able to go out on occasion, spending more in SeaTac at the Bullpen Pub or Olive Express, two small businesses supporting Proposition 1.[51]

Everyone knew that Alaska Airlines had been growing and posting larger and larger profits, even while its own indirect employees stood in line at the food bank. The people in Abdi, Habiba, and Chris's world knew the reality on the ground, and they didn't buy in to the conventional "wisdom" that a raise for the poorest workers would somehow be bad for the local economy. Quite the reverse—the local economy had been *made* bad because of the decline in wages.[52]

SEIU's Sterling Harders reflects: "One of the keys to the election was mobilizing the voters who were least likely to vote in a low-turnout, off-year small-town municipal election: people like those in

Abdi and Habiba's communities—young voters, immigrant voters, voters of color, and new voters."[53] County council member Julia Patterson posed the following question when Proposition 1 campaigners visited her to ask for her endorsement: "It's the right thing to do, but how are you going to win when only the older and more conservative voters come out to vote?"[54] The path to victory was to change the electorate.

REGISTERING VOTERS AND EXPANDING THE ELECTORATE

In August and September 2013, as Alaska Airlines and the other businesses were busy filing lawsuits to keep Prop. 1 away from the voters, Working Washington and other coalition organizations were busy registering voters. In the end we registered over a thousand new voters, which was not a small feat in a city with such a tiny electorate. Almost all of these new voters were younger or were immigrants from East Africa, Mexico, or East or South Asia. Many people worked at the airport. Almost all had a family member or neighbor who did.

In September and October, the Yes for SeaTac campaign got mobilized for the final election push, beginning when ballots were sent out on October 16 for Washington's all-mail election. Knowing that fear is a strong motivator and that the "vote no" side would campaign on fear of job loss, Yes on SeaTac decided it would knock on the door of every single registered voter in SeaTac well before ballots hit, peaking the fieldwork the weekend when ballots were arriving.

Sterling Harders remembers, "It was unheard of to knock on every door—campaigns always 'target' voters, thereby leaving out those who aren't frequent voters, or are perceived to be undecided, or who are already leaning your direction. But our strategy was to grow the electorate and to talk to every voter in town at least once. And instead of a typical campaign door-knock where a volunteer leaves literature and makes a soft, polite ask, we asked for a commitment. 'Would you put a sign in your yard or window? Will you sign a pledge card to vote yes?' If you didn't say yes to one of those questions, we didn't count you as a solid supporter. We would go back out and work even harder to get to the number of 'yes' votes we knew we needed to win."[55]

Competing groups of volunteers—pro– and anti–Prop. 1—went door to door in SeaTac. One big difference was that SeaTac workers themselves, and other volunteers from the local community, formed the backbone of the Vote Yes contingent. SEIU organizer Artie Nosrati recalls knocking on the door of a SeaTac resident named Kenji. "I told him what we were doing, and he said he'd heard about it. He was a fueler with ASIG making only about $10 an hour," Nosrati said. "He didn't know anything and he got involved when we talked about it. He wanted to come and door knock with us. He was out on the doors with me two days later, talking to other workers in SeaTac."[56]

The Vote No team, in contrast, consisted of paid staffers from the conservative rural town of Wenatchee, Washington, hundreds of miles away. They did not reach out to the new voters, or the immigrants. An article in the *Seattle Times* told the following story:

> On the other side of the Prop. 1 campaign is Jac Cates, an athletic, ruddy-faced extrovert who roams SeaTac's more affluent neighborhoods of single-family homes with an iPad Mini and a mobile-canvassing app called Ground Game.
>
> "The people who own the homes are decidedly against it," said Cates, 45, who was hired by a consulting firm for Common Sense SeaTac, a business-backed political committee opposed to Prop. 1. "They understand that the administrative costs of having to enforce it will fall on property owners."[57]

Note that Cates's targeted constituency is relatively affluent white property owners. The fault lines in the community mirrored the fault lines between the bosses and the workers.

The get-out-the-vote effort was of epic proportions. The Yes for SeaTac campaign made forty thousand door knocks during the final three weeks of the campaign alone, contacting ten thousand people. Organizer Abdi Mohamed said of the effort, "Imagine knocking all those doors in SeaTac, sometimes hundreds of times. We didn't need GPS—by the end we knew all of the locations by heart."

THE STORY GOES GLOBAL

The press had been covering the SeaTac campaign in fits and starts for most of 2012 and 2013. When workers called a press conference to raise awareness about health and safety conditions at the airport, plenty of local news cameras and a few print reporters were on hand.

Each time there was a new health and safety complaint filed against an airport contractor, there was some amount of local press coverage. When aircraft fuelers threatened to go on strike in 2012, there was plenty of local news coverage. Each fact-finding report by local community and the research organization Puget Sound Sage generated a story, as did every large march, rally, or mobilization. Press attention really ramped up in the summer of 2013. There was an enormous amount of legal activity being covered as the business coalition including Alaska Airlines and the Washington Restaurant Association filed motion after motion in court trying to prevent a vote.

Once the race was on, though, we discovered we had more than just a local story on our hands. We had been used to plenty of attention from local papers, blogs, and TV and radio. But now came PBS and the *New York Times*. Soon the BBC showed up. NPR, ABC, NBC, Fox, CBS, the *Huffington Post, Politico, Bloomberg, Forbes, The Guardian*, and so on.[58] *The Guardian* wrote, "For a highly local campaign the nature of the argument was surprisingly 'big picture': a battle of competing ideas about the national economy. It was either 'middle-out' economics versus 'trickle down,' or 'free-enterprise' versus 'big government,' depending on your political leanings."[59]

THE FINISH LINE

At the end of election day, after more door knocks, TV ads, billboards, yard signs, phone calls, and emails than had ever been experienced in a SeaTac municipal election, voters passed Prop. 1—by a mere seventy-seven votes.

It was a victory, but not a clean one. Common Sense SeaTac announced it would request a recount from King County (election rules say a group may request a recount if costs are covered, though state law provides no automatic recount for local ballot measures). Meanwhile, Prop. 1 organizers tracked down every last ballot that didn't have a verified signature, recovering eighty-eight in all. Organizers made herculean efforts to find voters whose ballot signatures were in question. One organizer recalls searching for a particular voter all over the Seattle area—and when he finally found her forty miles from her home, he convinced her to let him drive her all the way back to SeaTac to cast a replacement ballot.

The recount in December did not change the election results, and within weeks, Alaska Airlines and the business coalition went to court again to try to stop implementation of Prop. 1. To our great disappointment, a King County Superior Court judge ruled that the new law did not apply to the airport because it is controlled by the Port of Seattle, not the City of SeaTac. At dispute was a decades-old law that gave the Port the right to manage "operations" of the airport. The question of whether Prop. 1 could be applied to airport property would have to be decided by the State Supreme Court

But it was a mixed verdict: the judge also ruled that Prop. 1 would go into effect *outside* airport property, for businesses such as hotels, parking lots, and off-site rental car businesses that were located on private property within the city of SeaTac. So on January 1, 2014, some 1,600 workers outside of airport property saw their wages raised to $15. But for the 5,000 or so workers on airport property, the ongoing court battle was justice delayed. Airport worker Habiba Ali said, "I didn't believe we would win. It seemed like too much, that they wouldn't let us have $15. And they still don't want to let us have $15. I feel bad about that."[60]

Despite the ongoing court battle, the bar had been raised and years of resistance crumbled at the Port. The Port had long claimed to have no jurisdiction over wages at the airport, but the summer after Prop. 1 passed, it reversed course and adopted a policy on wages, sick leave, and employee retention that would raise wages on airport property to $13 by 2017.[61] (Though the Port finally did the right thing for workers, it also hedged its bets and deferred the implementation of its policy until forty-five days after the State Supreme Court's final decision on Prop. 1—which ended up taking another year.)

Of course, Alaska Airlines and the rest of them went to court to try to stop the Port from raising wages, too. But on December 19, 2014, the U.S. District Court for the Western District of Washington upheld the Port's policy on the basis that the agency *does* have the authority to enact worker-protective legislation.[62]

A few unusual things happened shortly after January 1, 2014, when wages suddenly jumped to $15 for hospitality and travel-related businesses in the city of SeaTac.

Several weeks after the election, Cedarbrook Lodge announced it would be breaking ground on a new wing of the hotel, almost doubling the bed capacity of the hotel, adding two presidential suites and a luxury spa. Why? Because the hotel investors wanted to maintain the same level of profitability, and apparently the only way to do that in light of the higher wage costs was to increase the number of rooms available and the number of customers the hotel could take on at once. So instead of cutting jobs, Cedarbrook would be hiring—first construction workers and then permanent hotel staff.

What about MasterPark, whose operator threatened to replace his employees with kiosks? A few weeks into 2014, he hung a large sign on his property: "Now hiring at $15 an hour." When a reporter called to ask about the threatened layoffs, he said it wasn't that good of an idea after all: his customers actually expected customer service. He said it would be "foolish" to lay them off and described his employees as "happy campers."[63]

SeaTac's city manager also reported that one year later there had been no impact on sales tax or property tax and no change in the number of business licenses issued.[64] Writing in the *Washington Post*, Dana Milbank concluded that SeaTac had raised wages "without raising havoc."[65]

In August 2015, the Washington State Supreme Court returned a landmark decision that agreed with Milbank's assessment. "We hold that Proposition 1 can be enforced at the Seattle-Tacoma International Airport," the court ruled, "because there is no indication that it will interfere with airport operations."[66] Though airport workers had lost more than $15 million in wages while waiting for the court's decision, they celebrated as they finally realized the promise of Prop. 1: $15 an hour, plus paid sick leave and job protections.

At a press conference announcing the victory, Reverend Jan Bolerjack said, "Now, possibly, our food pantry lines will go down. A living wage is the only fair thing, the only just thing, for workers working a full shift."[67]

If at the beginning of 2013 you had asked anyone in SeaTac or any political observers of Washington State elections whether they thought a $15 living-wage policy was likely to be adopted before the end of the year, no one would have said yes. But a reasonably small number of people got organized and built a campaign around a demand for $15 that ultimately proved resonant with voters. For most of the two years that workers were organizing at the airport, what they really hoped to do was get a union recognized so that they could bargain wages, benefits, hours, and working conditions with their employers. Instead they ended up writing a de facto union contract directly into city law.

They would not have won if they had accepted the other side's terms of the debate. Some people no doubt continue to believe that higher wages will kill jobs (a prediction that so far hasn't come true in SeaTac), but for those looking for reasons to support Prop. 1, we provided a counternarrative to forty years of trickle-down orthodoxy: if workers have more money, businesses will have more customers, and that will be good for the community and the economy.

Prop. 1 would also not have passed had the "unorganizable" voters not turned out in great numbers. It's nearly unheard of for campaigns to spend resources registering new voters in these sorts of low-turnout, off-year elections; knock on the doors of registered voters who hadn't bothered to vote in the last presidential election; or print literature in Spanish, Ukrainian, Somali, Korean, and Vietnamese. But without those efforts, Proposition 1 would have been hundreds, if not thousands, of votes behind when it counted.

As former King County and City of SeaTac council member Julia Patterson said, "The SeaTac campaign was a very American phenomenon. It gave me hope that the promise of representative democracy was still alive, that people could exercise their power, their voice, and make a change. You hear about it on the evening news, but to have the fight here was very exciting. There were door knockers in my neighborhood talking to people, there were flyers left at my doorstep. It's representative democracy at the most basic grassroots level you can imagine."[68]

There was something happening in America. Something we hadn't anticipated that made the SeaTac story into national news and made so much of the local political establishment lend their support to this measure. Wages and income inequality were becoming a breakthrough issue, and the media and politicians were taking notice.

5

Fifteen for Seattle

From the outside, Seattle may have seemed like an unlikely place for the nation's first successful $15 minimum-wage campaign. Seattle is a large, expensive, and wealthy city, to be sure. But it's not the nation's largest (New York), its most expensive (Honolulu and Washington, D.C.), or its wealthiest (San Francisco or Brookville, New York).[1]

However, Seattle *is* a city with a long-established history of pro-worker activism, dating back to the city's founding as a timber town and gold-rush way station. In 1919, Seattle workers held the first city-wide general strike in American history, with tens of thousands of workers from multiple industries walking off the job at the same time.[2] And as we saw in chapter 3, Seattle was also the home of the largest labor uprising of the late twentieth century, when tens of thousands of workers gathered to protest the World Trade Organization in 1999.

Seattle's rich history of worker militancy wasn't constrained to the maritime, timber, and aerospace industries for which it is famous. From the dawn of the twentieth century to the present day, some of Seattle's least powerful workers have organized to fight for better wages, while the presence of strong unions and a strong progressive infrastructure have helped Seattle workers win what might have been losing fights in other parts of the country.

ALICE LORD

Alice Lord, a twenty-three-year-old restaurant server in Seattle, was fed up about low pay, long hours, and seven-day workweeks. Seattle had a booming economy, a relatively strong labor movement even in an era of generally weak unions, and plenty of middle-class and upper-class citizens who sympathized with the lower-paid workers' plight. But its restaurant workers weren't sharing in the city's prosperity, and Alice, together with some co-workers, decided to do something about it.

One of the city's newspapers reported that skeptics had their doubts. The idea that a group of low-wage women could extract meaningful wage gains from an industry that had historically proven difficult to organize seemed a tall order. Nevertheless, Alice and a few dozen other women who worked in the city's restaurant industry organized a brand-new union. Critics dismissed it as "something of a joke." [3]

The workers organized; they learned to strike, negotiate, and lobby. They made demands on the employers in the restaurant industry as well as on the city council and the state legislature. They built coalitions with more conservative, male-dominated traditional unions, and with politically active sympathizers among the city's middle class and wealthy, and with women's rights organizations in particular.

Barely more than a year after the workers held their first meeting, they had helped pass legislation limiting the number of hours they could be required to work in a single day. By the following year, they had negotiated pay increases that more than doubled the pay of the lowest-paid workers and improved the pay of top earners by 60 percent. It was an incredible amount of progress in a short period.

The year was 1900 when Alice Lord announced the formation of the Seattle Waitresses Union Local 240. In 1901, the Washington state legislature passed a law establishing a ten-hour workday for women. By the fall of 1902, the Seattle *Union Record* reported that wages for waitresses had increased from between $3 and $6 to between $8.50 and $10 per week. [4]

More than a century later, another group of restaurant workers would follow in her footsteps.

CAROLINE DUROCHER

One hundred and thirteen years after Alice Lord called the first waitress union meeting, a twenty-one-year-old Taco Bell employee named Caroline Durocher became the first fast-food worker in Seattle to walk off the job and go on strike demanding $15 an hour. On the night of May 29, 2013, as supporters and news cameras looked on, she emerged through the front door of her workplace on a nondescript street corner in a residential neighborhood called Ballard. Within an hour, her two night-shift co-workers had joined her on a makeshift picket line, and the Taco Bell shut down. "It's the right thing to do, and that's all it comes down to," Durocher told one reporter at the scene, citing low wages, lack of benefits, and part-time hours. "What we're getting now isn't fair and it's not right. They keep us all below part-time, so we don't get benefits." She continued, "When my Taco Bell shut down, I felt like a person again. I wasn't a Taco Bell employee; I was a human being."[5]

The following day, thousands of other fast-food workers and their supporters joined in strikes across the city. Some of the strikes were planned; others occurred spontaneously as workers heard news of the citywide strike on the radio, Twitter, or Facebook. Workers at one Subway had planned to strike, and when they walked off the job they spread out and convinced workers at five other nearby Subway stores to join them.

According to federal data, at the time there were approximately 33,000 fast-food workers in the Seattle metro area. They earned a median wage of $9.50 an hour—one of the lowest wages of any occupation in the region.[6] But even that overstates the annual earnings of most fast-food workers, who are typically limited by their managers to fewer than the "full time" thirty hours a week that qualifies workers for health care, vacation, and other benefits. " 'Exactly 29.75,' laughed striking Arby's worker Amanda Larson when asked about her weekly hours," reported *The Stranger*.[7] Fast-food workers nationally work an average of only twenty-four hours a week; a twenty-four-hour-a-week worker making the Seattle median fast-food wage of $9.50 an hour earns only $11,856 a year.[8]

Fernando Cruz, a Taco Del Mar employee, spoke out about his working conditions during the strike. "I like this job. I like talking to customers," he said while picketing. But Cruz earned only $10.50 an hour and wanted "a better salary, benefits, and, most importantly, respect."[9] Another worker told the TV news that "I need a higher wage for the same reason a lot of people do—I can't afford to eat in this city. I can't afford to eat at the restaurant I work for."[10]

It was the opposite of a traditional union strike. None of the workers were union members, and the strikes weren't occurring to protest an overdue contract settlement, a stingy wage offer, or a labor law violation by their employers. They were striking against an industry and against poverty in general. The picket lines were undisciplined, energetic, and chaotic. They spread organically from one restaurant to the next. Rumors circulated that some gas station workers had walked off as well.

TV and radio news amplified the strikes all day. Flipping channels on TV or news radio it was impossible to avoid news of the strikes, which aired as the number one story on most outlets. Roaming picket lines and demonstrations appeared, then vanished, frustrating news crews competing for the freshest footage. At noon in the city's hip, busy Capitol Hill retail district, over a thousand workers and supporters blocked traffic. A mobile rally snaked past dozens of fast-food outlets while workers put down their aprons, turned off their fryers, and locked doors behind them to join in.

Some strikers received threats of illegal retaliation from their employers, but strike organizers had already asked politicians like state senator Ed Murray to step in to help prevent this. Murray was a prominent state senator best known for leading the historic legislative and ballot measure campaign to pass marriage equality legislation in Washington State. One journalist called Murray "a deliberative social justice Democrat."[11] He said, "When I learned of the situation, I placed a call to the manager of the restaurant and asked him to not retaliate against these low-income workers who are acting peacefully to seek better wages and working conditions. I will be joining fast food workers at their rally later this afternoon."[12]

Will Pittz, one of the community organizers who supported the strike, said that the strike was "resonating" with the general public. "I know we were getting a lot of honking and waving from passers-by," he said. "Everyone knows someone who works in the fast-food industry."[13]

No one really knows how many workers walked off the job that day or how many restaurants shut down (at least eight and as many as fourteen restaurants had to shut down completely).[14] But as a political statement it was a home run. Every major news outlet covered the strike as a top story and interviewed strikers about their lives and the economics of earning the minimum wage. The *Seattle Times* reported the story that evening, quoting a food-service employee who said, "You know the pay is bad when managers of higher-paid employees use the threat of fast-food wages to intimidate. They'll say 'If you don't like it, you can go work at McDonald's.' "[15]

SEATTLE'S ECONOMY IN 2013

Seattle is only fifteen miles north of SeaTac, but in 2013 their economies couldn't have been more different. While SeaTac was an inner-ring suburb struggling with poverty and decline, Seattle was a boomtown. Cranes dotted the skyline as new upscale neighborhoods continued to rise from formerly blighted neighborhoods. Biotech, software, aerospace, and health care were fast-growing industries. Microsoft founder Paul Allen's real estate development company, Vulcan, and Seattle e-commerce giant Amazon were busy transforming the north end of downtown from empty parking lots, cheap motels, and car dealerships into new high-rise offices, apartments, and condos for hordes of twentysomething urbanites arriving to seek or accept employment in one of Seattle's many growing technology-related industries.

Meanwhile, poorer Seattleites were finding it harder to make a home there. Seattle is one of the richest cities in the United States. It has the fourth-highest percentage of households earning over $150,000 a year in the nation.[16] But high incomes drive up the cost of living—studies estimate that it costs $93,000 per year to live comfortably in Seattle, while a worker making Washington's minimum wage is netting less than $20,000 per year.[17] And the cost to live a basic, self-sufficient life (with minimal help from government assistance or food banks) has gone up 38 percent in the past fifteen years, according to researchers at the University of Washington.[18] As the executive of Seattle's King County, Dow Constantine, summarized, "It's people doing really well, and people making espresso for people who are doing really well."[19]

Since 1999, 95 percent of new households in King County have been either rich or poor (more than $125,000 a year or less than $33,000). A mere 5 percent could be considered middle income.[20] Nevertheless, Seattle is rightly considered a progressive city when it comes to workers' issues. In recent years, Seattle had become one of the first municipalities in the United States to pass a law on paid sick leave, requiring all but the tiniest employers to provide some amount of paid sick leave to employees. It was among the first to pass a "wage theft" ordinance, making it a criminal offense for employers to steal workers' wages by not paying overtime, not allowing for required breaks, requiring workers to work "off the clock," or similar infractions. Seattle had also passed a local prevailing-wage ordinance (requiring contractors on public works projects to pay area standard wages and benefits), a local hire ordinance (incentivizing public works contractors to hire local residents), and a "ban the box" ordinance (prohibiting employers from inquiring about criminal backgrounds prior to an interview).

And it was in this environment that a movement arose that would demand a previously unthinkable minimum wage and inspire the nation with the knowledge that—at least in one city in the upper-left-hand corner of the United States—workers no longer needed to accept the low-wage status quo.

MEET THE FAST-FOOD STRIKERS

Seattle's lopsided economy and high-cost housing was the backdrop to the showdown between struggling workers and the city's dominant poverty-wage industry. But it took individual workers, restaurant by restaurant, to set things in motion. Their demand, as stated on their Facebook page, Good Jobs Seattle, was simple: "I make $15 per hour or less and I am worth more."

Brittany Phelps, twenty-four, participated in the first fast-food strike in May 2013. Phelps was making minimum wage working thirty-seven hours per week. She lived in a two-bedroom apartment in a cheaper suburb of Seattle with five other family members, all of whom she was helping with their expenses. She didn't make enough to get her own place with her five-year-old daughter while helping her family. Phelps said her ambition is to go to culinary school or open a restaurant, though she said, "In the condition I'm in right now, I don't see a way to get there." Why? Because, as Phelps said, "People have been working for [McDonald's] for ten years and only make 90 cents more than I do. So I'm like ok, we're going to fight for this change, because that's a shame."[21]

Jason Harvey, a forty-two-year-old navy veteran who works at Burger King, also went on strike that May. He said he felt moved to action because he had seen colleagues become victims of wage theft, slashed hours, and an overall "lack of respect."[22] He had worked at Burger King for eight years and still made minimum wage, and was also being assigned fewer hours than in previous years. Harvey had lived in the same government-subsidized studio apartment for twelve years, explaining that he "can't afford to live anywhere else." Once he makes $15 an hour, he added, "I may have to pay a higher rent, but I'll be able to afford to go to the grocery store. The food stamps would be the first thing to go. I don't like living off of the charity of others and the government." So he decided to join the other workers going on strike: "I was scared out of my boots," he said, "especially the first strike. It was a new experience for me and definitely moving out of my comfort zone. It's not something that you do because it feels fun, but I had to do it."[23]

Crystal Thompson, thirty-four, had worked in fast food for most of her life. After five years at Domino's Pizza, she was still making minimum wage. "I enjoy my job. I enjoy the people," she said. "And it helps pay the bills. But your week starts Monday, and you don't see your schedule until Sunday night. You don't have the same schedule every week, so you can't plan your life." Thompson shared a small living space with her young son and a roommate. Her son slept on the couch. "There's just not a way out yet," she said. "I just keep doing what I'm doing. All my money goes to bills. It's tough." When she first started protesting, Thompson admitted, "I was scared to be on strike. . . . I was scared of losing my job. But it was kind of empowering. I just felt good to be heard, to be a voice for the rest of the workers in the city that don't have a chance to speak out, giving them a chance for their troubles and their problems to be heard too." Thompson has received support from her fellow fast-food workers. "My coworkers think it's cool," she said. "That it's awesome that someone actually has the guts to get out there and do it. Because nobody else had the guts before."[24]

FIFTEEN DOLLARS BECOMES A POLITICAL FLASHPOINT

It is safe to say that none of the candidates for Seattle mayor had thought much about a $15 minimum wage when they were deciding to throw their hat into the ring during the winter and spring of 2013. But by the time the race was heating up in late spring and early summer, it was one issue that was unavoidable.

Seattle was the seventh city in the country to be hit by fast-food strikes, after New York in 2012 and Chicago, St. Louis, Detroit, Milwaukee, and Harrisburg, Pennsylvania, in early 2013. The Seattle fast-food campaign was led by Working Washington, the SEIU-backed labor-community partnership that we formed in 2011 to organize unemployed and low-wage workers, with the goal of holding politicians and corporations accountable for good jobs.

Like the SEIU-funded fast-food efforts in other large cities, Working Washington organizers, (together with the immigrant rights group OneAmerica and the antipoverty group Washington Community Action Network,) visited fast-food stores around the city—and found that the workers were excited about fighting for a raise.

When Seattle fast-food workers struck on May 30, 2013, it was the first time the call for $15 was heard on the streets of Seattle and the first time in the series of strikes when stores actually shut down.[25] And even more so than in other cities, news of the strike dominated the day's local news headlines.[26]

The May fast-food strikes took place at the beginning of what was to be an important election season in municipal Seattle. One-term incumbent mayor Mike McGinn was running for reelection against a field of eight challengers, including a current and a former city council member, a popular state senator, and five long-shot candidates. The four "major" candidates were McGinn, state senator Ed Murray, city councilman Bruce Harrell, and former city councilman Peter Steinbrueck.

Throughout the summer the issue of a $15 minimum wage was raised at almost every candidate debate and public forum. It was impossible to avoid. Candidates were asked about it everywhere they went. Within fifteen miles of each other in SeaTac and Seattle, two campaigns were developing that would find synchronicity on the ballot in November of 2013.

As a strategy, we could not have done better than the combination of a movement that was coming into its own just as a major election season was ramping up. Even those who were opposing $15 in SeaTac realized that this was a turning point toward an inevitable wage hike in Seattle. The campaign in SeaTac had business interests on alert. In August, the Seattle Chamber of Commerce called a meeting of its policy council to discuss the $15 movement. One participant explained,

"So that's why we are engaging on both levels, bringing all the stake-holders together in Seattle to say the first line of defense is to defeat it in SeaTac, that sends a message. I'm already getting calls from [Seattle City] Council members saying 'you should start your discussions now because the living wage is coming.'"[27]

A chamber member at the meeting even went so far as to acknowl-edge that the current minimum wage was not livable: "It's going to be an interesting battle. The rhetoric from the unions is pretty much [that] people have such difficulty supporting themselves on a mini-mum wage. . . . I don't think anybody can argue with that and I don't think anyone should argue about sick leave either, it's very popular."[28] In other words, even those in the business community who were op-posing the $15 wage campaign acknowledged that they couldn't win by arguing against a minimum-wage hike while a city election cam-paign was under way.

Six of the eight Seattle mayoral hopefuls appeared at a candidate forum at SEIU's downtown headquarters on a Saturday in June 2013. Such forums were a weekly, sometimes daily, occurrence during the height of the campaign season, with everyone from downtown business groups to neighborhood associations to climate advocates holding can-didate debates. But this particular candidate forum was unique. The subject matter of the ninety-minute forum was exclusively restricted to "low-wage worker issues," bringing the issue of the poverty-wage econ-omy to the center of political debate. Sponsored by a dozen worker and antipoverty groups, the low-wage worker forum was televised gavel-to-gavel by the Seattle Channel, the city's equivalent of C-SPAN, and covered by reporters from both major Seattle newspapers and several TV network affiliates. The auditorium at the union hall was packed to capacity.[29]

Moderating the debate was local political journalist and city hall reporter Erica Barnett. The panel of questioners consisted entirely of low-wage workers, including Burger King employee Aaron Larson, Taco Del Mar employee Alfonso Arellano, child care worker Kellie Baird, and Safeway grocery chain employee Tracie Champion.

The workers asked each candidate a series of questions about issues of importance to low-wage workers, including:

How would you live on the minimum wage?

What would you do as mayor to improve fast-food workers' lives?

What would you do to support better child care policies?

What would you do to support union organizing rights?

What should we do about companies pushing health care and other costs onto workers and the community?

What would you do to keep low-wage employers out of our neighborhoods?

Then, during Q&A, an audience member levied a challenging question to the candidates: "Would you support a $15 minimum wage in the city of Seattle?" When it came to raising the city minimum wage to $15 per hour, every candidate hedged to some extent. Harrell said, to laughs from the audience, "I heard everyone dodge the question except for Kate [Martin]." But Murray chimed in, "I said yes, Bruce."[30]

Each candidate was asked to explain to the audience how he or she would balance a household budget on the Washington minimum wage (then $9.19 an hour). They were given a blank budget worksheet to fill out with the usual household expense categories—rent/mortgage, utilities, groceries, health care, education expenses, entertainment, transportation cost, child care, etc. Their responses were unanimous—this was, in Steinbrueck's words, "an unworkable, below poverty line budget."[31]

The debate ended with no clear winner—except, that is, for Seattle's low-wage workers. Never before had there been a mayoral debate devoted exclusively to low-wage worker issues. But because of the broad coalition of organizations hosting the debate, no major candidate was willing to miss it—doing so might cost a candidate an endorsement from a major labor or civic organization.

Primary election day didn't bring many surprises in the mayor's race. As many political observers expected, the front-runners, incumbent Mike McGinn and state senator Ed Murray, emerged as the top two vote getters and victors of Seattle's nonpartisan primary, each with about 30 percent of the vote. They would go on to face each other in the general election. Both McGinn and Murray had been supportive of the fast-food worker strikes and had made public statements supporting a higher minimum wage. Neither had made a hard-and-fast commitment to the $15 number, although Murray had come the closest.

However, there was one big shocker on primary day in the Seattle City Council election. In the race for council position number 2, where sixteen-year incumbent Richard Conlin was widely perceived as having no meaningful opposition and being guaranteed an easy ride to reelection, two candidates appeared on the ballot against him: a young Democratic Party activist named Brian Carver and Socialist Alternative candidate Kshama Sawant (the Socialist Alternative party is the U.S. branch of a British-based Trotskyist labor party).

Both Sawant, then a forty-one-year-old community college economics professor, and Carver had run unsuccessfully in past elections, and neither raised much money nor garnered endorsements from popular elected officials or organizations. Conlin seemed to have no way to lose.

Conlin did indeed come in first in the primary, but with less than half of the vote—never a reassuring sign for an incumbent. It meant that more than half of the primary voters had voted for someone else. Even more surprising, Sawant had come in second, with 35 percent of the vote to Conlin's 47 percent. Sawant would face off against Conlin in the general election, the first socialist to advance to a general election in Seattle since 1991.[32] For a supposedly frivolous "protest" candidacy, Sawant's had done surprisingly well.

Moreover, Sawant had based her candidacy almost entirely on the message of a $15 minimum wage. She had effectively hitched her fate to the fast-food workers' strikes and the SeaTac initiative, both of which were dominating local and national media coverage throughout the summer. Sawant called the win in SeaTac "the mother of everything that came after it. It changed the landscape—before that, people were hesitating to talk about a $15 minimum wage." She also credited the fast-food strikers, saying, "The fast-food workers were in many ways the political backbone for the entire movement. The strikes were a real turning point and a sign of the changing consciousness of the most marginalized workers."[33]

SUMMER HEAT—AND AN ELECTION SURPRISE

On August 1, eight fast-food workers and community activists were arrested demonstrating in front of a downtown McDonald's. After police had hauled them away from a sit-down picket at the busy franchise, *The Stranger* reported,

> Well, somebody finally got arrested over complaints of criminal wage theft at Seattle fast food restaurants, only it wasn't the employers accused of stealing wages by refusing to pay for mandatory overtime. [The] arrests are an indication of the courage of the protestors, as well as the passion with which the strike's participants approach their cause.
>
> It's one thing to hide behind bandanas while hurling rocks. . . . It's another thing to stand your ground and demand arrest. This sort of civil disobedience certainly isn't new, but it's heartening to see this renewed embrace of the tactic.[34]

Then on August 29, the first day of coordinated national fast-food strikes occurred, marking the fiftieth anniversary of the 1963 March on Washington. The strikes reached sixty cities around the United States.[35] Within a few weeks, mayoral candidate Ed Murray huddled with a group of advisers to craft an economic policy platform that his campaign would release later in the month. I was part of that group. So were political consultants Christian Sinderman and Sandeep Kaushik, civil rights leader Pramila Jayapal, retired labor lobbyist Ellie Menzies, and former Clinton White House speechwriter and technology executive Eric Liu.

Murray had been criticized by his opponent, incumbent Mayor Mike McGinn, for being too close to the Chamber of Commerce and other special interest business lobbies. So Murray needed an economic platform that would place him squarely in Seattle's progressive mainstream. And he needed to solidify his support among labor unions. Unions were splitting their endorsements, with some for McGinn, some for Murray, and others staying out of the race. But the biggest endorsements so far had gone to McGinn, including the Machinists,

UFCW, and UNITE HERE. The large SEIU locals had so far not endorsed any candidate.

Endorsing a $15 minimum wage would be a bold move. It would brand Murray as a clear progressive in the race, and make it laughable to attack him as a shill for big business. It would also carry a lot of risks. Fifteen dollars was becoming a normal thing to talk about in Seattle, but it was far outside the parameters of the national conversation about wages, and it was certain to confuse or even infuriate some of his business supporters.

After several drafts, Murray released an "Economic Opportunity Agenda for Seattle" in September 2013. At a press conference at his campaign headquarters, he stood with Burger King striker Aaron Larson as he detailed his proposal. The six-page document covered several topics from wages to worker training to affordable housing. Here is what it said about wages:

> As Mayor, Ed Murray, who has personally endorsed finding an appropriate pathway to moving towards a $15 living wage, will work with City Council, businesses, labor and community partners . . . and the City Council to adopt a phased-in approach to implementing a strong living wage standard that substantially improves the living standards of low-wage workers in the City of Seattle. Seattle should not wait for state or federal action.[36]

The point was made: being for $15 an hour, in Seattle at least, was no longer outside of the mainstream. In fact, two weeks later, McGinn joined Murray in calling for $15 an hour. He even appeared to up the ante by saying that $15 was "a fair starting point," and that he'd support a wage *above* $15 if it had support on the city council.

So with a month to go before the election, not one but *both* candidates for Seattle mayor had endorsed a demand for a city minimum wage of $15. That was something that most observers would have dismissed as an impossibility back on May 29 when Caroline Durocher walked out of Taco Bell.

Adding fuel to the fire was the insurgent candidacy of Kshama Sawant, given credibility by her strong showing (and Conlin's weak one) in the primary. Hers wasn't a traditional campaign—she didn't have a budget for TV ads, many mailings, or paid phone calls. Her organizational outreach was thin to nonexistent. She would sometimes show up at rallies organized by fast-food workers carrying a bullhorn and expect to be invited to speak. It was the ultimate outsider, protest-candidate-style campaign.

But in addition to riding the coattails of the fast-food workers movement and the SeaTac campaign, Sawant also had *The Stranger* in her corner. *The Stranger* is Seattle's largest alternative newsweekly. For many readers, it's a source for movie and music reviews, concert and club listings, sex and relationship advice, personal ads, and ads for clothing boutiques, tattoos, escorts, and weed. But it's also a serious newspaper, with real news, investigative journalism, and editorial pieces in a retro-hip format: muckraking, well researched, accurately reported, opinionated, snarky, and decidedly liberal and antiestablishment. On a fraction of the budget and with a fraction of the staff of a mainstream daily, *The Stranger* may be the only remaining alt-newsweekly in the country to function simultaneously as a serious newspaper.

The Stranger's candidate endorsements are probably the most widely read in the city. They matter. And in the Sawant-Conlin race, *The Stranger* did more than endorse Sawant. It actively campaigned for her, with a front-page feature article about her campaign and with positive coverage in every week's edition and on its popular news blog. *The Stranger's* news and editorial staff were big fans of the fast-food strikes, big fans of SeaTac Prop. 1, and big fans of Sawant. They used the power of their publication to aggressively promote all three.

On Tuesday, November 5, 2013, elections took place throughout Washington State for various local offices and local ballot measures. In SeaTac, Proposition 1 appeared to be passing comfortably, although as late votes were tallied over the following two weeks the margin would shrink to less than 1 percent. In Seattle, Ed Murray was elected mayor by a margin of 53 to 47, defeating one-term incumbent Mike McGinn in an election where each candidate tried to outdo the other in support of higher wages and other worker issues.

But surprising everyone—including her—was the narrow victory by socialist city council challenger Kshama Sawant over incumbent Richard Conlin.[37] Sawant was the first socialist elected to the Seattle City Council since 1877.[38]

The cause of $15 wages had scored a trifecta in Seattle-area elections: Proposition 1 in SeaTac, Ed Murray, and Kshama Sawant.

GETTING TO $15

The next step would take just as much work and just as much skill—it was time to mobilize this newfound political power to get a $15 policy passed. There were four key ingredients to get to a meaningful $15 minimum wage:

- Murray's administration—particularly his income inequality committee
- Ongoing pressure from workers and the community
- The participation of the business community
- Policy expertise and public education

The goal was to have workers and coalitions organizing in the streets and in the halls of government, while others worked inside the official government process to land the right policy recommendations. And the public needed to be included every step of the way with events and relevant policy information.

GETTING TO $15: MURRAY'S ADMINISTRATION AND THE INCOME INEQUALITY COMMITTEE

A month after the election, Mayor Murray announced the formation of an Income Inequality Advisory Committee (IIAC) tasked with developing a new minimum-wage policy for Seattle. During the campaign, Murray had promised to bring together a representative group of stakeholders from business and labor to make a recommendation on how to get to $15 citywide.

Making good on his pledge, Murray named me and Seattle hotel and hospitality investor Howard Wright as the committee's co-chairs, representing labor and business, respectively. The other members included three city council members (including Sawant), the CEO of the Seattle Chamber of Commerce, venture capitalist Nick Hanauer, a host of business owners and business association representatives, and leaders from philanthropy, labor, and community groups.[39] Murray gave us four months to develop recommendations.

Murray laid out his charge for us at a press conference, asking, "Is this going to be a city of the rich? Or is this going to be a city that is diverse economically, racially, and ethnically? The issue of economic disparity is really the driver. People should have a wage that's livable; you can't have an economy that's built on low-wage jobs."[40]

Murray made a few things clear. The subject matter of the IIAC's recommendation was limited to the minimum wage—an important point given that business groups had been agitating for a "broader" (read: much longer) discussion that would include housing costs, educational access, and the like. He also reiterated his personal support for a minimum wage of $15 an hour, while holding open the possibility that the IIAC might reach a different recommendation.

"The path I'm choosing," Murray said, "acknowledges the urgency and avoids an ugly fight in an election year."[41] This wasn't just an issue of who got credit for passing $15, but more importantly of trying to cobble together a center-left coalition that would allow $15 to move forward without turning Seattle in 2014 into one giant and expensive war between labor and business.

The composition of the committee was crucial to its chances of success. Brian Surratt, adviser to the mayor and primary staffer on the committee, believed that "the most important starting point was the strong co-chairs, who each had credibility with their constituencies and had an interest in getting a deal done." Of the twenty-four members, eight were representatives of either pro-$15 organizations or pro-$15 elected members of the city council. In choosing the other committee members, Surratt said, "When we looked across Seattle's DNA in the business community we had to make sure the restaurant and hospitality community was there, and that those representatives would be brash, would poke holes, and would have credibility."[42]

The Washington Restaurant Association planned for the seven hospitality industry members on the IIAC to do more than poke holes, saying that the Seattle Restaurant Association had "fought hard to have these individuals on the Committee to ensure that the hospitality industry's voice is *leading* any negotiations that take place."[43] But even the hotel association leader on the IIAC, David Watkins, acknowledged that the mayor "put together a group of diverse, well-balanced individuals," that the IIAC was "very composed and respectful, with open dialogue," and that we built a "a sense of trust and comfort, even though we'd be on opposite ends of an issue."[44]

Although the IIAC had broad agreement on the most important topics, we got stuck at times in deep disagreement over others. Our early agreements were:

- There was agreement among almost all committee members that we should *raise the minimum wage to $15.*
- Almost all committee members were supportive of a *phase-in* for the minimum wage.
- All of the committee members supported a *no exemptions* policy—no type of business or employer should be exempt from the minimum-wage requirement.
- Although there had been a lot of talk about what types of employee benefits should "count" toward an employer's responsibility to pay a worker $15 an hour, only two types of compensation rose to the top: *tips and health care.*

On the other hand, we were quickly focusing on a limited set of questions with sharp differences of opinions on the committee:

- How long should the phase-in be to $15 per hour?
- Should the phase-in be different for large and small businesses?
- Should tips count toward the $15 per hour?
- Should employer-paid health benefits count toward the $15 per hour?

These would become the critical issues that the committee would have to wrestle with as we got down to hashing out a final recommendation. In particular, counting tips and health care as compensation toward a $15 wage became one of the most contentious issues in our negotiations.[45] These two issues, along with other forms of compensation such as 401(k) matches, bonuses, and tuition credits, were referred to by business leaders as a "total compensation" approach. Labor advocates argued against including the cost of such benefits toward a $15 wage, arguing "a wage is a wage."

A joint City Council–IIAC public hearing in March was the first official public forum for citizens to give feedback on raising the wage. Seattle's Town Hall can seat up to eight hundred people and was filled to capacity. Local TV news reported that "people stood out in the rain hours before the meeting even began so they could tell the City Council and the Mayor's advisory committee why the minimum wage should be raised."[46] Council member Sally Clark kicked off the meeting, telling the audience, "We have a moment in Seattle where people are hungry to talk about income inequality and how it affects our city."[47]

For hours on end, people gave testimony both for and against a $15 minimum wage, though most of the testimony was supportive. Vinon Goswami testified, "We're not asking for a yacht, or an airplane. We're asking for living wages to have a roof over our head and [to] pursue the American Dream."[48] Andy Moxley told the committee that an "economic apocalypse has already happened to working people and young people. I have a college degree and spent four years working in a restaurant but was never paid more than $10 an hour." He added that the concerns of small business "don't mean my landlord will wait, or my utilities will cost less."[49]

The banner headline in the *Seattle Times* the next day read: "Historic Moment: Hundreds Pack Minimum Wage Hearing." The article went on to report that "about 700 people, many wearing red T-shirts with '15' on the front, cheered calls to enact a pay increase in the city."[50]

Another key moment in the IIAC's outreach and education work was the Income Inequality Symposium at Seattle University. The "for and against" rhetoric was heating up in the media, and we wanted to lift up the discussion and have a serious, daylong set of civic conversations about income inequality. I saw the conference as a way of organizing support for the $15 proposal by bringing together national experts, think tankers, academics, and elected officials from Seattle and other cities to focus the city's attention for a day on this issue.[51] Council member Licata said, "I think what we're doing here today is of national importance. No other city in the nation has pulled together council members and academic experts from other cities, put them all into one room, and invited the public for an open discussion."[52] Hundreds attended; the conference center at Seattle University was packed to capacity.[53]

A panel of workers particularly hit home with their stories about trying to survive in Seattle on low wages. The panel included a hotel worker making just over $15, a McDonald's server who says she takes home about $1,100 a month, and a shelter counselor at the Downtown Emergency Service Center. The homeless shelter counselor, Jesse Inman, lives with his wife in a basement studio in an inexpensive neighborhood of Seattle but said he was still barely able to afford to stay in the city. "I've grown up in Seattle and have watched as rent and the cost of living has gone up tremendously. That's something I'm struggling with and that a lot of my coworkers are struggling with," he said, "the ability to live in the city that we serve."[54]

GETTING TO $15: COALITION PRESSURE AND THE POLITICS OF THE STREET

From the beginning, street-level political activism was key to keeping the pressure on the politicians and the IIAC—and keeping media attention focused squarely on low-wage workers' issues. While the IIAC was working with the mayor and council in city hall, the activist action out in the streets kept heating up. Building on the wins in SeaTac and Seattle, SEIU-backed Working Washington and a broad coalition of labor, community, faith, and immigrant organizations took the campaign to the next level.

One month after the election, Working Washington organized what they described as a "15-mile march to bring $15 from SeaTac to Seattle." On a clear but cold day, about a hundred bundled-up marchers set off early in the morning from SeaTac for an eight-hour march that began in SeaTac. They paraded through neighboring Tukwila, South Seattle, Central Seattle, Chinatown, and finally headed downtown to city hall. The marchers stopped for brief rallies and protests at fast-food restaurants along their route and were joined by Sawant supporters, students, and additional workers at different points throughout the day. As Dallas Brazier, a Burger King employee who marched for the entire day, told reporters, "If you make enough noise, then somebody's gonna have to listen."[55]

By the time they arrived at city hall at dusk, the crowd was several hundred strong. All four local news stations had followed them from SeaTac and throughout the march, featuring the marchers on morning, noon, and afternoon newscasts; Al Jazeera and Spanish-language station Univision also had reporters on the ground. As the marchers headed up Fourth Avenue toward City Hall Plaza, some stations carried their arrival live. In addition to Sawant, who had joined the march along the route, four other council members greeted the tired and cold marchers as they piled into the plaza.

The street heat kept growing as the months went on, with $15 supporters turning out en masse to the annual Martin Luther King Jr. march and rally on January 20. Thousands of people marched from Garfield High School in the historically African American Central District neighborhood to downtown's Westlake Park under the theme of the day: "Rise Up. Restore the Dream." Working Washington's website reported that "news helicopters followed and local journalists jogged on the sidewalks trying to keep up with the brisk pace down to our ending point."[56]

While Working Washington, the labor and community coalition, and fast-food workers were lobbying legislators and telling their stories, Kshama Sawant's group 15 Now began a drumbeat about a possible ballot measure. In mid-February, 15 Now held a daylong event to train hundreds of their activists on the mechanics of ballot measure qualification and how to organize and talk to voters about the merits of a $15 minimum wage.[57] The group's organizer, Jess Spear, facilitated the event, during which both Sawant and I spoke. It was followed by workshops on door knocking, picketing, and signature gathering on buses and in fast-food restaurants.

The same week in February 2014, U.S. senator Patty Murray and U.S. representative Suzan DelBene brought their call for a $10.10 federal minimum wage to town with a news conference featuring supportive small business owners. Both legislators highlighted the fact that boosting the wage would particularly benefit women, who account for most minimum wage workers. "When women succeed, Americans succeed," DelBene said.[58]

Only a few days later, fast-food workers were in the news again, this time calling for a one-day "big burger boycott" of the three major burger chains: McDonald's, Burger King, and Wendy's. The one-day action was dubbed "Boycott McPoverty."[59] Workers and supporters spread out to restaurants around the city to picket. Burger King worker Jason Harvey told the TV news, "We want this so we can pay our own bills and pay our own way. We wouldn't be out here saying something if we weren't hurting."[60]

GETTING TO $15: POLICY EXPERTISE AND PUBLIC EDUCATION

We realized early on that winning the public argument with facts would be a key piece of the puzzle to pass $15. The Income Inequality Advisory Committee needed detailed information to develop its recommendations, and we knew that minimum-wage opponents would undoubtedly trot out old but incorrect arguments about how a higher minimum wage wasn't necessary, or would cost jobs, or would cause businesses to fail or leave. We wanted to present solid answers.

One of the most relevant questions when crafting a living-wage policy is this: how much does a living wage actually need to be for workers to live at a minimum acceptable level, free of public assistance? Researchers often answer this question by looking at the cost of a "market basket" of common consumer goods, including the daily items that most of us need to buy in order to live a normal life: housing costs (rent or mortgage), groceries and food, child care and education costs, transportation, energy including gas, health care, taxes, utilities, clothing, and a bit for recreation and entertainment. This living-wage approach doesn't assume that you'd have enough money to see a movie in a theater, afford cable TV, take a vacation, or invest for retirement.

Two research groups presented information on the market basket for the Seattle area:

The Workforce Development Council of Seattle-King County's "self-sufficiency standard" estimates one's most basic living expenses based on age and the age of any dependent children. According to the calculator, a single thirty-year-old adult with one eight-year-old child would need an annual income of $42,000 to live in a bare bones but potentially self-sufficient way in Seattle. That's $20.25 per hour. And as we saw earlier, the cost of living has gone up fast over the past fifteen years—almost 20 percent in the past five years alone.[61]

Another market-basket report we examined, one created by the Alliance for a Just Society, calculates the cost of basic household budgets in the states across the country to determine the living wage for certain household types and measure the availability of living-wage jobs. The Alliance defines a living wage as one that "allows families to meet their basic needs, without public assistance, and that provides them some ability to deal with emergencies and plan ahead. It is not a poverty wage." The Alliance estimated the basic costs of living in the Seattle area (King County) for a single adult with no children at $3,042 per month, or $17.55 per hour at forty hours per week:[62]

Figure 5.1: The most basic daily cost of living in the Seattle area

	Single adult	Two working adults with two children
Food	$ 7	$24
Housing & utilities	$30	$37
Transportation	$20	$45
Health care	$ 4	$17
Child care	$ 0	$52
Taxes	$14	$28
Savings	$ 9	$17
Miscellaneous	$16	$31
Daily expenses:	*$100*	*$250*
Wage needed:	*$17.55/hr*	*$22.01/hr per adult*

The research included costs for different-sized households—with or without toddlers, school-aged children, and with one or two adults with or without two jobs. This budget is more realistic, though still very insecure—the cost of food, in particular, would be almost impossible to match for most Americans, let alone workers living in a city as expensive as Seattle. And the wage required is *still* above $15 per hour. In its most recent report from 2013, which we used in the IIAC process, the Alliance found that living wages for a single adult working full-time year-round ranged from $13.94 an hour in Montana to $16.13 an hour in Washington State, and $22.10 an hour in New York City. For a single adult with two children, living wages ranged from $24.82 an hour in Montana, to $28.71 in Washington, and $39.09 an hour in New York City.[63]

The Alliance study found living wages were two to three times greater than the federal poverty guidelines, which are calculated by multiplying a basic food budget by three (food made up a much larger percentage of the average American's budget when this standard was set in the 1964).

In sum, there was no minimum wage in any state in 2013 that provided a basic standard of living for an individual or a family.

THE IMPACT OF INCREASING THE MINIMUM WAGE

So now we knew something about the kind of wage that would provide a basic standard of living in Seattle. But what would be the impact of raising the minimum wage that high? We asked researchers at the University of Washington and University of California to analyze exactly who would be affected by an increase in Seattle's minimum wage, how laws in other localities were designed, and what we know about the impacts of local wage mandates on workers and businesses.

Professors Marieka Klawitter, Mark Long, and Robert Plotnick at the University of Washington's Daniel J. Evans School of Public Affairs researched the first question—who would be impacted by the $15 minimum wage in Seattle? They found that about a hundred thousand Seattleites currently earned less than $15 and would, therefore, be directly affected by the raise. As one would expect, they found that low-wage workers were more likely than the average Seattleite to be young, female, a person of color, have a lower educational level, be poor, and receive public assistance.

The most common occupations and industries for low-wage workers were food service, hospitality, personal care, retail, transportation, moving, and educational and social service.

The UW researchers also found that:

- Increasing the minimum wage to $15 per hour was simulated to reduce Seattle's poverty rate from 13.6 to 9.4 percent, if employment and hours did not change.
- Notably, half of all poor adults in Seattle were *working* poor.
- Minimum-wage workers work a median of one thousand hours a year—essentially half-time.

- For a family of three living on one full-time minimum-wage paycheck, food stamp benefits could drop from $348 to $75 if $15 passed (drops would be less for those working fewer hours or with smaller households).
- While 75 percent of Seattle businesses employed ten or fewer workers, those businesses accounted for only 12 percent of all employment. The vast majority of employees—88 percent—worked for larger firms.[64]

Three researchers at the University of California at Berkeley conducted a second study. As of early 2014, nine cities had raised their minimum wages above their state minimum-wage level. These local experiments in wage setting provided real-life case studies of what might happen if we raised the minimum wage significantly in Seattle.

The Berkeley researchers were tasked with examining how existing laws are designed, what we know about the impacts of local wage mandates on workers and employment, and whether businesses move outside city or county borders in response. What they found, in the words of San Jose city council member Don Rocha about his city's major minimum-wage increase, was that "The sky did not fall." (He added that nine thousand new businesses had been created in San Jose since the increase.)[65]

Each of the Berkeley study's research questions found evidence that the sky would, in fact, remain aloft after a major minimum-wage increase. Looking at similar increases around the country, the researchers found that increasing the minimum wage does:

- Boost income for workers at the bottom rungs of the labor market. These increases include both directly affected workers (those earning between the old and the new minimum wage) as well as those indirectly affected (those earning above, but near, the new minimum wage).
- Reduce income inequality, pushing up the wage floor compared to the median wage.
- Lift wages for women and people of color in particular, and mostly affect adults—not teenagers.

- Reduce poverty and use of public benefits such as food stamps.

The researchers also found that increasing the minimum wage *does not*:

- Result in higher unemployment, hours cuts, or reduced health or pension benefits, even in low-wage industries such as restaurants.
- Cause businesses to relocate to nearby cities or states with lower wages.
- Lead to a drop in the hiring rates of young people or people of color.
- Result in significant price increases. Some areas saw onetime price increases in the restaurant industry of about 0.7 percent following a 10 percent minimum-wage increase, but not in other industries.[66]

The Berkeley researchers found that wage increases had positive impacts for employers by reducing employee turnover, which translated into a reduction in direct costs (recruitment, selection, and training of new workers) and a reduction in indirect costs (lost sales, lower-quality service, and lost productivity as the new workers learn on the job). They also found that the local economy would likely benefit, because "low-wage workers and their families are likely to spend a significant portion of those increased earnings."[67]

So the bad things that naysayers predicted would happen in Seattle if we raised the wage just hadn't happened in other cities. This includes places like Santa Fe, where the minimum wage had been raised 85 percent over the state minimum wage. We will spend some more time on these questions in chapter 7, but as it relates to the work of the IIAC in Seattle, this research clearly gave ammunition to advocates of a $15 minimum wage.

THE HOT-BUTTON ISSUE OF TIPS

Probably the single most emotionally charged issue that we dealt with was tips. Tipped workers, who make up a significant portion of the low-wage workforce, are employed at restaurants, hotels, parking lots, car washes, nail salons, and airports. The largest numbers are employed in food service—waitstaff, bussers, and food delivery workers.[68] Most jobs in restaurants and hotels are low-wage jobs, and these are large industries. Unsurprisingly, restaurants, and to a lesser degree hotels, became incredibly mobilized around this issue during the IIAC process.

Tips were included under the "total compensation" argument that business-side negotiators made, along with health care, retirement plans, on-site child care, tuition credits, bonuses, profit sharing, stock options, and just about every other type of compensation that they could think of. "Total compensation" was a new term that restaurants had invented after political advisers told them that the term "tip credit" was too toxic, but it expanded to include these other forms of compensation. The idea was that all of an employee's benefits should count toward the $15 number. Under this proposal, employees who received no tips, no health care, no retirement, no bonuses, and so forth would get $15 an hour, and employees who received any of that wouldn't get $15.

Labor advocates nationally have been trying for years to get rid of the "tip credit" system, which functionally consigns many if not most restaurant servers to subminimum wages. It's been an uphill fight, but so far seven states, including Washington, have eliminated the tip credit, so that tipped workers are guaranteed the same minimum wage as any other worker.[69] (The other states are Alaska, Montana, Nevada, Minnesota, California, and Oregon.) This was a choice Washington State had made in 1988, when the voters approved Initiative 518, which also raised the state minimum wage from $2.30 to $4.25 over two years (an 85 percent hike).[70]

The other forty-three states have a lower minimum wage for tipped employees than for untipped employees, and require employers to make up for any wages that fall below the minimum wage. (Twenty-six states and the District of Columbia have a tipped minimum wage that is above $2.13 but lower than the regular minimum wage.)[71]

Although the law says the employer has to make up the difference if your tips don't amount to the difference between $2.13 and your state or the federal minimum wage, this rarely happens: more than one in ten tipped workers report that they earn actual hourly wages below the full federal minimum wage.[72] From 2010–12, the U.S. Department of Labor conducted nearly nine thousand investigations of full-service restaurants and found an 84 percent noncompliance rate. The Wage and Hour Division recovered $56.8 million in back wages for nearly 82,000 workers and assessed $2.5 million in civil money penalties, but of course that was only the tip of the iceberg of what was stolen from tipped workers.[73]

Saru Jayaraman, founder of the Restaurant Opportunities Center, wrote an entire book on the experience of restaurant employment, *Behind the Kitchen Door.* "The biggest workforce in America can't put food on the table except when they go to work," Jayaraman says. "It's an incredible irony that the people who put food on our tables use food stamps at twice the rate of the rest of the U.S. workforce. They don't use food stamps because they want to; they use food stamps because their wages are so low, and they face higher levels of food insecurity than other worker. They can't afford to eat."[74]

Jayaraman also noted that while people of color represent 26 percent of the Seattle workforce, 33 percent of the tipped workers here are people of color. She explained why tipping is not just about low wages, but also perpetuates a pernicious social system:

> Women have to sell themselves, to please the customer, because a portion of their income comes from their customer instead of from their employer. Almost everywhere I go, a woman comes up to me and says that she's been sexually harassed on the job, but never did anything about it because it was never as bad as when she was a young woman working in restaurants. This is how we are exposing our daughters to the world of work— a world in which they can be touched and treated and talked to in any which way. Ultimately, tips are not wages.[75]

As the IIAC's work and negotiations continued, it became more and more clear that tips would be one of the issues that determined our success or failure—and one of the most difficult negotiating points. It appeared nearly impossible to cut a deal that made both sides happy on the issue of tips.

GETTING TO $15: WORKING WITH THE
BUSINESS COMMUNITY

After $15 passed in SeaTac, the tone changed among the mainstream of the Seattle business establishment. For many business leaders, it was no longer a question of *whether* the minimum wage would be $15, but rather *how* and *with what policy specifics*. Businesses had learned a valuable lesson from the SeaTac campaign: when it comes to higher wages, "no" isn't a good answer. Voters wanted higher wages—as evidenced by victories in SeaTac, the Seattle mayor's race, and the Sawant race.

Now, instead of just saying "no," businesses were primarily concerned about building a long phase-in and getting credit for tips and health care. But the one thing they feared the most was a SeaTac-style initiative that would usher in a $15 rate all at once, with no exceptions, no phase-ins, no tip credits, no consideration for health care, no different rate for small businesses, and so forth.

Crucially, Murray didn't want "15 Now" either. He feared a business-labor ballot measure war that would divide and distract the city for a year, and regardless of outcome make it harder to accomplish many of his other key platform agenda items and campaign promises. For him, avoiding an initiative war was a benchmark measure of success. As Surratt noted, "Both sides were scared to death of the alternative. Business was afraid of an outcome like SeaTac, so it was in their interest to be proactive and avoid taking a 'hell no' posture."[76]

Co-chair Howard Wright is from a wealthy, well-connected, fourth-generation Washington State family—it would be harder to find any bluer blood in town. He is the CEO of the Seattle Hospitality Group of Companies, an investment firm with holdings up and down the West Coast. Many of his companies, particularly hotels, employ primarily low-wage workers. He understood the business side of low-wage work.

But Wright also had a genuine concern about the growing gap in the United States between the wealthy and everyone else. He sincerely felt the middle class in America was at risk and that *something* had to be done to restore earning power to working people in the interest of both the economy and democracy. "I'd become concerned that our society and middle class are unraveling at the edges," he said.[77]

Wright is emblematic of the type of business leader who could sit down with people from all backgrounds and hammer out a fair deal. He came into the process already believing that a $15 minimum wage was the right thing to do. That meant that from the very beginning it wasn't a question between us of *what* to do, but *how*. Wright's reading and research led him to the conclusion that an appropriate minimum wage would be at least $15 an hour. "The $15 minimum wage," he said, "is within a few cents of what it took to live an average functional life in 1968, after adjusting for inflation. If you look at $9.32, we're basically contributing to a poverty wage. We can make a difference by getting to $15 in a reasonable way." He had also come to believe that a dramatic increase in the minimum wage was a political inevitability, and that if voters were given a chance to do so, they would raise it. Wright believed that many at the Seattle Chamber of Commerce were in denial that $15 would come to Seattle after the victory in SeaTac, or that they could defeat it if it did. "Personally, I wasn't opposed to $15," he said. "I was opposed to 15 *now*. I thought that if we in the employer community did not get out in front of it, it would get out in front of us, and we'd end up with something we found unacceptable. I firmly believed at the time that it was going to pass in SeaTac and Seattle, so I wanted to make something mostly acceptable to most of the people."

Wright summarized his stance going into the process: "I operated out of two buckets of fear: First, our middle class is unraveling. Second, [Kshama Sawant's] people were going to hand us something really unpalatable. But I didn't operate only out of fear—I wanted to be *proactive*." [78]

So the IIAC chair chosen to represent the business community in negotiations was someone who was a successful businessman, a CEO, and an investor; a well-known donor in arts and philanthropic circles; an employer of low-wage workers; and an opponent of the SeaTac initiative. And he was simultaneously someone who was legitimately concerned about the trajectory of wages and the middle class and who believed that Seattle had a moral and civic obligation to act on income inequality for the health of the economy and our democracy.

As the process went on, some elements of the business community began to push back. After the Income Inequality Symposium, some of them were beginning to feel like they were losing the debate; not only had the Berkeley report largely dismissed and debunked concerns about business failure and job loss, but most of the speakers at the symposium were decidedly pro-$15 and many were skeptical about tip credits in particular. Several groups emerged from the business community to try and organize to counter the pro-$15 forces, which consisted of the 15 for Seattle Coalition (the "big table" coalition that unions helped lead), SEIU-backed Working Washington, and 15 Now (an offshoot of Kshama Sawant's Socialist Alternative party). The anti-$15 groups never gained much traction, though, and their meetings for workers were poorly attended. A planned rally of restaurant workers in favor of the tip penalty (organized by restaurant owners and their trade association, not by workers themselves) got canceled, apparently due to lack of interest.

One constituency that was barely present for much of the debate was the franchised national fast-food chains: McDonald's, Burger King, Wendy's, Pizza Hut, KFC, Taco Bell, Subway, etc. These were companies whose workers had walked out on strike in Seattle and around the nation, but the companies had been curiously quiet in the debate. The perception inside city hall was that these companies must have realized that they were not the best spokespeople for the restaurant industry—as national brands that make billions of dollars a year and pay their CEOs millions, yet pay their workers next to nothing.

What is important to note and worth repeating: the mainstream of the Seattle business community never went to the mat against $15 minimum wage. What they did was try to advocate to make the eventual $15 wage more acceptable to them. As Dave Freiboth said, "It was more of a begrudging, 'let's make the most of it.' "[79] They wanted tip credits (which labor organizers redubbed "tip penalties") they wanted a slow phase-in, and they wanted a total compensation approach that would take a lot of employers off the hook for meaningful wage increases if their employees earned tips, health care benefits, and 401(k) contributions.

But the chamber and most of the other respected business groups never really argued against $15. They tried to delay it as much as possible. And many certainly had not wanted to have the discussion about $15 to begin with. But one of the lessons of the SeaTac campaign for the dominant and most politically astute Seattle businesses was *not* to try to fight against $15, but to make it work on their terms.

THE HOME STRETCH

As the IIAC process continued to move forward and our deadline neared, the strikes, public demonstrations, "street heat," media coverage, public turnout at town halls and council meetings, compelling speeches by low-wage workers relating their stories, strong support of the mayor and a number of council members, the national echo chamber of fast-food workers continuing to strike around the country, academic analysis, the policy reports . . . everything was coming together to create an atmosphere of possibility, and even probability, around a $15 minimum wage in Seattle.

But the clock was ticking. On April 14, the socialist spin-off group 15 Now had filed language for a charter amendment with the city clerk. It could now begin the process of collecting the thirty thousand signatures legally required to get the amendment on the fall ballot. But 15 Now was still using the amendment as a threat rather than a promise, calling it "the people's safety net in the event City Hall cannot deliver a solution this year."[80]

The labor unions and community organizations who were part of the $15 for Seattle Coalition saw the risks as well as the potential rewards of using the initiative tool. On one hand, initiatives gave you the ability to write policy directly into city code without compromise. On the other hand, going the initiative route raised the possibility of allowing large national corporations and billionaires to pour in unlimited resources to campaign against them. While the SeaTac living-wage measure was narrow and targeted to travel-related large employers, the Seattle campaign was far broader in scope—we aimed to raise the wage to $15 for everyone in an entire city. And even more than that, as Surratt stated, "labor knew it needed to be inclusive if the model was to translate and spread further than progressive Seattle."[81]

Inside the 15 for Seattle coalition, our view was that we should be absolutely prepared to wage and win an initiative war if necessary. But we felt that a peaceful settlement of the issue without resorting to a costly and risky initiative would be even better, because the victory would be more certain and potentially more sustainable.

By early April 2014, the IIAC had only a few weeks left before our deadline. The IIAC had come close to breaking up in rancor amidst a business-side collective tantrum at what it had seen as the pro-$15, anti-tip balance of speakers at the previous week's income inequality symposium. But the process wasn't broken yet. We had clearly defined the four key issues that separated us from a deal: length of phase-in, treatment of different sized businesses, tips, and health care. There were plenty of other issues still on the table, but if we could solve these four we would be most of the way to a deal.

We had known all along that as the IIAC's work progressed we would end up needing a small group of core negotiators to bring the deal together. Howard Wright and I had urged the mayor to pull together such a group. And now it was desperately needed. The mayor and his staff team called in Howard Wright, Maud Daudon, Bob Donegan, and David Watkins from the business side and myself, David Freiboth, and Sarah Cherin from the labor side. We met several times a week, late at night, on weekends, and many times into the early hours of the morning, doing the hard bargaining to bring a deal together.

The issues had coalesced: labor wanted a fast path to $15 for all workers and no credits for tips or health care benefits, but was open to a slower path for small businesses. Business groups wanted a slow path to $15 with permanent credit for tips and health care and the same phase-in schedule for small and large businesses.

It was at an evening meeting at city hall on April 14 that the first real breakthrough came. It was Seattle Chamber of Commerce CEO Maud Daudon who sketched an impromptu graph on a conference room whiteboard. An upper line represented the rate and steps at which big businesses would need to get to a $15 minimum wage on a faster timetable. The lower line represented the rate at which small business would need to get to a $15 minimum wage on a slower time line. In the intervening years, before they both reached an inflation-adjusted $15, small businesses could make up the difference between their minimum wage and the large-business minimum-wage rate with tips or health care costs, but by the end of the phase-in period, small business credit for tips and health care costs would be phased out entirely. For small businesses without tips or health benefits, the higher rate would apply.

As Robert Feldstein summarized, "you get tip compensation at the beginning—which helps smaller businesses get [to $15] quicker—and a clean minimum wage at the end." Small restaurant and hotel employers would get the credit they had been fighting for, for tips and health care. But they wouldn't get it forever. Eventually the same rules would apply to everyone.

It was messy. It was also brilliant. To accept the parameters of Maud's impromptu drawing as a policy settlement, each side would need to part with some dearly held principles while being able to claim victory on others.

But many days later, after nights camped out in city hall in negotiations, we still hadn't reached consensus in the larger committee. Seattle news website *Publicola* referred to the minimum-wage discussions as "deadlocked."[82] Just in time, advisers Brian Surratt and Robert Feldstein came in with a proposal that broke through the rancor and indecision:

- For employees of large businesses (a term that had yet to be defined), minimum wages would rise to $11 in 2015, $13 in 2016, and $15 in 2017.
- For employees of large businesses enrolled in an employer-paid health plan (equal to the value of an Obamacare "Silver" plan), an extra year would be added to the phase-in, yielding $11 in 2015, $12.50 in 2016, $13.50 in 2017, and $15 in 2018. After that, it would be adjusted for inflation.
- For employees of small businesses (also a term that had yet to be defined), "guaranteed minimum compensation" would jump to $11 in 2015 and then $1 per year until reaching $15 in 2019. Guaranteed minimum compensation would be a new legal concept that included wages, tips paid through a paycheck (but not cash tips), and health care premiums.
- But this concept was only intended to be in effect until 2021, when the minimum wage of $15 would be reached—for everyone! That's $15 an hour in your paycheck, with no "tip credit" or reduction for health care premiums.
- After that, the minimum wage would adjust faster than inflation until 2023 before dovetailing with the large

business rate. The projected wage in 2023 would be $17.29, after which every employee in the city would have the same minimum wage, adjusted upward for inflation annually.

So a small business employee with no tips or employer-paid health care would get to a minimum wage of $15 by 2019. For those with tips and/or health care, the employer would be responsible for guaranteeing that the combined total of wages, tips, and health care reached $15 by 2019, of which $12 would have to be wages and as much as $3 could be the tips and health premiums. After 2019, the allowance for tips and health care would shrink each year until 2023, when it phased out entirely, and minimum wages would rise together from then on.

Of the two large issues still on the table, business size for the phase-in schedule and the treatment of franchises, the mayor ultimately made the call on business size: "small businesses" would have fewer than five hundred employees, the same definition used by the U.S. Small Business Administration. We believed that we could reach conceptual agreement on the inclusion of franchises in the category of "large business," knowing that we'd have to fight off amendments once we got to the city council and potential lawsuits after that. I made it clear that under no circumstances should the very workers whose courage and heroism had started this whole movement—the fast-food workers who worked for giant multinational brands—be left out of the higher and faster minimum-wage increase.

As we fought it out over the final issues, our "outside game" dramatically intersected with the "inside game": one day in late April, hundreds of pro-$15 demonstrators from Working Washington and the 15 for Seattle coalition converged on city hall for a rally while the negotiators were hammering out details of the agreement upstairs in the mayor's office. Supporters formed a giant picket line that completely surrounded city hall, holding over 1,200 feet of banners with all the reasons they needed $15.

Support our families.
Afford to survive.
Live on our own.
Pay the bills.

Women.
Youth.
Immigrants.
People of color.
Workers.
EVERYONE.

The activists surrounding city hall on the outside were a powerful visual message of the public's expectation: that those of us on the inside would reach a deal to bring $15 to Seattle—and soon. KIRO TV reported from the scene, "Hundreds are rallying for a living wage in one of the most expensive cities in the country."[83] Many of the progressive IIAC members attended the rally and mingled with the demonstrators. As I was leaving city hall for the afternoon, I was able to speak with several of the other progressive leaders who had not been a part of the most recent negotiations. The initial feedback was overwhelmingly positive. People liked the deal, thought the tradeoffs were reasonable, and were relieved that we seemed to have been approaching a consensus.

The mayor scheduled a celebratory press conference to announce the deal—except it turned out that we didn't yet have one. With the press conference only minutes away, a final agreement slipped away from us again, and the mayor, Howard Wright, and I went in front of the assembled national press without much to say. Robert Feldstein recalled that the agreement "felt too brittle and shaky to take to the public—this opportunity was too big to go out the door based on a shaky understanding. It took great courage and it was not what anyone would have chosen."[84]

Journalist Josh Feit later summed up the main problem: "the inability of the business reps to get sign-off from their varied memberships."[85] It took another few days for the business IIAC members and the constituencies inside the chamber of commerce, the Restaurant Alliance, and the Hospitality Association to reconcile themselves to what their own negotiators understood was inevitable: $15 was here and it was happening. The broad parameters of the deal had been signed off on by the top negotiators for business, labor, the council, and the mayor's office on the IIAC. The business representatives began to understand that they needed to get to "yes," then appease the angry members of their own constituency—restaurant owners in particular. The final vote on the IIAC was twenty-one to three. We had a supermajority recommendation for getting to $15 in Seattle. A year of rallies, boycotts, walkouts, and arrests in the street—along with the mayor's stakeholder-consensus strategy—had won a raise for one hundred thousand workers.

The following day was May 1, International Workers' Day—celebrated in most countries but not generally in the United States. In Seattle it was the traditional day for a large annual march and rally for immigrant rights. A week earlier, we'd had the disastrous press conference minutes after the IIAC's deal had fallen apart. On the morning of May 1, Mayor Murray, Howard Wright, and I again faced the press, joined by council member Nick Licata—this time with a victory to declare.

JUST A FEW WEEKS LATER, GETTING THROUGH COUNCIL

The next step in the Seattle process was to get our nine-member city council to enact a law enshrining the minimum-wage deal we had just spent four months negotiating. The council had already been involved—it had held hearings and council work sessions of its own, it had been involved in the March town hall and the March symposium, and three council members had been IIAC members. Howard and I had held meetings with all of the council members at least once during the IIAC process, and I had kept several of the more interested members updated throughout the endgame of negotiations.

Based on these conversations, we felt there was almost no chance that the council would out-and-out reject the IIAC recommendations. However, time is the enemy of deals, and there was risk that various constituencies would see the council process—which had been scheduled to run for two months after the IIAC process concluded—as a way of re-litigating issues that they hadn't prevailed on during the IIAC.

A group of mainly Asian immigrant–owned restaurants came late to the debate, largely uninvolved in the IIAC process until our recommendations were public. They out-and-out opposed the $15 recommendation and wanted it not to happen at all. At worst, they hoped to get small immigrant businesses exempted from the law altogether.

After the events of the last year, this was highly unrealistic. Brian Surratt wished that the mayor's staff had made different choices at the beginning of the process regarding these businesses. "It would've been great to have the voices of more ethnic business representatives," he said. "The immigrant community tried to build their coalition [late in the process], but we would have been better served to have their representatives" on the IIAC.[86]

The other group of restaurateurs that came alive in opposition to the deal was the franchises—McDonald's, Subway, and the like. Despite being part of multinational corporations, they wanted to be treated like small businesses rather than large ones. But they, too, had largely been outmaneuvered by the time that the IIAC recommendations hit the media—the mayor, the unions, and the business negotiators had already signed off on including franchises as large businesses.

In addition to those two groups—who largely wanted to undo the recommendations or rewrite major provisions—some of the organizations that were party to the IIAC recommendations saw the council process as a second bite at the apple, where they could get amendments adopted by council that weren't part of the IIAC recommendations. And on the opposite side, 15 Now and Socialist Alternative were still talking of a ballot measure, even while most of the 15 for Seattle coalition was focused on lobbying for five or more votes on the council for the IIAC's proposal.

On the afternoon of May 1, hours after the IIAC proposal was announced, thousands of marchers and demonstrators flooded streets in the annual immigration rights march that takes place in Seattle. But this year, working with march organizers, Working Washington and the 15 for Seattle coalition had arranged for the march to have twin demands: immigration reform on a federal level and a $15 minimum wage in Seattle.

The day before, we had spoken with our (and the mayor's) pollster, Ian Stewart of EMC Research, and commissioned a poll of public opinion about the recommendations. The initial poll taken in January 2014 had shown 68 percent support for the $15 minimum wage—an incredibly strong result.[87] We wanted to know where we stood with voters after four additional months of intensely public debate. We thought it was entirely possible that our support had dropped. EMC conducted the poll of likely voters during the first week of May.

On May 14, we released the results of our new poll to the public: an astounding 74 percent of Seattle voters supported the $15 minimum-wage proposal made by the IIAC.[88]

- Voters preferred it to the "$15 now" concept of an immediate jump to $15 without any additional policy nuances.
- They preferred it to a hypothetical lower, slower proposal of a $12.50 minimum wage.
- They didn't want permanent tip credits.
- They didn't want to see weakening amendments such as a permanent subminimum training wage.
- And the vast majority reported that they were paying close attention to the debate.

The poll was a home run, and we quickly released it to the news media. *The Stranger's* Anna Minard reacted: "There's been a lot of fear the council could be swayed by their imminent reelection campaigns (the district elections measure that passed in November forces all nine to go back to voters in 2015). Would that mean that big business money would sway them to the right? Now we can ask: Will what appears to be the clear will of the voters sway them to the left?"[89]

On May 15, fast-food workers walked off the job again as part of an international day of action coordinated by fast-food organizers and coalition partners in each city. It was the largest fast-food strike yet on a national basis, and in Seattle it occupied the day's media, just as the previous strikes and days of action had done. Workers at stores across the city walked off their jobs or did not report for duty. Local station KIRO TV reported that one protester, Julia Depape, said that though she'd held a steady job for three years at the minimum wage of $9.32 an hour, she was still homeless. "I've never had the opportunity to save and I work very hard," she said. "I live with friends, pay them what I can. I can't even get my daughter a new pair of shoes and this is my life and my stability and my independence."[90]

But this day of action was no longer about pure hope—we had a proposal on the table. Two weeks later, it became law. On May 29, in a packed hearing room, the Seattle City Council's Committee on Minimum Wage and Income Inequality heard its final public testimony and then voted to pass the IIAC recommendation together with the amendments we'd expected, by a vote of 9–0. There was vigorous debate on the amendments, with 15 Now and Sawant arguing against each amendment that was supported by business. But even Sawant, who had voted against it on the IIAC out of fear that it would be further weakened in council, was ultimately a yes vote on the whole package.

We had a unanimous decision, exactly a year to the day from when Caroline Durocher and her two co-workers walked out of a Ballard Taco Bell. Murray told reporters, "I appreciate the good work of the City Council to make clarifications and technical fixes to our minimum-wage legislation while keeping the overall framework of the deal we announced on May 1st intact."[91]

Despite the enormity of the win (or because of it), our opponents hadn't given up entirely. Just as in SeaTac, legal fights came fast on the heels of victory. The coming weeks would see right-wing ballot initiative entrepreneur Tim Eyman and the Forward Seattle Coalition both try and fail to gather sufficient signatures to get their anti-$15 measures on the ballot. A trade association of international franchisers also announced a lawsuit, but one so flawed that legal observers had a hard time taking it seriously. It was ultimately shot down by the federal courts. In denying the claim, the federal court held that the franchisers "did not provide persuasive evidence showing that the public interest would suffer as a result of allowing the ordinance to take effect, failed to raise serious questions going to the merits of any of its claim, and failed to show that an injunction was in the public interest."[92] Mayor Murray chided the chain restaurants that "rather than investing in lawyers to prevent workers from earning higher wages, it is time for these large businesses to begin investing in a higher minimum wage for their employees."[93]

THE LESSONS OF SEATTLE

A $15 minimum wage wasn't on anyone's radar screen as a potential civic issue before the first of the fast-food strikes happened in New York in November 2012. However, it would be almost exactly a year from the first Seattle strike in May 2013 to a unanimous council vote to raise the wage to $15 an hour—with the support of 74 percent of the public.[94]

The speed with which the deal went through city council was a testament to the political credibility of the process that the mayor had designed six months before and to the work of the IIAC members and their constituencies in getting behind a realistic agreement. Politically, it was a home run for Murray. Among the flurry of press covering the legislation, *Bloomberg Businessweek* reported, "In what may be a model for other cities and states, Murray put business leaders, union bosses, and community advocates in a room for months with simple instructions: work out your differences, or else. The 'or else' was that Murray and the city council would do it without them. He had the political momentum to back up the threat."[95]

Danny Westneat of the *Seattle Times* gave some serious credit to the labor unions and the workers we had organized: "Unions are back with city-by-city wage campaign," he said. "Suddenly these are looking like the best days for unions in decades," he said. "Instead of trying to organize workers business by business—the 'rusty old machine called collective bargaining'—the idea is to wage broader, public-spirited campaigns like the $15 wage fight. It's old school union bargaining. You take what you can get. Especially if you can then use the win to seek a bigger prize. Maybe these successes will turn out to be a blip. But it's been decades since anyone said this: Unions are back."[96]

It mattered significantly that we had union leaders willing to make the demands of largely nonunion workers their top political priority. It mattered that we elected a mayor who deeply and empathetically felt that it was his calling to attack income inequality, and who wished to try to do so in a negotiated, stakeholder-based process that kept the city united. It also mattered that we had a business community willing to sit down and negotiate rather than just say no. It mattered that we had individual leaders like Nick Hanauer and Kshama Sawant each playing a role in changing the debate substantially—Nick by making the argument that higher minimum wages are actually pro-business and Kshama by providing the left flank that gave many of the rest of us cover and the room to compromise.

Once again, as in SeaTac, the most critical element was workers themselves taking action. In this case, it was the fast-food workers going on strike, holding mayoral debates, organizing boycotts, marches, weeks of action, street demonstrations, and attendance at city hall forums, public debates, and town halls. By taking direct action, workers changed the terms of the debate as well as public perception of their value from that of *French fry cooks* to their value as *human beings, parents, neighbors, citizens,* and focused public attention on the fact that no one could live with dignity in Seattle on a $9.32 minimum wage.

Once again advocates and organizers also refused to accept the right-wing, trickle-down economic theory that minimum-wage increases kill jobs. Instead, we advanced Nick Hanauer's concept of "middle out" economics, that more wages will actually mean more customers for business and a virtuous cycle in which rising economic tides in fact lift all boats. And the credible research commissioned by the IIAC and done by local groups like Puget Sound Sage largely bore that out.

We were also operating in a changed public opinion environment post-Occupy, when income inequality and wage stagnation were finally becoming among the principal moral issues of our time. After forty years of stagnant and declining wages, people had had enough.

But the Seattle $15 struggle also had some new lessons to teach.

First, in Seattle the government was very clearly on the side of the workers. Going into 2014, we had a mayor-elect and a city council majority that had already declared their support for $15. The question then became how to get there in a way that was both sound policy and sound politics. Mayor Ed Murray positioned himself as the convener of the debate and negotiations were held in city hall itself. The research and staff work were paid for by city dollars. When talks broke down, Murray threatened and cajoled to get them restarted.

Murray used the bully pulpit and his own political capital to advance the debate. And the message was sent to the business lobby: the government is committed to addressing worker poverty and income inequality, so if business wants to influence how that happens, it had better claim a seat at the table, not just say no. *Having a government that operated openly on* the *workers' side* was one reason we got done peacefully in Seattle what it took a fight to accomplish in SeaTac and far more than we have become accustomed to expecting from Congress.

Second, the campaign in Seattle proved the value of having an organized and demanding left wing of the debate. Kshama Sawant, Socialist Alternative, and 15 Now were disruptive of the political status quo, frightening many city hall incumbents and much of the city's business elite. For that matter, they often drove the labor-community-progressive coalition crazy with their "our way or the highway" approach to strategy and their unwillingness to consider compromise or collaboration. But despite how frustrating they could sometimes be to work with, they were also an essential part of the dynamic unfolding in Seattle: if business elites, mainstream politicians, and even the business-as-usual elements of the labor-progressive coalition didn't get on board to produce a center-left minimum-wage proposal, they were certain to face a far-left proposal on the ballot that had a good chance of success. Sawant and Socialist Alternative helped create a hard-left edge to the debate in a way that the Tea Party produces a hard-right edge in much of the Republican electoral coalition, and it kept many Democratic and progressive leaders looking over their shoulders and motivated to find agreement. As labor leader Dave Freiboth said, "15 Now was helpful in making us look very moderate. We were the good cops."[97]

Third, business doesn't have to be the enemy. In Seattle, there were certainly parts of the business community that ended up wanting to say "hell no" to any minimum-wage agreement, but they were *decidedly in the minority*. And although the restaurant lobby in particular was slow to come to the table, there were many, many businesspeople like Howard Wright, David Watkins, Nick Hanauer, and Maud Daudon, who recognized that in the long term economic inequality is bad for everyone, even the rich.

Some business leaders agreed to negotiate because they were afraid of a worse outcome if Sawant ran a ballot measure. Some agreed because the mayor and city hall generally were clearly heading toward $15 and they didn't want to lose a chance to influence the policy. And some genuinely believed that the time had come to do something about income inequality and do the right thing for workers. (Wright and Hanauer would certainly fall into the latter category.) Together, the three overlapping subgroups—those who were afraid of Sawant, those who wanted a seat at the table with the mayor, and those who felt an obligation to improve lives for workers—formed a functional majority of the Seattle business establishment.

Even leaders of the local chamber of commerce and the local restaurant association played far different roles than the U.S. Chamber and National Restaurant Association play in Washington, D.C., contributing to the debate and even in some cases offering support for the final deal. Wright said of his role on the IIAC, "I took a lot of flak [from business], but we're different here in Seattle. We try to take care of our own."

If the victory in SeaTac seven months earlier had been a national and global news story, the victory in Seattle was even more of one. While some of the reporting in SeaTac had indeed suggested that it was about the "nation's highest minimum wage," the fact is that the SeaTac ordinance remained a living-wage measure attached to certain travel- and hospitality-related large businesses and benefiting a few thousand low-wage employees in those industries. But it had not been a true minimum-wage measure.

The victory in Seattle, by contrast, would lift wages for one hundred thousand people, far more than just about any union leader could ever hope to do at the bargaining table. And over ten years, it would transfer $3 billion in income away from corporations and business owners and to the workers who help make those businesses successful.

Just as we had said on election night in SeaTac and as I had repeated to reporters many times since then, voters were sending a message: they were tired of waiting for congressmen and CEOs to do the right thing and were taking matters in to their own hands at the state and local levels. *The Stranger*'s Anna Minard took a top-level look at the Seattle win:

> A lot of people deserve credit for getting the $15 minimum wage from the streets to City Hall. . . . But most of all, a bunch of people who work for terrible wages, and who have little power in a world that strives to disempower them, decided to take enormous personal risk and walk off the job, walk in a picket line, sit in the street, even get arrested. Congratulations to them, though the fight's not over yet. The fact that this debate has happened at all is thanks to low-wage workers fighting back.[98]

6

An American Wage for a Stronger America

The Case for $15

Will the uprisings of the national "Fight for 15" and the victories in SeaTac, Seattle, and elsewhere become the first victories ultimately leading to a stronger and more vibrant America? Or will they be viewed as brief blips on the radar screen during America's descent into a Third-World economy of poverty and inequality?

To start to answer these questions, we need to have a clear sense of what it is we are fighting for, why we want it, and what it would mean for the greater good. It is increasingly clear that Americans understand that what is good for American workers is ultimately good for the country as a whole. The question is whether our leaders—elected leaders in public office and business leaders in the C-suites—are willing to listen to the patriots instead of the plutocrats and unite around a vision of robust and shared prosperity in America that will once again let all boats rise together.

This chapter shows how a $15 minimum wage will make our nation stronger.

A $15 minimum wage will increase pay for as many as half of all American workers; restore the lost earning power of millions of Americans; decrease poverty and income inequality in America; allow more Americans to pursue an education; increase the time that American families and communities can spend together; improve America's collective physical and mental health; reduce America's dependence on public assistance programs; grow America's federal, state, and local tax revenues; and create demand in local economies that will help grow businesses and employment.

$15 WILL RAISE WAGES FOR HALF OF THE AMERICAN WORKFORCE

As we saw in chapters 1 and 2, a shockingly high percentage of American jobs are now low-wage jobs, and these jobs are no longer held primarily by teenagers. A $15 minimum wage would have a major impact on American workers: about 30 percent of all hourly workers are now making "near minimum-wage," $10 and under.[1] And *a full 42 percent of all American workers make less than $15 an hour.* Because the minimum wage sets pay scales in low-wage industries, a $15 minimum wage will transform jobs in restaurants, hotels, and warehouses from dead end to living wage.

Current proposals for increasing the federal minimum wage haven't reached high enough to make this kind of difference in workers' lives. We've seen proposals for $12 by early 2015 and $15 by mid-2015—but there has been significant political resistance in Congress even over proposals for $9 or $10.10 minimum wages. The *New York Times* correctly called out the idea of reaching $12 by 2020 as both "too low and too slow."[2] These low, slow, incremental proposals by Congress fail to directly affect a majority of American workers: a raise in the federal minimum wage to $9 would impact only a few million workers. A raise to $15 would impact tens of millions.

Some workers will benefit directly from raising the minimum wage to a living wage, while others will benefit indirectly through "spillover" wage effects—employers often increase the wages of workers earning slightly above the new minimum to maintain incentives to move up the pay scale.[3] Taking into account these spillover effects, many workers that are currently earning over $15 may see a raise as well—bringing the total affected by a $15 minimum wage to 50 percent of American workers.[4]

Fifteen dollars is so powerful because it sets a livable new standard, leaving the inadequate federal minimum wage in the dust. Workers around the nation are struggling on sub-$15 wages, wages that often never significantly increase despite years of service for an employer. Seattle security guard Tim Allen makes $12.60 an hour, but still is barely able to pay his rent in a subsidized apartment. "When my rent goes up this year," he said in early 2015, "then I'll be in the hole $5 a month. It's really tight. I can't go to the movies, or do much of anything." And of course, the future is uncertain for the fifty-seven-year-old. "I'm not sure there's much chance of ever retiring, due to the financial situation," he said.[5]

In Charlotte, North Carolina, McDonald's employee Kwanza Brooks has found that the stingy raises offered by McDonald's don't amount to much—and she needs more. When McDonald's announced in April 2015 that it would increase wages at its company-owned restaurants, Brooks wasn't impressed. "Up until the announcement this week that my wage was going up, I was trying to raise my kids on $7.25 an hour," Brooks told the New York Times. "Now I'll be trying to raise my kids on $8.25 an hour. That's still impossible! Let me be clear: raising wages only a little—and only for a small fraction of your 1.7 million workers—isn't change. It's a PR stunt." Ashley Wiley, who works for a company-owned McDonald's in New York City, agreed. "'It's not making a difference in my life at all,'" said Ms. Wiley, 26, who relies on food stamps and Medicaid to help support her three sons." She currently earns $9.19 an hour and will receive a 56-cent raise.[6]

$15 WILL HELP TO RESTORE PURCHASING POWER

A $15 wage would begin to restore some of the purchasing power that workers have lost over the past forty years. Workers are getting squeezed by a decrease in purchasing power, which the Levy Institute at Bard College found has been higher than is generally assumed: almost all workers have seen a drop of about one-fifth in their purchasing power from 1980 to 2013, while the cost of living has increased 67 percent in the past twenty-five years.[7]

People making less than $15 an hour (again, currently 42 percent of workers) are often faced with difficult choices about how to cover the essentials—rent, gas and groceries, health care and child care. This is a precarious and stressful way to live. But it's also a drag on local economies, because when workers have to ration their spending on the basics, it means they're *not* shopping for goods and services and spending the money in the local economy that would create demand and create jobs.

When Los Angeles passed a $15.37 minimum wage for hotel workers (a high percentage of whom live in poverty) in 2014, hotel housekeeper

Magdali Martinez had been making $11.42 an hour. Martinez, a forty-four-year-old working mother of three, responded to news of the raise, saying, "I'm overjoyed. This is really going to help my family. We don't have enough money coming in. We often have to choose between falling behind on our gas bill or our phone bill." Martinez, whose husband works at an auto body shop, said the raise would help send their son to dental school.[8]

Figure 6.1: Minimum wage compared to the wages of typical U.S. workers

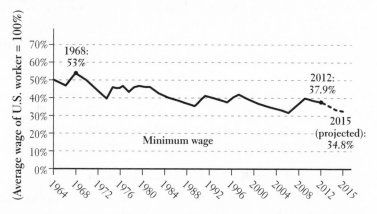

Source: David Cooper and Doug Hall, "Raising the Federal Minimum Wage to $10.10 Would Give Working Families and the Overall Economy a Much-Needed Boost," Economic Policy Institute, Briefing Paper No. 357, March 13, 2013.

One of the reasons that most workers can't make ends meet on to-day's minimum wage—or even many dollars above it—is because the wage has never been adjusted for inflation, and loses buying power over time unless Congress authorizes an increase. The minimum wage's current level of $7.25 is now far below its peak value in 1968, and has been unchanged since 2009.[9] In other words, today's ridiculously low minimum wage buys even less than it used to. Congress regularly raised the wage from the 1940s through the 1970s before doing nothing throughout the 1980s. The purchasing power of the minimum wage eroded 30 percent between 1979 and 1989. After a few raises in the 1990s, it was once again ignored until 2007, when a series of small increases began phasing in.

The value of the minimum wage has also tanked compared to the average worker's wage, which now stands at $21.50 an hour. In 1968, the minimum wage was more than half of the average wage, but by 2013 it had fallen to a third.[10]

In sum, Congress hasn't been even a minimally effective advocate for low-wage workers since the 1970s. And let's be clear—even a wage of $10.75 or $10.90 is far from adequate, just as $1.60 an hour wasn't a living wage in 1968. But in 1968, few minimum-wage earners were trying to survive solely on that income. Today, minimum-wage earners are almost all adults, and many are trying to support families on these low wages.

PRODUCTIVITY DOESN'T PAY (ANYMORE)—BUT $15 CATCHES WORKERS UP

In the past twenty years, the U.S. economy has grown nearly 60 percent. This huge increase in productivity is partly due to automation, communications technology, and other improvements in efficiency.

But it's also the result of Americans working harder.[11]

For decades, economists taught a relatively simple concept: wages tend to rise when productivity rises. The more goods or services workers produce or deliver per hour the more workers earn.

Though you wouldn't know it from their paychecks, today's American workers are the most productive they've ever been: from 1968 to 2008, the productivity of workers in the United States grew by 112 percent. Productivity growth (which means the growth of output per hour worked) has traditionally fueled the growth of living standards. The most productive nations have the highest standards of living, no matter what their level of GDP.

Higher productivity should translate into higher wages, and it used to: wages and productivity grew in tandem from the post–World War II period through the 1970s.[12] But today, productivity and compensation have completely come uncoupled. From 1979 and 2013, median wages rose a total of only 5 percent after inflation—while workers in the bottom 10 percent saw a wage *decline* of 5 percent. The tight labor market of the mid to late 1990s was the only period when wages increased for everyone.[13] Trends since the early 2000s are even more pronounced: wage growth from 2003 to 2013 was either flat or negative for the entire bottom 70 percent of earners, while at the same time one in ten Americans lost their employer-provided health care.[14]

Today, the gap between productivity and compensation for the typical worker is larger than at any time since World War II. If wages had been indexed to productivity since 1968, the minimum wage would now be $21.72 an hour. Productivity grew *eight times* faster than typical worker compensation. If minimum-wage workers received only half of the productivity gains over the period, the federal minimum would be $15.34.[15]

Figure 6.2: Growth in workers' productivity far exceeds their total compensation (salary plus benefits)

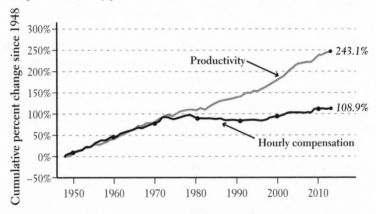

Source: Bureau of Labor Statistics, "Labor Productivity and Costs," U.S. Department of Labor, accessed August 11, 2015, http://www.bls.gov/lpc/.

This wage depression affected both college- and non-college-educated workers as well as blue- and white-collar workers at the same time that workers at all wage levels are better trained and educated than they were in 1979. Only a fifth of low-wage workers had any education above high school then, compared to 40 percent in 2008. But neither increased productivity nor higher education levels has managed to stem the decline in wages. And there is no evidence of upward pressure on wages—let alone acceleration of wages—and little evidence that corporations will raise wages on their own.[16]

So where are all of the gains in productivity going, if they're no longer being broadly shared with workers? To the income of the top earners and the profits of the top businesses.[17] Corporations and people at the higher end of the income distribution have received far more of the income produced by the economy since the 1980s. Almost all of the growth, in fact, has gone directly to the top, as Thomas Piketty documented in *Capital in the Twenty-First Century.*[18] And as Lawrence Mishel and Alyssa Davis of the Economic Policy Institute explain in their report on CEO pay, rising executive pay "reflects income that otherwise would have accrued to others in the economy." [19]

This is why, as economists Atif Mian and Amir Sufi observed, "the widening gap between productivity and median income is a defining issue of our time. It is not just about inequality—important as that issue is. The widening gap between productivity and median income has serious implications for macroeconomic stability and financial crises." [20]

A $15 MINIMUM WAGE REDUCES POVERTY

In 2013, more than 45 million Americans were living in poverty. The federal poverty threshold, an annual income of $23,624 for a family for four, is itself considered a sub-basic standard of living by many researchers. [21] Even more alarmingly, the prevalence of extreme poverty has increased 130 percent from the mid-1990s. Kathryn Edin and H. Luke Shaefer, the authors of the book $2.00 *a Day: Living on Almost Nothing in America,* estimated that in 2011 there were 1.5 million households, with 3 million children, scraping by on cash incomes of no more than $2 *per person per day.* Edin and Shaefer write, "That's about one of every 25 families with children living in a kind of poverty so deep that most Americans don't think it even exists here." [22]

Research shows what should be obvious, but bears repeating: raising the minimum wage reduces poverty. A $15 minimum wage would have a major impact on the number of Americans living in poverty, reducing the poverty rate by 19 percent in states that pay the federal minimum wage.[23]

Low-income families are almost always by definition working at low-wage jobs, and though these individuals are doing what society asks of them, they in return are not paid enough to get by. The fairest and most effective way to remedy that ill is to raise wages.

University of Massachusetts economist Arindrajit Dube has shown that higher wages: (1) increase incomes at the bottom of the family income distribution, (2) effectively reduce the percent of individuals living below the poverty line, and (3) reduce extreme poverty (families with incomes less than one-half the poverty line) in particular. The reductions in poverty are somewhat larger for black and Latino individuals, for those with less education, and for children.

Dube's careful research showed that for each 10 percent increase in the minimum wage, the poverty rate immediately decreases by 2.4 percent, and leads to an overall reduction of 3.6 percent in the longer run.[24] He finds that a higher minimum wage will lead to a significant boost in incomes not just for those earning the minimum wage, but also for other people just above the bottom of the income spectrum. Total household income increases when a minimum-wage worker gets a raise, lifting whole families up the economic ladder.[25]

Higher minimum wages also reduce the depth and severity of poverty—Dube finds that minimum-wage increases lead to "sizable reductions" in severe poverty (those living at half the poverty level).[26] The poverty-reducing effects of raising the minimum wage most strongly affect people living under the federal poverty level up through those making 50 percent more than the poverty level.

A few examples help to underscore the effect of a higher minimum wage on poverty:[27]

- In New York City, raising the wage from $8.75 to $15 per hour wage was estimated to reduce poverty by 18 percent for nonelderly adults and by 19 percent for children. Poverty was reduced for individuals in all race and ethnicity groups, but the effects were largest for Hispanics, with a 20 percent reduction in poverty.[28]
- The New York City comptroller found that raising the wage to $15 would significantly decrease the number of households earning low incomes while increasing the

number of families earning from $30,000 to $39,999 by
almost 67,000 households.[29]

- In Seattle, raising the wage to $15 was projected to reduce
  the number of people in poverty by a quarter, dropping the
  poverty rate from 14 to 9 percent.[30]

Contrary to trickle-down mythology that people living in poverty are nonworking "welfare queens," an overwhelming majority of
Americans living in poverty—75 percent—do have jobs, the majority
of which are full-time.[31] With a median wage of $8.85, a fast-food cook
with a family of three lives in poverty even if she never takes a day off.[32]
And while overall employment has increased since the Great Recession, that growth has come largely in low-wage jobs that do not pay
enough to cover basic needs. That means new jobs—nearly half—do
not provide enough to cover workers' bills.[33]

Figure 6.3: Broadly shared prosperity could have eradicated poverty

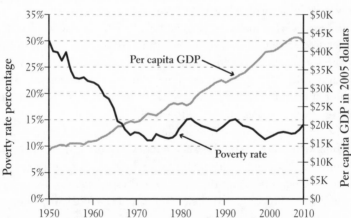

Source: Josh Bivens, Elise Gould, Lawrence Mishel, and Heidi Shierholz, "Raising America's Pay: Why It's Our Central Economic Policy Challenge," Economic Policy Institute, June 4, 2014.

Economic growth used to be associated with significant poverty
reduction. But since the 1970s, the relationship has largely decoupled.

The "simulated poverty rate" model predicts the poverty rate based on per capita GDP, and was quite accurate from 1959 and 1973. But since the mid-1970s, the actual poverty rate stopped falling when growth occurred and instead fluctuated within 4 percent of its 1973 low point. If the relationship between per capita GDP growth and poverty had held, the poverty rate would have fallen to zero in the mid-1980s.[34] Broadly shared prosperity could have led to a near eradication of poverty in the United States.

Even mainstream economic institutions and actors worry that America's high-level relative poverty rates are a long-term economic threat. The *Washington Post* wrote that lifting the minimum wage "isn't a thing that people proposing an inequality agenda just happened to throw on the table. A higher minimum wage is a substantial response to the challenges of inequality."

$15 REDUCES INCOME INEQUALITY (ESPECIALLY FOR WOMEN AND COMMUNITIES OF COLOR)

Raising the minimum wage to a more livable level is also an effective way to strike at income inequality. Much time and research have gone into studying the huge wage gap that exists between the top 1 percent of income earners and those at the bottom of the pay scale. But there is also a wide gap between middle earners and low-wage workers. The eroding value of the minimum wage, which has not been adequately adjusted for inflation by Congress, has contributed to a growing gap between wage earners at the bottom and those in the middle.

Economists agree that raising the minimum wage reduces income inequality by pushing up the wage floor, which brings low and middle incomes closer together (though raising the minimum wage does not address the gap between the median and top earners).[35] Economists Josh Bivens, Lawrence Mishel, Elise Gould, and Heidi Shierholtz found that the gap between low and middle earners was primarily due to the eroding real value of the minimum wage and high levels of unemployment.[36] Economists David Autor, Alan Manning, and Christopher L. Smith also found that most of the increase in low-end inequality from 1979 to 2009 was due to the decline in the value of the minimum wage. Economist Jared Bernstein confirmed that "the decline in the minimum wage's relative value has contributed to the increased [inequality] in wages over the past few decades—particularly among low-wage women, whose pay tends to be more closely tied to the minimum wage than low-wage men's pay." [37]

Women represent nearly two-thirds of minimum-wage workers, while 22 percent of minimum-wage workers are women of color. More than half of African American workers and close to 60 percent of Latino workers make less than $15 per hour and are overrepresented in low-wage workplaces—your server at a fast-food restaurant in Seattle, for instance, has even odds of being a person of color, despite the fact that minority workers make up only about 30 percent of the city's workforce. [38]

The overrepresentation of women and people of color in low-wage industries means that they benefit disproportionately from minimum-wage increases (and also explains much of the gender and race pay gap). Research shows that if the federal wage were raised by even a few dollars, the wage gap between men and women would decrease by 5 percent. Larger raises would reduce the gap even more. The decreasing value of the minimum wage during the 1980s may explain up to 30 percent of the concurrent increase in wage inequality for women. [39]

$15 WOULD SUBSTANTIALLY REDUCE DEPENDENCE ON GOVERNMENT WELFARE PROGRAMS

When workers make too little to survive, they turn to government-subsidized programs that help them make ends meet. Low-wage workers are eligible for a variety of benefits aimed at boosting incomes or helping them afford basics, such as housing, health care, or child care. This is important since many basics, especially health care, child care, and housing, are too expensive at market rates for low-income workers and their families—child care alone can eat up a large portion of minimum-wage workers' income. [40]

A $15 minimum wage would allow millions of American workers to reduce or eliminate their use of public assistance programs. It would also save billions of federal dollars per year, freeing up funds for other areas of need. A study by the Economic Policy Institute found that half of all workers making under about $10 an hour receive public assistance, totaling over $45 billion each year. The majority of the assistance spending is for health care—Medicaid and the Children's Health Insurance Program.[41]

Researchers using a similar methodology found that 60 percent of spending on food stamps and 47 percent of spending on Temporary Assistance to Needy Families (i.e., cash welfare) is provided to members of *working families*. The researchers found that more than half of families of fast-food workers are enrolled in one or more public programs, at an annual cost of nearly $7 billion. Low wages were the main predictor of public program enrollment.[42]

It may seem obvious that raising the minimum wage reduces reliance on public assistance programs. But how much? University of California at Berkeley minimum-wage researchers Rachel West and Michael Reich analyzed state and federal minimum-wage increases from 1990 to 2012 and found that, on average, a 10 percent increase in the minimum wage reduces food stamp program enrollment by about 3 percent and program expenditures by 2 percent.[43]

In states where the current federal minimum wage applies, a raise to $15 would decrease food stamp enrollment by almost 17 percent and program outlays by almost 10 percent. Beyond food stamps, research shows that a $1 increase in hourly wages reduces the percentage of people receiving *any* government assistance by 4 percent, in line with Reich's findings.[44]

And this is where even business-oriented fiscal conservatives start paying attention to higher minimum wages. Ron Unz is one of the best-known right-wing proponents of raising the wage. The former publisher of the *American Conservative*, a Silicon Valley entrepreneur, and once a Republican gubernatorial candidate in California, Unz even ran his own 2014 campaign to raise California's state minimum wage to $12 an hour ($2 more than the state legislature recently approved). Though the campaign was ultimately unsuccessful in getting off the ground, Unz and his ideas have gained a national stage. Interviewed by the liberal magazine *The Nation*, Unz was asked what raising the minimum wage would achieve. He replied,

> A lot of social welfare programs tend to be leaky buckets. One reason people don't want their taxes to be increased is they have

a sense a lot of the money will be burned up in the system and will never really go to the beneficiaries. Well, with the minimum wage the money goes straight to the person who has a paycheck. At a stroke, so many workers are no longer so poor [so] they no longer qualify for antipoverty programs—which makes conservatives much happier. The minimum wage is basically people working at their jobs. We're talking about raising income by $5,000 for an individual and $10,000 for a couple.

The $250 billion spent on social welfare programs for the working poor are really less of a subsidy for workers and more for their low-wage employers. If these workers had to actually survive on their own paychecks, they wouldn't be able to come to work in the morning; they wouldn't have food, rent money, they wouldn't be able to afford to live.

Whether you're a liberal or a conservative, having the government give hundreds of billions of dollars in subsidies to these low wage businesses doesn't make a lot of sense. Take the sweatshop industry, it's competing on prices and wages with companies in Bangladesh, and that doesn't make any sense. Why should the government be subsidizing sweatshops in the United States?[45]

Calling government welfare programs "a hidden government subsidy to low-wage businesses," Unz directly counters many of the arguments put forward by business and the right-wing. Because most low-wage jobs are in the parts of the service sector that can't be easily outsourced or cheaply automated, he says, a higher minimum wage would result in "the workers keeping their jobs at much higher pay, while their employers would simply pass along most of the increased labor costs to their customers in the form of higher prices. But the resulting price hikes would be so small that most consumers probably wouldn't even notice them."[46]

Unz summarized that "increasing the value of work, cutting social welfare spending, eliminating hidden government subsidies, and saving taxpayer dollars have always been important goals of conservatives and free market advocates, and a higher minimum wage achieves these."[47]

Unz is not alone. Other prominent conservatives such as Phyllis Schlafly, Bill O'Reilly, and economics writers at the *National Review* have also endorsed higher minimum wages. And the *Daily Caller*, one of the most widely read conservative publications, recently highlighted the conservative case for supporting a minimum wage hike with the headline, "$12 an hour is conservative rocket fuel."[48]

Unz has said, "I'm very glad that more and more conservatives are now coming around to supporting the conservative side of this issue, joining liberals who are supporting a wage hike for all sorts of liberal reasons." And he is calling on the rest of conservative America to join him. "I think America is at a sad point," Unz added, "when the political heirs of Ronald Reagan believe the solution to our poverty problem is more welfare spending while the political heirs of the Great Society are supporting efforts to make work pay and to cut welfare."[49]

Democrats and independents are sympathetic to these arguments as well. Several Democratic lawmakers have thrown their support behind a bill that would boost Oregon's state minimum wage to $15 by 2018. Senator Chip Shields said, "People in my district want a chance, not charity."[50]

As *The Guardian* recently reported, though, American corporations are currently all too happy to accept government welfare for their workers—and even encourage them to apply for it. A mother of two in Chicago, who had worked at McDonald's for ten years, called the McDonald's employee help line and found herself counseled to apply for food stamps and Medicaid.[51]

For Seattle Burger King worker Jason Harvey, getting a raise to $15 and not having to rely on government assistance would be a huge step in the right direction. "Right now I have a debt that I'm trying to pay off," he said. "I actually need to have food stamps. It was go get the food stamps, or go hungry for one or two meals. It was necessary. But first thing when we get $15 [per hour] is I would definitely forget to renew the food stamps! I mean, I don't like living off of the charity of others and the government, and that would be the first thing to go. I would go and buy my own food. I will still be watching the sales and doing coupons, but it will be buying it with my own money. I won't have to tell the government how much I'm making or how much I have in my account. It would feel really good."[52]

$15 HELPS GROW TAX REVENUES (WITHOUT NEEDING TO RAISE TAX RATES ON LOW- AND MIDDLE-INCOME EARNERS)

Lifting the wage not only cuts government expenses but also raises revenue by turning millions of net tax recipients into net taxpayers. Raising the federal minimum wage to $15 an hour would increase overall U.S. wages by 23 percent, or a $1.45 *trillion* gain for workers.[53]

And this new income would of course be taxed, and taxed again if it is spent on purchases (sales tax) or housing costs (property tax).[54] And although Americans are famously tax-averse to a fault, they also want good schools, healthy communities, a strong infrastructure of roads, bridges, airports, and transit, and a safe country. Higher wages mean more taxpayers and higher revenue collection *without* having to raise tax rates on working people. The lowest quintile of earners pay very little in taxes—and they shouldn't, given that they're struggling to provide even the basics for their families, are heavily indebted, and need a variety of government support programs.[55] But workers that earn enough to make it out of poverty also become net taxpayers. More economic activity and more taxes paid into the public coffers will further stabilize our society—both economically and socially.

$15 HELPS GROW AMERICAN BUSINESS FROM THE MIDDLE OUT BY STIMULATING DEMAND

Lower-income households spend every penny they make—and more, because they're borrowing to make ends meet. And when they do spend, the money flows directly into the economy.[56] New research shows that employment often *increases* when the minimum wage is raised, because the infusion of cash into the local economy creates jobs.[57] One example: when households making under $20,000 per year begin to make more livable wages, their spending at restaurants increases by nearly 45 percent. But trickle-down economics has left wages low and consumer demand weak. At this point, it's better for growth for lower-income workers to earn better wages than it is for business owners to sit on their capital.[58]

This is pretty much exactly the opposite of what we've been told for the past thirty years about how economic growth happens. The core assumption of trickle-down economics is that there is a trade-off between broadly shared prosperity—higher wages—and economic growth. Although it's counterintuitive, it's been repeated enough to become an accepted myth and now a cornerstone of the conventional policy framework in D.C. and on Wall Street.

The new economic narrative is based on decades of accumulated evidence that in a twenty-first-century technological capitalist economy, growth is a product of the *virtuous cycle between innovation and demand*—and that the policies that drive both innovation and demand are the ones that ensure that everyone gets a piece of the growth.[59] Not just because it's fair and good for society—but because it's good for business.

Venture capitalist Nick Hanauer was part of the Seattle negotiations, and was one of the earliest leaders of the fight for $15 back in 2012. He was one of the first investors in Amazon.com. Now he's a self-described "gazillionaire." He has built and sold businesses in aerospace, defense, information technology, and biotech. He is the CEO of a pillow and bedding manufacturing company. He and some friends own a bank. Hanauer fits the VC and CEO stereotype in so many ways: he lives in a mansion, owns a private jet and a yacht, has several vacation homes, and sends his kids to the best private schools.[60]

But as a businessman, Hanauer began to observe the damaging effects of income inequality on demand for his companies' products. Now he's a top-drawer figure in the fight against income inequality, frequently appearing on national TV, writing articles and books, and speaking around the country. Hanauer is an appealing spokesperson for the cause of defeating income inequality precisely because he's a wealthy venture capitalist worth hundreds of millions of dollars. He admits that the current rules are written to benefit wealthy capitalists like him. So, you might ask, why does Hanauer care about wages for people who make less, much less, than he does? "Ironically," he says, when "you earn less, and unemployment is high, it even hurts capitalists like me."

Hanauer has developed a narrative that turns trickle-down economics on its head. "The fundamental law of capitalism," he argues, is that "if workers have more money, businesses have more customers. Which makes middle-class consumers, not rich businesspeople like us, the true job creators. Which means a thriving middle class is the source of American prosperity, not a consequence of it. The middle class creates us rich people, not the other way around."[61]

This is not trickle-down economics: this is middle-out economics. It's the idea that if you focus economic policy on and generate demand from the middle class, "you'll both create more entrepreneurs to drive innovation, and essentially, a sale cycle and a hiring cycle for business that generates a virtuous cycle of increasing returns that benefits everybody," explains Hanauer.[62]

As he wrote in *Politico*, "Raise wages, and you increase demand. Increase demand and you increase jobs, wages, and innovation. The real economy is simply the interplay between consumers and businesses. On the other hand, as we've learned from the past forty years of slow growth and record stock buybacks, not even an infinite supply of capital can persuade a CEO to hire more workers absent demand for the products and services they produce."[63]

Most people understand that personal consumption drives the American economy. This concept was first formulated by economist John Maynard Keynes during the Great Depression, and drove the great government stimulus projects that helped America recover from the Depression. Keynes's general idea was that consumer demand stimulates business output, which provides business with capital, and capital provides employment. So functionally, employment depends on consumer demand.[64]

Personal consumption represents 70 percent of our nation's GDP—so the modern U.S. economy is directly fueled by consumers with money to spend. But Nobel Prize–winning economist Joseph Stiglitz notes that our current fiscal policy interferes with the virtuous cycle of demand-output-employment:

> America is full of creative entrepreneurial people throughout the income distribution. What creates jobs is demand: when there is demand, America's firms (especially if we can get our financial system to work in the way it should, providing credit to small and medium-sized enterprises) will create the jobs to satisfy that demand.
>
> And unfortunately, given our distorted tax system, for too many at the top, there are incentives to destroy jobs by moving

them abroad. This growing inequality is in fact weakening demand—one of the reasons that inequality is bad for economic performance."[65]

The Center for American Progress (CAP) has embraced and advanced the middle-out philosophy. Their perspective is that "investments in human capital, innovation, and infrastructure have a proven track record of growing the economy. The reason some countries grow and others do not is differences in productivity—not the small differences in labor and capital produced by tax incentives that trickle-down economics emphasizes."[66]

CAP points out that the Reagan tax cuts did not grow the economy; according to a study by Reagan's own chief economist, there is no evidence that the 1981 tax cuts increased employment. The U.S. economy in fact grew significantly faster after Bill Clinton raised the top tax rate and the capital gains tax rate. "If raising taxes were the key to economic growth then the 1994 tax increase should have killed the economy. Instead, the [U.S.] economy achieved the only consistent real income gains for median families over the past three decades."[67]

$15 DRIVES ECONOMIC GROWTH—EVEN BANKS AGREE THAT (WAGE) GROWTH IS GOOD

Many policy thinkers and institutions have woken up to these realities—and not just on the left. Nearly one thousand business owners and executives, including former Costco CEO Jim Sinegal, U.S. Women's Chamber of Commerce CEO Margot Dorfman, Addus Health Care CEO Mark Heaney, Credo Mobile president Michael Kieschnick, ABC Home CEO Paulette Cole, and small business owners from all fifty states signed a Business for a Fair Minimum Wage statement supporting a major increase in the federal minimum wage. As their statement explained, "higher wages benefit business by increasing consumer purchasing power, reducing costly employee turnover, raising productivity, and improving product quality, customer satisfaction and company reputation."[68]

Even former New York mayor and capitalist Michael Bloomberg worked to raise the minimum wage in 2012. "Raising the minimum wage will put much-needed cash in the pockets of more than

1.2 million New Yorkers, who will spend those extra dollars in local stores," he said. "The minimum wage is a vital part of the social safety net. By raising it, we can help more people escape poverty and avoid government dependency—strengthening communities from Brooklyn to Buffalo."[69]

Such wild-eyed leftist organizations as Standard & Poor's, the World Bank, and the IMF have also called for higher wages to reduce income inequality—not because "it's the right thing to do," but because it supports sustained economic growth. Research indicates that for every $1 added to the minimum wage, low-wage worker households spent an additional $2,800 the following year.[70] Researchers have found that increasing the national minimum wage by about $3 an hour would result in a net increase in economic activity of approximately $33 billion during the phase-in period alone, and would add approximately 140,000 new jobs to the tax rolls.[71]

Global economic powerhouses agree—we need wage growth to power the economy:

- Standard & Poor's sees extreme income inequality as a drag on long-run economic growth. "At extreme levels, income inequality can harm sustained economic growth over long periods. The U.S. is approaching that threshold. We've reduced our 10-year U.S. growth forecast to a 2.5% rate. We expected 2.8% five years ago."[72]
- The World Bank said that "too much of the focus in the debate about inequality has been on the top earners, rather than on how to lift a significant portion of the population out of poverty—which would be a good thing for the economy . . . extreme inequality can impair economic growth."[73]
- The International Monetary Fund (IMF) called on the United States to raise its federal minimum-wage rate in 2014, describing the U.S. minimum wage as low by both historical and international standards. This marked the first time that the IMF has endorsed raising the U.S. minimum wage. IMF managing director Christine Lagarde said that doing so would help raise the incomes of millions of poor

and working-class Americans and "would be helpful from a macroeconomic point of view." In other words, it would be good for the whole economy.[74]

- IMF economists Andrew Berg, Jonathan Ostry, and Jeromin Zettelmeyer examined economic growth between 1950 and 2006, and found that the "level of inequality may be the key difference between countries that enjoy extended, rapid expansion and those whose growth spurts quickly dissipate. In short, promoting greater equality may also improve efficiency in the form of more sustainable long-run growth." They found that a 10 percent decrease in inequality increases the expected length of a growth spell by 50 percent.[75]
- The Federal Reserve Bank of Chicago reported that raising the federal minimum wage from $7.25 to $9.00 would increase household spending by roughly $48 billion in the short term, increasing GDP by 0.3 percent. It also found that increasing the minimum wage by $1 an hour results in an increase in spending by affected families of $800 per quarter, and families spent that money mostly on debt payments and on durable goods—particularly cars.[76]
- The New York City comptroller found in 2015 that increasing its minimum wage to $15 would lead to increased household spending by $10 billion, distributed across more than 1 million New York City households, implying an average increase of about $10,000 per household.[77]

Weak consumer demand is not just inhibiting consumer spending—it's depressing new hiring and holding us back from full employment. The *Wall Street Journal* conducted a poll of fifty-three economists and found that 65 percent cited a lack of demand as the main reason for a lack of new hiring by employers.[78]

In a 2015 report, the Center for American Progress details the importance of a strong middle class for economic growth:

1. A stronger middle class that consumes more of its income than do the rich increases business certainty about demands

for goods and services. This makes investment more attractive to large and small businesses alike and boosts entrepreneur confidence.

2. A stronger middle class increases social mobility, which means people are better able to match their talents to jobs, boosting growth in general.

3. A strong middle class demands good governance, property rights, infrastructure, education, and the trustworthy legal structures necessary for a thriving, stable economy.

4. A weakened middle class has to borrow more during times of need, destabilizing the consumer base and hurting long-term growth.

5. People raised in strong middle-class families are more likely to the have the education and training needed to boost broad economic productivity and start a business. The greater macroeconomic stability associated with a strong middle class also gives entrepreneurs greater confidence about taking risks based on informed investment decisions.[79]

In sum, the economic activity spurred by a $15 minimum wage is inarguably positive not just for the low-wage workers who are finally getting a decent paycheck, but for the economy writ large.[80]

$15 WOULD ALLOW MORE YOUNG PEOPLE TO PURSUE HIGHER EDUCATION OR OTHER CAREER GOALS

Angie Garcia, a twenty-year-old single mom who earns $9.60 an hour at a Seattle McDonald's, has already planned how she is going to spend the extra money she earns from a 2015 minimum-wage increase: education. "It's going to change everything," she said. "Because I can go back to school, I can start my college, so that is really big for me, like a really, really big help."[81]

Garcia and her four-month-old daughter Sophia live with her mom and stepdad. She departs for work at 4:30 a.m., leaving her daughter with her mom, who is injured from a recent car accident. She would like to be able to pay her mom for child care while she's at work, and soon school. "I feel bad because I can't pay her," Garcia said. "She understands, but I'd feel better if I can pay her a little bit."[82]

Lifting the wage floor to $15 isn't just about staying out of poverty—it's also about increased opportunity, and having a realistic shot at moving into the middle class. Though many people with college educations are now having a hard time getting by, education is still one of the best ways to increase your chances of moving up in the world.

But since 1978, U.S college tuition and fees have increased by a whopping 1,120 percent. During that same period, the price of food has increased 244 percent and medical expenses 601 percent—but still tuition dwarfs all other price increases, going up four times faster than the consumer price index, according to a report by Bloomberg. The average amount an in-state student paid to attend a public university is 60 percent higher in the current academic year than just five years ago.[83]

In 1978, working a minimum-wage job full-time for seven weeks was enough to pay for a year of in-state tuition at a university—in other words, you used to be able to cover your college tuition with a summer job. Today, a student has to work full-time for half a year to make enough money to pay a year's worth of in-state tuition.[84]

According to Edvisors, 70 percent of students borrow to go to college, taking on an average of $33,000 in student loans. Total student loan debt in the United States has ballooned to $1.2 trillion, now eclipsing the amount of credit card debt Americans hold. This trend is not slowing down.

These unprecedented levels of student loan debt have only been worsened by a lackluster economy—about 50 percent of people under twenty-five with bachelor's degrees are either unemployed or underemployed, according to the Associated Press, and stagnant wages mean that a college education is increasingly unaffordable for most students. One indicator of these problems is that more than 30 percent of loans are currently in deferment, forbearance, or default.[85]

Daryle Wallette of the Spokane, Washington, area tells a story that is increasingly familiar. After growing up in one of the poorest neighborhoods in the state, Wallette has been trying to improve her chances at a better job by going to school while working. "I've been the front service clerk at French Cleaners for about six months, and I work as hard as I can. My boss tells me that I'm doing a great job at work, but covering the costs of basic needs is a daily struggle. I'm trying to make things better for myself. I decided to start attending school at Spokane Community College," she said, "but in order to cover costs, I had to accept an $8,000 student loan. As it is, I'm currently unable to save any money for emergencies and feel like I'm being kept at the bottom by the system. Barely surviving is not quality living."[86]

Wallette is a low-wage worker, already in precarious economic circumstances, taking a big financial risk by attending school for the sole purpose of securing a living-wage job upon completion. The reality is that Wallette and many others like her will face the grim reward of highly uncertain job prospects after graduation. For a student like Wallette, a $15 minimum wage wouldn't solve all of these problems. But it would reduce the daily struggle of meeting her basic needs, allow for a bit of savings for emergencies, and let her continue to make education a priority in her life.

$15 MEANS WORKERS HAVE MORE TIME TO SPEND WITH THEIR FAMILIES AND COMMUNITIES

Seattle Tacoma Airport worker Socrates Bravo, whom we met in chapter 4, makes about $12 an hour, with no sick time or benefits. He says the national minimum-wage debate is about more than finances; it's about families. As a ramp agent for Sea-Tac subcontractor Menzies Aviation, Bravo has to work more than twenty hours of overtime per week to try to make ends meet. His hectic schedule means sacrificing valuable quality time with his two-year-old daughter. "She is asleep when I get home and still sleeping when I leave for work," he says. "It's very sad but missing our children growing up is the reality for me and other coworkers."[87]

Low-wage workers are not just hurting for money—they're hurting for time. The average two-parent American family worked an average of 26 percent more hours in 2009 than in 1973. They also earned 23 percent more in 2009 than they did in 1973 after inflation. If you take away that extra time on the job and factor in that wages haven't gone up at all for the median family in more than forty years, it is clear that even though workers have grown more productive their wages have actually *decreased*.[88]

MIT researchers estimate that a typical two-adult, two-child family "needs to work more than three full-time jobs (a sixty-eight-hour workweek per working adult) to earn a living wage." The National Center on Children in Poverty's Basic Needs Budget Calculator suggests, "Even in lower-cost localities where access to better paying jobs are limited, a single parent with two children needs a job that pays more than twice the federal minimum wage in order to provide for her family." And more often than not for low-wage families, that actually means two jobs.[89]

More hours at work means less time to spend helping kids in school, less time around the dinner table, less ability to stay home with a sick child or take her to the doctor, and less quality time as a family. Low-wage workers are not only forced to take more hours to make ends meet, but also working increasingly erratic and punishing schedules with last-minute work assignments, impromptu cancellations of work shifts without pay, or the chaos of being "on call"—committed to working shifts for which they might or might not be needed. As we saw in chapter 2, one example is clopening, the growing practice of managers scheduling the same workers who close up at night to open the store the next morning.

These policies don't just hurt low-wage families from day to day—they fundamentally interfere with social mobility. Rich parents can afford to spend more time and money on their kids, a gap that is continuing to grow. Over the past four decades, high-income families have gone from spending four times as much as low-income families on their kids' education and enrichment activities to nearly seven times as much.[90] Children in poverty also have less access to early childhood education, attend under-resourced schools, and are less likely to attend or complete college.[91]

And there's no recovering from a slow start. Research now conclusively shows that effects of inequality begin in the first few years of life. Stanford professor Sean Reardon explains, "Rich students are increasingly entering kindergarten much better prepared to succeed in school than middle-class students," and they're staying that way. In a 1995 study, University of Kansas researchers found that children in professional families heard an average of 2,100 words an hour, working-class kids heard 1,200, and those from families on welfare heard only 600. By the age of three, a child from a high-income home had heard about 30 million more words than a poor child.[92]

And if there's any remaining doubt that money matters to families, one study showed that children's math and reading skills were improved by programs that increased parental income and employment, but not by programs that increased employment alone.[93] Having a job isn't enough. It also has to pay.

$15 WILL IMPROVE OUR COLLECTIVE PHYSICAL AND MENTAL HEALTH

Poor adults are more likely to be in poor health, to be uninsured, and to die at a younger age than nonpoor adults, according to the Centers for Disease Control.[94] The effects of low income on health are pervasive, but a simple example can be helpful. Researchers at the National Bureau of Economic Research found in 2009 that a $1 decrease in the real minimum wage was associated with a 6 percent average increase in an individual's body mass index (BMI). The connection was significant across all gender and income groups, but the largest effect was found for people with the highest BMI. The study showed that decreases in the real value of the minimum wage explains 10 percent of the increase in the U.S. BMI since 1970 and concluded that "the declining real minimum wage rates has contributed to the increasing rate of overweight and obesity in the United States."[95]

Mental health is also strongly linked to low income. There is strong evidence that reducing poverty and generally increasing income to middle-class levels is a "reliable and effective way to reduce the incidence of depression and associated medical spending," wrote blogger Kas Thomas.[96] The numbers also show that nonelderly adults living below the poverty level ($11,500 per year if you're single) have roughly five times greater risk of depression than adults making 400 percent or more above poverty level ($46,000 per year).

Numerous studies show that poverty is also associated with an increased risk of having other psychiatric disorders, including anxiety and even schizophrenia. While people with severe mental disorders are more likely to become poor, innovative studies have shown that poverty actually significantly increases the risk for mental illness.[97] (See Figure 6.4.)

For poor children, family income directly influences development and lifetime health outcomes. Families with lower incomes have less access to the resources needed for healthy development, such as nutritious meals, enriched home environments, high-quality child care settings, and health care resources. Overcrowded housing and difficulty finding adequate, nutritious food are only some of the most prominent challenges lower-income families face; the wide variety of stressors that low-income children encounter on a daily basis contribute to their diminished economic mobility.[98]

Figure 6.4: Depression and poverty (U.S. adults 20 and over have far greater incidence of depression if they are under the poverty line)

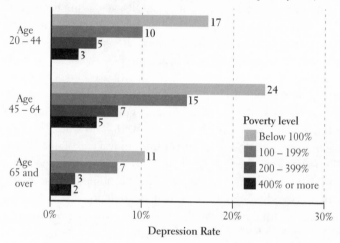

Source: National Center for Health Statistics, *Health, United States, 2011: With Special Feature on Socioeconomic Status and Health* (Hyattsville, MD: U.S. Department of Health and Human Services, 2012).

Sadly, but not surprisingly, children living in poverty have been found to be much more likely to develop learning problems, attention deficits, depression, serious behavioral problems, and an array of other troubles.[99] Neuroscientists recently discovered that the brains of children from families earning less than $25,000 a year had less surface area than those whose families earned $150,000 or more, due to reduced mental stimulation in poorer children's environments. The lead researcher on the study said, "We've known for so long that poverty and lack of access to resources to enrich the developmental environment are related to poor school performance, poor test scores and fewer educational opportunities. But now we can really tie it to a physical thing in the brain. We realized that this is a big deal."[100]

From a psychological perspective, the stress of living in poverty also has a profound effect on parents, contributing to depression, anxiety, and other forms of psychological stress that can negatively impact their interactions with children. Even when parental stress does not manifest itself in observed changes in mental health, it can contribute to a harsh and less supportive parenting style, according to a body of research dating back to the Great Depression.[101]

An unexpected recent finding has been that income inequality is not just bad for people at the bottom of the income spectrum, but also negatively affects the well-being of our entire society. A growing body of research shows that inequality damages the social fabric of our communities. Researchers have shown that health and social problems are between two and ten times as common in more unequal societies—not just for low earners but for *everyone*. These problems, including mental illness, drug addiction, obesity, loss of community life, imprisonment, unequal opportunities, and poorer well-being for children, go all the way up the income ladder, which led researcher Ichiro Kawachi to describe inequality as a "social pollutant."[102] Kawachi says that his research shows that "the more egalitarian the country, the healthier its citizens tend to be."[103]

The social pollutant of inequality is thought to hurt even high-income earners in unequal societies like the United States because it erodes social cohesion. Increasingly, people from different income strata are living drastically different lives, with lower-income individuals unable to participate in the civic or cultural life of the society in any meaningful way. Unable—and even unwilling. Kawachi's research shows that "income inequality leads to psychosocial effects where people become less trusting, less cohesive, and less likely to contribute to public spending."[104]

But there is hope for more unequal nations like the United States—raising our minimum wage has significant effects in reducing income inequality between low and median earners. In more equal developed nations, life expectancy is longer, infant mortality is lower, child well-being is better, drug use is decreased, teenage birth rates are lower, mental illness is less common, homicide rates are lower, and levels of interpersonal trust are even higher.[105] Not a bad payoff.

$15 HAS WIDESPREAD PUBLIC SUPPORT

There is growing evidence that the American public understands the effects of decades of wage erosion and misbegotten trickle-down policy, and that a shrinking middle class is shouldering a disproportionate social burden for soaring corporate profits.

Nowhere is this understanding more clear than in polling support for higher minimum wages. In every state and every part of the partisan and ideological spectrum, a majority of Americans support a significantly higher minimum wage.

- A major 2015 poll found 63 percent support for a $15 federal minimum wage, phased in over a number of years.[106]
- Seventy-one percent support increasing the tipped minimum wage (currently $2.13) to guarantee all workers the same wage floor, and 82 percent support automatic annual adjustments to the minimum wage.
- A 2014 poll showed that a striking 60 percent of self-described conservative Republicans favor the government giving preference to businesses that pay their employees a living wage and provide benefits such as health care and sick leave.[107] The same poll found that 71 percent of voters supported a significantly higher minimum wage for businesses that have government contracts.
- Eighty-eight percent of voters also believe that the growing gap between the rich and everyone else is a problem in the country, including 79 percent of Republicans and 88 percent of independents.
- Sixty-two percent of voters rate low-wage workers favorably, much higher than CEOs (26 percent favorable) and Wall Street (24 percent favorable). Congress receives the lowest ratings among voters, earning only a 17 percent favorable rating.[108]

- Polls show that voters are more likely to elect legislators who support minimum-wage legislation in 2016: by nearly two to one, registered voters say they would be more likely to support a member of Congress who votes to raise the minimum wage than one who did not. The same was said by a strong majority of independents, as well as voters who were living in states that voted for Mitt Romney in 2012.[109]

Although the federal government hasn't yet raised the minimum wage in response to this wave of public support, many cities and states did, with a flurry of raises in 2014 and 2015—many passed by the people themselves via initiatives.

These are among the cities to enact raises:

In San Francisco, voters passed a referendum for $15 an hour overwhelmingly in November of 2014.

Both the city and county governments of Los Angeles voted in the summer of 2015 to raise the minimum wage to $15.

In San Diego, the city council voted to raise the wage to $11.50 by 2017, overriding Mayor Kevin Faulconer's veto. But opponents gathered enough signatures to force the council to put the issue on the ballot in June 2016.[110]

In Chicago, the city council approved Mayor Rahm Emanuel's plan to raise the wage to $13 by 2019.[111] What is all the more surprising is that by many accounts Emanuel had opposed even a $9 minimum wage when he served as White House chief of staff.

In New York, Mayor Bill de Blasio proposed a $15 minimum wage (which would take a state law change and a city law change). New York governor Andrew Cuomo used his executive authority to convene an industry wage board that recommended a $15 minimum wage for fast-food industry workers. The recommendation went into effect in 2015.

Lawmakers in Connecticut, Delaware, Hawaii, Maryland, Massachusetts, Michigan, Minnesota, Rhode Island, Vermont, West Virginia, and D.C. also enacted increases during the 2014 session. In Massachusetts, the state legislature raised the minimum wage to

$11 by 2017—the highest state wage in the country. The Washington, D.C., city council raised the wage to $11.50 by 2016.

Wage increases were passed by the people in even some of the unlikeliest places—the solid red states of Alaska, Arkansas, Nebraska, and South Dakota all approved minimum-wage increases through ballot measures.[112] And while electing a Republican governor in the same election, Illinois voters also approved an increase in the state minimum wage to $10. All told, twenty states implemented minimum-wage increases on New Year's Day 2015 via the ballot, legislation, or automatic annual increases. These raises are estimated to boost the incomes of 3.6 million low-paid workers, about 2 percent of the American labor force.[113]

Four additional states and the District of Columbia have approved raises for the coming years. Including all state and local raises, the Council of Economic Advisers estimates that more than 7 million workers will benefit from minimum-wage increases between 2013 and 2017—almost 5 percent of the American labor force.[114]

The 2014 crop of state minimum-wage increases alone will also generate $827 million in new economic growth, increasing to more than $1 billion in 2015 as low-paid workers spend their increased earnings on basic necessities like food, gasoline, and housing.[115]

Voters or legislators passed minimum-wage increases in ten cities and ten states—*in a single year.*[116] And the movement isn't slowing down as more cities and more states introduce minimum-wage legislation. Voters are sending a message: they are tired of waiting for Congress and CEOs to do the right thing and are taking matters into their own hands at state and local levels.

7

But Won't the Sky Fall?

Throughout a century of public debate, business lobbyists, trade associations, and the economic right have portrayed minimum wages as harmful to business. The criticisms raised by minimum-wage opponents display a remarkable consistency over the past hundred years, despite huge changes in our economy. Data and experience, in other words, have been irrelevant to those who oppose higher minimum wages. This is not because minimum wages actually cause widespread harm to business—the evidence is quite the opposite. It has nothing to do with the greater good of the American economy or the average American worker. It is because some conservative politicians, low-wage industry lobbyists, and large business associations (such as the National Restaurant Association and the U.S. Chamber of Commerce) habitually reject any "interference" in their pursuit of corporate profits.

But it's not just the big-business–right-wing nexus that has created a political environment in which wage hikes are seen as potentially toxic moves. Over the past four decades, liberals also have largely accepted the trickle-down explanation of what growth is (higher profits, rather than more jobs and higher wages) and where growth comes from (lower taxes and less regulation on businesses and the wealthy). Since the late 1970s, even most liberal Democratic proposals have done little more than tinker around the edges of century-old minimum-wage laws, increasing the wage by a quarter here and fifty cents there, allowing its value to erode precipitously over the past decades, afraid to claim the moral and economic center.

And so through Republican and Democratic administrations alike, corporate America has fought for and won less regulation, lower taxes, and higher profits, while middle-class America has gotten the shaft— policies that helped lead to the economic disaster of the Great Recession and the slow recovery that followed. For a generation, America's political class has lacked the vision or courage to articulate or defend the true interests of American workers and the middle class.[1]

THE SKY IS ALOFT

The National Employment Law Project (NELP) examined a hundred years of criticism of the minimum wage and found three distinct themes that persistently reappear in criticisms of the minimum wage: (1) raising the minimum wage would impair the economy; (2) a higher minimum wage would ultimately harm the very workers it is intended to help (otherwise known as "concern trolling"); (3) the minimum wage violates America's commitment to freedom and liberty.

When a federal minimum wage was first proposed in 1937, Gary Harrington of the National Publishers Association said, "Rome, 2,000 years ago, fell because the government began fixing the prices of services and commodities. We, however, know what has always happened when governments have tried to superintend the industry of private persons. The final result has always been distress, misery and despair."[2]

In the years since Harrington made his dire prediction, the minimum wage would rise over two dozen times and nearly identical predictions of job loss and economic contraction—without regard or reference to the effects of earlier raises—would be voiced each and every time. This is despite "nothing short of a sea change in [economists'] understanding of the effects of minimum wage increases": that raising minimum wages does far more good than harm. NELP calls these criticisms "little more than articles of faith repeated by the adherents of a stubborn ideology and expressed without reflection on the prevailing economic or political conditions."[3]

The real-world, experiential data are ever clearer—raising wages lifts workers out of poverty, creates new customers, boosts the economy, leads to imperceptibly small price impacts, and does not reduce job growth. And yet the same old scare stories that have been repeated for the past century are trotted out every time a minimum-wage increase is proposed—even though the sky has yet to fall.

In this chapter, we will address a hundred years of data-resistant anti-minimum-wage messages, one myth at a time. As economist Jared Bernstein states, raising the minimum wage achieves its "goal of boosting the earnings of low-wage workers, most of whom really need the extra resources, with virtually no budgetary costs and few unintended consequences."[4]

MYTH: LOW-WAGE WORKERS ARE TEENAGERS

Iconic American films like *Grease* and *American Graffiti* feature the teenage heroes and heroines working part-time at burger joints, putting in a few hours to earn spending cash before peeling out in classic cars to rebel against society. Our cultural understanding of minimum-wage workers doesn't seem to have evolved much since these movies were made in the 1970s. One of the most common reactions to proposals to raise the minimum wage is: "That's for teenagers. It's just a starter wage." And that was true through the 1970s.[5]

But here in 2015, things have changed: 88 percent of minimum-wage earners are over the age of twenty. Now the average minimum-wage earner is thirty-five years old.[6] These aren't teenagers who are being supported by their parents while making a little money on the side. In 1979, 27 percent of low-wage workers were teenagers, but by 2013 it was only 12 percent. Minimum-wage workers are older and have greater family responsibilities than is often portrayed in the media and minimum-wage debates—they are breadwinners and they need higher wages to keep themselves and their families out of poverty.[7] (Though even if this myth were true, it would not justify paying teens subpoverty wages.)[8]

Yet minimum-wage opponents can't seem to hear the data. In 2014 Art Laffer, a former economic adviser for Ronald Reagan, called the federal minimum wage the "black teenage unemployment act." He recommended that it be abolished or lowered to $4 an hour for some workers.[9] The conservative Heritage Foundation claimed in 2013 that "a hike in the minimum wage primarily raises pay for suburban teenagers, not the working poor."[10] And the National Federation of Independent Business, the largest U.S. association of small businesses, testified before the Washington State Senate in 2015: "It will forever bear repeating that the minimum-wage rate is an entry-level wage earn[ed] almost entirely by teens and young adults starting out on their working lives. Raising it has mainly one effect, and that is to remove the first rung up the economic ladder for tens of thousands of young people."[11]

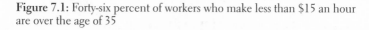

Figure 7.1: Forty-six percent of workers who make less than $15 an hour are over the age of 35

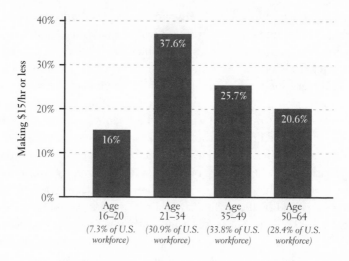

These days, only 6.4 percent of workers affected by a significant wage increase would be "suburban teenagers."[12] Part of the reason for the shift in the age of minimum-wage workers is that more kids are staying in school and spending more time on their studies, says student employment expert Charles Hirschman of the University of Washington.[13] But even more important, the lack of jobs—especially middle-class jobs—has pushed older workers down the economic ladder.

These older, more experienced, and better-educated workers have an edge on teenagers in the job market, said Andrew Sum, director of Northeastern University's Center for Labor Market Studies. "It's a real weakness in our labor market right now," he said. "We're going to need a big increase in demand to turn this around in the short run."[14]

A related myth is that youth employment, as well as employment for minorities, will be harmed by wage increases. As the American Enterprise Institute recently opined, "Why not support increasing the minimum wage? Because it will make it more expensive for businesses to hire young and low-skill workers at a time of crisis-level unemployment."[15]

Although they make up a tiny segment of the labor force, teenagers are the subject of a lot of minimum-wage research because they are the "lowest skilled" workers and are therefore thought to be "last hired, first fired." But the best studies, which make comparisons to nearby states or counties to control for regional economic trends, find no statistically significant negative effects on employment or hours for specific groups of workers such as teens. These studies also do not find substitution effects (such as shifts in hiring away from black and Latino teens).[16]

In his 2013 review of minimum-wage research, John Schmitt of the Center for Economic and Policy Research considered whether employers will simply switch to hiring more skilled workers after a minimum-wage increase, hurting the employment prospects of less educated workers and, in particular, black and Latino teens.[17] Schmitt reviewed several studies that have explicitly researched this question and found that studies that thoroughly controlled for regional and local differences did not find evidence of shifts from teens or minority workers. Economists Sylvia Allegretto, Arindrajit Dube, and Michael Reich examined the impact of the minimum wage on the employment of white, black, and Hispanic teens, covering the period from 1990 to 2009. After improving on previous research by controlling for regional differences, they found no statistically significant negative effects on employment or hours for teens, regardless of race or gender.[18]

MYTH: LOW-WAGE EMPLOYERS ARE SMALL STRUGGLING LOCAL BUSINESSES

Another pervasive myth about minimum wages is that they disproportionately affect small businesses, mom-and-pop stores serving ice cream and selling auto parts to local customers. Combining these two common myths of teenage workers and small-business owners, the conservative American Enterprise Institute (AEI) claimed that a $15 minimum wage would "impose a significant burden for many small businesses that can't pass the costs on to consumers (and a gift to big business that can). Worse, it would make it that much harder for un-skilled workers to get their first job." [19]

But this "concern" flies in the face of the facts. Two-thirds of low-wage workers are actually employed by large firms: 66 percent are em-ployed by companies with more than a hundred employees, and half work in firms with more than five hundred employees. [20] And these firms aren't hurting—the fifty largest employers of low-wage workers are in strong financial positions: 92 percent were profitable in 2011, executive compensation is up from before the recession, and share-holders have seen strong returns from these companies. [21] At the larg-est low-wage employers in the nation—Walmart, McDonald's, Target, and Yum! Brands (the operator of fast-food chains such as Pizza Hut, KFC, and Taco Bell)—profits, cash holdings, and dividends have not only rebounded but are now substantially higher than before the 2007 recession. All are growing and have hired more workers in recent years.

So who hasn't seen a strong recovery? Low-wage workers. More workers who are slipping down the ladder from the middle class to poverty wages as middle-wage jobs eliminated during the Great Reces-sion are replaced with sub-$15 service jobs.

For McDonald's, the company's profit, after wages are paid, works out to $18,200 per employee—more than most McDonald's workers make in a year. Walmart makes over $13,000 in pretax profits per em-ployee (after paying them), which comes to more than 50 percent of the earnings of a forty-hour-per-week wage earner. Four members of the Walmart family made a combined $20 billion from their invest-ments last year; less than half of that would have given every U.S. Walmart worker a $3-an-hour raise, enough that many employees would no longer need taxpayer-subsidized public assistance. [22]

As the National Employment Law Project reported in 2012, "as their profits have rebounded, these companies have awarded their top executives multi-million dollar compensation packages. At the same time, a very large amount of firm revenue . . . has been returned to shareholders through dividends and stock buybacks. Taken together, the scale of the executive compensation packages, dividends and stock buybacks illustrate the resources readily available to cover the cost of a higher minimum wage."[23]

These companies represent the modern service industry on steroids—massive companies, low prices, low wages, huge profits. This matters even more right now because low-wage workers make up more than half of the entire service-industry workforce, the segment of our economy that is growing the fastest.[24] And because the service sector, and these companies in particular, employ such a significant share of America's lowest-paid workers, the wages that prevail in these sectors help set standards for the bottom end of the labor market as a whole.[25] Where Walmart goes, the service industry follows—and its impact as the world's largest private sector employer can't be underestimated for its suppliers, competing businesses, and workers alike: a 2012 report found that only the Chinese People's Liberation Army and the U.S. Department of Defense had more people working for them.[26]

Figure 7.2: Top employees of low-wage workers[27]

	Wages for frontline employees	PROFITS (2013)	CEO pay	Stock price 2010–2015
Walmart *1.4 million employees (1% of U.S. workforce)*	$9/hr; $10/hr after a 6-month training program	$17 billion	$20.7 million	Up 37%
McDonald's *440,000 employees*	Less than $9/hr for most, some at $9.90	$5.5 billion	$13.8 million	Up 30%
Yum! Brands *539,000 employees*	Less than $8.50/hr	$1.6 billion	$14.2 million	Up 48%
Target *366,000 employees*	About $9/hr	$3 billion	$28.2 million	Up 35%

While big businesses keep wages low—effectively setting wages for their industries—and rake in the profits, most small business owners actually support minimum-wage increases. Small businesses know they can adjust to minimum-wage increases, because those increases usually also affect their direct competitors. A 2014 survey found that 61 percent of small business owners support a significant increase in the minimum wage. And a majority of small business owners also believe that a higher minimum wage would (1) benefit business by increasing consumer purchasing power; (2) help the economy; and (3) result in lower employee turnover, increased productivity, and higher customer satisfaction.[28]

Figure 7.3: The single most important problem for businesses is poor sales

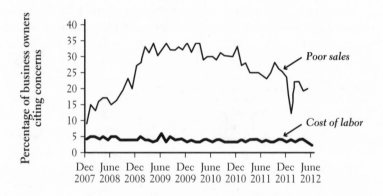

Another survey found that the biggest problem faced by small businesses is not labor costs but consumer demand. The 2012 poll, conducted by none other than the National Federation of Independent Business (NFIB), indicated that small business owners identify poor sales as their main economic concern, not the cost of labor. The takeaway is that the real concern among small businesses is not that their low-wage workers earn too much, but that their customers earn too little. While labor costs concerned only about 5 percent of small businesses, 34 percent cited poor sales as their biggest problem in 2009 and 2010.[29]

Despite the NFIB's own opposition to minimum-wage increases, many small business owners get it—wages need to go up. And people need to make decent wages for their businesses to thrive. The lobbying organizations and mega-corporations are the ones behind the organized opposition to higher wages. They have the resources, and they are making a conscious choice to maximize profits and shareholder returns instead of sharing a bigger portion with the workers and boosting consumer demand. And they hide behind small businesses to shield their true intentions.

MYTH: HIGHER WAGES KILL JOBS BECAUSE BUSINESSES WILL CHOOSE TO HIRE FEWER WORKERS

Another common refrain is that if the minimum wage increases, businesses will hire fewer workers. "When you raise the price of employment, guess what happens? You get less of it," said Representative John Boehner in 2013. Senator Marco Rubio added that "the impact of minimum wage usually is that businesses hire less people."[30] The American Enterprise Institute said in 2014 that "if the 'living wage' movement had its way, we would surely have many more Americans receiving government assistance, because many fewer Americans would be able to find a job at all."[31] Even during the huge uptick in our economy in 1995, the NFIB predicted a national minimum-wage increase from $4.25 to $5.15 would be "a regressive and job-killing scheme which will put a big dent in small-business hiring."[32]

It seems like basic economics: increasing the cost of labor causes competitive employers to cut employment, hurting the very low-skilled workers that the policy was designed to benefit in the first place. The problem with this logic? It's not actually how employers behave. Cutting employees, it turns out, is a last-ditch response to increased labor costs, not a first line of defense. Given a certain level of demand, companies need to produce products and deliver services, and they need employees to do that—even if it starts to cost a little more. Ramping down output is simply not as profitable as other options.

And the research proves it. A meta-review of sixty-four studies on minimum-wage increases found no discernible effect on employment.[33] Economists generally support minimum-wage increases—in

2014, more than six hundred economists (seven of them Nobel Prize winners in economics) signed a letter to Congress and the president supporting a significant increase. The economists wrote,

> In recent years there have been important developments in the academic literature on the effect of increases in the minimum wage on employment, with the weight of evidence now showing that increases in the minimum wage have had little or no negative effect on the employment of minimum-wage workers, even during times of weakness in the labor market.
>
> Research suggests that a minimum-wage increase could have a small stimulative effect on the economy as low-wage workers spend their additional earnings, raising demand and job growth, and providing some help on the jobs front.[34]

And this is why the conventional "wisdom" is wrong. The 1995 minimum-wage increase that would put a "big dent" in hiring? Instead of suppressing small business hiring, that wage hike was followed by the creation of 2 million new small business jobs over the next five years.

One perceived problem with studying minimum-wage increases is that regions that choose to raise their wages may be unique in ways that make such increases possible—perhaps they have a stronger local economy or different mix of businesses. Maybe a wage hike works in giant Los Angeles, this line of thinking goes, but not in tiny Lima, Ohio. So a 2010 study by economists Arindrajit Dube, T. William Lester, and Michael Reich set out to test this idea, producing one of the most sophisticated minimum-wage studies to date. The study controlled for differences between local economies by comparing pairs of neighboring U.S. counties that straddled a state border and had different minimum-wage levels.

After controlling for unrelated differences between local economies, the authors found that higher wages do not result in adverse employment effects on earnings and employment in restaurants and other low-wage sectors—in other words, that minimum-wage increases did not cost jobs.[35] A companion study published in April 2011 found that these results hold true even during periods of recession and high unemployment.[36]

Another widely cited study by economist John Schmitt at the Center for Economic and Policy Research, reviewed the past two decades of research on the impact of minimum-wage increases on employment and also concluded that "the weight of the evidence points to little or no effect of minimum wage increases on job growth."[37]

Watching a significant wage increase take effect on the local level is quite telling. A 25 percent minimum-wage increase in San Jose, California, took effect in 2013. The *Wall Street Journal* reported that the increase "didn't cause the region's fast-food franchises to stop hiring. But it might have caused some heartburn."[38] After a 2012 ballot initiative started by San Jose State University students resulted in a $2 increase to the city's minimum wage, opponents of the increase said it would lead to job losses that never materialized.

Figure 7.4: Fast-food restaurant hiring grows faster than ever before, after a major minimum-wage increase

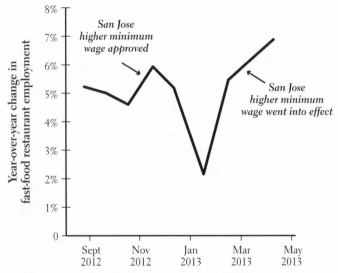

Source: Eric Morath, "What Happened to Fast-Food Workers When San Jose Raised the Minimum Wage?," *Wall Street Journal*, April 9, 2014.

But my favorite example is from right here in Seattle, where even the business press admits that a higher minimum wage is not killing restaurant jobs (our wage began phasing in during April 2015). Jeanine Stewart of the *Puget Sound Business Journal* wrote a cover piece in October 2015 declaring "Apocalypse Not: $15 and the Cuts That Never Came." Stewart cites the fact that Seattle's King County has issued a record number of new food-service permits in 2015, including for "many new eateries run by the law's fiercest critics, such as [Tom] Douglas."[39] Some of the chefs who are opening restaurants at a "dizzying pace," she notes, "are the ones who had issued dire warnings of empty tables and shuttered rooms as a result of the wage law." Douglas, a celebrity chef who owns and operates fifteen different high-end, white-tablecloth restaurants in Seattle, predicted that a $15 minimum wage would cause the city "to lose maybe a quarter of the restaurants in town." But a year and a half later, he was forced to recant, admitting that his restaurant empire has continued to expand and that he was "naive" to think that restaurants would raise pay on their own. One of Douglas's own head chefs, Dezi Bonow, gave kudos to the $15 minimum wage for "legitimiz[ing] cooking as a craft."[40] Stewart concludes that "the thunder in the city's already booming restaurant scene contrasts with the early fears of shuttered cafes and empty tables."[41]

Internationally, countries that pay low-wage workers more actually show *higher* job creation than lower-paying nations. Looking at advanced economies comparable to the United States, the OECD found a strong relationship between higher wages for lower-earning workers (the lowest 10 and 20 percent) and higher employment levels in the following years.[42] So the more you pay your low-wage workers, the more jobs you create. Countries like Italy, Korea, Japan, and the United States, which have the lowest wage levels, also have the lowest employment rates, while economies like Switzerland, Denmark, Sweden, and Canada, which pay low-wage workers better, also generate more jobs and have higher employment rates.

So let's get real—minimum-wage increases don't have a negative impact on employment. And even if a small number of jobs were lost due to a minimum-wage increase—which overall economists say is not the case—the economic benefits to low-wage workers and local economies are simply enormous. Minimum-wage opponents aren't really concerned about a few lost jobs. They're concerned about their profits.

MYTH: MINIMUM-WAGE INCREASES DON'T HAVE AN IMPACT ON POVERTY BECAUSE EMPLOYERS CUT HOURS

Minimum-wage opponents also raise the possibility that even if employment is not negatively affected, there are "hidden" negative impacts to raising the wage. For example: we know that the minimum wage has at worst a neutral impact on employment. But what about hours? Might employers choose to reduce workers' hours in response to minimum-wage hikes instead of reducing the total number of workers on payroll?

The same principle applies for hours as for employment—firms need to provide services to meet demand, and will be loath to reduce their output if they can avoid it. They tend to rely on increased employee productivity, other businesses efficiencies, and small price increases post–wage increase. But even if employers did cut hours for some employees, the reduction would not necessarily reduce total wages, because employees are now earning more per hour.[43]

The best study on minimum-wage impacts (by Arindrajit Dube, T. William Lester, and Michael Reich in 2011) found that "the fall in hours is unlikely to be large" after a minimum-wage increase.[44] A different review of the evidence, by economists more skeptical of the minimum wage, still concludes that "the question of how employers adjust average hours in response to a minimum-wage increase is not yet resolved."[45]

Another study by Dube in 2007 compared restaurants in San Francisco and the adjacent East Bay before and after implementation of a citywide San Francisco minimum wage in 2004 that raised the minimum from $6.75 to $8.50, with further increases indexed annually to local inflation. The study didn't find any significant effects on employment or hours.[46] And a 2011 study of quick-service restaurants found that two-thirds of the minimum-wage cost increases were offset by higher menu prices, and that slightly higher prices rather than cuts in employment or hours was the most important channel of adjustment for this type of firm.[47]

But even if there were a small decrease in some employees' hours after a wage increase (for which there is no evidence), there is a pretty big elephant in the room when this argument is made: employers, especially low-wage employers, have been cutting low-wage workers' hours for years. They are using scheduling software that breaks up employees' shifts into erratic pieces that often don't add up to a full-time schedule, and they are making sure that employees keep their total hours under overtime limits—and under the level where they might have to pay employees any benefits according to their own policies. More often than not, these benefits are just window dressing for employees who never get enough hours to qualify for them. These employees are commonly said to be working "part-time involuntarily."

Rates of involuntary part-time employment have escalated since 2006, especially among hourly employees.[48] A recent study found significant fluctuations in work hours for workers under thirty-two and an especially low average number of minimum weekly hours among people working part-time.[49]

Even the conservative American Enterprise Institute agrees with this assessment. AEI's Desmond Lachman, a former managing director at Salomon Smith Barney, told the *New York Times*: "Corporations are taking huge advantage of the slack in the labor market—they are in a very strong position and workers are in a very weak position. They are using that bargaining power to cut benefits and wages, and to shorten hours." According to Lachman, that strategy "very much jeopardizes our chances of experiencing a real recovery."[50]

MYTH: HIGHER WAGES WILL KILL JOBS BECAUSE BUSINESSES WILL CLOSE

When business associations and their defenders want to heat up the rhetoric even more, they turn to the next minimum-wage myth: higher wages will force businesses to close their doors. When Congress was considering a federal minimum-wage increase in 1991, a Hardees VP said, "I don't know what kind of dream world they're in. When [the cost of] your labor component goes up, it ultimately gets passed on to the consumer. [If another wage increase were enacted], we'd probably be out of business at some point."[51] Hardees, is, of course, still churning out fast food to this date.

In 2003, San Francisco voters adopted a citywide minimum-wage law. The Golden Gate Restaurant Association called it a job killer that would "bankrupt many restaurants." But as we've seen before, the city saw no statistically significant negative effects on the number of firms or employment as a result of the San Francisco law, In fact, firm growth was actually higher in the city than in neighboring cities, unemployment was below the statewide average, and job growth in bars and restaurants led the region.[52] Though we don't see net negative effects on business closure, there's no doubt that wage hikes do require businesses to make changes to absorb the new costs.

Paying higher wages can require thought and change on the part of small businesses. But we know that after even major wage hikes in San Francisco, the number of businesses didn't shrink—it grew. And let's keep our eye on the other prize: employees are taking home more money to allow them to (still, barely) survive in one of the nation's most expensive cities.

After the $15 minimum wage passed in Seattle last year, local lifestyle glossy *Seattle Magazine* ran an article with the inflammatory headline "Why Are So Many Seattle Restaurants Closing Lately?"[53] It claimed that a number of recent restaurant closures were in part due to the wage increase.

Conservative pundits jumped all over the article. The right-wing think tank the Washington Policy Center went straight for the most hyperbolic anti-raise argument: $15 was shutting down businesses and depriving unfortunate low-wage workers of their jobs. "The shutdowns have idled dozens of low-wage workers, the very people advocates say the wage law is supposed to help," it claimed. "Instead of delivering the promised 'living wage' of $15 an hour, economic realities created by the new law have dropped the hourly wage for these workers to zero."[54]

Forbes covered the story, with an article titled "We Are Seeing the Effects of Seattle's $15 an Hour Minimum Wage."[55] But when the *Seattle Times* went and actually talked with these businesses, they found that none of them listed the $15 minimum wage as a reason for ceasing operations. Renee Erickson was indeed closing her Boat Street Cafe, but she runs three others and is in the process of opening two more. Asked in an e-mail about the closure being associated with $15, she replied, "That's weird, no, that's not why I'm closing Boat Street. . . . I'm totally on board with the $15 min. It's the right thing to do. . . . Opening more businesses would not be smart if I felt it was going to hinder my success."[56]

A different *Forbes* commentator, Rick Ungar, entered the discussion, penning an article titled "Minimum Wage Increase Killing Seattle Restaurants? Anatomy of a Lie from Inside the Bubble." Ungar wrote of the *Seattle Magazine* piece, "It was a headline that opponents of the citywide minimum wage increase could not resist—and the facts could not be allowed to stand in the way." [57]

Surprisingly, the fiscally conservative news outlet even told the straight truth about raising the minimum wage: it doesn't result in closures. "Research shows," it said, quoting a 2006 study by the Fiscal Policy Institute, "that small businesses have not been hurt in states that raise their minimum wages above other states." The study found that jobs at small businesses, as well as the total number of small businesses, actually grew faster in states with higher minimum wages. This highlights how the minimum wage is ultimately a very small factor affecting job growth, including at small businesses. [58]

Even business stalwarts like *Crain's New York Business* have become fed up with the same old disproven arguments. In 2012 it ran an editorial stating, "Critics of [the minimum wage] proposal are making the same arguments as the last time the Legislature increased the minimum wage, in 2004. If the change had a cataclysmic effect on businesses that depend heavily on minimum-wage workers, we certainly missed it. [The] objections are essentially objections to the very existence of a minimum wage, which has been a fixture in the U.S. since 1938 and has never stopped our economy from flourishing." [59]

We know that the evidence points toward neutral effects on business closures in the wake of a minimum-wage increase, though there may be an uptick in what economists call "churn" as businesses close and open more quickly than before an increase. Economists at the Federal Reserve of Chicago found that the small percentage upturn in firm "exit" after minimum-wage increases, but "more surprising," they said, "we find a simultaneous increase in firm entry . . . roughly matched by the losses induced by exit." The authors reported that overall employment did not change. [60]

Ken Jacobs, chairman of the Berkeley Center for Labor Research and Education, agreed with the Reserve's findings. "There is considerable churn among small businesses. Firms are going out of business and new businesses are rising all of the time. What is important from the research is that you do not see a net decline in employment as a result of the minimum-wage ordinances."[61]

So whether anti-minimum-wage arguments are cynical (business associations) or born from uncertainty (some small businesses), in either case the arguments are overblown. Businesses can adapt to minimum-wage increases, and it's more than worth it for them to try.

MYTH: WORKERS ARE PAID WHAT THEY'RE WORTH "IN THE MARKET"

Another common refrain during minimum-wage debates is that government has no place setting wages—the market "decides" what workers are worth. If we interfere in the wage-setting function of the market, the thinking goes, we introduce distortions into the free market. Why demand that labor be valued more highly than employers are willing to pay? The reality is that wage rates respond to what workers demand to be paid, reflecting their bargaining power in the market. Some business models just aren't possible if workers demand more money—and that's okay.

Another more pernicious line of thinking about workers' worth in the market (one that is more rarely admitted to in public) argues that low-wage workers are inherently less deserving of higher wages. The assertion is usually followed by a suggested solution—if these workers really think they deserve higher wages, they should educate themselves and gain skills valuable in the market. However, research shows that workers are more educated than ever, far more than workers were in the better-compensated 1950s and 1960s. Moreover, even if this were not the case, the costs of education and skills training have skyrocketed, making advancement functionally out of reach for those closest to the bottom of the economic ladder.

There are market-based reasons that wages in some sectors are more subject to downward pressure. But these pressures can be managed, if wages are a national priority. The Russell Sage Foundation's recent series of books *Low-Wage Work* deeply examined low-wage work in Europe and the United States through case studies and other data. The studies illustrate how differences in the degree of unionization, the structure of ownership (national or multinational), the generosity of social insurance, regulations on minimum wages, and working hours and conditions all shape the quality of jobs. It found that overall "quality and incidence of low-wage work is more a matter of national choice than economic necessity."[62]

Not all work is going to be compensated equally. But we do not have to accept that some work is paid poverty wages. The primary reason that so many service jobs are increasingly low wage is not because American workers are increasingly unskilled or uneducated (which simply isn't true) but because worker bargaining power is waning as union density declines.

There are tiers of pay that make some intuitive sense, based on educational investment, rarity of skills, and so forth. But fundamentally there is no invisible-hand "market." There is only what we believe, and we can choose to believe something different. It's particularly important to weaken this mythological link because it disproportionately hurts women and minorities who are overrepresented in the service economy; and of course their overrepresentation in service is also the reason that service work is low-paid. An unfortunate example of this phenomenon is the decline in wages for veterinarians as more women have entered the once male-dominated field; as the profession has become "feminized," wages have dropped.[63]

Let's look at some specific examples that rebut the "you're paid what you're worth" myth. Fifty years ago, when General Motors was the largest employer in America, the average GM worker made $35 an hour, adjusted for inflation. Today, America's largest employer is Walmart, and the average Walmart worker makes about $9 an hour.[64]

Some may counter that the reason autoworkers now need to accept lower pay is because of the global market, and the cost pressures of increased competition. And yet if we compare autoworker pay in the United States and Germany, in an industry serving global markets and facing very similar globalized competitive pressures, we see that wages are in fact a function of employees' bargaining power and a national choice, as well as a function of what the market will bear.

In 2010, Germany produced more than 5.5 million automobiles; the U.S. produced 2.7 million. At the same time, it didn't have to sacrifice wages to achieve its dominant competitive position—the average autoworker in Germany made more than $67 per hour, including both salary and benefits, while the average U.S. autoworker made only about $34. Yet Germany's big three car companies, BMW, Daimler, and Volkswagen, saw strong sales and profits even in the midst of the weak consumer markets in 2011 in Europe and the United States.

Historian Kevin C. Brown writes, "The salient difference is that, in Germany, the automakers operate within an environment that precludes a race to the bottom; in the United States, they operate within an environment that encourages such a race."[65] The German constitution encourages "works councils" in every factory, where management and employees work together on matters like shop floor conditions and work life. Horst Mund, the head of Germany's autoworkers' union, pointed out that "against all mainstream wisdom of the neo-liberals, we have strong unions, we have strong social security systems, we have high wages. So, if I believed what the neo-liberals are arguing, we would have to be bankrupt, but apparently this is not the case. Despite high wages . . . despite our possibility to influence companies, the economy is working well in Germany."[66]

But what happens when German car companies come to the United States? They pay the wages that are required here. At Volkswagen's Chattanooga plant, nonunionized new employees earn just $14.50 an hour, rising to $19.50 after three years.[67] Where Volkswagen must pay high wages, it will. Where it doesn't, it won't.

This is true even when the government is a significant actor in setting pay, as it is in home health care work. For the same work, home care workers in Washington State will make an average wage of $14.37 under their current union contract, but nonunion home care aides in South Carolina only earn $9.70.[68] Why? Most of the home care workers in Washington are unionized, with union caregivers earning more than $14 an hour. The workers have lobbied state government and fought for higher wages year after year. Their successes have also pushed up the wages offered to nonunion caregivers in the state.

Fast-food worker pay is another telling example. In Denmark, $20 an hour is the lowest wage that the fast-food industry can pay workers. This is not due to a minimum-wage requirement, but rather a binding agreement between Denmark's largest union and the Danish employers group Horesta, which includes Burger King, McDonald's, Starbucks, and other restaurant and hotel companies. Denmark has strong labor laws, and Danish employees have bargaining power.

Danish Burger King worker Hampus Elofsson, twenty-four, told the *New York Times,* "You can make a decent living here working in fast food. You don't have to struggle to get by." Elofsson reports that he is able to pay his rent and all his bills, as well as put some money into his savings account—yet still had money for nights out on the town.[69] In the United States, on the other hand, fast-food workers earn an average of $8.90, wages so low that half of these workers rely on some form of public assistance.

Prices are higher in Denmark, and fast-food restaurants are less profitable. "We have to acknowledge it's more expensive to operate," said Martin Drescher, general manager of HMSHost Denmark, which runs restaurants at the airport. "But we can still make money out of it—and McDonald's does, too. Otherwise, it wouldn't be in Denmark. The company doesn't get as much profit, but the profit is shared a little differently."[70]

John Schmitt of the Center for Economic and Policy Research summarized: "We see from Denmark that it's possible to run a profitable fast-food business while paying workers these kinds of wages." Denmark is not an isolated example. The minimum wage for adult workers in Australia is almost $15 an hour, and a further 15 percent raise is to take effect by 2017. And France, with a $12 minimum wage, has more than 1,200 McDonald's stores. Despite the higher wages, McDonald's actually earns more revenue in Europe than it does in the United States.[71]

Finally, there is the not-at-all small matter of CEO compensation. From 1978 to 2013, average CEO compensation ballooned about 937 percent. Current CEO compensation is far higher than it was at any time from the 1960s to the 1990s. The ratio of CEO pay compared to the average worker was 20 to 1 in 1965. But by 1995 it was 123 to 1, then tripled in just five years to peak at 383 to 1 in 2000. In 2013 the CEO-to-worker compensation ratio stood at 296 to 1.[72] (See Figure 6.2 on page 170.)

Kevin Drum at *Mother Jones* quipped, "Over the past three decades, the growth rate in justifications for skyrocketing executive compensation has been nearly as high as the growth rate of executive compensation itself." The list of justifications offered by Drum include "Globalization makes a great CEO more valuable than ever.

Companies are bigger these days. The skill sets of modern CEOs dwarf those of past eras." And last but not least, "pay is more closely linked to performance."[73]

Is CEO pay linked to performance? If it was, wouldn't we see pay-for-performance packages that rewarded the best CEOs significantly more than their peers at comparable companies? That is not what we see. We see 90 percent of major U.S. companies setting their executive pay *at or above the median of their corporate peer group*.[74] CEO pay is driven up by peer comparisons—a higher-paid CEO is seen as a symbol of corporate success.

CEO pay as a whole does track with one kind of performance, though: the stock market. To a large degree, CEO's compensation gains reflect the value of generous stock option grants for corporate executives. It might seem only fair to incentivize executives to boost their companies' share prices—until you consider how few of these gains have trickled down to the average American worker.

University of Massachusetts at Lowell economics professor William Lazonick notes that a huge chunk of these stock market gains have been the result not of business growth, but of downsizing and cost-cutting (including payroll costs) that is viewed favorably by the market. Those stock market gains come from someone's pocket, in other words—just not the CEOs. The fact that CEO pay soars along with stock prices, notes Lazonick, only underscores the disconnect between pay and companies' true underlying performance.

Revenue, which is a better metric of what companies are actually producing, grew only 7 percent in 2011, while companies in the S&P 500 posted profits of 47 percent that year. CEO pay growth tracked profits, not revenue growth.[75] As Josh Harkinson summarized in *Mother Jones*, "a 7 percent pay hike for CEOs might have been fair; a 27 percent raise looks a lot more like profiting off the misery of the people who once worked for you."[76]

At its most extreme, the "worth in the market" myth can mean that workers are not worth anything at all. The pure free market at work is not pretty—in desperate circumstances, workers are willing to indenture themselves for even the chance of a better life. Child labor is permissible. Companies use the land and water to enrich themselves, and leave it degraded. Food is unmonitored. This is not the world we want.

We have to create the world we want to see. Companies are not necessarily ethical actors without the guidance of human social ethics. Claude Barfield, a scholar with the American Enterprise Institute, when asked why the German car companies behave so differently in the United States than they do in Germany, answered, "Because they can get away with it so far."[77]

MYTH: INCREASING THE MINIMUM CAUSES INFLATION THAT ERASES WAGE GAINS

Some minimum-wage opponents fear that wage hikes will trigger inflation, an overall rise in prices. Inflation doesn't mean that all prices go up, but that the *average* price of goods and services goes up. Some may go up a lot, some a little, and some may actually fall. A spokesman for the Florida Retail Federation fretted that adjusting to the higher state minimum wage, which went up from $7.67 to $7.79 in 2012, would force businesses to raise prices, "And then you get to this inflationary spiral where higher prices lead to higher cost of living."[78]

This idea is not completely irrational, because companies do pass on part of the increase in wages to customers as small price increases.[79] But these increases will generally occur only at companies that employ a significant amount of low-wage labor, such as restaurants. Because these price increases are so small *and* apply only to a minority of firms, the impact on overall price inflation is very minimal.

In response to a reader question about this issue, economics columnist Arthur MacEwan of *Dollars & Sense* analyzed the evidence and concluded that "any inflation generated by an increase of the minimum wage is likely to be small."[80] A 2008 paper by economist Sara Lemos reviewed the existing studies on the impact of minimum-wage hikes on prices and inflation, finding that "despite the different methodologies, data periods and data sources, most studies found that a 10% US minimum wage increase raises food prices by no more than 4% and overall prices by no more than 0.4%. This is a small effect."[81] Journalist Jeannette Wicks-Lim notes that this level of price increase would raise the average annual inflation rate of 2.6 to 2.7 percent—a change so small that it is smaller than the margin of error for the Department of Labor's estimate of inflation.[82]

Lemos summarizes that "the overall reading of the evidence on price effects, together with the evidence in the literature on wages and employment effects is that the minimum wage increases the wages of the poor, does not destroy too many jobs, and does not raise prices by too much." Though MacEwan adds that even if there is a small amount of inflation that results from raising the minimum wage, "a little inflation is probably good for economic growth. One of the factors retarding economic growth currently is that firms are sitting on larger amounts of cash. A bit of inflation could induce them to invest, which might yield more rapid economic growth. If the gains from growth, as in recent years, continue to be captured by the very wealthy, this is not so good. But at least growth opens some possibilities."[83]

AGAINST THE STEREOTYPE: HOW AMERICAN COMPANIES ARE COMMITTING TO HIGHER WAGES AND STILL SUCCEEDING

The conventional wisdom seems to be that many companies have no choice but to offer bad jobs. It's globalization, it's competition, it's high input prices, it's uncertainty, it's the need to please the stock market, it's poor demand. . . . It's always something. Especially for retailers with business models that are all about low, low prices, jobs that pay low, low wages are just assumed to be part of the deal. Their hands are tied; they can't raise prices or they'll lose customers. So it's easy to conclude that firms that offer higher wages can do so only because they cater to more elite clientele—their customers are *willing* to pay higher prices.

But according to a growing number of business experts like Zeynep Ton of MIT, the presumed conflict between employee compensation and low prices is a false one. High-performing companies like QuikTrip convenience stores and Costco wholesale clubs "not only invest heavily in store employees but also have the lowest prices in their industries, solid financial performance, and better customer service than their competitors," says Ton. "They have demonstrated that, even in the lowest-price segment of retail, bad jobs are not a cost-driven necessity but a choice. And they have proven that the key to breaking the trade-off is a combination of investment in the workforce and operational practices that benefit employees, customers, and the company."[84]

So it's not just government policy that matters to wage growth, it's changing our understanding of what makes a company successful. Decades of management philosophy has pointed toward labor as a cost to be minimized, never placing people on the "assets" side of the balance sheet. This is not just a choice (that can be reversed), it's a *poor* choice for corporate growth and *long-term* profitability.

Let's dig into some examples of this pro-growth, pro-worker strategy in action.

COSTCO VERSUS WALMART

The most talked-about example of a company that pays fairly, and is doing better economically, is Costco. Its primary competitor is Walmart, and the contrast between the two retailers is stark. A 2005 article in the *New York Times* even named Costco "The Anti-Walmart." Discount retail is an extremely low-margin, highly competitive industry, with usual profit margins of 1 or 2 percent.[85] But that's where the easy similarities end between Costco and Walmart: the starting wage for Costco's employees is $11.50 an hour, and their average wage is nearly $21 an hour. Walmart, meanwhile, pays its entry-level staff less than $9 an hour and has an average wage of less than $13 for nonsupervisory staff.[86]

Given the large gap in employee compensation between the two, one might expect Costco to have lower profitability—but this isn't the case. Costco's investor returns from 2005 to the present have been almost five times those of Walmart. Its revenue has grown 52 percent from 2010–15, while Walmart's revenue has only grown 18 percent.

And Costco's market share may also be growing—with Costco's membership fee revenue rising from $459 million to $528 million in the year from 2013 to 2014, "it's pretty clear," said one commentator, "that a significant number of customers are moving over to the retailer to do their discount shopping."[87] Costco benefits from extraordinary customer loyalty, as well as employee loyalty: yearly employee retention rates are over 85 percent, and turnover for Costco employees who stay at least a year is just 5.5 percent.[88] On *Forbes*'s list of the best companies to work for, it's—surprisingly—a retail company, Costco, that takes the second-place spot (only Google is better rated).[89]

Costco's (relatively) high wages and generous benefits are intentional business decisions. Costco co-founder Jim Sinegal said in the *New York Times* that Costco's higher productivity, better customer service, and lower employee turnover rates provide an advantage for Costco versus the competition. "This is not altruistic," he said. "This is good business." Costco's pro-worker, pro-growth model took the national stage in 2013, when CEO Craig Jelinek wrote a public letter urging Congress to increase the federal minimum wage, saying, "We know it's a lot more profitable in the long term to minimize employee turnover and maximize employee productivity, commitment and loyalty."[90]

Over at Walmart, on the other hand, the policy has been to push wages down as far as legally possible. As Bob Ortega pointed out in his 1998 book *In Sam We Trust*, Walmart founder Sam Walton "deliberately used superficial forms of paternalism to gain the loyalty of his workers while keeping labor costs at rock bottom." Ortega quoted Walton as saying, "We really didn't do much for the clerks except pay them an hourly wage, and I guess that wage was as little as we could get by with at the time."[91] The companies' attitude toward unions mirrors their stances on wages: fifteen thousand Costco workers belong to a union, while the federal National Labor Relations Board has repeatedly ruled against Walmart for interfering with workers' right to organize.[92]

Walmart's wage policies have not only hurt its 1.4 million American workers, but its customers as well. *Forbes* nailed it: "Walmart service now pretty much sucks—and customers don't like it."[93] Walmart's poor customer service is directly related to its low wages, which result in high turnover and leave less experienced employees working the floor. Evidence also increasingly points to a direct relationship between wages and productivity—people work harder when they're given a raise.[94] Walmart also aggressively keeps its staffing ratios low, cutting employment by 1.4 percent even as it increased its store count by 13 percent. Is it any surprise that sales per employee at Costco are almost double those at Walmart's Sam's Club?[95]

Costco's high wages have translated into revenue and stock growth, while Walmart's stingy policies have led it into a less competitive position relative to Costco. Journalist Dante Atkins writes on the difference between Walmart and Costco, "A minimum wage increase may interfere with a low-wage, low-satisfaction business model—but that doesn't mean it interferes with the ability of businesses to be profitable."[96]

QUIKTRIP VERSUS TYPICAL GAS STATIONS

An even more surprising example of a company succeeding—while treating its employees far better than the industry average—is Oklahoma-based QuikTrip, a chain of six hundred convenience stores and gas stations in twelve states. Convenience stores are a competitive, low-margin growth industry. But while most stores try to make do with as few workers as possible, QuikTrip prioritizes service, even maintaining a force of hundreds of floaters who can fill in for employees who get sick, are on vacation, or have an emergency. While the average convenience store worker makes $20,000 a year, QuikTrip pays its full-time store associates $40,000, including a yearly bonus, and adds a full suite of benefits, including vacation and sick time, 401(k) matching, profit sharing, and tuition reimbursement.

While most retail chains skimp on training, entry-level hires at QuikTrip are trained for two full weeks before they start work, learning the QuikTrip way in everything from ordering merchandise to cleaning the bathroom. And while most convenience store employees are stuck in a dead-end job, most QuikTrip store managers are promoted from within, giving employees a reason to work hard. "They can see that if you work hard, if you're smart, the opportunity to grow within the company is very, very good," says company spokesman Mike Thornbrugh. The company even aggressively expands its stores to new areas to provide employees with a path to advancement: CEO Chet Cadieux notes that "without store growth, good employees will exit."[97] Cadieux's commitment to staff shows in the company's turnover numbers: in an industry with more than 100 percent yearly turnover, QuickTrip loses just 10 percent of its full-time employees every year and 30 to 40 percent of its part-timers.

An industry profile of QuickTrip (QT) by *Convenience Store and Fuel News* describes the customer service benefits of its policies: "One of QT's longstanding secrets," it said, "is its effervescent, clockwork chemistry. Its team of store associates routinely cover for each other, much like a veteran basketball team, whose members implicitly know where the other will be with nary a nod or gesture."[98]

QuikTrip's excellent customer service has bolstered the chain's sales, revenue, and growth: with revenue of $11.5 billion per year, it is the twenty-seventh largest private company in the United States. When it comes to sales performance, QuikTrip is in a league of its own. Its store sales per square foot are $804, while the average convenience store chain makes only $522 per square foot. QuikTrip's sales per labor hour are 66 percent higher than those of an average convenience store chain, and 50 percent higher than even the average of the top quartile convenience store.[99]

QuikTrip consistently shows up as a top employer on national ratings lists; it's currently number 21 on Glassdoor's national list of best places to work. Jim Fram, senior vice president for economic development for the Tulsa, Oklahoma, Chamber of Commerce, credits the chain's above-average industry pay and the fact that QuikTrip promotes from within. "[Employees] have their anniversary date on their name badges," Fram says. "You don't see very many people who have worked there only a few months. They are all long-term employees."[100]

But QuikTrip's high-road practices haven't cost it anything in terms of competitiveness. As *Convenience Store and Fuel News* notes, "high wages didn't stop QuikTrip from prospering in a hostile economic climate. While other low-cost retailers spent the recession laying off staff and shuttering stores, QuikTrip expanded."[101]

QuikTrip's competitors are paying attention, which may mean that its model will spread to other chains. Jim Griffith, CEO of Oklahoma-based convenience store chain OnCue Express, calls QuikTrip "one of the best retailers in the country," acknowledging that his chain looks to it for new ideas and inspiration. "I just think the world of them," he says. "Someday maybe I can grow up and be QuikTrip."[102]

When it comes to QuikTrip's culture of employee retention, Griffith said, "My hat is off to them. It takes a lot of work. Anytime you can reduce turnover, you reduce costs." And in the cutthroat retail industry, cutting costs is the only game in town. It just turns out that also seeing labor as an asset, instead of just a cost, is key to winning it.

IN-N-OUT VERSUS THE FAST-FOOD INDUSTRY

In-N-Out is a classic hamburger chain whose employees wear 1950s-style red and white uniforms, and its wrappers and cups feature biblical quotes. It has also achieved a cult-like following, including the late Julia Child.

The fast-food industry doesn't have many chains like In-N-Out. The reputation of fast food has tanked in recent years, with protests over low wages and scandals over food quality— think "pink slime" burgers. Founded in 1948 and family-run ever since, In-N-Out may not be a behemoth corporation like McDonald's or Burger King—the chain has only 280 stores in five western states, and has long resisted both franchising and going public. But In-N-Out is profitable, with an estimated $625 million in revenue last year and a 5 percent annual growth rate.[103]

From the beginning, In-N-Out has chosen to pay high wages as part of its business model. Its founder Harry Snyder paid $1 an hour (plus one burger per shift) when California's minimum wage was 65 cents. The lowest-paid jobs at In-N-Out now average above $10 an hour, with some nonmanagement jobs starting at more than $13 an hour. Assistant managers average $51,200 annually, or $25 an hour.[104] Full-time employees receive medical and dental benefits, life insurance, vacation and sick time, free meals, discounted gym memberships, and frequent raises.[105]

And employees love working for In-N-Out. It is currently listed eighth on Glassdoor's list of best places to work in the United States, and by *Forbes* as 2015's second most attractive place to work in retail. A whopping 91 percent of employees on Glassdoor would recommend In-N-Out to a friend seeking employment.[106] That's pretty impressive for a burger joint.

Customers consistently rate In-N-Out as their favorite quick-serve restaurant.[107] It's loved even in areas of the country that are generally hostile to other fast-food companies like McDonald's. Local business leaders in San Francisco's local food mecca Fisherman's Wharf opposed every other fast-food chain *except* In-N-Out, because the leaders "wanted to maintain the flavor of family-owned, decades-old businesses in the area" and residents would ordinarily "be up in arms about a fast-food operation coming to Fisherman's Wharf." But, they said, "this is different."[108]

Fairly compensated employees have helped make In-N-Out not only wildly popular with customers but highly profitable as well. Its revenue per hour is higher than Burger King, McDonald's, and other fast-food chains.[109] But almost all of McDonald's wages hover near legal minimums, under $8 an hour, with poor benefits. *USA Today* and 24/7WallSt.com have said that McDonald's—more than any fast-food chain—was one of "eight companies that most owe workers a raise."[110]

Critics have fearmongered that if fast-food workers get a raise to $15 an hour, future Big Macs will shoot up in price. Yet an In-N-Out cheeseburger costs about $2.20, french fries just $1.50—more evidence that claims of a "$10 Big Mac" are just another far-fetched anti-minimum-wage fantasy.[111]

One of the reasons In-N-Out has chosen to grow slowly and retain control of its business operations has been to avoid compromising its quality or customer service by growing too fast; instead, its business practices have been noted for "employee-centered personnel policies." In its case study of In-N-Out, business textbook *Exploring Management* notes that the firm treats "employees as long-term partners instead of disposable resources" and "prefers to focus on its formula for success instead of conventional definitions like shareholder returns or IPOs."[112]

In-N-Out, like QuikTrip, has chosen to make money by making employee retention a priority. Former CEO Rich Snyder said, "Why let good people move on, when you can use them to help your company grow?" Snyder instituted a system to professionalize management, including In-N-Out University and a limited growth strategy that would expand to new restaurants only as quickly as the internally cultivated management roster would allow. The result was "that many part-timers came for a summer job and stayed for a career." When Snyder was planning to expand his chain in the 1980s, he sought the advice of a food industry consultant. The expert told Rich that if he slashed salaries, In-N-Out could save a "ton of money." Snyder was infuriated, saying that it was exactly the kind of advice you would expect "from a guy who wears a suit and who thinks you don't pay a guy who cooks hamburgers that much money."[113]

In-N-Out's leaders knew from the beginning that the "guy who cooks hamburgers" was the key to well-run stores and happy customers in its restaurants. Seventy years later, In-N-Out isn't just a place that customers and employees love but proof that taking the high road—even in fast food—can lead to sustainable profitability.

COOPERATIVE HOME CARE ASSOCIATES (CHCA)

The home care industry, as we saw in chapter 3, historically has provided minimum wage—or subminimum wage—jobs with no benefits and little chance of advancement. In the early 1980s, Rick Surpin, Peggy Powell, and a team of like-minded colleagues recognized that existing home care services in New York City were not prioritizing quality patient care, nor were they providing decent jobs. The average starting wage for a New York City home care aide at that time was $3.75 an hour, though many workers were paid the minimum wage of $3.35, with erratic hours and no benefits or sick time.[114]

Private home care companies in the area were structured, as they still are today, like temporary employment agencies, working from a roster of aides, many of whom signed up with multiple agencies. Once hired, aides bounced from one short-term job to another, often only working a half-day for a particular client before receiving a new assignment. Virtually all of the home care workers in the area were, and are, African American and Latina women with little formal education or better job prospects.

So the team decided to start a new home care company based on two then-radical premises: First, if workers own their own company, they can maximize wages and benefits. Second, good jobs would result in higher quality care—which is not possible without quality jobs. Surpin believed that home care jobs had the potential to be more than dead-end, low-wage, poorly trained piecemeal work. He reasoned that if they provided more training and meaningful managerial support to workers who were currently isolated and ignored, they could provide better care than their competitors *and* bargain for higher wages.

In 1985, Surpin and his colleagues founded Cooperative Home Care Associates (CHCA) in the Bronx, the first worker-owned home care cooperative in the United States. Their aim was to change the entire home health care industry by modeling a philosophy of "quality care through quality jobs." Now they just had to show that it could actually be done.

The team had done its research, and knew their plan would work only if the organization created a sizable enterprise with a high percentage of full-time positions—an uphill battle from the beginning but "without which all attempts to improve the quality of work life for the home care [workers] would fail." [115] CHCA's initial business plan assumed 70 percent full-time positions compared to an industry norm of 30 percent. Starting salaries would be $4.25 an hour, nearly $1.00 more than the norm; health care and other benefits were unaffordable at the beginning, but workers would receive training from CHCA. And, crucially, the company's first major client was chosen for its interest in improving client care, when most agencies weren't all that concerned with client care standards above the minimum legally required.

CHCA faced negative profits and managerial chaos during the first years but actively learned and adapted. They soon stabilized their business operations with employee growth from fifty workers in 1985 to almost three hundred in 1992, with two hundred of those being worker-owners who had paid into the company to become part owners of the cooperative. Profits went from negative to net positive, and the company's net worth grew to almost $1 million, with annual sales at $4 million in 1992.

Along with corporate growth came wage growth, in line with CHCA's values: wages rose to $5.90 for entry-level employees by 1992, with pay at $6.70 for workers with more than three years' seniority. [116] Employee turnover declined along with rising wages, from 27 percent in 1985 to 11 percent in 1992.

Today, CHCA employs 2,300 people, and about half that are worker-owners. Over 90 percent of worker-owners are women of color. [117] Today, workers become owners with a buy-in of $1,000, paid over time. Wages have continued to rise, standing at $16 an hour, including generous benefits. Workers also are represented by a union, SEIU 1199.

Even more important to many workers than high wages are the regular hours provided at CHCA—workers enjoy an average of thirty-six guaranteed hours a week, compared to an industry norm of twenty-five to thirty.[118] Turnover is still very low, at 15 percent, compared to an industry standard of almost 60 percent.

CHCA has accomplished these impressive outcomes with a tightly networked and highly supportive working environment. At CHCA's Bronx office, peer-mentors answer caregivers' calls at desks, while other caregivers socialize in the cafeteria. In the PHI training lab, workers in training learn what it's like to be both a caretaker and a patient.

But deeper improvements within the home care sector were needed to support a high-road company like CHCA, its clients, and workers in a race-to-the-bottom industry. To raise industry standards, CHCA started the worker-run Paraprofessional Healthcare Institute (PHI) under the leadership of Steve Dawson in the mid-1980s. PHI advocates for policies that support quality home care and fund-raises for CHCA's training program. PHI has been instrumental in the current fight to extend the Fair Labor Standards Act's minimum-wage and overtime protections to home care workers. In 1993, Dawson was also instrumental in replicating the CHCA cooperative home care model by founding Home Care Associates of Philadelphia, which today has grown to a two-hundred-member worker cooperative. In honoring Dawson's induction into the Cooperative Hall of Fame in 2013, the Cooperative Development Foundation said that he "understood that much of what affects the quality of work for direct-care workers emanates from public policy" and saw the need to develop a "national research, policy analysis, and technical assistance organization that works for the benefit of all direct-care workers."[119]

In 2000, CHCA founded the Independence Care System (ICS), a nonprofit managed-care company with a commitment to helping adults with physical disabilities live in their homes independently. ICS served two purposes for CHCA: it filled a market need for quality home care serving disabled individuals, while also creating its own primary customer to fuel CHCA's growth. ICS is now a multibillion-dollar company generating $267 million in annual revenue, responsible for a large share of CHCA's business.

CHCA has created deep change in the lives of the clients it serves and the workers it employs. Before Zaida Ramos joined Cooperative Home Care Associates, she was raising her daughter on public assistance, shuttling between dead-end office jobs, and not making ends meet. "I earned in a week what my family spent in a day," she recalled. But after seventeen years as a home health aide at CHCA, Ramos recently celebrated her daughter's college graduation. She's paying half of her son's tuition at a Catholic school, and she's a worker-owner in a business where she enjoys flexible hours, steady earnings, health and dental insurance, plus an annual share in the profits. She's not rich, she says, "but I'm financially independent. I belong to a union, and I have a chance to make a difference." When asked if worker-owned businesses like CHCA can lift families out of poverty, Ramos replied, "They did mine."[120]

THE GOOD JOBS STRATEGY

Companies like Costco, QuikTrip, and CHCA have consciously constructed business models that—even in low-margin, low-price segments of the economy—allow them to reap the rewards of investing deeply in their employees. Because they've figured out how to optimize their businesses in other ways, they're able to capitalize on the benefits of a well-trained, loyal, motivated base of employees. This is not charity or altruism. This is a business advantage.

For more than twenty years, MIT's Zeynep Ton has studied firms that operate this way, which she calls the "good jobs strategy." In her influential book *The Good Jobs Strategy*, she argues that firms that invest in employees often lead their industries because they are more operationally efficient. They don't just cut costs—they cut costs in the right places.[121]

To compete against companies with lower labor costs, these firms need to be more careful in other aspects of their businesses. They have to design and manage their operations to increase employee productivity and reduce other costs. They boost customer satisfaction and financial performance with tightly managed operations and superior customer service. They eliminate waste in everything, but not at the expense of their employees or their employees' performance. As Ton states, good jobs companies are "obsessed with eliminating waste and improving efficiency" and "choose excellence over mediocrity in everything they do."

Ton has found that good jobs companies operate better in four key areas:

1. Good jobs companies offer fewer choices. They focus on the products, store hours, and amenities customers want most, and offer "everyday low prices" instead of a revolving menu of labor-intensive promotions. Good jobs companies Trader Joe's and Costco carry only about 4,000 products, compared with the supermarket industry average of approximately 39,000, and QuikTrip offers only high-demand products.

2. Good jobs companies standardize their processes and procedures—but also empower employees to contribute information that will improve product offerings and operations. "Low level" employees are closest to the customer and are in the best position to choose the mix of products offered (like at QuikTrip), or feed information up the chain to managers.

3. Good jobs companies cross-train, making the most of every employee's skills to provide flexibility and resilience in the company's labor pool. When customer traffic is high, employees at QuikTrip focus on customer-related tasks; when traffic is low, they stock shelves or clean the store. QuikTrip employees can also easily move from one store to another as needed, because all stores are intentionally designed to allow it—they are all designed the same.

4. Good jobs companies operate with slack in staffing. They deliberately overstaff to ensure that customer service— and employee morale—doesn't suffer from inevitable gaps when employees call in sick or there's a sudden uptick in customer demand. "Instead of responding to short-term pressures by automatically cutting labor," Ton says, "stores should strive to find the staffing level that maximizes profits on a sustained basis. In many cases, that will mean adding workers."

The key to maintaining this focus on excellence over the long run is to explicitly prioritize employees and customers ahead of investors. For companies that are publicly held, resisting short-term performance pressure is not easy.

Costco has deliberately weathered Wall Street's disappointment in its earnings during some quarters, in order to keep its focus on its business model. "Each miss was an opportunity for Wall Street to remind the company's executives that Costco did not *have to* miss earnings targets," says Ton. Analysts urged the company to take a look at its expenses—especially employee expenses—and find a way to reduce those in order to meet its earnings expectations. Or the company could find a way to increase prices.

Costco ignored the advice and saw significant drops in its stock whenever it missed its earnings targets. Co-founder and former CEO Jim Sinegal responded that "on Wall Street, they're in the business of making money between now and next Thursday. I don't say that with any bitterness, but we can't take that view. We want to build a company that will still be here 50 and 60 years from now." [122]

Jim Kelly, the chairman and former CEO of another good jobs company, UPS, agreed:

> We think our share owners should get treated well and should get a fair return, but we're not as concerned with whether they're going to get a fair return tomorrow or a year from now or five years from now. We've always thought that the long term was the important thing. If we were to start dancing for the folks on Wall Street because they expect something in the quarter, it would be counterproductive. [123]

Good jobs companies also lead their industries by investing in their employees. Companies with the discipline and vision to operate with excellence are also able to "unlock" the advantages of investing more in their employees, further driving up long-term performance and growth in a virtuous cycle. In a well-managed company, well-paid, well-trained employees create even more wealth than they cost. Labor economists call this phenomenon "efficiency wages," noting that higher wages can motivate employees to work harder, to treat customers better, make them more reluctant to leave their jobs, and help them to bring fewer worries and distractions to work. All of which feeds into higher productivity numbers, and reduces the costs associated with worker turnover and supervision.

Economist Adam Posen says in the *Financial Times*, "Snobbery and current wage disparities favoring the highly educated should not blind us to the fact that all jobs can be done better or worse, and that lower-paid workers respond to incentives other than just fear of losing their job." [124] Good jobs companies get this, and invest heavily in their employees, "start[ing] with the mentality of seeing employees as assets to be maximized," says Ton, "not as a big, scary expense to be kept under tight control." She continues, "This is not a matter of happy talk, PR, and employee-of-the-month awards. This is concrete policy, manifested not only in wages and benefits but also in recruitment, training, scheduling, equipment, in-store operations, head count, and promotion. Investment in employees includes setting and enforcing high standards for employee performance." [125]

These two good jobs strategies go hand-in-hand: solid operational choices reduce costs and increase labor productivity, making high investment in employees possible. At the same time, it is the high investment in skillful and motivated employees that makes these operational choices work well. A poorly trained employee with low morale, who is thinking about her sick kid or her unpaid bills instead of the customer in front of her, is not as strong an asset to her company as one who is prepared, motivated, and ready to give her full attention to her work.

In retail, where investors and employers often think there is no way to increase labor costs and stay profitable and competitive, firms like QuikTrip and Trader Joe's have proven them wrong. There are real business reasons for more investment in employees, according to Ton, even in low-cost retail.

First, it takes a lot of human effort and judgment to get the right product to the right location at the right time and to make an efficient transaction. "It's the low-paid employee," says Ton, "not the inventory-management software, who notices that a shelf looks messy or that some of the products are in the wrong place." [126] Second, the interactions between customers and employees have significant consequences for overall customer satisfaction, sales, and growth. "It's the employee who notices a customer standing in the aisle looking lost and offers help," notes Ton. "It's the employee who can read from a familiar customer's face that he's had a bad day and could use a friendly smile." [127]

At good jobs company Trader Joe's, the starting wage for full-time employees is between $40,000 and $60,000 a year, more than twice what some competitors offer. Sales per labor hour are also more than 40 percent higher than those of an average U.S. supermarket, while sales per square foot are three times higher. Doug Rauch, the former president of Trader Joe's, says that the company invests a lot more in its employees than its competitors do because "nowadays you can go through an entire day without a single person acknowledging your existence. But don't forget that we are people who generally like connecting with other people." He stressed that Trader Joe's had found it profitable to invest in employees, even for a supermarket that competes on the basis of low prices, noting that most online grocers have not found a way to make money because in the extremely low-margin grocery business, attentive customer service really matters for the bottom line.[128]

Another example of the good jobs strategy at work is Southwest Airlines. Ton points out that after September 11, instead of laying off employees like most airlines did, Southwest took measures to improve on-time performance and urged its employees to suggest ways of cutting costs. In the face of sharp decreases in ridership and increases in other costs, Southwest employees—more than 80 percent of whom belong to a union—helped reduce operating expenses by almost 3 percent.[129] Southwest was then well positioned to take advantage of other market opportunities after September 11, expanding into new cities and ending up with more total market share than before the attacks. As Warren Buffett is fond of saying, "be greedy when others are fearful."[130] That's a strong way of stating the principle, but Southwest was able to aggressively seize the opportunity to grow because other companies degraded their own ability to perform.

Southwest's business improvements didn't just allow them to grow during one strategic moment—they "outlasted the circumstances that spawned them." If an airline lays off employees because demand has dropped, notes Ton, it has to hire them back when demand recovers, saying, "The savings are convenient for a time, but only temporary." But if Southwest responds to the same drop by improving operations, she adds, "it can keep that performance even when demand comes back. That's how the company has maintained its profitability forty years in a row from 1973 through 2012."[131]

Companies that pursue the good jobs strategy are able to achieve something that others cannot: they satisfy employees, customers, and investors all at the same time. Good jobs companies perform better than their competitors and also enjoy strategic advantages that boost their long-term competitiveness: They adapt more quickly to changes in the marketplace and are better at differentiating themselves from their competitors "by creating relationships with their customers and giving them reasons to shop there," Ton says.[132]

In sum, we know that highly successful retail chains such as Quik-Trip and Costco, which are highly dependent on tight operations and excellent customer service, have the lowest prices in their industries, solid financial performance, and better customer service than their competitors. They have demonstrated, says Ton, that "even in the lowest-price segment of retail, bad jobs are not a cost-driven necessity but a choice."[133]

CORPORATE WAGE HIKES—THE BEGINNING OF BETTER JOBS?

The good jobs movement started to pick up significant momentum in 2014 and 2015. Starbucks, Ikea, and TJ Maxx announced raises last year, along with the Gap, which boosted its starting wage from $9 to $10 by the middle of 2015 for 65,000 U.S. employees. Though this is a small wage increase, Gap CEO Glenn Murphy's strategy seems to be working already: job applications are up 10 percent since the announcement. (Imagine what $15 would do!) Murphy said the purpose of the raise was to "attract and retain great talent," and that "our decision to invest in frontline employees will directly support our business, and is one that we expect to deliver a return many times over."[134]

But these are, of course, inadequate and largely symbolic raises compared with what's needed. A much better example unfolded when health insurance company Aetna surprised the nation by introducing a $16-an-hour minimum wage for its employees. The raise increase will affect about 5,700 of Aetna's employees, or 12 percent of its workforce, who will also pay less for their health care. CEO Mark Bertolini is not concerned about the cost of the raise, saying it will largely pay for itself by making workers more productive. "We wanted people at the front lines who took care of our customers to not have the kind of stress associated with being able to provide health coverage for their families and food for their families, worrying while they were on the job. To make sure that they were bringing their best selves to work every day." Because of the productivity gains, he believes that "it's a pretty good bet that we're going to find a way to cover those costs in the long run. We don't see it as suffering at all." [135]

Bertolini's motivation is ethical as well as business-oriented—he has reportedly given his fellow executives copies of *Capital in the Twenty-First Century* by French economist Thomas Piketty, which demonstrated how much inequality has risen in the United States and Europe since the 1970s.[136] "When you look at it you say, wow, we are a Fortune 50 company and we have employees who are on food stamps and putting their kids on Medicaid," he said.[137] Bertolini has become known as an evangelist on this subject among other CEOs, handing out a how-to packet to encourage them to look closely at boosting their low-income workers' compensation. He says he's getting positive feedback from many.

The myths that business lobbyists and anti-worker politicians have propagated for over a century are just that—myths. Low wages are not an economic inevitability caused by globalization and competition. Low wages are a choice. Some cities and states, and now even some companies, are beginning to buck the stereotypes and mythologies of the past decades and make a choice that is better for America.

8

Toward a Different Future

$15 and Beyond

"It wasn't always this way, and it doesn't have to be this way."

Those words, a rallying cry of the Occupy Wall Street movement in 2011, still aptly sum up the state of working America five years later.

It wasn't always this way.

Our wages weren't always stagnant; our middle class wasn't always under attack; the American Dream wasn't always receding into distant memory.

And it doesn't have to be this way.

Many of America's traditional allies and first-world peer nations— Canada, Germany, the Scandinavian countries—are figuring out how to protect their middle classes, right now in the twenty-first century.

And historically impoverished countries like Brazil and China— now U.S. competitors and trading partners—are figuring out how to grow and expand their middle classes for the first time.

Right-wing pundits and think tanks want us to believe that America's best days are behind us, that the era of livable wages and a growing middle class is now just a part of history, and that there's nothing we can do to rebuild a future of broadly shared prosperity.

We've been told that we've somehow become lazy, that decades of high taxes, reckless social spending, regulation, and union work rules have hobbled our economy.

We've been told that the only way to achieve prosperity is to shower favors like low taxes and weak regulations on billionaires and corporations, hoping that they'll choose to let some of the economic benefit trickle down to the rest of us.

We've been told that in a globalized economy we can no longer sustain high wages in the face of worldwide competition for labor.

We've been told that if we want to get ahead, we should concentrate only on furthering our education in light of the purported "skills gap" that prevents American workers from getting hired into the high-wage, high-tech jobs of the future.

These are lies, now repeated often enough in our popular media that they ring true.

America is more wealthy and productive than ever. We have among the lowest effective tax rates for corporations and the wealthy among our competitor nations. We have some of the weakest government regulations, weakest unions, and lowest social-sector spending as a percentage of GDP. And our corporate CEOs and large shareholders have hardly been asked to tighten their own belts, even as they prescribe austerity for the rest of us.

It's true that global labor-market competition explains a lot about why sectors such as clothing manufacturing and customer-service call centers have have been offshored to countries with lower labor costs. But it doesn't explain why high-wage countries like Germany now produce more cars than the United. States. Nor does it explain why tens of millions of *unexportable* service-industry jobs in retail, food service, health care, heavy labor, transportation, and construction are increasingly low-wage, poverty-level jobs.

And Americans are more educated than ever. About 20 percent of American jobs *require* a college degree, and around 33 percent of Americans *have* a college degree. So although college and post-college education are powerful factors in determining lifelong earning potential for individuals, as an explanation for why American wages have declined and why the American middle class is shrinking it falls flat.

In a narrow sense, the thesis of this book has been that we should raise our national minimum wage to $15 to restore American workers' earning power and grow the economy. In a broader sense, it advances the very idea that *it wasn't always this way, and it doesn't have to be this way.*

As we saw in chapter 6, a $15 minimum wage would directly or indirectly benefit about half of all American wage earners. It would reduce poverty, reduce inequality, and help the economy grow from the middle out. Adopting a $15 minimum wage would be the single most important thing the government could do to restore earning power and hope to tens of millions of Americans.

But it's crucial to acknowledge that a higher minimum wage is not the end of the story—rather, it would be the first, indispensable chapter of a new account of what America could and should become.

HOW TO CREATE A MIDDLE CLASS

In a 2015 article we wrote for *Democracy*, Nick Hanauer and I discuss what it means to be middle class:

> "Middle class" is less of an income distinction and more of a social one. Typically, middle-class Americans purchase homes, they educate themselves and their children, they participate in their community, they spend money on leisure and other discretionary purchases, and they save for retirement. Over the course of their lives, middle-class Americans build personal wealth, however modestly, and sometimes they start businesses. And they can do all these things because they have the confidence and wherewithal—the economic security—to plan for the future. Or, to use a word our nation's business leaders would surely understand, a functional middle class enjoys *certainty*.[1]

Looking back at the past forty years, it's not just the erosion of income and wealth alone that has threatened the middle class, it's also the lack of certainty: "Will I have a job?" "Will my wages stay the same or shrink?" "Will I be able to afford food, medicine, child care, and rent?" "What if I get sick?" "Can I (or my child) afford college?" "Will I ever be able to retire?" As a union organizer for almost a quarter century, I hear workers asking these sorts of questions every day.

Workers living with this much uncertainty aren't middle class, at least not in the cultural and social sense of the word. For decades in America, pollsters and public opinion scientists noted that even relatively low-income Americans described themselves as middle class. In other words, even the poor experienced sufficient certainty and optimism about their economic lives that they felt secure. As recently as 2008 (just before the Great Recession), in a Pew Research poll 53 percent of Americans described themselves as "middle class" while only

25 percent described themselves as "lower middle or lower class." But even this generations-long trend in public opinion has begun to shift. In 2014 (five years into the "recovery"), the same poll found that 44 percent of respondents identified as "middle class" while 40 percent described themselves as "lower middle or lower class."[2]

Workers without economic security and a degree of certainty aren't part of a functional middle class. They feel like they're on their own, living in uncertain times, trying to navigate the economy without anyone else on their side: not their employers and not even their own government. An insecure, uncertain, shrinking middle class is less likely *either* to drive up consumer demand and help create jobs today *or* to take a risk on the future by starting a business or taking on added debt to go to school or buy a home. It's a recipe not just for short-term personal gloom but for national economic underperformance in the long run.

Beyond setting wages at a level that would enable everyone who works full-time to live free of poverty, what other strategies should we pursue to provide workers with the certainty they need and usher in an era of prosperity that is broadly shared among Americans?

Four recent reports by prestigious public policy researchers and economists help point the way toward a robust policy agenda for a growing middle class. In 2012, Demos published its report *Millions to the Middle: 14 Big Ideas to Build a Strong and Diverse Middle Class.* Also in 2012, Yale University scholars Jacob Hacker and Nate Lowentheil published their book *Rebuilding Prosperity: Building an Economy for All.* In January 2015, the Center for American Progress released a *Report of the Commission on Inclusive Prosperity,* recommendations from a blue-ribbon panel chaired by former U.S. treasury secretary Lawrence Summers and former British cabinet member Ed Balls. And in May 2015, the Roosevelt Institute published a report by Joseph Stiglitz titled *Rewriting the Rules: An Agenda for Growth and Shared Prosperity.*[3] Each of these reports attempts a comprehensive set of policy prescriptions for fixing America's broken economy for workers and the middle class.

In addition to these reports and the organizations that produced them (CAP, Roosevelt Institute, and Demos), a number of other respected organizations have done important work on which broad policies would support and sustain a middle class. These include the National Employment Law Project, the Center for Popular Democracy, the Center for Community Change, the Center on Budget and Policy Priorities, and the Economic Policy Institute. I also spoke with some of the nation's smartest organizational leaders and thought leaders. And I looked at innovative legislation in cities and states. I tried to answer the question: what does a pro-worker, pro–middle class agenda for America look like?

Broadly speaking, strategies to renew the promise of a middle class for working Americans fall into three categories:

- Renewing the employment contract for the twenty-first-century economy
- Establishing a twenty-first-century set of shared benefits for all Americans
- Changing how economic and political power work for and against working people in America, so that government acts *for* rather than *against* American workers

The next section examines what each of these strategies could look like and what policies we should enact to achieve them.

A TWENTY-FIRST-CENTURY EMPLOYMENT CONTRACT

American workers need a new deal from American employers. In chapters 1 and 2, we saw the lengths to which many employers have gone to lower wages, avoid paying benefits, and exploit their superior bargaining power over their workers. In addition to paying a minimum of $15 an hour, Americans should demand that employers abide by a minimum set of legally enforceable expectations for how employers treat employees.

Pay Equity
In the twenty-first century, there is no excuse for persistent gaps in pay between white male workers and their colleagues who are women or people of color. According to the U.S. Census, women who work full-time, year-round are paid only 78 cents for every dollar paid to a male working in that same position. And that gap only gets worse for women of color: African American women get paid only 64 cents and Latinas only 56 cents for every dollar paid to white, non-Hispanic men.[4] This problem is not just simply one of fairness. Pay disparities affect our

economy's stability, and structural discrimination serves as a drag on our economic performance.

Tools such as the federal Paycheck Fairness Act would strengthen the ways that workers have to fight back against wage discrimination by fully compensating victims of gender-based discrimination; providing skills that empower women to negotiate their wages; expanding collection of pay discrimination data to lead to stronger, more effective enforcement; and preventing employers from retaliating against workers who discuss their wages with co-workers.[5] Governments should also require large public and private employers to conduct independent audits of their pay equity metrics and post or link the results on their human resource recruitment websites and job announcements.

Paid Leave Time

Alone among workers in developed nations, Americans aren't guaranteed any paid time off from work for vacation, health needs, or caring for their families. According to the national advocacy group Moms-Rising, "Right now, only 13 percent of Americans have access to paid family leave through their employer and only 37 percent have personal medical leave provided through an employer."[6] This translates to at least 43 million private sector workers in the United States who lack access to paid sick days, forcing them into a precarious situation fraught with uncertainty and fear of becoming ill.[7] And because low-wage workers are disproportionately affected by the lack of employer-provided paid family and medical leave, it forces the most vulnerable members of the workforce—those employees who can least afford to miss a paycheck—to choose between coming to work sick, which puts their own health and the public in danger, or being able to make ends meet that month for their families.[8]

When it comes to paid vacation and holidays, the United States similarly lags behind the rest of the world. Not only do major industrialized nations such as Japan, France, Germany, and Australia require that employers offer paid vacations and holidays, but so do developing nations such as Costa Rica, Niger, and Nepal. Even Iraq, which the United States occupied for a decade, requires that employers offer twenty paid vacation days per year.[9]

This is an easy problem to solve if we simply do what most of the world already does. Governments (again, it should be federal, but could start at the state or local level) could simply require that every worker earn a minimum of 0.04 hours of paid vacation time and 0.02 hours of paid medical leave (usable for prevention, illness, or family care) for every hour worked. For a full-time worker, that adds up to ten days (or two weeks) of vacation per year for a full-time worker and five days of medical leave.

Predictable, Family-Friendly Scheduling

We saw in chapter 2 how both involuntary part-time work and involuntary overwork create chaos and economic distress in the lives of low-wage workers in sectors like retail, food service, and customer service, all powered by predictive scheduling software.[10] According to the *Washington Post*:

> Here's what that looks like in practice: Handing out schedules based on what times of day or the month you expect the most business, splitting up hours across a large workforce that's available on a moment's notice and sometimes sending people home if traffic is slow. . . . That helps companies optimize their labor costs, but it wreaks havoc on the lives of low-wage workers, who don't know how much they're going to make from week to week, and often can't schedule anything else around work.[11]

Now, municipalities around the United States are beginning to look at ways to intervene on behalf of workers. Legislation like San Francisco's Retail Worker Bill of Rights, which went into effect in July 2015, set parameters for how employers treat workers with respect to scheduling. Under the San Francisco law, chain retail employers have to post employee schedules two weeks in advance, pay workers extra for last-minute schedule changes or on-call status, offer full-time work to existing part-time workers before hiring more part-timers, and treat part-time workers equally with respect to hourly pay and earned leave time.[12]

Universal, Prorated, and Portable Benefits

And what about all of the new economy workers who don't have traditional employers, like the worker who hires out for gigs on TaskRabbit, or makes deliveries through PostMates, or works as a home care aide through HomeHero? What about temporary workers and freelancers? How can we cover these workers under *existing* protections and benefits for traditional "employees" as well as potential new ones such as mandated vacation and sick leave?

Again, it turns out not to be that hard. As Nick Hanauer and I proposed in our 2015 *Democracy* article, we could simply require that those platforms or companies who pay on-demand economy workers or who employ traditional part-timers, freelancers, or temporary employees be required to pay an hourly prorated share of the cost of a set of universal employee benefits into a secure account where the worker can use them exclusively for the designated benefits when needed.

Payments from different service purchasers or employers could then be pooled and used to purchase health care insurance, invest in retirement plans, pay for income lost due to an accident, and accumulate vacation and sick pay. With the right legislative changes, they could also be used to pay both the employee and employer portion of Social Security and Medicare, as well as state workers' compensation and unemployment insurance funds.

Such "shared security accounts" could be required by government action and administered by worker co-ops, credit unions, or labor unions employing benefits experts and investment professionals with a fiduciary duty to act on behalf of their worker-customers. Such a system would enable gig-economy workers, temporary workers, part-time workers, and freelancers to enjoy the fundamentals of economic security that traditional employees get, but in a portable and prorated way. And since these benefits would be universal, it would diminish the employer incentive for misclassifying workers as independent contractors, cutting full-time workers' hours, or outsourcing to a lower-cost subcontractor.[13]

TWENTY-FIRST-CENTURY SOCIAL BENEFITS

As we saw in chapter 2, many Americans no longer work for a single employer in a traditional employment relationship. Many experience relatively long periods of unemployment or involuntary part-time employment, working as an independent contractor or on-demand worker, working for multiple employers, or simply working for one employer at a time in rapid succession. In this world, expecting employers to take primary or exclusive responsibility for providing insurance or social benefits that have lifelong value—such as education, child care, and retirement—but won't necessarily be used during a worker's employment with that firm seems increasingly archaic. Beyond the employer-employee relationship, creating a stable middle class for the twenty-first century will require a set of universal policies that benefit all Americans, no matter where (or if) they are working. These social benefits should specifically *not* be tied to employment and shouldn't be financed primarily through employer payroll costs, but rather through taxes or social insurance premiums.

Child Care

Child care and early education together constitute another area where the United States trails its global partners and competitors. According to the Commonwealth Fund, the United States has among "the least well-developed early childhood policies at the national level." [14] As a result, while wealthy Americans can afford top-notch child care and early education programs for their kids, most low- and middle-wage earners can't. This has an impact on household income in one of two ways or in both of them. Either one parent (almost always the mother) stays home for a few years and can't contribute to needed household earnings, or by necessity the mother keeps working but the family spends almost as much (or even more) of their household income on child care as they do on rent—leaving less for health care, nutrition, recreations, savings, debt service, etc.

As for the kids, decades of research now demonstrates that later-in-life educational attainment and earning power increase when children receive high-quality early childhood education. A child's earliest educational experience from birth to age three even impacts brain development. So our failure to provide free or affordable child care and early education to every child from birth to age five is just one more way that we force poor and working-class kids to start life already behind.

Every U.S. parent and child should be offered high-quality child care and preschool education, with a hard cap on the percentage of household income required for a child to participate. And this doesn't really even require creating new government programs, simply expanding and adapting the most successful of the ones already in place in various states, municipalities, and school districts.[15]

Career and Higher Education

A generation ago, it was typical for students to be able to attend college and graduate without debt. This was due to relatively low tuition rates and much more generous grants (as opposed to loans). Today, student loan debt has tripled to more than $1 trillion, and tuition has risen faster than inflation consistently over the past three decades. Seventy percent of today's bachelor's degree graduates leave college owing money. But until the 1980s, most students could pay a year's worth of tuition simply by working a summer job. So it's not surprising that the percentage of Americans earning college degrees has begun to lag behind some of our competitor nations for the first time in decades.

For the majority of Americans who will enter careers that don't require a college degree, we have a patchwork of support for community colleges and apprenticeships. U.S. apprenticeship programs enroll only a few hundred thousand students a year, despite having an incredible track record of success in preparing students for skilled trades and other living-wage jobs.

We need a new organizing principle for how we treat postsecondary education. Instead of seeing it as a private benefit to the student, we need to understand it as a public good that will foster rising incomes, higher employment rates, more lifelong self-sufficiency, and greater innovation in our economy. Either we could follow the lead of Germany, Mexico, Brazil, and many other countries in simply making tuition free at community colleges and state-sponsored four-year schools. Or we could do what Australia and New Zealand do, capping annual loan repayments at between 0 and 8 percent of income, based on how much you earn. And for the non–college bound, we should resource a national system of apprenticeships for high-demand careers that require hands-on learning.[16]

Retirement

Americans aren't prepared to retire. Social Security, once intended only to be a supplement to private employer-based pension plans, has now become the default retirement plan for most Americans. Half of all households don't have any retirement account at all, and even most people aged fifty-five or over have saved only a fraction of what it will take to retire.[17] The median 401(k) account balance reported by Vanguard in 2013 was enough for $1,200 *per year* in retirement income.[18] For those with 401(k) accounts, usurious fees can cost future retirees between a quarter and a third of the eventual value of their plans.[19]

Meanwhile, the hundred largest CEO retirement funds are worth a combined $4.9 billion, equal to the entire retirement account savings of 41 percent of American families (at least those families lucky enough to have any retirement savings at all). In other words, *one hundred* CEOs will retire with the same total nest egg as *116 million* other Americans.[20] According to the Center for Effective Government and the Institute for Policy Studies, most Fortune 500 firms offer special unlimited-contribution, tax-deferred accounts for their executives, while ordinary workers face strict limits on how much pretax income they can invest each year in their retirement plans. Most Fortune 500 executives also have defined-benefit pension plans, while fewer than one in five American workers still has access to a traditional pension.[21] "These privileged few," the Center for Effective Government concludes, "are free to shelter unlimited amounts of compensation in these special pots. . . . The CEO-worker retirement divide turns our country's already extreme income divide into an even wider economic chasm."[22]

America needs to add a new leg to our retirement stool: in addition to Social Security and private savings (401(k)s, IRAs, and defined pension plans), we need a new American retirement benefit plan that is universal (i.e., not optional), portable, individually held, collectively and professionally managed, and low-fee and from which assets can't be withdrawn except in the form of pension annuities upon retirement or permanent disability. Such a benefit would be similar to the "public option" IRAs that Joseph Stiglitz proposes in *Rewriting the Rules* and the American Retirement Accounts that Demos proposes in *Millions to the Middle*—except that it would be universal. It would also be similar to what Hacker and Lowentheil propose in *Rebuilding Prosperity*, except that it would coexist with, and not replace, 401(k)s.

Additionally, we should take the easiest, most commonsense

approaches to increasing America's retirement security: eliminating the cap on Social Security contributions enjoyed by those earning six figures or above in annual income, levying Social Security taxes on investment income, and capping fees charged by managers of 401(k) plans.[23]

Health and Long-Term Care

First, the good news. The Patient Protection and Affordable Care Act (ACA, or "Obamacare") is working. Its passage was not only a "big f——ing deal," in the words of Vice President Joe Biden, but also the first giant step forward in decades for American workers who had grown accustomed to seeing the federal government repeatedly fail to act in their economic interests.

As a result of the Affordable Care Act, 17 million more Americans have health insurance coverage. The ACA curbed or eliminated many onerous insurance company practices such as lifetime out-of-pocket maximum coverage, denial of coverage for preexisting conditions, and cancellation of policies. The ACA expanded preventive medical care and coverage for young adults. It expanded Medicaid eligibility, closed significant gaps in Medicare coverage, and made it much easier for consumers to shop for individual or family health coverage.[24] And with or without the ACA, there is broad consensus within the U.S. health care system that our insurance plans and our health delivery systems need to change dramatically in order to promote the best quality care at the most affordable price leading to the best health outcome for patients (the health care "triple aim").

The bad news is that there is still work to do. For now, the ACA largely keeps in place the employment-based health care insurance system, making large employers primarily responsible for the health care insurance of their employees (a cost borne by almost none of their global competitors). Health care costs are still likely to keep rising faster than inflation. Too many "catastrophic" plans require significant and often unaffordable co-pays. Too many health care dollars are spent on care that isn't necessary, or is actually harmful, or that doesn't provide the best health outcome for the dollar. And long-term care such as home care and nursing home care isn't covered either by Medicare or by the ACA's individual health insurance mandate, making private long-term care insurance unaffordable and exposing individuals and families to huge costs for long-term services and end-of-life care.

The gold standard for health care reform is undoubtedly a "Medicare for all" system that would cover all Americans, take employers out of the health care picture, allow the government to use its bargaining power to hold down prices and prevent unnecessary or harmful practices, and cover long-term care through a new Medicare Part L.

But even short of a perfect solution on a short timeline, there's a lot we can do on a step-by-step basis. There are still twenty-one states that have not yet expanded Medicaid, a no-brainer to further expand health care coverage. The ACA's bronze (i.e., high-deductible) plans should be phased out so that low-wage workers and low-income families don't end up having to bankrupt themselves due to high out-of-pocket costs. We could enact a public health insurance option (discarded during negotiations over the 2010 law) to keep insurance companies honest. We could reestablish consumer health purchasing cooperatives that were defunded in 2012 so that there would be at least one nonprofit, consumer-governed health plan in each state.

Better yet: we could cheapen, simplify, and clarify pricing simply by making Medicare or Medicaid reimbursement rates the law of the land for private plans, thereby sharply reducing health care inflation and making prices transparent for consumers. And states can pilot universal long-term care insurance plans for their own residents, becoming laboratories for eventual national policy.[25]

Direct Employment to Fix America

What should the social contract look like between government and citizens when the economy turns bad and jobs are lost? Or for all of the on-demand economy workers, temps, freelancers, independent contractors, guestworkers, and others who may be in and out of the workforce periodically and who may stumble from gig to gig, attempting to piece together something like full-time work?

The irony is that in the United States, government fiscal policy tends to make matters worse during recessions, as public spending contracts and further exacerbates loss of household and firm spending power, joblessness, and tax revenue—in turn making matters worse once again.[26]

For the largely disposable and stateless (temp, part-time, freelance, on-demand, etc.) workers in the new economy, their contracts and gigs are often the first to go when economic times turn tough and both firms and households cut back on discretionary spending. And they are the least likely to have personal savings or unemployment insurance to fall back upon.

At the same time, our nation has a gigantic backlog of public infrastructure needs. According to a 2014 report by the American Society of Civil Engineers, between now and 2020 there's a $3.6 trillion need to repair, replace, and update our airports, bridges, dams, drinking water infrastructure, energy grid, levees, public parks, ports, public transit systems, schools and universities, railways, roads, wastewater treatment systems, waste disposal capacity, and waterways.[27] This number doesn't even include the longer-term expenditures necessary to convert America to green fuels and stabilize our climate, estimated by one report to be around $200 billion per year.[28]

Imagine how many workers we could put to work each year updating our infrastructure and greening our economy, accelerating these expenditures during business cycle downturns to provide counter-cyclical economic stimulus and jobs for the unemployed or underemployed. Hacker and Lowentheil suggest that for every $1 billion in expenditures, we create between four thousand and eighteen thousand mainly middle-class jobs.[29] This won't just have the impact of shortening recessions and tightening labor markets when needed but also of dramatically upgrading our nation's economic backbone and improving competitiveness.

A GOVERNMENT ON THE WORKERS' SIDE

Finally, if America wants to succeed at building and maintaining a strong and stable middle class over the long haul, we need to rewrite the rules of economic and political power that have stacked the deck against working people. This isn't just about improving jobs or writing more pro-worker policies, it's about who gets to make the big decisions, how those decisions get made, who wields power in our economy, and who benefits. Government needs to take a side: it should be unapologetically on the side of American workers.

Trade Agreements

One-sided trade agreements represent one way that the deck has been stacked against American workers in manufacturing, information technology, and other fields that are susceptible to global outsourcing. Trade and globalization are, on balance, good for economic growth and have helped many of our partner nations create jobs and grow their middle classes. And trade agreements have helped many American companies grow in foreign markets. But too often this has been at the expense of American workers or on terms that don't create a level playing field, as American workers are forced to compete in a global race to the bottom.

To correct these imbalances, the president should negotiate, and Congress should approve, only trade agreements that help create win-win, high-road outcomes for workers in the United States and abroad. Trade agreements should give workers parity with investors in seeking enforcement action; penalize currency manipulation by trading partners; require trading partners to honor the UN Declaration of Universal Human Rights and other international norms regarding slavery, child labor, and the right to form unions; and promote transparency in state-owned or -subsidized enterprises. Trade agreements should be negotiated in a transparent way, with worker and human rights advocates enjoying the same access to the negotiating table as corporate lobbyists and lawyers. And Congress should end tax policies that encourage global outsourcing while strengthening "buy American" provisions in public contracting and investment.[30]

Criminal Justice

Reforming our criminal justice system is another necessary step to unstack the opportunity deck for millions of Americans, a disproportionate share of whom are black men. America incarcerates more of its residents than any other nation and does so with a consistent racial bias. Never colorblind to begin with, our criminal justice system suffers from racial inequities exacerbated by the war on drugs beginning in the 1970s, resulting in the mass incarceration over time of millions of African Americans, as well as other people of color and poor people. As a result, formerly incarcerated Americans find themselves virtually unemployable not just upon release from prison but for much of their subsequent adult lives.

Far from "paying one's debt to society" and then being released, today's formerly incarcerated Americans face lifelong barriers to full economic and political participation. In many cases this is a consequence of relatively minor drug infractions, property offenses, or petty crimes committed when they were very young. It impacts their own lifelong earning power, to be sure (as well as access to education, housing, social services, and the right to vote), but also the long-term economic well-being and future earning potential of their families and communities. As household and community earning power dimishes in black neighborhoods and other poor communities, it becomes harder for communities to spend and create local demand for goods and services (and therefore jobs), accelerating the downward economic spiral that in turn leads to a higher likelihood of individual recidivism and a reduction in economic opportunity for the next generation.

To provide opportunity for employment, wage growth, and fuller economic participation, we need to reform our criminal justice system. A good start would be for Congress and state legislatures to end mandatory minimum sentencing without judicial discretion, provide for automatic expungement of criminal records for nonviolent property and drug offenses after a certain amount of time, prohibit employers from inquiring about criminal history early in the job application process for entry-level positions, and end the treatment of juveniles as adults in criminal proceedings.[31]

Immigration Reform

Legalizing the status of an estimated 11 million undocumented workers and providing them a path to citizenship would increase worker earning power, job mobility, and our overall GDP. It would also make it harder for employers to exploit vulnerable workers who don't have full legal protections. Today, these 11 million workers work primarily for very low wages, pay their taxes, and yet don't enjoy the right to enforce employment and labor laws without fear of retribution or even deportation. This holds down their wages, helps impoverish the communities they live in, and makes it harder for them to move up the income ladder and difficult for them to seek higher education in many states. And by effectively suppressing wages for undocumented low-wage workers, our broken immigration system pulls down wages for other low-wage, low-skill employees.

The extremist policy solution preferred by some in the Tea Party and many right-wing talk show hosts—deportation—would be as impossible to achieve as it would be a moral and human rights disaster. And it would immediately throw the country into a recession if millions of productive wage earners suddenly left.

The only economically sane and morally defensible answer is for Congress to provide a path out of the shadows for these often low-wage and exploited workers. By eliminating the underground economy that employs and exploits undocumented immigrants, we would see these workers able to enforce their rights on the job, openly seek better employment, pursue training and education, participate more fully in the economy, and increase their spending power, in turn lifting the economies of their cities and communities. According to research by Robert Lynch and Patrick Oakford, legalizing the status of undocumented workers would result in $1.4 trillion in GDP growth over ten years, add $791 billion in new personal income, and add 203,000 jobs per year.[32]

Corporate Governance
In chapter 1 we saw how corporate behavior toward workers changed from the 1970s through the 2000s. Facilitated by deregulation, the shareholder revolution of the 1980s, and changes in how the federal government treats CEO pay and share buybacks, American corporations abandoned strategies for long-term investment and growth and instead adopted an obsession with share prices and quarterly numbers. As a result, today corporations are actually disincentivized from making long-term investments for the good of the company, its workers, its community, and its long-term investors. Instead, CEO pay is often tied to share price and company management can manipulate the price of shares by engaging in buybacks and issuing dividends. By reducing the supply of stock (through buybacks) or increasing the apparent value of the stock (through dividends), companies increase the value of each share without improving overall profitability, productivity, innovation, or the long-term health of the enterprise.

In a groundbreaking article in *Harvard Business Review,* William Lazonick exposed the degree to which these ethically corrupt practices have contorted boardroom behavior. From 2003–12, S&P 500 companies spent 54 percent of their earnings on share buybacks and another 37 percent on issuing dividends. That's a shocking 91 percent of earnings unavailable for research and development, increasing worker pay, or infrastructure investment. The solution? Says Lazonick: "Corporations should be banned from repurchasing their shares on the open market. Executives' excessive stock-based pay should be reined in. Workers and taxpayers should be represented on corporate boards. And Congress should reform the tax system so it rewards value creation, not value extraction."[33]

Both *Rewriting the Rules* and the *Inclusive Prosperity Commission* report make similar recommendations. Corporations should pay tax on CEO compensation in excess of $1 million, the SEC should ban or sharply regulate share buybacks, and a financial transactions tax on high-frequency trades should raise the cost of speculative trading. What's more, we should require that publicly traded corporations end the practice of stocking their boards of directors primarily with CEOs and instead require that a significant percentage of each corporate board include representatives of a company's rank-and-file workers, its unions (if any), institutional investors, and representatives of the public.[34]

Monetary Policy

Ironically, the one federal agency with a mandate to achieve full employment—the Federal Reserve—is also the agency that often acts to *prevent* full employment by raising interest rates when any sign of inflation, particularly *wage* inflation, appears on the horizon. That means it costs more to borrow money and firms have less to pay workers. This contributes to loose labor markets, higher unemployment rates, and suppressed wages. But modest annual wage inflation is actually a good thing—it means wages are going up, and thus labor markets are more likely to tighten. Companies will have to pay more to attract and retain workers, in turn leading to increased spending power and demand-driven economic growth. And lower interest rates also ease consumer borrowing, helping workers buy homes and cars or start a small business.

Instead of prioritizing anti-inflationary measures to the exclusion of full employment measures, the Federal Reserve should adopt a more balanced approach and develop specific targets for unemployment, underemployment, and involuntary part-time employment, keeping interest rates low and even encouraging mid- to single-digit inflation to help tighten labor markets, raise wages, and lower joblessness.[35]

Current Federal Reserve chair Janet Yellen has taken a step in the right direction by keeping interest rates low since 2006. She put the kibosh on a planned rate hike in September 2015, citing flat wages and economic fragility. In announcing the Fed's decision, Yellen confirmed that "The main thing that an accommodative monetary policy does is put people back to work."[36]

Campaign Finance Reform

One of the most important barriers to improving the lives and working conditions of American workers actually has very little to do with work and employment—at least not on the surface. But our corrupt system of financing elections in America guarantees that ordinary working people aren't heard and that legions of corporate chieftans and lobbyists have constant access to elected officials from city hall to Congress.

Most Americans already understand this intuitively. Our democracy has long been in crisis, as more and more money is required to win elections and only those companies and individuals who have lots of money to contribute get access to elected officials. That's why it's so easy for corporations and business lobbies to get their way with the government and so hard for everyday working people to be heard.

Perhaps the best and most outrageous example occurred during the 2008–9 financial crash, when the federal government bailed out banks, insurance companies, and the automobile industry but never adopted needed relief and protections for home owners, the unemployed, and those driven into bankruptcy by Wall Street's irresponsible decisions. The power of big money in politics also goes a long way toward explaining why raising the federal minimum wage is so hard. Despite support from a supermajority of Americans and even a majority of Republicans, Congress listens primarily to corporations and business lobbyists, and the wage stays where it is.[37]

In a remarkable 2014 article, professors Martin Gilens and

Benjamin Page analyzed data on 1,779 separate policy issues and concluded that economic elites and business lobbies almost always get their way with the federal government, while individual citizens and large membership organizations almost never have any impact at all.[38] It's hardly surprising, given that many members of Congress spend much of their time fund-raising from, being lobbied by, and socializing with the 1 percent.

The solutions? In the long run, we need a constitutional amendment to overturn *Citizens United*, the U.S. Supreme Court decision that equates money with speech and made corporations into citizens, allowing unlimited corporate speech in elections. But even before *Citizens United*, America had long experienced the corrupting influence of money in politics. Ultimately, we'll need a comprehensive approach.

Some of the best ideas in this arena come from Harvard's Lawrence Lessig and from clean elections advocates David Donnelly at Every-Voice and Josh Silver of Represent.Us. These proposals include: full public financing of elections, allowing small donations by regular citizens to be matched by public funds, prohibiting elected officials from soliciting or receiving money from businesses they regulate (including executives and trade associations representing those businesses), prohibiting fund-raising by elected officials during working hours, and barring elected officials from working as lobbyists for ten years after leaving office.[39]

These ideas all have merit, but my personal favorite would be either full-scope public financing or restricting election financing exclusively to crowd-sourced small donations. Getting money out of politics won't be quick and it won't be easy. But it's ultimately hard to see how working people in America ever get heard as long as we're on our current road to plutocracy.

Worker Bargaining Power

As we saw in chapter 1, between the 1930s and the 1970s, unions and collective bargaining helped to power the creation of America's vast middle class. Unions smoothed the distribution of wealth over the entire economy, constraining the percentage of wealth and income concentrated at the top of the economy while lifting up the bottom and the middle. But union strength has been on the wane since the

1950s and, beginning in the 1980s, suffered a catastrophic free fall in the private sector that continues to this day. The ability to join a union and bargain collectively is inaccessible to more than 93 percent of private sector workers. As we've seen, that's a major reason why working people have experienced forty years of wage stagnation even as the economy grew and the rich got richer.

Most progressive economists, scholars, think tank analysts, and centrist or left-of-center politicians in the United States agree: the scale has tipped too far in favor of business and away from workers. Generally, they support government measures to rebalance the power of capital and labor by improving the conditions for union organizing. Such measures include banning the permanent replacement of striking workers, increasing penalties for labor law violations by employers, allowing workers to achieve union representation more quickly and simply, requiring binding arbitration in labor contract disputes, and repealing the 1947 Taft-Hartley Act (which restricted or banned many effective union tactics and permitted states to go "right to work" and cripple many unions financially).

But these sorts of federal legislative strategies, which attempt to augment or restore America's collective bargaining framework, have failed repeatedly for the past fifty years. That's in part because American enterprise-based collective bargaining is an inherently weak model of industrial and labor relations compared to the possible alternatives.

Under America's current "enterprise bargaining" framework, agreements are reached between a single union and a single employer. Under enterprise bargaining, the right to a voice in the workplace is considered an *optional* right that workers must *opt into* on a workplace-by-workplace basis via a majority vote. This means that only a minority of workers are ever likely to benefit from collective bargaining, which weakens political support for unions and worker bargaining rights. It also means that employers are highly incentivized to avoid unions before they form or to crush them once they exist. Where unions do form and exist, employers who agree to union demands often perceive that they have been placed at a competitive disadvantage on price or flexibility within their industries—unless a supermajority of their competitors is also unionized. In addition, under the current system of enterprise bargaining, unions can't require that employers negotiate over some of the most important factors in worker prosperity, such as the overall strategic direction of a firm; worker equity in a firm; or worker control of health, pension, and training funds.

The confluence of these facts means that unions are hard to form, difficult to maintain, and limited in the scope of their bargaining, and they face constant workplace and political opposition from employers. That political opposition in turn leads to the repeated failure of labor law reform. As Marx once speculated about capitalism, we can now say with some certainty about our system of collective bargaining: it sowed the seeds of its own destruction.

Organized labor's legislative strategy since the 1950s—restoring the old model of union bargaining—is unlikely to prevail in the twenty-first century. That model thrived in an era of standardized industrial production, long-term or even lifelong employment in an industry or firm, and the relative geographic immobility of both workers and capital. This was also a period that witnessed mass worker militancy and industrial strikes and rampant interunion competition—overlaid with fears of communism abroad. And added to this mix was a domestic Communist Party that trained skilled anticapitalist organizers; organized crime syndicates that cynically promoted unions so they could loot union treasuries and extort employers; and a federal government broadly committed to using collective bargaining to maintain industrial stability during world wars, cold wars, and depressions. One could no more bring back such a unique set of historical factors and conditions than one could repeal refrigeration, globalization, or the Internet (each of which also in its own way helped hasten union decline).

But workers still need mechanisms to exercise power and to do so at a scale that improves the lives of millions of workers, as well as build organizations that can sustain worker bargaining power for the long haul. If twentieth-century-style unions as we knew them aren't going to play that role, we'll need to invent new forms of powerful, scalable, sustainable worker organizations if we want any effort to rebuild the middle class to succeed.

Such organizations might take several forms. Borrowing from labor law in other countries, from U.S. history, and from promising experiments happening in the United States today, there are several potential overlapping strategies for how future forms of worker power might operate and for what U.S. labor policy might eventually look like.

Geographic and/or sectoral bargaining. With changes in federal law, unions could represent workers throughout an entire industry and not on a firm-by-firm basis, eliminating much of the dysfunction of firm-by-firm bargaining. But even without federal statute changes, cities or states could develop stakeholder or tripartite (government, company, and union) bargaining by geography or by industry. Wage-setting boards, for example, were commonplace at the state and municipal levels in the early twentieth century. Representatives of workers, employers, and government could determine legally binding standards for wages and benefits throughout an industry or within a geographic area. This is similar to the stakeholder process we used in Seattle for the minimum-wage negotiations and exactly how New York's fast-food workers achieved a $15 wage policy in 2015.

Codetermination. Common in Europe, codetermination allows employees a greater role in the management of a company, increasing worker voice and aligning incentives for quality and productivity between labor and management. Germany is the most successful example of this model, but a variation is used in the United States by health giant Kaiser Permanente. Under codetermination, labor agreements are made at the national level by unions and employer associations, and then local plants and firms meet with works councils to adjust the national agreements to local circumstances.

Worker ownership. Through worker-owned cooperatives or employee stock ownership plans (ESOPs), workers gain an equity stake in the firms where they work and gain control over the selection of a management team, reinvestment in the firm, and compensation. With no federal statute changes, cities and states could provide tax breaks and other incentives to help these sorts of businesses grow and expand.

Control of work distribution platforms. The majority of the new on-demand applications (discussed in chapter 2) are similar to technologically enhanced union hiring halls—a mechanism for selling labor to consumers and distributing work among workers. Through bargaining, codetermination, or co-ownership, these work distribution apps could be transformed from mechanisms for suppressing wages into ones for fairly allocating the proceeds of labor, maximizing hours, and collaborating on multiworker tasks. One could even imagine algorithm-based smartphone applications that allow on-demand economy workers to effectively bargain with—or strike against—work-distribution platforms.[40]

Labor standards enforcement. Voluntary worker associations could develop the capacity to "represent" workers through onsite worker-led enforcement of labor standards and employment laws within a geographic area or an industry. This could take the form of publicly financed organizations that advocate for workers under municipal law. Experiments with these sorts of worker-community organizations are already happening in San Francisco and Seattle. Or it could take the form of organizations that empower workers to set and enforce labor standards across employers. Promising private sector efforts of this sort are already under way among Florida tomato workers, Austin construction industry employees, and California janitors, in each case paid for by contributions from employers or upstream purchasers.

Certification and labeling. The LEED standard signifies excellence in environmental design for new construction, and the Fair Trade label indicates ethical supply chain practices for coffee, tea, and chocolate. Similarly, a worker organization could develop, or a government could even require, an ethical workplace certification and labeling system for consumer-facing brands, businesses, products, and services. Like a health department letter grade on a restaurant, consumers would know to what extent an employer, manufacturer, or service provider follows best practices in paying living wages, offering benefits and paid leave, implementing fair scheduling procedures, practicing gender and racial equity in hiring and promotion, and adhering to labor and employment laws. Like LEED and Fair Trade, businesses could earn such a label (let's call it a WorkScore) by registering with a worker-led nonprofit organization, adhering to certain minimum standards, and agreeing to workplace audits by the worker organization. Consumers could then easily "vote with their feet" and economically reward businesses for doing the right thing.

Benefits administration. In a world of increasingly short-term, temporary, and employer-less employment, worker organizations could replace employers as the primary provider and administrator of worker benefits that are universal, portable, and prorated. Nick Hanauer and I proposed a Shared Security System in 2015, which we now refine one degree further to add that these universal, portable benefits would be administrated by worker advocacy organizations.[41] The system would be similar to the health and welfare funds administered by unions in the construction industry, which provide workers with health, pension, and training benefits, and to the Ghent system of collective unemployment insurance in several northern European countries.

When it comes to how workers exercise collective power over wages, benefits, hours, and working conditions, now is the time for risk taking and experimentation in search of a new model that can replace traditional union collective bargaining. Government at all levels should promote, finance, encourage, and protect such experiments. Just as twentieth-century labor law was originally prototyped at the city and state levels, today's workers and their supporters should demand that mayors and city councils, governors and state legislatures enlist in the search for the next labor movement.

Afterword

Something's Happening

It's becoming ever clearer that Americans are ready for a change.

A January 2015 poll showed that 63 percent of Americans support a $15 minimum wage.

The April 15, 2015, strikes for $15 that SEIU helped organize were joined not just by fast-food workers but also by home care aides, child care aides, adjunct faculty, airport workers, and retail workers. These strikes took place in an astounding 236 U.S. cities. Workers in forty other countries joined solidarity protests.

Chicago raised its minimum wage to $13. Los Angeles joined Seattle and San Francisco in raising the minimum wage to $15. Emeryville, California, raised its minimum wage to $16. The mayors of Boston, New York, St. Louis, and Kansas City all proposed minimum-wage increases to $15. Activists in Washington, D.C., are organizing to put a $15 wage on the June 2016 municipal ballot.

In Congress, from 2010 through 2014 proposals for a $10.10 wage were considered extreme ($9.00 was the more centrist number, while most conservatives wanted no change). But in the spring of 2015, a group of senators publicly called for a $12 national minimum wage, blowing past years of more cautious and tepid Capitol Hill politics on wages. In the summer of 2015 another group of senators and representatives finally introduced a bill to go to $15.

In 2014, thousands of service workers at Johns Hopkins Hospital won a new union contract that included a $15 minimum wage for long-time employees, while tens of thousands of nonteaching workers in the Los Angeles Unified School District bargained a $15 minimum wage in their union contract. In the spring of 2015, union hospital workers in Minnesota did the same. Home care workers in Massachusetts bargained a new union contract in June 2015 that will raise starting wages to $15 by 2018. Home care workers in Washington State saw their highest wage rates rise to above $15 under their July 2015 contract and won retirement benefits for the first time.

In New York, Mayor Bill de Blasio proposed a $15 minimum wage in 2014, which would require a state law change and a city law change. Governor Andrew Cuomo initially dismissed the figure as unrealistic. In early 2015, when the state assembly proposed raising the state minimum wage to $15, Cuomo scoffed, "God bless them—shoot for the stars."[1] He then put forward his own plan to slowly raise the minimum wage to $11.50 in New York City and $10.50 elsewhere in the state. But the $15 movement moved Cuomo as well—and quickly. By the middle of 2015, he had appointed an industry wage board for the fast-food industry, which recommended raising the wage to $15. The recommendation is now law, and fast-food workers are set to make $15 an hour by 2018 in New York City and by 2021 in the rest of the state.

Sensing the change in the political winds, Cuomo then even went a step further in September 2015, announcing a proposal to increase the *state* minimum wage to $15 an hour for all workers. "Fifteen dollars an hour will be the highest statewide rate in the nation," Cuomo said, "and will herald a new economic contract with America—and it's about time."[2] By November, he put his money where his mouth was and unilaterally established a $15 minimum wage for all state government workers—the highest such minimum wage in the nation.[3] That's a long way for a politician to come in less than a year.

The *New York Times* editorial page editor's blog ran a headline in June 2015 that summed up what seemed to be on the nation's mind: "A Starting Wage of $15 an Hour: The New Normal?"[4] And this all happened months *before* the 2016 presidential race really got under way in Iowa and New Hampshire. The upcoming elections offer an opportunity for Americans to organize and mobilize for $15 like never before.

WE CAN DO IT

Every great movement for justice in American history has begun with a seemingly implausible demand:

- The abolition of slavery . . . when the entire economy of the South was built on slavery and the U.S. Constitution was written to ensure its political survival.
- An end to child labor . . . when one in five American workers was under sixteen years old.[5]
- Women's suffrage . . . at a time when urban political machines, major religious faiths, and powerful industries all feared losing power or income if women gained the right to vote.
- An eight-hour day . . . when full-time manufacturing and construction employees worked an average of a hundred hours a week.[6]
- An end to Jim Crow laws and the passage of federal civil rights and voting rights laws.
- Medicare, Medicaid, and (eventually) Obamacare to dramatically expand health insurance coverage.
- Marriage equality for LGBT Americans.

Impossible?

The fight for $15 has also been called impossible, even "near insane,"[7] "killing flies with a shotgun,"[8] and "an economic death wish."[9]

Yet the movements to end child labor, establish a fair workweek, and expand civil and human rights all produced powerful policy victories that created a more just society within a generation. As we've seen, the fight for $15 movement, while only a few years old, has already won major victories for workers.

The challenges of poverty, income inequality, and slow economic growth are only becoming more acute. Main Street needs higher wages, and though Wall Street fights it, it has proven itself a poor steward of the American economy.

This issue is not going to fix itself. That's the job of government and those who own it—in other words *us*. Now is the time for the people and our representatives—presidential candidates and members of Congress, statehouses, and city councils—to seize the easy opportunity presented to them: the chance to be a part of a historically significant national moment, and do something both hugely popular and hugely valuable for American workers.

One hundred years from now, few people living in America today will be remembered by name. What people *will* remember is whether or not our generation had the courage to stand up for the American Dream when it was at its greatest moment of risk, and whether we left a vibrant middle class to the generations that came after us.

Let us hope we give them reason to remember us with appreciation.

NOTES

Introduction

1. Lynn Thompson, "Workers See $15 Wage as 'Peace of Mind,' " *Seattle Times*, June 1, 2014.
2. All stories from ibid.

1: America at 200: The American Dream Versus the War on the Middle Class

1. Harold Meyerson, "Work in the Age of Anxiety: The Forty Year Slump," *American Prospect*, November 12, 2013.
2. Jennifer Erickson, ed., "The Middle-Class Squeeze: A Picture of Stagnant Incomes, Rising Costs, and What We Can Do to Strengthen America's Middle Class," Center for American Progress, 2014, 5; Meyerson, "Work in the Age of Anxiety."
3. Pew Research Center, Social and Demographic Trends, "Fewer, Poorer, Gloomier: The Lost Decade of the Middle Class," August 22, 2012.
4. Erickson, "Middle-Class Squeeze."
5. David Leonhardt and Kevin Quealy, "Losing the Lead," *New York Times*, April 22, 2014.
6. Max Roser, "Income Inequality," OurWorldInData.org, 2015; Wikipedia, "The Gini Coefficient," accessed August 12, 2015, https://en.wikipedia.org/wiki/Gini_coefficient.
7. Alicia Parlapiano, Robert Gebeloff, and Shan Carter, "The Shrinking American Middle Class," *New York Times*, January 26, 2015.
8. Kendra Bischoff and Sean F. Reardon, "State of the Nation: No Middle Ground," *Boston Review*, May 1, 2012.
9. Lawrence Katz and Claudia Goldin, *The Race Between Education and Technology* (Cambridge, MA: Harvard University Press, 2008).
10. Algernon Austin, "The Unfinished March: An Overview," Economic Policy Institute, June 18, 2013.
11. Nina Pavcnik, "Globalization and Within-Country Income Inequality," chap. 7 in *Making Globalization Socially Sustainable*, ed. Marc Bacchetta and Marion Jansen (Geneva: International Labour Organization and World Trade Organization, 2011).

12. Meyerson, "Work in the Age of Anxiety."

13. In 1978, the top 1 percent of wealth holders were 220 times richer than the average family. But by 2012, they were 1,120 times richer. Emmanuel Saez and Gabriel Zucman, "Wealth Inequality in the United States Since 1913: Evidence from Capitalized Income Tax Data," National Bureau of Economic Research Working Paper Series, October 2014.

14. Ibid. Since 1988, it has been 8 percent per year.

15. Colin Gordon, "Growing Apart: A Political History of American Inequality," Inequality.org, June 18, 2013.

16. Among households with net worth of $500,000 or more, 65 percent of their wealth comes from financial holdings, such as stocks, bonds, and 401(k) accounts, and 17 percent comes from their home. Among households with net worth of less than $500,000, just 33 percent of their wealth comes from financial assets and 50 percent comes from their home. Richard Fry and Paul Taylor, "A Rise in Wealth for the Wealthy; Declines for the Lower 93%," Pew Research Center Social and Demographic Trends, April 23, 2013.

17. Ibid.

18. Saez and Zucman, "Wealth Inequality," 3.

19. Paul Krugman, "Why We're in a New Gilded Age," *New York Review of Books*, May 8, 2014.

20. Tom Kertscher, "Michael Moore Says 400 Americans Have More Wealth than Half of All Americans Combined," PolitiFactWisconsin, March 10, 2011; Aimee Picchi, "How America's 400 Highest Earners Are Doing," CBS MoneyWatch, April 10, 2015.

21. Gordon, "Growing Apart."

22. Dave Gilson, "Charts: Income Growth Has Stalled for Most Americans," *Mother Jones*, September 18, 2013.

23. Saez and Zucman, "Wealth Inequality"; Dave Gilson, "Chart: It's Never Been a Better Time to Be Rich," *Mother Jones*, September 25, 2014.

24. Josh Bivens and Lawrence Mishel, "The Pay of Corporate Executives and Financial Professionals as Evidence of Rents in Top 1 Percent Incomes," Economic Policy Institute, Working Paper No. 296, June 20, 2013.

25. Lawrence Mishel and Alyssa Davis, "CEO Pay Continues to Rise as Typical Workers Are Paid Less," Economic Policy Institute, June 12, 2014.

26. "Labor share" is the share of output accounted for by employees' compensation; it is thus a measure of how much of the economic pie goes to all workers. Susan Fleck, John Glaser, and Shawn Sprague, "The Compensation-Productivity Gap: A Visual Essay," *Monthly Labor Review* 134, no. 1 (January 2011): 57; Elise Gould, "Why America's Wage Earners Need Faster Wage Growth and What We Can Do About It," Raising America's Pay, Economic Policy Institute, Briefing Paper No. 382, August 27, 2014.

27. Olivier Giovannoni, "What Do We Know About the Labor Share and the Profit Share? Part III: Measures and Structural Factors," Levy Economics Institute of Bard College, Working Paper No. 805, May 2014.

28. Ibid. The decrease is even larger when the consumer price index is used instead of gross domestic product in these calculations, because prices have increased more than GDP.

29. Quoted in Patricia Cohen, "Middle Class, but Feeling Economically Insecure," *New York Times*, April 10, 2015.

30. Joseph E. Stiglitz, *Rewriting the Rules of the American Economy: An Agenda for Growth and Shared Prosperity* (New York: Roosevelt Institute, 2015).

31. Jared Bernstein, "Increasing Inequality: It's Happening, It Matters, and We Can Do Something About It," Center for Budget and Policy Priorities presentation, January 6, 2015, http://jaredbernsteinblog.com/wp-content/uploads/2015/02/Inequality-Presentation_1_6_15-Final.pptx. Data derived from "Distribution of Household Income and Federal Taxes, 2011," Congressional Budget Office, November 12, 2014, https://www.cbo.gov/publication/49440.

32. Tami Luhby, "Why Isn't the Middle Class Earning $156,000 a Year?," CNN Money, July 1, 2015.

33. Gilson, "Chart: It's Never Been a Better Time to Be Rich."

34. Joe Maguire, "How Increasing Income Inequality Is Dampening U.S. Economic Growth, and Possible Ways to Change the Tide," Standard & Poor's, August 5, 2014.

35. Joseph E. Stiglitz, "Of the 1%, By the 1%, For the 1%," *Vanity Fair*, May 2011.

36. Dave Gilson and Carolyn Perot, "It's the Inequality, Stupid," *Mother Jones*, April 2011.

37. Gilson, "Charts: Income Growth Has Stalled for Most Americans."

38. John Komlos, "Income Inequality Begins at Birth and These Are the Stats That Prove It," *PBS NewsHour*, May 4, 2015, http://www.pbs.org/newshour/making-sense/plight-african-americans-u-s-2015/.

39. Gilson, "Charts: Income Growth Has Stalled for Most Americans"; Stiglitz, *Rewriting the Rules of the American Economy*; Economy Policy Institute, "Why It's Time to Update Overtime Pay Rules," August 4, 2015, http://www.epi.org/publication/time-update-overtime-pay-rules-answers-frequently/. In addition, this report mentions that the median worker saw a real (inflation-adjusted) hourly wage increase of just 6.1 percent between 1979 and 2013, despite overall productivity growth of 64.9 percent.

40. Mishel and Davis, "CEO Pay Continues to Rise as Typical Workers Are Paid Less."

41. Jonathan Karl, "Transcript: Freedom Partners Forum: Ted Cruz, Rand Paul and Marco Rubio in Conversation with ABC's Jonathan Karl," ABC News, January 26, 2015.

42. Economic Innovation Group, "Beneath the Recovery: Obstacles to Growth and Opportunity in the New Economy," March 2015.

43. Lawrence H. Summers and Ed Balls, "Report of the Commission on Inclusive Prosperity," Center for American Progress, January 15, 2015, 41.

44. Lawrence Mishel, Josh Bivens, Elise Gould, and Heidi Shierholtz, "Hourly Wages of All Workers, by Wage Percentile, 1973–2011 (2011 Dollars)," in *The State of Working America*, 12th ed. (Ithaca, NY: Cornell University Press, 2012).

45. Nelson Schwartz, "Low-Income Workers See Biggest Drop in Paychecks," *New York Times*, September 2, 2015.

46. John Komlos, "America Can Be a Full-Employment Economy Once Again," *PBS NewsHour*, March 15, 2015.

47. Michael Greenstone, Adam Looney, Jeremy Patashnik, and Muxin Yu, "Thirteen Economic Facts about Social Mobility and the Role of Education," Brookings Institution, June 2013.

48. Carrie Gleason and Susan J. Lambert, "Uncertainty by the Hour: The Fair Workweek Initiative," Center for Popular Democracy, accessed August 10, 2015, http://www.gistfunders.org/documents/UncertaintybytheHour_GleasonLambert_OSIFutureofWork.pdf.

49. Alicia Parlapiano, Robert Gebeloff, and Shan Carter, "The Shrinking American Middle Class," *New York Times*, January 26, 2015.

50. Ibid. The authors note that "there is no universal definition of middle class, of course. Some definitions are based on occupation or wealth; others take regional cost of living into account. We have chosen a simple one starting at about 50 percent above the poverty level for a family of four ($35,000) and topping out at six figures of annual income ($100,000), adjusting for inflation over time. We realize many households making more than $100,000 consider themselves middle class, but they nonetheless are making considerably more than most households— even in New York or San Francisco."

51. Dave Gilson, "Overworked America: 12 Charts That Will Make Your Blood Boil," *Mother Jones*, July–August 2011.

52. Heather Boushey, "Understanding How Raising the Federal Minimum Wage Affects Income Inequality and Economic Growth," Washington Center for Equitable Growth, March 12, 2014; Cohen, "Middle Class, But Feeling Economically Insecure."

53. Parlapiano et al., "Shrinking American Middle Class."

54. Derek Thompson, "The Typical Millennial Is $2,000 Poorer Than His Parents at the Same Age," *The Atlantic*, January 31, 2015. Thompson notes that "the median income of young adults today is $2,000 less today than their parents in 1980, adjusted for inflation. The earnings drop has been particularly steep in the rust belt and across the northwest."

55. Parlapiano et al., "Shrinking American Middle Class."

56. Kim Philips-Fein, "Why Workers Won't Unite," *The Atlantic*, April 2015.

57. Jacob S. Hacker and Nathaniel Loewentheil, "Prosperity Economics: Building an Economy for All," September 2012.

58. Lawrence Mishel, "Unions, Inequality, and Faltering Middle-Class Wages," Economic Policy Institute, August 29, 2012.

59. Gerald Mayer, "Union Membership Trends in the United States," Congressional Research Service, August 31, 2004.

60. Bureau of Labor Statistics, "Union Members Summary," January 23, 2015, http://www.bls.gov/news.release/union2.nr0.htm.

61. Kevin Drum, "Why Screwing Unions Screws the Entire Middle Class," *Mother Jones*, March–April 2011.

62. Lance Compa, *Unfair Advantage* (New York: Human Rights Watch, 2000).

63. "Union Membership Rates and U.S. Incomes," Demos, accessed August 10, 2015, http://www.demos.org/data-byte/union-membership-rates-middle-class-incomes.

64. Mishel, "Unions, Inequality, and Faltering Middle-Class Wages."

65. Drum, "Why Screwing Unions Screws the Entire Middle Class."

2: The New Work: Fissured, Flexible, Insecure

1. U.S. Government Accountability Office, "GAO-15-168R Contingent Workforce," April 20, 2015.

2. Bud Meyers, "Temp Workers Aren't Temporary," blog post, February 21, 2015, http://bud-meyers.blogspot.com/2015/02/temp-workers-arent-temporary-theyre-norm.html; "Intuit 2020 Report: Twenty Trends That Will Shape the Next Decade," Intuit, October 2010; U.S. Government Accountability Office, "GAO-15-168R Contingent Workforce"; Laura Forlano and Megan Halpern, "Design as Advocacy and the Future of Work: Lessons from a Participatory Design Workshop on Reimagining Work," Future of Work Project, Open Society Foundations, Summer 2014. Forlano and Halpern note, "According to temp firm Kelly Services, the contingent workforce has increased 70% since 2008."

3. David Weil, *The Fissured Workplace: Why Work Became So Bad for So Many and What Can Be Done to Improve It*, Kindle ed. (Cambridge, MA: Harvard University Press, 2014), loc. 4835–37; Freelancers Union, "Freelancing in America: A National Survey of the New Workforce," September 4, 2014.

4. Mary Beth Maxwell, "Contingent Workforce: Size, Characteristics, Earnings, and Benefits," U.S. Government Accountability Office, April 20, 2015, http://www.gao.gov/assets/670/669899.pdf.

5. Weil, *Fissured Workplace*, Kindle loc. 122.

6. Ibid.

7. Ibid., Kindle loc. 4863–64; Carrie Gleason and Susan J. Lambert, "Uncertainty by the Hour: The Fair Workweek Initiative," Center for Popular Democracy, accessed August 10, 2015, http://www.gistfunders.org/documents/Uncertaintyby theHour_GleasonLambert_OSIFutureofWork.pdf.

8. Bureau of Labor Statistics, "Table 8-A: Employed Persons by Class of Worker and Part-Time Status," U.S. Department of Labor, economic news release, accessed November 2, 2015, http://www.bls.gov/news.release/empsit.t08.htm.

9. Bureau of Labor Statistics, "The Employment Situation—July 2015," news release, U.S. Department of Labor, August 7, 2015, http://www.bls.gov/news.release /archives/empsit_08072015.pdf.

10. U.S. Government Accountability Office, "Employment Arrangements: Improved Outreach Could Help Insure Proper Worker Classification," July 2006,

http://www.gao.gov/products/GAO-06-656; Steven Greenhouse, "A Part-Time Life, as Hours Shrink and Shift," *New York Times*, October 27, 2012.

11. Greenhouse, "Part-Time Life."

12. Ibid.

13. Gleason and Lambert, "Uncertainty by the Hour."

14. Steven Greenhouse, "A Push to Give Steadier Shifts to Part-Timers," *New York Times*, July 15, 2014.

15. Gleason and Lambert, "Uncertainty by the Hour."

16. Donald M. Kerwin and Kristen McCabe, "Labor Standards Enforcement and Low-Wage Immigrants: Creating an Effective Enforcement System," Migration Policy Institute, July 2011, http://www.migrationpolicy.org/research/labor-standards-enforcement-immigration.

17. Josh Sanburn, "Fast Food Strikes: Unable to Unionize, Workers Borrow Tactics from 'Occupy,'" *Time*, July 30, 2013.

18. Gleason and Lambert, "Uncertainty by the Hour."

19. Ibid., chap. 2.

20. Erin Hatton, *The Temp Economy: From Kelly Girls to Permatemps in Postwar America* (Philadelphia: Temple University Press, 2011), 55; Sarah Jaffe, "Forever Temp?," *In These Times*, January 6, 2014.

21. Freelancers Union, "Freelancing in America.".

22. Maxwell, "Contingent Workforce," 12.

23. Freelancers Union, "Freelancing in America."

24. Dhanya Skariachan and Jessica Wohl, "Wal-Mart's Everyday Hiring Strategy: Add More Temps," Reuters, June 13, 2013.

25. Jaffe, "Forever Temp?"; Meyers, "Workers Aren't Temporary."

26. Maxwell, "Contingent Workforce."

27. According to one study, the distribution of blue-collar and office and administrative occupations within this industry reversed completely between 1990 and 2001. In 1990, office and administrative support workers constituted 42 percent of those in staffing services, and blue-collar workers made up 28 percent. By 2001, blue-collar workers peaked at 53 percent and office and administrative support was at 24 percent. Matthew Dey, Susan N. Houseman, and Anne E. Polivka, "Manufacturers' Outsourcing to Employment Services," Upjohn Institute, Working Paper No. 07-132, 2006, doi:10.17848/wp07-132.

28. U.S. Government Accountability Office, "Contingent Workforce: Size, Characteristics, Earnings, and Benefits," April 20, 2015. Employment includes 1.3 percent agency temps and 3.5 percent on call.

29. Peter S. Fisher, Elaine Ditsler, Colin Gordon, and David West, "Nonstandard Jobs, Substandard Benefits," Iowa Policy Project, July 2005, http://www.cfcw.org/Nonstandard.pdf.

30. Ibid.

31. Maxwell, "Contingent Workforce," 6.

32. Catherine Ruckelshaus, Rebecca Smith, Sarah Leberstein, and Eunice Cho, "Who's the Boss: Restoring Accountability for Labor Standards in Outsourced Work," National Employment Labor Project, May 2014.

33. See David Autor and Susan Houseman, "Do Temporary-Help Jobs Improve Labor Market Outcomes for Low-Skilled Workers? Evidence from 'Work First,' " *American Economic Journal: Applied Economics* 2, no. 3 (2010): 96–128. Additional research is summarized in Rebecca Smith and Claire McKenna, *Temped Out: How the Domestic Outsourcing of Blue-Collar Jobs Harms America's Workers* (New York: National Employment Law Project and National Staffing Workers Alliance, 2014).

34. Susie Poppick, "Temps Make 10% Less Than Full-Time Employees for the Same Work," *Money*, May 20, 2015.

35. Center for a Changing Workforce, "Permatemps," accessed August 10, 2015, http://www.cfcw.org/permatemps.html.

36. Claire McKenna, "The Job Ahead: Advancing Opportunity for Unemployed Workers," National Employment Labor Project, February 2015.

37. Rebecca Smith and Claire McKenna, "Temped Out: How Domestic Outsourcing of Blue-Collar Jobs Harms America's Workers," National Employment Law Project and National Staffing Workers Alliance, September 2, 2014.

38. Millennials are more likely to freelance than older workers—38 percent of millennials are freelancing, compared to 32 percent of those over age thirty-five, and are significantly more likely to search out work that has "a positive impact on the world" or is "exciting." Freelancers Union, "Freelancing in America."

39. Ibid.

40. Small Business Majority, "Rise of the Freelance Economy," March 17, 2015; MBO Partners, "Majority of Workforce Will Be Independent by 2020," December 20, 2011. MBO Partners projects that by 2020 there will be 65 to 70 million independent/contingent workers, comprising more than half of all employees.

41. Sara Horowitz, Althea Erickson, and Gabrielle Wuolo, "Independent, Innovative, and Unprotected: How the Old Safety Net Is Failing America's New Workforce," Freelancer's Union, accessed August 10, 2015, http://fu-res.org/pdfs/advocacy/2010_Survey_Full_Report.pdf.

42. Lynn Stuart Parramore, "Cut-Throat Capitalism: Welcome to the Gig Economy," *Alternet*, May 27, 2014.

43. Steven Greenhouse, "In Service Sector, No Rest for the Working," *New York Times*, February 21, 2015.

44. Judith Warner, "Crunch Time," *Washington Monthly*, November 2014.

45. Steven Greenhouse, "McDonald's Workers File Wage Suits in 3 States," *New York Times*, March 13, 2014.

46. Dave Jamieson, "Jimmy John's 'Oppressive' Noncompete Agreement Survives Court Challenge," *Huffington Post*, April 10, 2015.

47. Ibid. Jamieson reports, "The agreement applies to 'competing' shops that derive 10% or more of their revenue from any kind of sandwich: 'Employee covenants and agrees that, during his or her employment with the Employer and for a period of two (2) years after . . . he or she will not have any direct or indirect interest in or perform services for . . . any business which derives more than ten percent (10%) of its revenue from selling submarine, hero-type, deli-style, pita and/or wrapped or rolled sandwiches and which is located within three (3) miles

of either [the Jimmy John's location in question] or any such other Jimmy John's Sandwich Shop.' "

48. Ibid.

49. Steven Greenhouse, "Noncompete Clauses Increasingly Pop Up in Array of Jobs," *New York Times*, June 8, 2014.

50. Jamieson, "Jimmy John's 'Oppressive' Noncompete Agreement."

51. National Guestworker Alliance and Pennsylvania State University, Dickinson School of Law's Center for Immigrant Rights, *Leveling the Playing Field: Reforming the H-2B Program to Protect Guest Workers and U.S. Workers*, n.d., http://www.guestworkeralliance.org/wp-content/uploads/2012/06/Leveling-the-Playing-Field-final.pdf.

52. J-1 Visa: Exchange Visitor Program, "Facts and Figures," Bureau of Education and Cultural Affairs, U.S. Department of State, accessed August 10, 2015, http://j1visa.state.gov/basics/facts-and-figures/.

53. Saket Soni, National Guestworker Alliance, personal interview, 2015.

54. "Report of the August 2011 Human Rights Delegation to Hershey, Pennsylvania," September 2, 2011, http://www.guestworkeralliance.org/wp-content/uploads/2012/05/Human-Rights-Delegation-Report-Hershey.pdf.

55. "Forced Labor on American Shores," editorial, *New York Times*, July 8, 2012, 2015.

56. National Guestworker Alliance, *Leveling the Playing Field: Reforming the H-2B Program to Protect Guestworkers and U.S. Workers*, June 2012.

57. Josh Eidelson, "Guest Workers as Bellwether," *Dissent*, Spring 2013.

58. Ibid.

59. "Forced Labor on American Shores."

60. "Harsh Conditions Create Public Support for Reform," Hearts and Minds Sweatshops, accessed August 10, 2015, http://www.heartsandminds.org/articles/sweat.htm; Bill Wallace, "70 Immigrants Found in Raid on Sweatshop / Thai Workers Tell Horror Stories of Captivity," *San Francisco Chronicle*, August 4, 1995.

61. Sarah Maslin Nir, "The Price of Nice Nails," *New York Times*, May 7, 2015.

62. Barry Estabrook, "Politics of the Plate: The Price of Tomatoes," *Gourmet*, March 2009.

63. Ibid.

64. The sharing economy is an economic model based on sharing underutilized assets from spaces to skills to stuff for monetary or nonmonetary benefits. Largely focused on peer to peer marketplaces. The peer economy is made up of person-to-person marketplaces that facilitate the sharing and direct trade of products and services built on peer trust. Assets are owned and exchanged person to person, facilitated by online platforms that set some or most terms, such as TaskRabbit, Lyft, and Airbnb.

65. Catherine Clifford, "The Future of the Sharing Economy Is a World Built Like Bitcoin," *Entrepreneur*, June 12, 2014.

66. Ingrid Lunden, "Uber Rides High, Dominates Transport App Revenues and Downloads Up to November," *TechCrunch*, November 24, 2014.

67. "Workers on Tap," *The Economist*, January 3, 2015.

68. Lunden, "Uber Rides High."

69. Jon Liss, "Uber and the Degradation of Working Class Jobs," Future of Work Project, Open Society Foundations, 2014, http://static.opensocietyfoundations .org/misc/future-of-work/taxi-drivers-uber-and-modernizing-the-taxi-industry.pdf.

70. Douglas MacMillan, "The $50 Billion Question: Can Uber Deliver?," *Wall Street Journal*, June 15, 2015; Douglas MacMillan and Telis Demos, "Uber Eyes $50 Billion Valuation in New Funding," *Wall Street Journal*, May 9, 2015.

71. Carolyn Said, "Worker Survey Reveals Challenges of Sharing Economy," *San Francisco Chronicle*, May 20, 2015. The drivers spent $521 on gasoline, and the rest on insurance ($285 a month), car maintenance ($115), and parking ($44). Delivery drivers spent a mean of $374 a month on car expenses. Those chauffeuring passengers and 16 percent of those making deliveries said they lack personal auto insurance.

72. Sarah McBride, "Uber Expected to Ride Out Employee Ruling, Maintain High Valuation," *Insurance Journal*, June 22, 2015; Kaja Whitehouse, "California Ruling Challenges Uber Business Model," *USA Today*, June 17, 2015.

73. Tim Devaney, "NLRB Rules Against Business in Pivotal Joint-Employer Decision," *The Hill*, August 27, 2015.

74. Carl Benedikt Frey and Michael A. Osborne, "The Future of Employment: How Susceptible Are Jobs to Computerisation?," Oxford Martin Programme on the Impacts of Future Technology working paper, September 17, 2013.

75. Edward Luce, " 'Rise of the Robots: Technology and the Threat of a Jobless Future', by Martin Ford," *Financial Times*, May 8, 2015.

76. Ibid.

77. John Duhamel et al., "Rethink Robotics: Finding a Market," Stanford University School of Engineering, June 3, 2013.

78. Margi Murphey, "Shell to Pilot AI Virtual Assistant Named Amelia," *Tech World*, December 5, 2014.

79. Thomas L. Friedman, "If I Had a Hammer," *New York Times*, January 11, 2014.

80. Lauren F. Friedman, "IBM's Watson May Soon Be the Best Doctor in the World," *Business Insider*, April 22, 2014.

81. Zoë Corbyn, "Robots Are Leaving the Factory Floor and Heading for Your Desk—and Your Job," *The Guardian*, February 9, 2015.

82. Ibid.

83. Martin Ford, "Robots Are Coming for Your Job: Amazon, McDonald's and the Next Wave of Dangerous Capitalist 'Disruption,' " *Salon*, May 10, 2015.

84. Duhamel, "Rethink Robotics."

85. Erik Brynjolfsson and Andrew McAfee quoted in Corbyn, "Robots Are Leaving the Factory Floor."

86. Ibid.

87. Martin Ford, *Rise of the Robots: Technology and the Threat of a Jobless Future* (New York: Basic Books, 2015).

88. David H. Autor, Frank Levy, and Richard J. Murnane, "The Skill Content of Recent Technological Change: An Empirical Exploration," *Quarterly Journal of Economics* 118, no. 4: (2003): 1279–333, doi:10.1162/003355303322552801.

89. Martha Laboissiere of McKinsey & Company, presentation at SEIU 21st Century Blueprint Committee, Oakland, CA, June 2013.

90. Timothy Aeppel, "Be Calm, Robots Aren't About to Take Your Job, MIT Economist Says," *Wall Street Journal*, February 25, 2015.

91. Corbyn, "Robots Are Leaving the Factory Floor."

92. Timothy Aeppel, "Robots May Look Like Job-Killers, But It's Hard to See in the Numbers," *Wall Street Journal*, April 30, 2015.

93. Lawrence Mishel, "The Missing Footprint of the Robots," Economic Policy Institute, May 13, 2015.

94. Autor et al., "Skill Content."

95. Lawrence Mishel, "The Robots Are Here and More Are Coming: Do Not Blame Them for Our Wage or Job Problems," Economic Policy Institute, January 22, 2014.

96. Mishel, "Missing Footprint of the Robots."

97. Aeppel, "Be Calm"; Aaron Smith and Janna Anderson, "AI, Robotics, and the Future of Jobs," Pew Research Center, August 6, 2014.

98. Frey and Osborne, "Future of Employment."

99. Aeppel, "Be Calm."

100. Jared Bernstein, "Future Tense: Concern About the Quantity and Quality of Future Jobs," *Washington Post*, June 1, 2015.

3: It Doesn't Have to Be This Way: Resistance, Unrest, and Innovation

1. Kim Phillips-Fein, "Why Workers Won't Unite," *The Atlantic*, April 2015.

2. Josh Eidelson, "Alt-Labor," *American Prospect*, January 29, 2013.

3. Wikipedia, "Justice for Janitors," accessed August 12, 2015, https://en.wikipedia.org/wiki/Justice_for_Janitors.

4. Stephen Lerner and Jong Shaffer, "25 Years Later: Lessons from the Organizers of Justice for Janitors," *In These Times*, June 17, 2015.

5. SEIU, "The 10 Mile March That Helped Launch a Social Justice Movement," June 2010, http://seiu.info/a/justice-for-janitors/justice-for-janitors-20-years-of-organizing.php.

6. Roger Waldinger, Chris Erickson, Ruth Milkman, Daniel J.B. Mitchell, Abel Valenzuela, Kent Wong, and Maurice Zeitlin, "Helots No More: A Case Study of the Justice for Janitors Campaign in Los Angeles," chap. 6 in *Organizing to Win: New Research on Union Strategies*, ed. Kate Bronfenbrenner, Sheldon Friedman, Richard W. Hurd, Rudolph A. Oswald, and Ronald L. Seeber (Ithaca, NY: Cornell University Press, 1998).

7. Ibid.

8. Nancy Cleeland, "Justice for Janitors: Janitors Victory Galvanizes Workers Across the Nation," *Los Angeles Times*, April 25, 2000.

9. Lerner and Shaffer, "25 Years Later."

10. Heidi Shierholtz, "Low Wages and Scant Benefits Leave Many In-Home Workers Unable to Make Ends Meet," Economic Policy Institute, November 26, 2013.

11. Wage and Hour Division, "Application of the Fair Labor Standards Act to Domestic Service," U.S. Department of Labor, January 1, 2015, https://www.dol.gov/whd/homecare/final_rule.pdf.

12. Bureau of Labor Statistics, "Occupational Outlook Handbook," U.S. Department of Labor, http://www.bls.gov/ooh/healthcare/home-health-and-personal-care-aides.htm#tab-1; Shierholz, "Low Wages and Scant Benefits." The $10.21 wage is for an agency-based direct-care aide, and the $11.09 wage is for a non-agency direct-care aide.

13. Shierholz, "Low Wages and Scant Benefits"; "Home Care Aides in Washington State: Current Supply and Future Demand," WWAMI Center for Health Workforce Studies, January 2011, http://depts.washington.edu/uwrhrc/uploads/Home_Care_Aides_Brief.pdf.

14. Wage and Hour Division, "Application of the Fair Labor Standards Act to Domestic Service."

15. David Moberg, "Union Blues Lift in Chicago," The Nation, April 9, 2005.

16. Harold Meyerson, "Caretakers Take Charge," LA Weekly, February 24, 1999.

17. Linda Delp and Katie Quan, "Homecare Worker Organizing in California: An Analysis of a Successful Strategy," Labor Studies Journal 27 no. 1 (Spring 2002): 1–23.

18. Steven Greenhouse, "In Biggest Drive Since 1937, Union Gains a Victory," New York Times, February 26, 1999.

19. Catherine Fisk, "Harris v. Quinn Symposium: Court Departs from Federalism, First Amendment Jurisprudence," SCOTUSblog, July 3, 2014.

20. Wikipedia, "Living Wage," accessed August 10, 2015, http://en.wikipedia.org/wiki/Living_wage#cite_note-17.

21. National Employment Law Project, "Living Wage Laws," accessed August 10, 2015, http://campaign.nelp.org/content/content_issues/category/living_wage_laws/.

22. Open Government Guide, "Public Contracting," accessed August 10, 2015, http://www.opengovguide.com/topics/public-contracting/.

23. David Moberg, "Martha Jernegons's New Shoes," American Prospect, November 30, 2000.

24. Partnership for Working Families, "Policy & Tools: Living Wage," accessed August 2, 2015, http://www.forworkingfamilies.org/resources/policy-tools-living-wage.

25. Moberg, "Martha Jernegon's New Shoes."

26. Ibid.

27. ThisNation.com, "What Is the History of 'Third Parties' in the United States?," http://www.thisnation.com/question/042.html; Wikipedia, "Ralph Nader," accessed August 10, 2015, https://en.wikipedia.org/wiki/Ralph_Nader#The_spoiler_controversy.

28. Harold Meyerson, "Dan Cantor's Machine," American Prospect, January 2014.

29. Wikipedia, "Electoral Fusion," accessed August 10, 2015, https://en.wikipedia.org/wiki/Electoral_fusion#New_York. "In order to obtain or maintain

automatic ballot access, a party's candidate for governor of New York must receive 50,000 votes on that party's line."

30. Sarah Jaffe, "The Third Party That's Winning," *In These Times*, March 3, 2014.

31. Meyerson, "Dan Cantor's Machine."

32. Working Families, "Ed Gomes Just Made History," February 25, 2015, http://workingfamilies.org/2015/02/ed-gomes-just-made-history/.

33. Jaffe, "Third Party That's Winning."

34. Harold Meyerson, "If Labor Dies, What's Next?," *American Prospect*, September 13, 2012.

35. Steven Greenhouse, "The Fight for $15.37 an Hour: How a Coalition Pushed for a Hotel Workers' Minimum Wage," *New York Times*, November 22, 2014; Meyerson, "Dan Cantor's Machine."

36. Meyerson, "Dan Cantor's Machine."

37. Ibid.

38. Greenhouse, "Fight for $15.37 an Hour."

39. Ibid.

40. Harold Meyerson, "What Does Labor Need to Do to Survive?," *American Prospect*, September 13, 2012.

41. Bud Meyers, "Temp Workers Aren't Temporary, They're the Norm," blog post, February 21, 2015, http://bud-meyers.blogspot.com/2015/02/temp-workers -arent-temporary-theyre-norm.html.

42. Ibid. Intuit, "Intuit 2020 Report: Twenty Trends That Will Shape the Next Decade," February 2010.

43. Steven Greenhouse, "Tackling Concerns of Individual Workers," *New York Times*, March 23, 2013.

44. Sara Horowitz, interview with author, January 2015.

45. Greenhouse, "Tackling Concerns of Individual Workers."

46. Dan Munro, "How Sara Horowitz Is Disrupting Healthcare for the 'Gig' Economy," *Forbes*, October 2, 2014; Greenhouse, "Tackling Concerns of Individual Workers."

47. Greenhouse, "Tackling Concerns of Individual Workers."

48. Paul Keegan, "The 5 New Rules of Employee Engagement," *Inc.*, December 2014–January 2015.

49. Zoe Henry, "Secrets of a Very Opaque Glass Door," *Inc.*, December 2014– January 2015.

50. Panos Ipeirotis, "How Big Is Mechanical Turk?," *Computer Scientist in a Business School* blog, November 18, 2012.

51. Danielle N. Shapiro, Jesse Chandler, and Pam A. Mueller, "Using Mechanical Turk to Study Clinical Populations," *Clinical Psychological Science* 1, no. 2 (2013): 213–20, doi:10.1177/2167702612469015.

52. Julian Dobson, "Mechanical Turk: Amazon's New Underclass," *Huffington Post*, February 19, 2013.

53. Turkopticon, accessed August 10, 2015, https://turkopticon.ucsd.edu/.

54. Dobson, "Mechanical Turk."

55. Sarah Kessler, "What Does a Union Look Like in the Gig Economy?," *Fast Company*, February 19, 2015.

56. Kevin Roose, "The Sharing Economy Isn't About Trust, It's About Desperation," *New York*, April 24, 2014; Nancy Scola, "In Newly Launched Peers.org, the 'Sharing Economy' Gets a Posse," *Next City*, July 31, 2013.

57. Jason Tanz, "How Airbnb and Lyft Finally Got Americans to Trust Each Other," *Wired*, April 23, 2014.

58. Scola, "In Newly Launched Peers.org."

59. Ibid.

60. Shelby Clark, "Our First 'Homegrown' Products, by Popular Request: Home-sharing Liability Insurance and Keep Driving," Peers, December 4, 2014, http://blog.peers.org/post/104320093099/our-first-homegrown-products-by-popular.

61. Scola, "In Newly Launched Peers.org."

62. Rachel Homer, "An Explainer: What's Happening with Domestic Workers' Rights?," *On Labor*, http://onlabor.org/2013/11/06/an-explainer-whats-happening-with-domestic-workers-rights/.

63. Janice Fine, *Worker Centers: Organizing Communities at the Edge of the Dream* (Ithaca, NY: ILR Press/Cornell University Press, 2006).

64. Micah Maidenberg, "Florida Employers Guilty of Slavery," *Labor Notes*, July 31, 2002.

65. Ibid.

66. Katrina vanden Heuvel, "Sweet Victory: Coalition for Immokalee Workers Wins," *The Nation*, May 23, 2008.

67. Ibid.

68. Eidelson, "Alt-Labor."

69. Ibid.

70. Linda Burnham and Nik Theodore, *Home Economics: The Invisible and Unregulated World of Domestic Work* (New York: National Domestic Workers Alliance, 2012); Sarah Jaffe, "In New Report, 2,086 Domestic Workers Speak Out," *In These Times*, November 27, 2012.

71. Andrea Cristina Mercado and Ai-jen Poo, "Domestic Workers Organizing in the United States," Association for Women's Rights in Development, 2008, http://www.awid.org/sites/default/files/atoms/files/changing_their_world_-_domestic_workers_organizing_in_the_united_states.pdf.

72. Burnham and Theodore, *Home Economics*.

73. Ibid.

74. E. Tammy Kim, "Home Is Where the Union Is," *American Prospect*, December 7, 2012.

75. Bob Edwards, "Profile: Restaurant Opportunities Center of New York," *Morning Edition*, NPR, April 22, 2004; William Finnegan, "Inside the Fast-Food Labor Protests," *New Yorker*, November 4, 2015.

76. Eidelson, "Alt-Labor."

77. Dan La Botz, "Immigrant Restaurant Workers Hope to Rock New York," *Dollars & Sense*, January–February 2004.

78. Ibid.

79. Eidelson, "Alt-Labor."

80. Harold Meyerson, "Labor's New Reality—It's Easier to Raise Wages for 100,000 Than to Unionize 4,000," *Los Angeles Times*, December 7, 2014.

81. Fine, *Worker Centers*.

82. Robert E. Scott, "The High Price of 'Free' Trade: NAFTA's Failure Has Cost the United States Jobs Across the Nation," Economic Policy Institute, November 17, 2003.

83. Harold Meyerson, "The Battle in Seattle," *LA Weekly*, December 1, 1999.

84. Howard Zinn, *A People's History of the United States* (New York: HarperCollins, 2003), 672.

85. Harold Meyerson, "Workers Toppled a Dictator in Egypt, But Might Be Silenced in Wisconsin," *Washington Post*, February 15, 2011.

86. Wikipedia, "2011 Wisconsin Protests," accessed August 10, 2015, https://en.wikipedia.org/wiki/2011_Wisconsin_protests#February.

87. Ibid.

88. "Wisconsin Assembly Passes Controversial Labor Bill," CNN, March 10, 2011, http://news.blogs.cnn.com/2011/03/10/wisconsin-assembly-poised-to-pass -controversial-labor-bill/.

89. Meyerson, "Workers Toppled a Dictator in Egypt."

90. Harold Meyerson, "Wisconsin and Beyond," *American Prospect*, April 4, 2011.

91. Wikipedia, "Occupy Wall Street," accessed August 10, 2015, https://en.wiki pedia.org/wiki/Occupy_Wall_Street.

92. Jeff Sharlet, "Inside Occupy Wall Street," *Rolling Stone*, November 10, 2011.

93. Wikipedia, "Timeline of Occupy Wall Street," accessed August 10, 2015, https://en.wikipedia.org/wiki/Timeline_of_Occupy_Wall_Street#October_2011; Wikipedia, "Occupy London," accessed August 10, 2015, https://en.wikipedia.org /wiki/Occupy_London; Wikipedia, "Anonymous (group)," accessed August 10, 2015, https://en.wikipedia.org/wiki/Anonymous_(group).

94. Jenny Brown, "In Walmart and Fast Food, Unions Scaling Up a Strike-First Strategy," *Labor Notes*, January 23, 2013.

95. Walmart employs almost five times as many people as IBM, the second largest employer. Wikipedia, "Walmart," accessed October 20, 2015, https://en .wikipedia.org/wiki/Walmart; Brown, "In Walmart and Fast Food."

96. Karen McVeigh, "Walmart Faces Fresh Protests over Workers' Rights and Conditions," *The Guardian*, May 29, 2014.

97. Sarah Jaffe, "The Bad Boss Tax," *In These Times*, July 21, 2014; Sue Sturgis, "Walmart Workers Plan Biggest-Ever Black Friday Mobilization," *Facing South*, November 26, 2014.

98. Brown, "In Walmart and Fast Food."

99. Reuters, "Walmart Illegally Closed Union Store, Court Says," *New York Times*, June 27, 2014.

100. Erica Smiley, "Target's Wage Increase Proves Walmart Sets Standards for the Entire Retail Industry," Jobs with Justice, March 20, 2015.

101. Andy Kroll, "Walmart Workers Get Organized—Just Don't Say the U-Word," *Mother Jones*, March–April 2013.

102. Worker Center Watch, "OUR Walmart Founding," accessed November 1, 2015, http://www.workercenterwatch.com/worker-centers/our-walmart/founding/.

103. Sturgis, "Walmart Workers Plan Biggest-Ever Black Friday Mobilization."

104. Dave Jamieson, "Walmart Workers Launch Black Friday Strike," *Huffington Post*, November 26, 2014.

105. Ibid.

106. Susan Berfield, "Wal-Mart Workers Plan a Fresh Protest, This Time in Bentonville," *Bloomberg Businessweek*, May 28, 2013.

107. "Walmart Workers Pave the Way for Real Change in Retail," *Walmart Watch Blog*, March 2, 2015.

108. Nathan Lane, "Target to Lift Minimum Wage to $9 an Hour, Matching Rivals," Reuters, March 18, 2015.

109. Bryce Covert, "Walmart CEO Divulges Why the Company Raised Its Minimum Wage to $10," *ThinkProgress*, February 19, 2015.

110. Erica Smiley, "Now Trending: Whistleblowers in Low-Wage Jobs Turn to Social Media," Jobs with Justice, April 10, 2014.

111. Brown, "In Walmart and Fast Food."

112. Kroll, "Walmart Workers Get Organized."

113. Making Change at Walmart, "Wal-Mart Workers Pave the Way for Real Change in Retail," March 2, 2015, http://makingchangeatwalmart.org/2015/03/02/10263/, citing Rana Foroohar, "The Real Meaning of $9 an Hour," *Time*, February 26, 2015.

114. Aaron Pacitti, "The Great Stagnation: Five Years into the Recovery and Americans Still Don't Feel It," *Huffington Post*, June 13, 2014.

115. Steven Greenhouse, "With Day of Protests, Fast-Food Workers Seek More Pay," *New York Times*, November 29, 2012.

116. Ibid.

117. SEIU, "SEIU: All Working People Stand to Gain When Fast Food Workers Can Afford to Help Drive the Economy Forward," news release, November 30, 2012, https://web.archive.org/web/20141006171443/http://www.seiu.org/2012/11/seiu-all-working-people-stand-to-gain-when-fast-fo.php.

118. Greenhouse, "With Day of Protests."

119. Cienna Madrid, Dominic Holden, David Goldstein, Anna Minard, and Callan Berry, "Fast Food Strike!," *The Stranger*, August 28 2013, http://www.thestranger.com/seattle/fast-food-strike/Content?oid=17608887.

120. Ned Resnikoff, "Historic Fast Food Strike Draws Lessons from MLK's Last Campaign," MSNBC, April 4, 2013.

121. Josh Sanburn, "Fast Food Strikes: Unable to Unionize, Workers Borrow Tactics from 'Occupy,' " *Time*, July 30, 2013.

122. William Finnegan, "Dignity: Fast-Food Workers and a New Form of Labor Activism," *New Yorker*, September 15, 2014.

123. "Labor, Then and Now," editorial, *New York Times*, August 31, 2013; Marcus Donner, "Protesters Rally in Seattle for Higher Minimum Wage (Video)," *Puget Sound Business Journal*, August 29, 2013.

124. "Labor, Then and Now."

125. Katie Johnston, "SEIU President Visits Boston to Map out 'Fight for $15' March," *Boston Globe*, March 28, 2015.

126. Samantha Stark, "Labor's $15 Wage Strategy," *New York Times*, March 30, 2015.

127. David Goldstein, "Eight Arrested Outside Downtown Seattle McDonald's as Fast Food Strike Gains Momentum," *The Stranger*, August 2, 2013, http://slog.thestranger.com/slog/archives/2013/08/02/eight-arrested-outside-downtown-seattle-mcdonalds-as-fast-food-strike-gains-momentum.

128. Barack Obama, "Remarks by the President at Milwaukee Laborfest," White House, Office of the Press Secretary, September 1, 2014.

129. Steven Greenhouse, "Movement to Increase McDonald's Minimum Wage Broadens Its Tactics," *New York Times*, March 30, 2015.

130. Eidelson, "Alt-Labor."

4: The Little City That Could: Winning a $15 Wage in SeaTac

1. Nicole Keenan and Howard Greenwich, *Below the Radar* (Seattle: Puget Sound Sage, 2013).

2. Port of Seattle, "Seattle-Tacoma International Airport," accessed August 10, 2015, http://www.portseattle.org/Newsroom/Fast-Facts/Pages/Airport-Basics.aspx.

3. Bureau of Labor Statistics, "Industry Wage Survey: Scheduled Airlines, August–November 1975," Bulletin No. 1951, 1977, available at https://fraser.stlouisfed.org/scribd/?item_id=499394&filepath=/docs/publications/bls/bls_1951_1977.pdf#scribd-open. Median wage for "ramp" classification was $61,208 in 1975.

4. Remarks by Representative Adam Smith (D-WA) at the Democratic National Convention, July 27, 2004.

5. Amy Martinez, "SeaTac Voters to Decide on $15 Minimum for Airport Workers," *Seattle Times*, July 25, 2013.

6. All worker stories in this section are from personal interviews with the named individuals, January 2015; Keenan and Greenwich, *Below the Radar*; David Mendoza, Howard Greenwich, Megan Brown, and Thea Levkovitz, *First-Class Airport, Poverty Class Jobs* (Seattle: Puget Sound Sage, OneAmerica, Faith Action Network, and Working Washington, 2012), 5–6.

7. Goldy, "Delta Contractor Lays Off Skycap Featured in Ad Campaign Demanding 'Good Jobs' at Sea-Tac," *The Stranger*, May 31, 2012.

8. Keenan and Greenwich, *Below the Radar*, 8.

9. Martin Associates, "2007 Economic Impact of the Port of Seattle," Port of Seattle, February 10, 2009, 53.

10. Miranda Dietz, Peter Hall, and Ken Jacobs, "Course Correction: Reversing Wage Erosion to Restore Good Jobs at American Airports," UC Berkeley Labor Center, January 1, 2013.

11. William McGee, *Attention All Passengers: The Truth About the Airline Industry*, Kindle ed. (New York: HarperCollins, 2012).

12. Dietz et al., "Course Correction," 5; McGee, *Attention All Passengers*.

13. Dietz et al., "Course Correction," 1.

14. Socrates Bravo, interview with author, January 2015.

15. Ibid.

16. Abdi Mohamed, interview with author, January 2015.

17. Socrates Bravo, interview with author, January 2015.

18. Mendoza et al., *First-Class Airport*, 5–6.

19. Nicole Vallestero Keenan and Howard Greenwich, "Economic Impacts of a Transportation and Hospitality Living Wage in the City of SeaTac," *Puget Sound Sage*, September 2013, 8.

20. Julie Chinitz, Scott Harrah, and Dennis Osorio, "Searching for Work That Pays: 2010 Job Gap Study," Alliance for a Just Society, December 2010, http://nwfco.org/wp-content/uploads/2010/12/2010-1209_2010-Job-Gap.pdf.

21. Mendoza et al., "First-Class Airport," 9.

22. Keenan and Greenwich, *Below the Radar*, 15.

23. Ibid., 11. Allegations were filed by workers from four aviation service companies operating at Sea-Tac Airport, including AirServ, ASIG, DAL Global Services, and Bags. Specific complaints cited here are from worker statements. The source documents are the Alleged Safety or Health Hazards complaint forms filed with Department of Labor and Industries Division of Occupational Safety and Health on November 26, 2012. Copies of the complaint statements were furnished to the authors upon request to Working Washington, which is listed on the complaint forms as the representative of employees.

24. Keith Ervin, "Sea-Tac Jet Fuelers Threaten Strike over Safety, Worker's Suspension," *Seattle Times*, October 3, 2012.

25. Keenan and Greenwich, *Below the Radar*, 15.

26. Mendoza et al., "First-Class Airport," 11.

27. Matthew Kaminski, "An Airline That Makes Money. Really," *Wall Street Journal*, February 4, 2012.

28. Mendoza et al., "First-Class Airport," 11.

29. Keenan and Greenwich, *Below the Radar*.

30. Dave Freiboth, interview with author, January 2015. Freiboth formerly headed the Inlandboatmen's Union of the Pacific, ILWU.

31. Ibid.

32. Leonard Smith, interview with author, January 2015.

33. Darrin Hoop, "High Stakes for Port Drivers," *Socialist Worker*, February 13, 2012; Jon Talton, "Stalemate as Port Labor Fight Continues," February 13, 2012, *Seattle Times*; Mike Lindblom, "Port of Seattle Truckers Rally as Walkout Passes Second Week," *Seattle Times*, February 13, 2012.

34. "A Veteran Shouldn't Have to Choose Between Filling Gas Tank or Feeding Family," *It's Our Airport*, April 4, 2012.

35. Jonathan Rosenblum, "Small City, Big Ideas," *International Union Rights* 21, no. 2 (2014): 8, doi:10.14213/inteuniorigh.21.2.fm.

36. Memo Rivera Gutierrez, interview with author, December 2014.

37. Leonard Smith, interview with author, January 2015.

38. Freiboth, interview.

39. Dietz et al., "Course Correction," 16.

40. SeaTac is a "code city" under Washington State law, meaning that it can choose to adopt the powers of initiative and referendum. It did so in 1990. "Initiative and Referendum Powers," MRSC Local Government Success, accessed August 10, 2015, http://www.mrsc.org/subjects/governance/initreflist.aspx.

41. Ballotpedia, "Minimum Wage on the Ballot," accessed August 10, 2015, http://ballotpedia.org/Minimum_wage_on_the_ballot.

42. Karen Keiser, interview with author, January 2015.

43. Goldy, "Eight Arrested Outside Downtown Seattle McDonald's as Fast Food Strike Gains Momentum," *The Stranger*, August 2, 2013.

44. Lewis Kamb, "$15 Wage Issue Back on Ballot," *Seattle Times*, September 7, 2013.

45. Amy Martinez, "Both Sides Brace for Impact of SeaTac Wage Measure," *Seattle Times*, November 23, 2013.

46. Goldy, "Face-Plant: The 'Small Business' Face of a Campaign to Oppose a Higher Minimum Wage," *The Stranger*, September 18, 2013.

47. Don Liberty, "Small Businesses Support SeaTac Prop 1," YouTube, accessed August 10, 2015, https://www.youtube.com/watch?v=wKgH9jZi6Hc.

48. "SeaTac Family Business, Bull Pen Pub, Appears in Television Ad Prop 1 Endorsed by Growing List of SeaTac Small Businesses," It's Our Airport, April 4, 2012.

49. Abdirahman Abdullahi, interview with author, January 2015.

50. Habiba Ali, interview with author, January 2015.

51. Chris Smith, "Guest Opinion: A Higher Minimum Wage Would Help Families and Revitalize SeaTac," *Puget Sound Business Journal*, October 31, 2013.

52. Working Washington, "Port of Seattle: Prosperity or Poverty," *Sea-Tac Good Jobs Gazette*, September 2011, http://seiumaster.3cdn.net/a78924ebe0a984 c1c5_ptm6vtc81.pdf.

53. Sterling Harders, interview with author, January 2015.

54. Julia Patterson, interview with author, January 2015.

55. Sterling Harders, interview with author, January 2015.

56. Artie Nosrati, interview with author, January 2015.

57. Amy Martinez, "Minimum-Wage Measure Puts SeaTac in Spotlight," *Seattle Times*, October 27, 2013.

58. "Interview with David Rolf, President, SEIU Local 775NW," PBS, http:// video.pbs.org/widget/partnerplayer/2365115515/?start=0; Kirk Johnson, "Voters in Sea-Tac, Wash., Back $15 Minimum Wage," *New York Times*, November 26, 2013.

59. Gavin Kelly, "SeaTac: The Small US Town That Sparked a New Movement Against Low Wages," *The Guardian*, February 22, 2014.

60. Habiba Ali, interview with author, January 2015.

61. Ashley Gross, "Port of Seattle Proposes Lifting Airport Workers' Minimum Wage to $13 by 2017," KPLU 88.5 News, June 24, 2014.

62. Dmitri Iglitzin, e-mail message to author, December 19, 2014; Soojin Kim, internal presentation, Port of Seattle, April 27, 2015, http://www.aci-na.org/sites /default/files/soojin_kim_-_april_17.pdf.

63. Amy Martinez, "$15 Wage Floor Slowly Takes Hold in SeaTac," *Seattle Times*, February 13, 2014.

64. Jake Whittenberg, "1 Year After $15 Minimum Wage, Little Impact in SeaTac," KING 5 News, December 31, 2014.

65. Dana Milbank, "Raising the Minimum Wage Without Raising Havoc," *Washington Post*, September 4, 2014.

66. *Supreme Court of the State of Washington, Alaska Airlines and the Washington Restaurant Association v. The City of SeaTac*, filed August 20, 2015, http:// www.courts.wa.gov/opinions/pdf/897239.pdf.

67. Joel Connelly, "State Supreme Court Rules SeaTac's $15 an Hour Minimum Wage Applies to Airport Workers," *Seattle Post-Intelligencer*, August 20, 2015.

68. Julia Patterson, interview with author, January 2015.

5: Fifteen for Seattle

1. Jonnelle Marte, "The Most Expensive Cities in the U.S.," *Washington Post*, August 26, 2015; "The 10 Richest Cities in the U.S.," *MarketWatch*, March 2, 2015; Prashant Gopal, "Where the Rich (Still) Live," *Bloomberg News*, March 17, 2009.

2. Pacific Northwest Labor and Civil Rights Projects, "Seattle General Strike Project," University of Washington, accessed November 1, 2015, http://depts.wash ington.edu/labhist/strike/.

3. Mildred Andrews, "Alice Lord: How One Waitress Changed Seattle," in "Women's Votes, Women's Voices," Washington State Historical Society, originally published in *Union Record*, February 1901 and October 1902 issues, http:// washingtonhistoryonline.org/suffrage/People/alord.aspx; Margaret Riddle, "Washington State Senate Approves an Eight-Hour Workday for Women on March 2, 1911," October 8, 2011, Historylink.org, http://www.historylink.org/index.cfm ?DisplayPage=output.cfm&file_id=8315.

4. Ibid.

5. Working Washington, "Strike Poverty: Raise Seattle," YouTube, accessed August 10, 2015, https://www.youtube.com/watch?v=W9uy8SrrACs.

6. Estimate from U.S. Census, "County Business Patterns, 2010 for Limited Service Restaurants (NAICS 722211) and Snack and Nonalcoholic Beverage Bars (NAICS 722213)," cited in Good Jobs Seattle, "August 29th National Fast Food Strike Fact Sheet," August 29, 2013, n1.

7. Goldy, "Supersize My Salary Now!," *The Stranger*, June 5, 2013.

8. Production and nonsupervisory workers in U.S. limited-service restaurants worked an average of 24.1 hours a week in 2011, and average hours in the industry have not gone above 24.7 hours a week for at least the past ten years. Good Jobs Seattle, "August 29th National Fast Food Strike Fact Sheet," n4.

9. Goldy, "Supersize My Salary Now!"

10. Working Washington, "Strike Poverty, Raise Seattle."

11. Josh Feit, "What Do We Want? $15! When Do We Want It? In a Little While!" *Seattle Met*, June 30, 2014.

12. Erica C. Barnett and Josh Feit, "With Labor Rocking Seattle Today, We Had One Question for All the Mayoral Cadidates," *Seattle Met*, May 30, 2013.

13. Eric Lacitis and Christine Clarridge, "Fast-Food Workers Demonstrate for Better Pay," *Seattle Times*, May 31, 2013.

14. Anna Minard, Cienna Madrid, Dominic Holden, Goldy, and Callan Berry, "Fast Food Strike!," *The Stranger*, August 28, 2013.

15. Lacitis and Clarridge, "Fast-Food Workers Demonstrate for Better Pay."

16. After San Francisco ($124,561), San Jose ($115,515), and Washington, D.C. ($108,092).

17. Erika Rawes, "The 10 Richest Cities in America," *USA Today*, January 25, 2015.

18. Diana M. Pearce, "The Self-Sufficiency Standard for Washington State 2014," Workforce Development Council of Seattle-King County, 2014, http://www.selfsufficiencystandard.org/docs/Washington2014.pdf.

19. Kirk Johnson, "Targeting Inequality, This Time on Public Transit," *New York Times*, February 28, 2015.

20. Gene Balk, "Mapping King County's Disappearing Middle Class," *Seattle Times*, March 7, 2015.

21. Working Washington, *Fifteen Stories: How Workers Struck Poverty and Won $15 for Seattle* (Seattle: Working Washington, 2014), http://www.workingwa.org/fifteen-stories.

22. Minard et al., "Fast Food Strike!"

23. Working Washington, *Fifteen Stories*.

24. Ibid.; Lynn Thompson, "Workers See $15 Wage as 'Peace of Mind,' " *Seattle Times*, June 1, 2014.

25. Minard et al., "Fast Food Strike!"

26. Kara Kostinich, "Fast Food Workers Striking in Seattle to Protest Low Wages," KOMOnews.com, December 2, 2013.

27. Goldy, "Anti-$15 an Hour Minimum Wage Lobbyist: 'I Don't Think Anybody Can Argue' That $9 an Hour Is a Living Wage," *The Stranger*, October 4, 2013.

28. Ibid.

29. Morning Fizz, " 'I Was You,' " *Seattle Met*, June 17, 2013; for complete video of the forum, see "Mayoral Candidate Forum: Low-Wage Workforce Issues," City of Seattle, June 17, 2013, http://www.seattlechannel.org/misc-video?videoid=x21773; for coverage of the debate, see "Low Wage Worker Town Hall," YouTube, June 19, 2013, https://www.youtube.com/watch?v=Eyb45qPgSRg.

30. "Mayoral Candidate Forum."

31. Ibid.

32. Wikipedia, "Kshama Sawant," accessed August 11, 2015, http://en.wikipedia.org/wiki/Kshama_Sawant.

33. Kshama Sawant, interview with author, January 2015.

34. Goldy, "Eight Arrested Outside Downtown Seattle McDonald's as Fast Food Strike Gains Momentum," *The Stranger*, August 2, 2013.

35. "Labor, Then and Now," editorial, *New York Times*, August 31, 2013.

36. Ed Murray for Mayor Campaign, "Economic Opportunity Agenda for Seattle," September 2013, https://web.archive.org/web/20150210020442/http://murray4mayor.com/wp-content/uploads/2013/09/Murray-Opportunity-Agenda.pdf.

37. Joel Connelly, "Conlin Concedes to Sawant," *Seattle Post-Intelligencer*, November 13, 2013.

38. Wikipedia, "Kshama Sawant."

39. City of Seattle, "Income Inequality Advisory Committee," January 2014, http://www.seattle.gov/Documents/Departments/IncomeInequalityAdvisoryCom mittee/one-pager.pdf. The IIAC members were: council member Nick Licata, council member Bruce Harrell, council member Kshama Sawant, venture capitalist Nick Hanauer, philanthropist Audrey Haberman, author and educator Eric Liu, Nucor Steel human resources executive Janet Ali, Seattle Chamber CEO Maud Daudon, small businessman Craig Dawson, pizzeria owner Joe Fugere, restaurant and nightlife impresario Dave Meinert, hotel owner Craig Shafer, Seattle Hotel Association president David Watkins, Capitol Hill Chamber of Commerce executive Michael Wells, Union Bank executive Ron Wilkowski, Ivar's restaurant chain CEO Bob Donegan, King County Labor Council leader Dave Freiboth, UFCW political director Sarah Cherin, SEIU hospital union president Diane Sosne, civil rights leader Pramila Jayapal, Puget Sound Sage researcher Nicole Vallestero Keenan, and antipoverty agency executive director Gordon McHenry.

40. KIRO 7, "Seattle Mayor-Elect Announces Minimum Wage Task Force," video, December 19, 2013, http://www.kirotv.com/news/news/seattle-mayor-elect -announces-minimum-wage-task-fo/ncQNG/.

41. Lynn Thompson, "Call for $15 Minimum Wage Moves North to Seattle," *Seattle Times*, December 4, 2013.

42. Brian Surratt, interview with author, January 2015.

43. Emphasis added. Washington Restaurant Association, "Restaurants Help Organize OneSeattle Coalition in Response to Push for Higher Minimum Wage," April 3, 2014, http://warestaurant.org/blog/restaurants-help-organize-one seattle-coalition-in-response-to-push-for-higher-minimum-wage/. The post also said, "The Seattle Restaurant Alliance (SRA), a chapter of the WRA, is working hard on behalf of the hospitality industry to promote its interests and develop a smart, reasonable solution to the Seattle minimum wage issue. The SRA was the first industry group to organize—starting in October 2013—on this issue. It is now helping to lead the other industries so they can help complement its efforts."

44. David Watkins, interview with author, 2015.

45. Relatively few committee members felt strongly that we should count other types of compensation against the base wage, including retirement contributions, child care, tuition, bonuses, profit sharing, and so on.

46. Tina Patel, "Hundreds Turn Out for Seattle's Town Hall on $15 Minimum Wage Issue," Q13 FOX, March 5, 2014.

47. Lynn Thompson, " 'Historic Moment': Hundreds Pack Minimum-Wage Hearing," *Seattle Times*, March 5, 2014.

48. Personal meeting notes, 2014.

49. Local NPR affiliate KUOW reported, "Testimony was heavily in favor of raising the minimum to $15 an hour." Deborah Wang, "Seattle Residents Testify For, Against $15 Minimum Wage at Packed Hearing," KUOW.org, March 6, 2014, http://kuow.org/post/seattle-residents-testify-against-15-minimum-wage-packed -hearing; Good Jobs Seattle, "Lining Up in the Rain, Seattle Speaks Out in Support of $15," March 7, 2014, http://goodjobsseattle.tumblr.com/post/78871231274 /lining-up-in-the-rain-seattle-speaks-out-in.

50. Thompson, " 'Historic Moment.' "

51. The audience heard from a total of thirty-seven speakers, ranging from academics to think tankers, business leaders, individual local business people, and low-wage workers themselves: venture capitalist Nick Hanauer; San Francisco supervisor John Avalos; Philadelphia City Council member Wilson Goode; Chicago aldermen Roderick Sawyer, Toni Foulkes, and John Arena; Seattle council members Nick Licata, Bruce Harrell, and Kshama Sawant; Lori Pfingst, Center for Budget and Policy; Dorian Warren, Columbia University; Michael Reich and Ken Jacobs, UC Berkeley; Marieka Klawitter and Bob Plotnik, University of Washington; Jasmine Donovan, Dick's Burgers; Saru Jayaraman, ROCUnited; Dick Conway, Puget Sound Forecast; Maud Daudon, Greater Seattle Chamber of Commerce; Heather Boushey, Washington Center for Equitable Growth; Paul Sonn, National Employment Law Project; and other national and local experts, employers, and stakeholders.

52. Bellamy Pailthorp, "Symposium on Income Inequality Pushing Seattle Toward $15 Minimum Wage," KPLU 88.5, March 27, 2014.

53. Wang, "Seattle Residents Testify For."

54. Ibid.

55. Shirley Qiu and Josh Feit, "Fast Food Workers Build Momentum for $15 Minimum Wage," *Seattle Met*, December 6, 2013.

56. Good Jobs Seattle, "The $15 Movement Walks in MLK's Footsteps," January 24, 2014.

57. Goldy, "Join Kshama Sawant and 15Now.org Tomorrow for a Day of Organizing, Education, and Music," *Slog* blog, *The Stranger*, February 14, 2014.

58. Donna Gordon Blankinship, "Murray, DelBene Bring $10.10 Wage Fight to Seattle," KOMO News, February 18, 2014.

59. KIRO 7, "Fast Food Workers Ask Seattle to Boycott McPoverty with a 1-Day Citywide Boycott of the Big Burger Chains," February 19, 2014, video available at https://drive.google.com/file/d/0B0uBA8WNYlhlbHpwSDFZdXBTaFk /edit?usp=sharing.

60. "Boycott McPoverty! Fast Food Workers Call For ONE DAY Fast Food Restaurant Boycott," YouTube, February 18, 2014, https://www.youtube.com/watch ?v=1BHsPjrSnsI.

61. The cost of living has increased 38 percent since 2001 (calculation based on a family of four). Self Sufficiency Calculator for Washington State, http://www

.thecalculator.org/; Diana M. Pearce, *The Self Sufficiency Standard for Washington State 2014* (Seattle: Workforce Development Council of Seattle-King County, 2014), 12, http://www.selfsufficiencystandard.org/docs/Washington2014.pdf.

62. Self Sufficiency Calculator for Washington State.

63. Alliance for a Just Society, "2012 Job Gap Report," accessed August 12, 2015, http://allianceforajustsociety.org/wp-content/uploads/2013/02/2012-Job-Gap -Report_National_FINAL.pdf; Pearce, *Self-Sufficiency Standard*, 8.

64. Marieka M. Klawitter, Mark C. Long, and Robert D. Plotnick, "Who Would Be Affected by an Increase in Seattle's Minimum Wage?," Seattle Income Inequality Advisory Committee, University of Washington, March 21, 2014, 3.

65. Michael Reich, Ken Jacobs, and Annette Bernhard, "Local Minimum Wage Laws: Impacts on Workers, Families, and Businesses," Seattle Income Inequality Advisory Committee, March 2014, http://murray.seattle.gov/wp-content /uploads/2014/03/UC-Berkeley-IIAC-Report-3-20-2014.pdf.

66. Ibid.

67. Ibid.

68. Raise the Minimum Wage, "Minimum Wage Question and Answer," National Employment Law Project, accessed November 2, 2015, http://www.raisethe minimumwage.com/pages/qanda; Klawitter et al., "Who Would Be Affected," 3.

69. Wage and Hour Division, "Minimum Wages for Tipped Employees," U.S. Department of Labor, January 1, 2015, http://www.dol.gov/whd/state/tipped.htm; Wikipedia, "Tipped Wage in the United States," accessed August 11, 2015, http:// en.wikipedia.org/wiki/Tipped_wage_in_the_United_States.

70. The initiative was approved by a whopping 77 percent of Washington voters. David Goldstein, "Washington Restaurants Already Weathered an 85 Percent Minimum Wage Hike (and Apparently Survived)," *Slog* blog, *The Stranger*, February 24, 2014, http://slog.thestranger.com/slog/archives/2014/02/24/washington -restaurants-already-weathered-an-85-percent-minimum-wage-hike-and-apparently -survived.

71. Wage and Hour Division, "Minimum Wages for Tipped Employees."

72. Ibid.

73. National Economic Council, Council of Economic Advisers, Domestic Policy Council, and the Department of Labor, "The Impact of Raising the Minimum Wage on Women and the Importance of Ensuring a Robust Tipped Minimum Wage," White House Report, Washington, DC, March 2014, https:// www.whitehouse.gov/sites/default/files/docs/20140325minimumwageandwomen reportfinal.pdf. The White House release of the report can be found at https:// www.whitehouse.gov/the-press-office/2014/03/26/new-white-house-report-impact -raising-minimum-wage-women-and-importance-.

74. Saru Jayaraman, " 'Behind the Kitchen Door' Author Encourages Diners to Speak Out," *Moyers & Company*, February 20, 2013.

75. Saru Jayaraman, *Behind the Kitchen Door* (Ithaca, NY: Cornell University Press, 2013).

76. Brian Surratt, interview with author, January 2015.

77. Howard Wright, interview with author, January 2015.

78. Ibid.

79. Dave Freiboth, interview with author, January 2015.

80. "With Seattle Charter Amendment Filed, 15 Now Leader at Capitol Hill Community Council Minimum Wage Panel This Week," *Capitol Hill Seattle Blog*, April 14, 2014.

81. Brian Surratt, interview with author, January 2015.

82. "Wednesday Jolt: Potential Minimum Wage Compromise," *Seattle Met*, April 16, 2014.

83. KIRO 7, "Seattle Mayor Set to Announce $15 Minimum Wage Plan," video, April 24, 2014, http://www.kirotv.com/videos/news/video-hundreds-rally-for -living-wage/vCYQrd/

84. Robert Feldstein, interview with author, January 2015.

85. Feit, "What Do We Want?"

86. Surratt, interview.

87. Goldy, "Vast Majority of Seattle Voters Support $15 Minimum Wage," *The Stranger*, February 12, 2014.

88. EMC Research, "New Polling on $15 Minimum," May 13, 2014, available at http://www.thestranger.com/images/blogimages/2014/05/14/1400088148-emc _research__15_minimum_wage_polling_memo__5-13_.pdf.

89. Lynn Thompson, "New Poll Shows Big Support for $15 Minimum Wage," *Seattle Times*, May 14, 2014; Anna Minard, "New Poll on the $15 Minimum Wage Shows Support in Seattle Is Higher Than Ever: 74 Percent," *The Stranger*, May 14, 2014.

90. Chris Francis, "$15 Minimum Wage Protesters, Rally, Walk Out," KIRO TV, May 15, 2014.

91. Matt Driscoll, "Boos, Hisses, and a $15-an-Hour Minimum-Wage Vote," *Seattle Weekly*, May 29 2014.

92. *International Franchise Association, Inc. v. City of Seattle, U.S. Court of Appeals*, filed September 25, 2015, http://cdn.ca9.uscourts.gov/datastore/opinions /2015/09/25/15-35209.pdf.

93. Office of Mayor Ed Murray, "Murray Statement on International Franchise Association Injunction Order Decision," March 17, 2015, http://murray .seattle.gov/murray-statement-on-international-franchise-association-injunction -order-decision/#sthash.NTCDZTy2.dpuf.

94. Office of Mayor Ed Murray, "Seattle Support Growing for Mayor Murray's $15 Minimum Wage Proposal," May 14, 2014, http://murray.seattle.gov/seattle-sup port-growing-for-mayor-murrays-15-minimum-wage-proposal/#sthash.6JFlm06J .dpbs.

95. Karen Weise, "How Seattle Agreed to a $15 Minimum Wage Without a Fight," *Bloomberg Businessweek*, May 8, 2014.

96. Danny Westneat, "Unions Are Back with City-by-City Wage Campaign," *Seattle Times*, May 3, 2014.

97. Dave Freiboth, interview with author, January 2015.

98. Anna Minard, "How a Few Striking Workers Changed Seattle Politics," *The Stranger*, May 18, 2014.

6: An American Wage for a Stronger America: The Case for $15

1. Drew Desilver and Steve Schwarzer, "Making More than Minimum Wage, but Less than $10.10 an Hour," Pew Research Center, November 5, 2014. This is true for non-self-employed workers eighteen and older.

2. Teresa Tritch, "Doesn't President Obama Know That $10.10 an Hour Is Not Enough?," *Taking Note* blog, *New York Times*, January 22, 2015.

3. Evidence for spillover effects was found by the following authors: Heidi Shierholtz, "Fix It and Forget It: Index the Minimum Wage to Growth in Average Wages," Economic Policy Institute, Briefing Paper No. 251, December 17, 2009; David Cooper and Doug Hall, "How Raising the Federal Minimum Wage Would Help Working Families and Give the Economy a Boost," Economic Policy Institute Issue Brief No. 341, August 14, 2012.

4. The 50 percent figure was derived using data from the following sources: Bureau of Labor Statistics, "May 2014 National Occupational Employment and Wage Estimates United States," U.S. Department of Labor, http://www.bls.gov /oes/current/oes_nat.htm#00-0000; Irene Tung, Yannet Lathrop, and Paul K. Sonn, "The Growing Movement for $15," National Employment Law Project, April 13, 2013; David Autor, Alan Manning, and Christopher L. Smith, "The Contribution of the Minimum Wage to U.S. Wage Inequality over Three Decades: A Reassessment," Finance and Economics Discussion Series, Divisions of Research & Statistics and Monetary Affairs, Federal Reserve Board.

5. Tim Allen, interview with author, January 2015.

6. Rachel L. Swarns, "McDonald's Workers, Vowing a Fight, Say Raises Are Too Little for Too Few," *New York Times*, April 5, 2015.

7. Heather Boushey, "Understanding How Raising the Federal Minimum Wage Affects Income Inequality and Economic Growth," Washington Center for Equitable Growth, March 12, 2014; Dave Gilson, "Overworked America: 12 Charts That Will Make Your Blood Boil," *Mother Jones*, July 2011.

8. Steven Greenhouse, "The Fight for $15.37 an Hour: How a Coalition Pushed for a Hotel Workers' Minimum Wage," *New York Times*, November 22, 2014.

9. Jared Bernstein and Sharon Parrott, "Proposal to Strengthen Minimum Wage Would Help Low-Wage Workers, with Little Impact on Employment," Center on Budget and Policy Priorities, January 7, 2014; Congressional Budget Office, "Baseline Economic Forecast—February 2013 Baseline Projections." The minimum wage of $1.60 an hour in 1968 would be $10.90 today when adjusted for inflation, according to the Bureau of Labor Statistics' Consumer Price Index. Raise the Minimum Wage, "Real Value of the Federal Minimal Wage," accessed August 11, 2015, http://www.raisetheminimumwage.com/facts/entry /amount-with-inflation/.

10. Economic Policy Institute, "Real Value of the Minimum Wage, 1960–2013 (2013 Dollars)," *State of Working America*, 12th ed., accessed August 11, 2015, http://stateofworkingamerica.org/chart/swa-wages-figure-4-ae-real-minimum-wage/. If the minimum wage were indexed to 50 percent of the average wage, roughly

where it was in 1968, it would currently be $10.08. Boushey, "Understanding How Raising the Federal Minimum Wage."

11. Gilson, "Overworked America: 12 Charts."

12. John Schmitt, "The Minimum Wage Is Too Damn Low," Center for Economic and Policy Research, March 2012.

13. Ken Jacobs, Ian Perry, and Jenifer MacGillvary, "The High Public Cost of Low Wages," UC Berkeley Labor Center, April 2015. The mid- to late 1990s is also when most of the 6 percent total wage increase between 1979 and 2013 occurred.

14. Justin Fox, "Farewell to the Blue-Collar Elite," *Bloomberg View*, April 6, 2015. About 58 percent of workers received health care from their employer in 2013.

15. Bureau of Labor Statistics, "Labor Productivity and Costs," U.S. Department of Labor, accessed August 11, 2015, http://www.bls.gov/lpc/; Schmitt, "Minimum Wage Is Too Damn Low"; Bernstein and Parrott, "Proposal to Strengthen Minimum Wage"; Raise the Minimum Wage, "Real Value."

16. Shierholz, "Fix It"; David Cooper and Doug Hall, "How Raising the Federal Minimum Wage to $10.10 Would Give Working Families and the Overall Economy a Much-Needed Boost," Economic Policy Institute, Briefing Paper No. 357, March 13, 2013.

17. Olivier Giovannoni, "What Do We Know About the Labor Share and the Profit Share? Part III: Measures and Structural Factors," Levy Economics Institute of Bard College, Working Paper No. 805, 2014, http://www.levyinstitute.org/pubs/wp_805.pdf. The decrease is even larger when the consumer price index is used instead of GDP in these calculations, because prices have increased more than GDP.

18. Thomas Piketty, *Capital in the Twenty-First Century* (Cambridge: Belknap Press of Harvard University Press, 2014). "After 1980, the lion's share of gains went to the top end of the income distribution, with families in the bottom half lagging far behind," Piketty notes.

19. Alyssa Davis and Lawrence Mishel, "CEO Pay Continues to Rise as Typical Workers Are Paid Less," Economic Policy Institute, June 12, 2014.

20. Atif Mian and Amir Sufi, "The Most Important Economic Chart," *House of Debt*, March 18, 2014.

21. Mark Gongloff, "45 Million Americans Still Stuck Below Poverty Line: Census," *Huffington Post*, September 16, 2014; Cooper and Hall, "How Raising the Federal Minimum Wage." Regarding researchers who deem the federal poverty line to be inadequate for the basics of daily living, see Thomas Edsall, "Who Is Poor?," *New York Times*, March 13, 2013. Researchers include Kathryn Edin, a professor of public policy and management at Harvard's Kennedy School; Shawn Fremstad of the Center for Economic and Policy Research; and Pat Ruggles, senior fellow at NORC at the University of Chicago. Poverty thresholds are 2012 levels for families of two (one adult, one child) and three (two adults, one child). Note that the poverty threshold for a family of one adult, two children is slightly higher ($18,498). Annual earnings are calculated assuming workers work full time (forty hours per week) and fifty-two weeks per year (i.e., with no vacation). Minimum

wage is deflated using CPI-U-RS. Source: authors' analysis of 2012 data from the U.S. Census Bureau and the Wage and Hour Division, U.S. Department of Labor; Carmen DeNavas-Walt and Bernadette D. Proctor, "Income and Poverty in the United States: 2013," U.S. Census Bureau, September 2014.

22. Kathryn Edin and H. Luke Shaefer, "Living on $2 a Day in America," *Los Angeles Times*, September 3, 2015.

23. Arindrajit Dube, "Minimum Wages and the Distribution of Family Incomes," University of Massachusetts at Amherst, Working Paper, December 30, 2013. This is a 19 percent reduction "over the longer term," according to Dube. Because some states have higher minimum wages, the total nationwide reduction in poverty would be somewhat less.

24. Ibid. The U.S. poverty rate is reduced by 1.5 percent for every 10 percent increase in the minimum wage. Dube found that a $10.10 federal minimum wage would reduce the number of people living in poverty in the United States by 4.6 million, or about a fifth of the working poor. Also see Boushey, "Understanding How Raising the Federal Minimum Wage."

25. Dube, "Minimum Wages."

26. Ibid.

27. Other recent studies, using less sophisticated statistical methods, also show that raising the minimum wage reduces poverty. The Council of Economic Advisers predicted that the proposal would lift 2 million people out of poverty, while the Congressional Budget Office estimated that $10.10 nationally would lift 900,000 people out of poverty. Reich et al., "Local Minimum Wage Laws."

28. Linda Giannarelli, Laura Wheaton, and Joyce Morton, "How Much Could Policy Changes Reduce Poverty in New York City?," Urban Institute, 2015, http://www.urban.org/sites/default/files/alfresco/publication-pdfs/2000136-How-Much-Could-Policy-Changes-Reduce-Poverty-in-New-York-City.pdf.

29. Scott M. Stringer, "Income Analysis of a $15.00 Minimum Wage in New York City," New York City Economic Brief, Bureau of Fiscal and Budget Studies, April 2015.

30. Marieka M. Klawitter, Mark C. Long, and Robert D. Plotnick, "Who Would Be Affected by an Increase in Seattle's Minimum Wage?," Seattle Income Inequality Advisory Committee, University of Washington, March 21, 2014, 3.

31. Fifty-two percent of workers in poverty were working full-time. DeNavas-Walt and Proctor, "Income and Poverty in the United States: 2013."

32. Catherine Ruetschlin and Amy Traub, "Ten Reasons Why Fast Food Workers Deserve a Raise," Demos, August 28, 2013.

33. Claire McKenna, "Data Points: Many of the Highest-Growth Occupations Are Low-Wage Jobs," Raise the Minimum Wage blog, April 2, 2015.

34. Ibid.

35. Autor et al., "Contribution of the Minimum Wage"; David Lee, "Wage Inequality in the United States During the 1980s: Rising Dispersion or Falling Minimum Wage?" *Quarterly Journal of Economics* 114, no. 3 (August 1999): 977–1023, doi:10.1162/003355399556197.

36. Josh Bivens, Elise Gould, Lawrence Mishel, and Heidi Shierholtz, "Raising America's Pay: Why It's Our Central Economic Policy Challenge," Economic Policy Institute, June 4, 2014; Boushey, "Understanding How Raising the Federal Minimum Wage." Though there is not yet agreement on the exact size of the effect, most economists agree with EPI's findings that the decline of the minimum wage has been a significant factor in the increase in inequality for the lower half of the income distribution. As we'll see in chapter 7, there is no conflict between raising the minimum wage and employment, because raising the wage does not increase unemployment.

37. Autor et al., "Contribution of the Minimum Wage"; Bernstein and Parrott, "Proposal to Strengthen Minimum Wage."

38. Nicole Keenan and Howard Greenwich, "Economic and Equity Outcomes of a $15/Hr Minimum Wage in Seattle," *Puget Sound Sage*, April 2014. Nearly 63 percent of Seattle food-service workers earn below $15 an hour.

39. National Women's Law Center, "Fair Pay for Women Requires a Fair Minimum Wage," May 13, 2015; National Employment Law Project, "The Growing Movement for $15," April 13, 2013. Nationally, African Americans make up about 12 percent of the total workforce but account for 15 percent of the sub-$15-wage workforce. Similarly, Latinos constitute 17 percent of the workforce but account for almost 23 percent of workers making less than $15 per hour. John DiNardo, Nicole Fortin, and Thomas Lemieux, "Labor Market Institutions and the Distribution of Wages, 1973–1992: A Semiparametric Approach," National Bureau of Economic Research, April 1995.

40. Boushey, "Understanding How Raising the Federal Minimum Wage."

41. The predicted declines in participation rates for the other public assistance programs are relatively small, but this is because even among low-wage workers the number and shares participating in these programs are fairly small to begin with. David Cooper, "Raising the Federal Minimum Wage to $10.10 Would Save Safety Net Programs Billions and Help Ensure Businesses Are Doing Their Fair Share," Economic Policy Institute Issue Brief No. 387, October 16, 2014, http://s4.epi.org/files/2014/safety-net-savings-from-raising-minimum-wage-final.pdf; Sylvia Allegretto, Marc Doussard, Dave Graham-Squire, Ken Jacobs, Dan Thompson, and Jeremy Thompson, "Fast Food, Poverty Wages: The Public Cost of Low Wage Jobs in the Fast Food Industry," Center for Labor Research and Education, University of California, Berkeley, 2013.

42. Ibid.

43. Rachel West and Michael Reich, "The Effects of Minimum Wages on SNAP Enrollments and Expenditures," Center for American Progress and Institute for Research on Labor and Employment, March 2014.

44. Cooper, "Raising the Federal Minimum Wage"; Bryce Covert, "Hate Government Spending? Here's Why You Should Love a Higher Minimum Wage," *Think Progress*, October 17, 2014.

45. Sasha Abramsky, "Ron Unz: Why I Dropped My Ballot Initiative to Raise California's Minimum Wage," *The Nation*, March 18, 2014.

46. Ron Unz, "The Conservative Case for a Higher Minimum Wage," republished from *Fox & Hounds Daily*, February 3, 2014.

47. Ibid.

48. Ron Unz, "The Minimum Wage and Illegal Immigration," Higher Wages for American Workers, January 22, 2014; Neil Munro, "$12 an Hour Is Conservative Rocket Fuel, Says Ron Unz," *Daily Caller*, January 10, 2014.

49. Unz, "Conservative Case for a Higher Minimum Wage."

50. Laura Fosmire, "Democrats Speak Out in Favor of $15 Minimum Wage," *Statesman Journal*, February 4, 2015.

51. William Finnegan, "Dignity," *New Yorker*, September 15, 2014; Lynsey Hanley, "The Way We Live Now," *The Guardian*, March 13, 2009.

52. Working Washington, *Fifteen Stories*.

53. Original research from CPS Merged Outgoing Rotation Groups (MORG) based on data from the National Bureau of Economic Research.

54. Cooper and Hall, "Raising the Federal Minimum Wage."

55. Wikipedia, "CBO Estimates of Historical Effective Federal Tax Rates Broken Down by Income Level, December 2013," accessed August 12, 2015, http://en.wikipedia.org/wiki/Economy_of_the_United_States#/media/File:Average_US_Federal_Tax_Rates_1979_to_2013.png.

56. Keenan and Greenwich, "Economic and Equity Outcomes." Households making over $70,000 spend only about two-thirds of their income. Households under $40,000 spend all of their income.

57. John Schmitt and David Rosnick, "The Wage and Employment Impact of Minimum-Wage Laws in Three Cities," Center for Economic and Policy Research, March 2011. They write, "Our estimated employment responses generally cluster near zero, and are more likely to be positive than negative. Few of our point estimates are precise enough to rule out either positive or negative employment effects, but statistically significant positive employment responses outnumber statistically significant negative elasticities."

58. Klawitter et al., "Who Would Be Affected."

59. The virtuous cycle of consumer demand and wages is Nick Hanauer's concept.

60. Nick Hanauer, "The Pitchforks Are Coming . . . for Us Plutocrats," *Politico Magazine*, July–August 2014.

61. Ibid., 2.

62. Nick Hanauer, "Why Capitalism Has Nothing to Do with Supply and Demand," *Making Sen$e* blog, PBS Newshour, July 28, 2014.

63. Nick Hanauer, "Whatever Happened to Overtime?," *Politico Magazine*, November 17, 2014.

64. Wikipedia, "Keynesian Economics," accessed August 12, 2015, http://en.wikipedia.org/wiki/Keynesian_economics.

65. Joseph Stiglitz, "Stiglitz: Why Inequality Matters and What Can Be Done About It," *Next New Deal* blog, Roosevelt Institute, April 1, 2014.

66. Center for American Progress, "Attacking the Trickle Down Tax Mantra," unpublished paper, 2014; William Easterly and Ross Levine, "It's Not Factor

Accumulation: Stylized Facts and Growth Models," unpublished paper, March 2001, http://www2.lawrence.edu/fast/finklerm/easterly_levine.pdf.

67. Martin Feldstein, "Supply Side Economics: Old Truths and New Claims," National Bureau of Economic Research, January 1986, http://www.nber.org/papers /w1792.pdf; Center for American Progress, unpublished paper, 2013.

68. Business for a Fair Minimum Wage, "Business Owners from Every State Say Higher Minimum Wage Helps Business," January 29, 2007.

69. Michael Bloomberg and Sheldon Silver, "New York Must Finally Raise the Minimum Wage," New York Daily News, February 2, 2012.

70. Daniel Aaronson, Sumit Agarwal, and Eric French, "The Spending and Debt Responses to Minimum Wage Increases," Federal Reserve Bank of Chicago WP 2007-23, February 8, 2011.

71. Cooper and Hall, "Raising the Federal Minimum Wage."

72. Jessica Schieder, "S&P: Reduce Inequality for a Better Economy," Center for Effective Government, August 14, 2014.

73. Roy van der Weide and Branko Milanovic, "Inequality Is Bad for Growth of the Poor (But Not for That of the Rich)," World Bank Group, Policy Research Working Paper No. 6963, July 2014.

74. Katie Little, "IMF Calls on the US to Hike Its Minimum Wage Rate," CNBC, June 16, 2014; Robert Schroeder, "IMF Urges U.S. to Raise Minimum Wage," MarketWatch, June 16, 2014.

75. Joe Maguire, "How Increasing Income Inequality Is Dampening U.S. Economic Growth, and Possible Ways to Change the Tide," Standard & Poor's Financial Services, August 5, 2014; Little, "IMF Calls on the US."

76. Daniel Aaronson, Eric French, and James MacDonald, "The Minimum Wage, Restaurant Prices, and Labor Market Structure," Journal of Human Resources 43, no. 3 (2008): 688–720; Daniel Aaronson and Eric French, "How Does a Federal Minimum Wage Hike Affect Aggregate Household Spending?" Chicago Fed Letter, no. 313, August 2013.

77. Stringer, "Income Analysis."

78. Phil Izzo, "Dearth of Demand Seen Behind Weak Hiring," Wall Street Journal, July 18, 2011.

79. Gadi Detcher, "Middle Class Series: About the Middle Class Project at the Center for American Progress," Center for American Progress, August 31, 2012.

80. Shierholz, "Fix It"; Izzo, "Dearth of Demand"; Hall and Cooper, "How Raising the Federal Minimum Wage."

81. Deborah Wang, "Seattle's $15 Minimum Wage Is 'Going to Change Everything,' " KUOW.org, March 30, 2015.

82. Ibid.

83. Amanda Reaume, "Will Tuition Ever Stop Increasing?," USA Today, November 8, 2014.

84. Laura Donovan, "Thousands Strike Nationwide to Protest Low Wages," ATTN., April 17, 2015.

85. Reaume, "Will Tuition Ever Stop Increasing?"

86. Alliance for a Just Society, "Washington," Job Gap Economic Prosperity series, accessed August 11, 2015, http://thejobgap.org/washington-low-wage-nation -2015/.

87. Socrates Bravo, interview with author, January 2015.

88. Jim Tankersley, "The Devalued American Worker," *Washington Post*, December 14, 2014.

89. Mike "Mish" Shedlock, "Jobs Numbers Are Far Worse Than They Look," *MarketWatch*, March 8, 2013.

90. Bernstein and Parrott, "Proposal to Strengthen Minimum Wage."

91. Daniel T. Lichter, "Poverty and Inequality Among Children," *Annual Review of Sociology* 23 (1997): 121–45, doi:10.1146/annurev.soc.23.1.121.

92. Sean Reardon, "The Great Divide: No Rich Child Left Behind," *Opinionator* blog, *New York Times*, April 27, 2013; "Choose Your Parents Wisely," *The Economist*, July 26, 2014.

93. Greg J. Duncan, Pamela A. Morris, and Chris Rodrigues, "Does Money Really Matter? Estimating Impacts of Family Income on Young Children's Achievement with Data from Random-Assignment Experiments," *Developmental Psychology* 47, no. 5 (2011): 1263–79, doi:10.1037/a0023875. A study of varying child benefits in Canada also found higher levels of child achievement (e.g., higher vocabulary scores) in children whose families received higher income supplements: Kevin Milligan and Mark Stabile, "Do Child Tax Benefits Affect the Well-Being of Children? Evidence from Canadian Child Benefit Expansions," *American Economic Journal: Economic Policy* 3, no. 3 (August 2011): 175–205.

94. National Center for Health Statistics, *Health, United States, 2011: With Special Feature on Socioeconomic Status and Health* (Hyattsville, MD: U.S. Department of Health and Human Services, 2012).

95. David O. Meltzer and Zhuo Chen, "The Impact of Minimum Wage Rates on Body Weight in the United States," National Bureau of Economic Research, Working Paper No. 15485, November 2009.

96. Kas Thomas, "Biggest Risk Factor for Depression: Low Income," *Blogorrhea*, March 11, 2013.

97. Mark W. Manseau, "Increase the Minimum Wage for Better Mental Health," Kevin MD blog, March 4, 2015; Jitender Sareen, Tracie O. Afifi, Katherine A. McMillan, and Gordon J. Asmundson, "Relationship Between Household Income and Mental Disorders: Findings from a Population-Based Longitudinal Study," *Archives of General Psychiatry* 68, no. 4 (April 2011): 419–27, doi:10.1001/archgenpsychiatry.2011.15.

98. Bernstein and Parrott, "Proposal to Strengthen Minimum Wage."

99. Manseau, "Increase the Minimum Wage."

100. Lyndsey Layton, "Study Links Kids' Brain Sizes to Affluence," *Winnipeg Free Press*, April 18, 2015.

101. Julia B. Isaacs, "Starting School at a Disadvantage: The School Readiness of Poor Children," Social Genome Project Research, Brookings Institution, March 2012.

102. Richard Wilkinson and Kate Pickett, "The Spirit Level Authors: Why Society Is More Unequal than Ever," *The Guardian*, March 9, 2014.

103. Amy Gluckman and Alissa Thuotte, "Inequality: Bad for Your Health: An Interview with Ichiro Kawachi," *Dollars & Sense*, January–February 2008, available at http://02d9ed5.netsolhost.com/kawachi.htm.

104. Ibid.

105. Richard Wilkinson and Kate Pickett, "The Spirit Level: Why Equality Is Better for Everyone," Equality Trust, 2009.

106. Guy Molyneu, "Support for a Federal Minimum Wage of $12.50 or Above," Hart Research Associates, January 14, 2015, http://nelp.org/content/uploads/2015/03/Minimum-Wage-Poll-Memo-Jan-2015.pdf; Mitchell Hirsch, "New Poll Shows Overwhelming Support for Substantial Minimum Wage Increase," Raise the Minimum Wage blog, January 15, 2015. Seventy-five percent of Americans—including 53 percent of Republicans—support raising the national minimum wage to $12.50 by 2020.

107. Greenberg Quinlan Rosner Research, "Voters Stand Behind Workers," November 13, 2014.

108. Ibid.

109. Molyneu, "Support for a Federal Minimum Wage."

110. Claire Trageser, "San Diego Minimum Wage Increase to Go on June 2016 Ballot," KPBS, October 20, 2014.

111. Chris McGreal, "Seattle Minimum Wage: $15 Figure Represents 'Historic Victory' for Workers," *The Guardian*, June 3, 2014.

112. South Dakota raised its state minimum wage to $8.50, with annual increases; Arkansas to $8.50 by 2017; Alaska to $9.75 by 2016; and Nebraska to $9.00 by 2016.

113. David Cooper, "20 States Raise Their Minimum Wages While the Federal Minimum Continues to Erode," Economic Policy Institute, December 18, 2014; Social Security Online, "Automatic Increases," accessed August 12, 2015, http://www.ssa.gov/cgi-bin/netcomp.cgi?year=2013; Matt Philips, "The Chart Obama-Haters Love Most—and the Truth Behind It," *Quartz*, November 4, 2014.

114. Executive Office of the President, "A Year of Action: Progress Report on Raising the Minimum Wage," August 12, 2014.

115. Emma Stieglitz, "20 States to Increase Minimum Wage on New Year's Day," Raising the Minimum Wage blog, December 31, 2014.

116. National Employment Law Project, "Minimum Wage Basics: City Minimum Wage Laws: Recent Trends and Economic Evidence," May 2015; National Conference of State Legislatures, "State Minimum Wages: 2015 Minimum Wages by State," November 10, 2015.

7: But Won't the Sky Fall?

1. National Employment Law Project and the Cry Wolf Project, "Consider the Source," March 2013.

2. Ibid.

3. Ibid.

4. Jared Bernstein and Sharon Parrott, "Proposal to Strengthen Minimum Wage Would Help Low-Wage Workers, with Little Impact on Employment," Center on Budget and Policy Priorities, January 7, 2014.

5. In 1979, 27 percent of low-wage workers (those making $10.10 per hour or less in today's dollars) were teenagers, compared with 12 percent in 2013, according to Janelle Jones and John Schmitt, "Update on Low-Wage Workers," Center for Economic and Policy Research, June 7, 2014.

6. Jared Bernstein, "Minimum Wage: Who Makes It?," New York Times, June 9, 2014; Heather Boushey, "Understanding How Raising the Federal Minimum Wage Affects Income Inequality and Economic Growth," Washington Center for Equitable Growth, March 12, 2014.

7. Robert Reich, "Seattle Is Right," blog post, June 5, 2014, http://robertreich.org/post/87896763410.

8. David Cooper and Douglas Hall, "Raising the Federal Minimum Wage to $10.10 Would Give Working Families, and the Overall Economy, a Much-Needed Boost," Economic Policy Institute, Briefing Paper No. 357, March 13, 2013.

9. Emily Arrowood, "Fox Regular Art Laffer: The Minimum Wage Is Just the 'Black Teenage Unemployment Act,' " Media Matters, January 8, 2014.

10. James Sherk, "Who Earns the Minimum Wage? Suburban Teenagers, Not Single Parents," Heritage Foundation, Issue Brief No. 3866, February 28, 2013.

11. NFIB Research Foundation, "16,000 Jobs Lost Under House Bill 1355: Minimum-Wage Legislation Would Take Huge Toll on State's Economy," April 5, 2015; Michael J. Chow, "Economic Impact Analysis of House Bill 1355 on Washington State Small Businesses," NFIB Research Foundation, March 24, 2015.

12. Heidi Shierholtz, "Fix It and Forget It: Index the Minimum Wage to Growth in Average Wages," Economic Policy Institute, Briefing Paper No. 251, December 17, 2009.

13. Ben Wolfgang, "Number of High-School Students with Jobs Hits 20-Year Low," Washington Times, May 24, 2012; Bureau of Labor Statistics, "Labor Force Statistics from the Current Population Survey," U.S. Department of Labor, accessed August 12, 2015, http://www.bls.gov/cps/minwage2010tbls.htm#1.

14. Wolfgang, "Number of High-School Students."

15. Keven A. Hasset and Michael R. Strain, "Why We Shouldn't Raise the Minimum Wage," Los Angeles Times, March 10, 2013.

16. Michael Reich, Ken Jacobs, and Annette Bernhard, "Local Minimum Wage Laws: Impacts on Workers, Families, and Businesses," Seattle Income Inequality Advisory Committee, March 2014, http://murray.seattle.gov/wp-content/uploads/2014/03/UC-Berkeley-IIAC-Report-3-20-2014.pdf.

17. John Schmitt, "Why Does the Minimum Wage Have No Discernible Effect on Employment?," Center for Economic and Policy Research, February 2013.

18. Ibid.; Sylvia Allegretto, Arindrajit Dube, and Michael Reich, "Do Minimum Wages Really Reduce Teen Employment? Accounting for Heterogeneity and Selectivity in State Panel Data," Industrial Relations 50, no. 2 (2011): 205–40.

19. Jonah Goldberg, "Martin O'Malley's Modern-Day Know-Nothingness," American Enterprise Institute, April 22, 2015.

20. National Employment Law Project, "Big Business, Corporate Profits, and the Minimum Wage," Data Brief, July 2012.

21. Raise the Minimum Wage, "Corporate Profits of Low-Wage Employers," accessed August 12, 2015, http://www.raisetheminimumwage.org/pages/corporate -profits.

22. Paul Buchheit, "Apple, Walmart, McDonald's: Who's the Biggest Wage Stiffer?," *Alternet*, July 28, 2013.

23. National Employment Law Project, "Big Business, Corporate Profits, and the Minimum Wage," Data Brief, July 2012, 5.

24. Ibid.

25. Ibid.

26. Martin Sandbu, "Why Walmart's Raise Is Good for Business," *Financial Times*, February 19, 2015.

27. Source: Glassdoor, "Walmart," accessed August 8, 2015, http://www .glassdoor.com/Salary/Walmart-Salaries-E715.htm; Michele Simon, "Walmart's Hunger Games," *Eat Drink Politics*, November 2014, http://www.eat drinkpolitics.com/wp-content/uploads/Walmarts_Hunger_Games_Report.pdf; Morning Star, "Wal-Mart Stores Inc," accessed August 12, 2015, http://perfor mance.morningstar.com/stock/performance-return.action?p=price_history_page &t=WMT&region=usa&culture=en-US; McDonald's, "McDonald's Reports Fourth Quarter and Full Year 2014 Results," news release, January 23, 2015, http:// news.mcdonalds.com/Corporate/Press-Releases/Financial-Release?xmlreleaseid =123060; Wikipedia, "McDonald's," accessed August 12, 2015, http://en.wikipedia .org/wiki/McDonald%27s; Glassdoor, "McDonald's Hourly Pay," accessed August 8, 2015, http://www.glassdoor.com/Hourly-Pay/McDonald-s-Hourly-Pay -E432.htm; Morning Star, "McDonald's Corp," accessed August 12, 2015, http:// quote.morningstar.com/Stock/chart.aspx?t=MCD&region=USA; Wikipedia, "Yum! Brands," accessed August 12, 2015, http://en.wikipedia.org/wiki/Yum! _Brands; Glassdoor, "KFC Salaries," August 7, 2015, http://www.glassdoor.com /Salary/KFC-Salaries-E7860.htm; Morning Star, "Yum Brands Inc.," accessed August 12, 2015, http://www.morningstar.com/stocks/XNYS/YUM/quote.html; Wikipedia, "Target Corporation," accessed August 12, 2015, http://en.wikipedia .org/wiki/Target_Corporation; Morning Star, "Target Corp," accessed August 12, 2015, http://quote.morningstar.com/Stock/chart.aspx?t=TGT&region=USA.

28. American Sustainable Business Council, "Small Business Owners Favor Raising Federal Minimum Wage," July 2014, http://www.businessforafairminimum wage.org/sites/default/files/BFMW_ASBC_Minimum_Wage_Business_Poll_Re port_July_2014.pdf; U.S. Department of Labor, "Minimum Wage Mythbusters," accessed August 12, 2015, http://www.dol.gov/minwage/mythbuster.htm.

29. Jack Mozloom, "Minimum Wage Won't Stay Dead," NFIB, May 17, 2012, http://www.nfib.com/article/?cmsid=60142; Eric Hoyt, "Poor Sales, Not High Wages, Worry Small Businesses," Center for Economic and Policy Research, July 10, 2012.

30. Igor Volsky, "Why Employers Won't Fire People If We Raise the Minimum Wage to $9," *Think Progress*, February 14, 2013; Travis Waldron, "Speaker Boehner Rejects Obama's Proposal to Raise the Minimum Wage," *Think Progress*, February 13, 2013.

31. Michael R. Strain, "No, Food Stamps Aren't Subsidies for McDonald's and Wal-Mart," *Washington Post*, April 17, 2015.

32. Peter Dreier and Donald Cohen, "Americans Deserve a Big Raise—Celebrating the 75th Anniversary of the Fair Labor Standards Act," *Huffington Post*, June 25, 2013.

33. Hristos Doucouliagos and T.D. Stanley, "Publication Selection Bias in Minimum-Wage Research? A Meta-Regression Analysis," *British Journal of Industrial Relations* 47, no. 2 (2009): 406–28, doi:10.1111/j.1467-8543.2009.00723.x.

34. "Over 600 Economists Sign Letter in Support of $10.10 Minimum Wage," Economic Policy Institute, January 14, 2014.

35. Arindrajit Dube, T. William Lester, and Michael Reich, "Minimum Wage Effects Across State Borders: Estimates Using Contiguous Counties," Institute for Research on Labor and Employment, University of California, Berkeley, Working Paper No. 157-07, November 2010, http://www.irle.berkeley.edu/workingpapers/157-07.pdf.

36. Arindrajit Dube, T. William Lester, and Michael Reich, "Do Minimum Wages Really Reduce Teen Employment? Accounting for Heterogeneity and Selectivity in State Panel Data," Institute for Research on Labor and Employment, University of California Berkeley, Working Paper No. 166-08, April 2011.

37. Schmitt, "Why Does the Minimum Wage."

38. Eric Morath, "What Happened to Fast-Food Workers When San Jose Raised the Minimum Wage?," *Wall Street Journal*, April 9, 2014.

39. Jeanine Stewart, "Apocalypse Not: $15 and the Cuts That Never Came," *Puget Sound Business Journal*, October 23, 2015.

40. Paul Constant, "You Should Read This Story About Seattle's 'Minimum Wage Meltdown That Never Happened,'" *Civic Skunk Works*, October 23, 2015.

41. Stewart, "Apocalypse Not."

42. *Growing Unequal? Income Distribution and Poverty in OECD Countries* (Paris: OECD, 2008), doi:10.1787/9789264044197-en.

43. Dube et al., "Minimum Wage Effects"; David Neumark and William Wascher, "Minimum Wages and Employment: A Review of Evidence from the New Minimum Wage Research," National Bureau of Economic Research, Working Paper No. 12663, November 2006.

44. Dube et al., "Minimum Wage Effects."

45. Neumark and Wascher, "Minimum Wages and Employment."

46. Arindrajit Dube, Suresh Naidu, and Michael Reich, "The Economic Effects of a Citywide Minimum Wage," *Industrial and Labor Relations Review* 60, no. 4 (2007): 522–43.

47. Barry T. Hirsch, Bruce E. Kaufman, and Tetyana Zelenska, "Minimum Wage Channels of Adjustment," *Industrial Relations: A Journal of Economy and*

Society 54, no. 2 (April 2015): 199–239, doi:10.1111/irel.12091; Mark Wilson, "The Negative Effects of Minimum Wage Laws," CATO Institute, September 2012.

48. Carrie Gleason and Susan J. Lambert, "Uncertainty by the Hour: The Fair Workweek Initiative," Center for Popular Democracy, accessed August 10, 2015, available at http://www.gistfunders.org/documents/UncertaintybytheHour_Glea sonLambert_OSIFutureofWork.pdf.

49. Claire McKenna, "Data Points: A Look at Involuntary Part-Time Work in Retail," Raise the Minimum Wage blog, March 3, 2015.

50. Michael Powell, "Profits Are Booming. Why Aren't Jobs?," *New York Times*, January 8, 2011.

51. Karen Ball, "Minimum Wage Increases on Monday, Labor Already Pressing for More," Associated Press, April 1, 1991, http://www.apnewsarchive.com/1991 /Minimum-Wage-Increases-on-Monday-Labor-Already-Pressing-for-More/id-c54 aa46le1fb599e9c31b6bfac7d8b28.

52. Dube et al., "Economic Effects"; Michael Reich, Ken Jacobs, Annette Bernhardt, and Ian Perry, "San Francisco's Proposed City Minimum Wage Law: A Prospective Impact Study," Center on Wage and Employment Dynamics, Policy Brief, August 2014.

53. Sara Jones, "Why Are So Many Seattle Restaurants Closing Lately?," *Seattle Magazine*, March 4, 2015.

54. Paul Guppy, "Seattle's $15 Wage Law a Factor in Restaurant Closings," Washington Policy Center, March 11, 2015.

55. Tim Worstall, "We Are Seeing the Effects of Seattle's $15 an Hour Minimum Wage," *Forbes*, March 16, 2015.

56. Bethany Jean Clement, "Truth Needle: Is $15 Wage Dooming Seattle Restaurants? Owners Say No," *Seattle Times*, March 19, 2015.

57. Rick Ungar, "Minimum Wage Increase Killing Seattle Restaurants? Anatomy of a Lie from Inside the Bubble," *Forbes*, March 22, 2015.

58. Tsedeye Gebreselassie, testimony before the New Jersey State Labor Department, "S-3: Increases the Minimum Wage to $8.50, Then Makes Annual Adjustments Based on CPI Increases," National Employment Law Project, March 8, 2012, http://nelp.org/content/uploads/2015/03/NewJerseyMinimumWageTestimony.pdf ?nocdn=1.

59. "Raise the Minimum Wage," *Crain's New York Business*, February 5, 2012.

60. Daniel Aaronson, Eric French, and Isaac Sorkin, "Firm Dynamics and the Minimum Wage: A Putty-Clay Approach," Federal Reserve Bank of Chicago, Working Paper No. 2013-26, November 2013.

61. Lynn Thompson, "Studies Look at What Happened When Cities Raised Minimum Wage," *Seattle Times*, March 12, 2014.

62. Jerome Gautie and John Schmitt, eds., *Low-Wage Work in the Wealthy World* (New York: Russell Sage Foundation, 2009).

63. Jeanne Lofsted, "Gender and Veterinary Medicine," *Canadian Veterinary Journal* 44, no. 7 (2003): 533–35.

64. Robert Reich, "The 'Paid-What-You're-Worth' Myth," blog post, March 13, 2014, http://robertreich.org/post/79512527145.

65. Kevin C. Brown, "A Tale of Two Systems," *Remapping Debate*, December 21, 2011.

66. Frederick E. Allen, "How Germany Builds Twice as Many Cars as the U.S. While Paying Its Workers Twice as Much," *Forbes*, December 21, 2011.

67. Ibid.

68. SEIU 775, "Washington State Legislature: Prepare for the Age Wave by Investing in Home Care," January 14, 2015, http://seiu775.org/washington-state -legislature-prepare-for-the-age-wave-by-investing-in-the-home-care-workforce/; Bureau of Labor Statistics, "May 2014 State Occupational Employment and Wage Estimates South Carolina," U.S. Department of Labor, accessed August 12, 2015, http://www.bls.gov/oes/current/oes_sc.htm.

69. Liz Alderman and Steve Greenhouse, "Living Wages, Rarity for U.S. Fast-Food Workers, Served Up in Denmark," *New York Times*, October 27, 2014.

70. Ibid.

71. Schmitt quoted in ibid.; Jordan Weissmann, "The Magical World Where McDonald's Pays $15 an Hour? It's Australia," *The Atlantic*, August 5, 2013.

72. Lawrence Mishel and Alyssa Davis, "CEO Pay Continues to Rise as Typical Workers Are Paid Less," Economic Policy Institute, Brief No. 380, June 12, 2014.

73. Kevin Drum, "CEO Pay: Still Skyrocketing, Still Undeserved," *Mother Jones*, October 3, 2011.

74. Ibid.

75. Mishel and Davis, "CEO Pay Continues to Rise."

76. Josh Harkinson, "CEO Pay Shoots Up at Expense of Workers," *Mother Jones*, April 5, 2011.

77. Allen, "How Germany Builds Twice as Many Cars."

78. Arek Sarkissian II, "Inflation Brings Boost to Minimum Wage in Fla.," *Tallahassee Democrat*, December 31, 2012.

79. Sara Lemos, "The Effect of the Minimum Wage on Prices," Institute for the Study of Labor, Discussion Paper No. 1072, March 2004, http://ssrn.com /abstract=524803. "Despite the different methodologies, data periods, and data sources, most studies found that a 10 percent U.S. minimum wage increase raises food prices by no more than 4 percent and overall prices by no more than 0.4 percent. This is a small effect."

80. Arthur MacEwan, "The Minimum Wage and Inflation," *Dollars & Sense*, July 2014.

81. Lemos, "Effect of the Minimum Wage."

82. Jeannette Wicks-Lim, "Minimum Wage Hikes Do Not Cause Inflation," *Truthout*, January 22, 2013.

83. Macewan, "Minimum Wage and Inflation."

84. Zeynep Ton, "Why 'Good Jobs' Are Good for Retailers," *Harvard Business Review*, January–February 2012.

85. Yahoo! Finance, "Costco Wholesale Corporation," accessed August 12, 2015, http://finance.yahoo.com/q/ks?s=COST+Key+Statistics.

86. Stacy Perman, "As Minimum Wages Rise, Businesses Grapple with Consequences," *New York Times*, February 5, 2014.

87. Rick Ungar, "Walmart Pays Workers Poorly and Sinks While Costco Pays Workers Well and Sails—Proof That You Get What You Pay For," *Forbes*, April 17, 2013.

88. Ton, "Why 'Good Jobs' Are Good"; Andrés Cardenal, "Why Costco Is Crushing Wal-Mart," *Motley Fool*, September 5, 2014.

89. *Forbes*, "America's Best Employers," accessed August 12, 2015, http://www .forbes.com/best-employers/list/.

90. Brad Stone, "Costco CEO Craig Jelinek Leads the Cheapest, Happiest Company in the World," *Bloomberg Businessweek*, June 6, 2013.

91. Philip Mattera, "Wal-Mart: Corporate Rap Sheet," Corporate Research Project, accessed August 12, 2015, http://www.corp-research.org/wal-mart.

92. UFCW, "Costco an Example of the 'Union Difference,' " blog post, October 23, 2013, http://www.ufcw.org/2013/10/30/costco-an-example-of-the-union -difference/; Chaz Bolte, "NLRB Decisions Admonish Walmart, McDonald's for Retaliatory Behavior, Union Obstruction," We Party Patriots, January 9, 2015.

93. Ungar, "Walmart Pays Workers Poorly."

94. Leonardo Becchetti, Stefano Castriota, and Ermanno C. Tortia, "Productivity, Wages and Intrinsic Motivations," *Small Business Economics* 41, no. 2 (August 2013): 379–99, doi:10.1007/s11187-012-9431-2.

95. Ton, "Why 'Good Jobs' Are Good."

96. Dante Atkins, "The 6 Most Ridiculous Arguments Against the Minimum Wage, Debunked," *ATTN:*, April 1, 2015.

97. Mitch Morrison, Angel Abcede, and Kelly Kurt Brown, "On the QT," *CSP Magazine*, March 2013.

98. Ibid.

99. Wikipedia, "QuickTrip," accessed August 12, 2015, http://en.wikipedia.org /wiki/QuikTrip#cite_note-9.

100. Morrison et al., "On the QT."

101. Ibid.

102. Kelly Kurt Brown, "Respecting QuikTrip: Top-Notch Convenience Retailer Is Competition, but Also Inspiration," *Convenience Store and Fuel News*, March 14, 2013.

103. Martin Michaels, "Expert: Fast-Food Industry Could Survive Giving Employees Living Wages," Mintpress News, August 6, 2013; Seth Lubove, "Youngest American Woman Billionaire Found with In-N-Out," *Bloomberg Business*, February 4, 2013; Caleb Melby, "Why In-N-Out Heiress Lynsi Torres Isn't a Billionaire Yet," *Forbes*, March 6, 2013.

104. Lubove, "Youngest American Woman Billionaire"; Steven Rosenfeld, "Fast Food Restaurants Don't Need to Pay Starvation Wages," *Salon*, September 11, 2013, reposted from Alternet.

105. "In-N-Out Burger Benefits," Glassdoor.com, accessed November 2, 2015, http://www.glassdoor.com/Benefits/In-N-Out-Burger-US-Benefits-EI_IE14276.0 ,15_IL.16,18_IN1.htm.

106. Clare O'Connor, "Best Places to Work in Retail in 2015: Costco, In-N-Out and More," *Forbes*, December 15, 2014.

107. "In-N-Out Burger Rated No. 1 in Customer Satisfaction Survey," QSR Web, January 28, 2009.

108. Wikipedia, "In-N-Out Burger," accessed August 12, 2015, http://en.wikipedia.org/wiki/In-N-Out_Burger#cite_note-sfgate-11.

109. Stacy Perman, "As Minimum Wages Rise, Businesses Grapple with Consequences," *New York Times*, February 5, 2014; Stacy Perman, "In-N-Out Burger: Professionalizing Fast Food," *Bloomberg Businessweek*, April 8, 2009.

110. Douglas McIntyre and Samuel Weigley, "8 Companies That Most Owe Workers a Raise," *USA Today*, May 13, 2013.

111. Michaels, "Expert: Fast-Food Industry Could Survive Giving Employees Living Wages."

112. John R. Shermerhorn, *Exploring Management* (New York: John Wiley & Sons, 2012), C-36.

113. Perman, "In-N-Out Burger: Professionalizing Fast Food."

114. Cooperative Home Care Associates, internal report, 1993.

115. Ibid.

116. Ibid.

117. Laura Flanders, "How America's Largest Worker Owned Co-Op Lifts People Out of Poverty," *Yes! Magazine*, Fall 2014.

118. Ibid.

119. Deanna Beebe, "PHI Founder and Past President Steven Dawson Recognized as 'Cooperative Hero,'" PHI National, November 15, 2012, http://phinational.org/blogs/phi-founder-and-past-president-steven-dawson-recognized-cooperative-hero.

120. Flanders, "How America's Largest Worker Owned Co-Op"; Independence Care System, IRS form 990, 2013, accessed January 25, 2016, www.guidestar.org/ViewPdf.aspx?PdfSource=0&ein=13-3964284.

121. Zeynep Ton, *The Good Jobs Strategy: How the Smartest Companies Invest in Employees to Lower Costs and Boost Profits* (Boston: New Harvest, 2014), 19; Adam Davidson, "Thinking Outside the Big Box," *New York Times*, January 5, 2014.

122. Ton, *Good Jobs Strategy*, 192–93, citing Steven Greenhouse, "How Costco Became the Anti-Wal-Mart," *New York Times*, July 17, 2005.

123. Ton, *Good Jobs Strategy*.

124. Adam S. Posen, "US Companies Pay Well and Do Better," Peterson Institute for International Economics, February 20, 2015, reprinted from the *Financial Times*.

125. Ton, *Good Jobs Strategy*, 16.

126. Zeynep Ton, "Retailers Should Invest More in Employees," *Harvard Business Review*, December 20, 2011.

127. Ibid.

128. Ibid.

129. Justin Bachman, "Southwest CEO's Cost Crusade: Haggling with Unions While Profits Soar," *Bloomberg Businessweek*, September 17, 2014.

130. Wikipedia, "Warren Buffett," accessed August 28, 2015, http://en.wikiquote.org/wiki/Warren_Buffett. Buffett also is a proponent of maximizing

employee performance. In the game of bridge, he said, "you behave in a way that gets the best from your partner. And in business, you behave in the way that gets the best from your managers and your employees."

131. Ton, *Good Jobs Strategy*, 200.

132. Ibid., 191.

133. Ton, "Why 'Good Jobs' Are Good."

134. Lindsey Rupp, "Gap Sees Job Applications Jump After Wage-Raise Pledge," *Bloomberg Business*, June 24, 2014.

135. John Ydstie, "Health Insurer Aetna Raises Wages for Lowest-Paid Workers to $16 an Hour," *All Things Considered*, NPR, April 30, 2015.

136. Martin Sandbu, "Why Walmart's Raise Is Good for Business," *Financial Times*, February 19, 2015.

137. Ton, "Why 'Good Jobs' Are Good."

8: Toward a Different Future: $15 and Beyond

1. Nick Hanauer and David Rolf, "Shared Security, Shared Growth," *Democracy*, Summer 2015.

2. Rakesh Kochhar and Rich Morin, "Despite Recovery, Fewer Americans Identify as Middle Class," Pew Research Center, January 27, 2014.

3. Amy Traub, David Callahan, and Tamara Draut, *Millions to the Middle: 14 Big Ideas to Build a Strong and Diverse Middle Class* (New York: Demos, 2012); Joseph E. Stiglitz, *Rewriting the Rules of the American Economy: An Agenda for Growth and Shared Prosperity* (New York: Roosevelt Institute, 2015); Lawrence H. Summers and Ed Balls, *Report of the Commission on Inclusive Prosperity*, Center for American Progress, January 15, 2015; Jacob S. Hacker and Nathaniel Loewenthiel, *Rebuilding Prosperity: Building an Economy for All*, Prosperity for All, September 2012, http://www.prosperityforamerica.org/wp-content/uploads/2012/09/prosperity-for-all.pdf.

4. National Women's Law Center, "Closing the Wage Gap Is Crucial for Women of Color and Their Families," April 9, 2015.

5. Abigail Bar-Lev, "Supporting the Paycheck Fairness Act Means Closing the Wage Gap for Working Women," National Women's Law Center, March 25, 2015.

6. MomsRising.org, "M: Maternity/Paternity Leave," accessed August 12, 2015, http://www.momsrising.org/issues_and_resources/maternity.

7. National Partnership for Women and Families, "The Healthy Families Act," fact sheet, February 2015, http://www.nationalpartnership.org/research-library/work-family/psd/the-healthy-families-act-fact-sheet.pdf.

8. Traub et al., *Millions to the Middle*.

9. Wikipedia, "List of Statutory Minimum Employment Leave by Country," accessed August 12, 2015, https://en.wikipedia.org/wiki/List_of_statutory_minimum_employment_leave_by_country.

10. Regarding "flexible jobs" and rights for part-timers, see Summers and Balls, *Report of the Commission on Inclusive Prosperity*.

11. Lydia DePillis, "The Next Labor Fight Is Over When You Work, Not How Much You Make," *Washington Post*, May 8, 2015.

12. Annie Sciacca, " 'Bill of Rights' for San Francisco Retail Workers Goes into Effect This Week," *San Francisco Business Times*, June 29, 2015.

13. Hanauer and Rolf, "Shared Security"; Steven Hill, *Raw Deal: How the "Uber Economy" and Runaway Capitalism Are Screwing American Workers* (New York: St. Martin's Press, 2015).

14. Neal Halfon, Shirley Russ, Frank Oberklaid, Jane Bertrand, and Naomi Eisenstadt, "An International Comparison of Early Childhood Initiatives: From Services to Systems," Commonwealth Fund, May 27, 2009.

15. Traub et al., *Millions to the Middle*; Stiglitz, *Rewriting the Rules*; Summers and Balls, *Report of the Commission on Inclusive Prosperity*; White House, "Fact Sheet: Helping All Working Families with Young Children Afford Child Care," January 21, 2015; and Children's Defense Fund, "Early Childhood Development and Learning," accessed August 12, 2015, http://www.childrens defense.org/policy/earlychildhood/.

16. Traub et al., *Millions to the Middle*; Stiglitz, *Rewriting the Rules*; Summers and Balls, *Report of the Commission on Inclusive Prosperity*; Catherine Rampell, "Data Reveal a Rise in College Degrees Among Americans," *New York Times*, June 12, 2013; and "How Does Germany Afford Free Tuition for All of Its Citizens?," *ATTN:*, March 27, 2015.

17. Suzanne Woolley, "The Retirement Savings Gap Between Haves and Have-Nots Is Getting Bigger," *Bloomberg Business*, March 12, 2015.

18. Brian Stoffel, "The Average American Has This Much Saved in a 401(k)— How Do You Compare?," *Motley Fool*, January 5, 2015; Vanguard, "How America Saves: 2014," accessed August 12, 2015, https://pressroom.vanguard.com/content /nonindexed/How_America_Saves_2014.pdf.

19. Stiglitz, *Rewriting the Rules*; Traub et al., *Millions to the Middle*.

20. Sarah Anderson and Scott Klinger, "A Tale of Two Retirements," Center for Effective Government and Institute for Policy Studies, October 28, 2015, http://www.foreffectivegov.org/two-retirements.

21. Monique Morrissey, "Private-Sector Pension Coverage Fell by Half over Two Decades," Economic Policy Institute, January 11, 2013.

22. Anderson and Klinger, "Tale of Two Retirements," 3.

23. Traub et al., *Millions to the Middle*; Stiglitz, *Rewriting the Rules*; Hacker and Loewenthiel, *Rebuilding Prosperity*.

24. White House, "Health Care That Works for Americans," accessed August 12, 2015, https://www.whitehouse.gov/healthreform/healthcare-overview.

25. Stiglitz, *Rewriting the Rules*; Ron Pollack, "What's Next for the Affordable Care Act? Life After King v. Burwell," *Health Affairs Blog*, June 29, 2015; White House, "Health Care That Works for Americans"; Ryan Cooper, "ObamaCare Is Working. Here's What's Next for Health Care Reform," *The Week*, April 7, 2015; Families USA, "A 50-State Look at Medicaid Expansion," July 2015, http://families usa.org/product/50-state-look-medicaid-expansion.

26. Traub et al., *Millions to the Middle*; Stiglitz, *Rewriting the Rules*; Summers and Balls, *Report of the Commission on Inclusive Prosperity*; Hacker and Loewenthiel, *Rebuilding Prosperity*.

27. American Society of Civil Engineers, "2013 Report Card for America's Infrastructure," accessed August 12, 2015, http://www.infrastructurereportcard.org/; Andrew Flowers, "Why We Still Can't Afford to Fix America's Broken Infrastructure," *Five Thirty Eight*, June 3, 2014.

28. Robert Pollin, Heidi Garrett-Peltier, James Heintz, and Bracken Hendricks, *Green Growth: A U.S. Program for Controlling Climate Change and Expanding Job Opportunities* (Washington, DC: Center for American Progress and PERI, 2014).

29. Hacker and Loewenthiel, *Rebuilding Prosperity*.

30. Traub et al., *Millions to the Middle*; Stiglitz, *Rewriting the Rules*; Summers and Balls, *Report of the Commission on Inclusive Prosperity*; Hacker and Loewenthiel, Congressional Progressive Caucus, "Principles for Trade: A Model for Global Progress," March 4, 2015, ; United Nations, "The Universal Declaration of Human Rights," accessed August 12, 2015, http://www.un.org/en/documents /udhr/; Adam Hersh and Jennifer Erickson, "Progressive Pro-Growth Principles for Trade and Competitiveness," Center for American Progress, March 11, 2014.

31. Stiglitz, *Rewriting the Rules*; National Employment Law Project, "Voices in Support: Fair Chance Gains Support Across the Spectrum," June 2015, http:// www.nelp.org/content/uploads/Voices-in-Support-Factsheet.pdf; Bruce Western, "The Impact of Incarceration on Wage Mobility and Inequality," *American Sociological Review* 67 (August 2002): 256–46; Bruce Western and Becky Pettit, "Incarceration & Social Inequality," *Daedalus*, Summer 2010, 8–19; Michelle Alexander, *The New Jim Crow: Mass Incarceration in the Age of Colorblindness* (New York: The New Press, 2010).

32. Stiglitz, *Rewriting the Rules*; Robert Lynch and Patrick Oakford, "The Economic Effects of Granting Legal Status and Citizenship to Undocumented Immigrants," Center for American Progress, March 20, 2013; Eunice Hyunhye Cho and Rebecca Smith, "How Immigration Reform Can Stop Retaliation and Advance Labor Rights," National Employment Law Project, February 2013.

33. William Lazonick, "Profits Without Prosperity," *Harvard Business Review*, September 2014, 46–55.

34. Nick Hanauer, "Why Capitalism Has Nothing to Do with Supply and Demand," *Making Sen$e* blog, PBS *Newshour*, July 28, 2014; Stiglitz, *Rewriting the Rules*; Summers and Balls, *Report of the Commission on Inclusive Prosperity*; Max Ehrenfreund, "The Fringe Economic Theory That Might Get Traction in the 2016 Campaign," *Wonkblog*, *Washington Post*, March 2, 2015.

35. Traub et al., *Millions to the Middle*; Stiglitz, *Rewriting the Rules*; Jared Bernstein and Jean Baker, "Full Employment: Don't Give It Up Without a Fight," Economic Policy Institute, January 2, 2002.

36. Jana Kasperkevic and Graeme Wearden, "Federal Reserve Puts Rate Rise on Hold—as It Happened," *The Guardian*, September 17, 2015.

37. "Minimum Wage Basics: Public Opinion on Raising the Minimum Wage," National Employment Law Project, May 2015.

38. Martin Gilens and Benjamin I. Page, "Testing Theories of American Politics: Elites, Interest Groups, and Average Citizens," *Perspectives on Politics* 12, no. 3 (September 2014): 564–81.

39. Josh Silver, "Discovered: A Cure for Political Corruption," *Huffington Post*, March 19, 2013; Every Voice, "Solutions: Our Plan," accessed August 12, 2015, http://everyvoice.org/solutions; Hacker and Loewenthiel, *"Rebuilding Prosperity"*; Jonathan Shaw, "A Radical Fix for the Republic," *Harvard Magazine*, July 2012, 46–55; Lawrence Lessig, *Republic, Lost: How Money Corrupts Congress—and a Plan to Stop It* (New York: Twelve, 2011).

40. Albert Wenger, "Labor Day: Right to an API Key (Algorithmic Organizing)," *Continuations*, September 1, 2014.

41. Hanauer and Rolf, "Shared Security"; Hill, *Raw Deal*.

Afterword: Something's Happening

1. Kenneth Lovett, "Andrew Cuomo Rejects Assembly Democrats' Plan to Raise Minimum Wage to $15 an Hour in 2018," *New York Daily News*, March 12, 2015.

2. Zeeshan Aleem, "New York Governor Andrew Cuomo Just Proposed a $15 Statewide Minimum Wage," *Mic*, September 10, 2015.

3. Jesse McKinley, "Cuomo to Raise Minimum Wage to $15 for All New York State Employees," *New York Times*, November 10, 2015.

4. Teresa Tritch, "A Starting Wage of $15 an Hour: The New Normal?," *Taking Note* blog, *New York Times*, June 26, 2015.

5. Irwin Yellowitz, "Child Labor," 2009, http://www.history.com/topics/child-labor.

6. Talal Al-Khatib, "Why Do We Work Eight Hours a Day?," *Discovery*, May 1, 2015.

7. Sara Jones, "Why Are So Many Seattle Restaurants Closing Lately?," *Seattle Magazine*, March 4, 2015.

8. Tim Worstall, "Nick Hanauer's Near Insane $15 an Hour Minimum Wage Proposal," *Forbes*, June 21, 2013.

9. Mark J. Perry, "Seattle's New Minimum Wage Law Takes Effect April 1 but Is Already Leading to Restaurant Closings and Job Losses," American Enterprise Institute, March 14, 2015.

INDEX

Page numbers in italics represent figures.

Publishing in the Public Interest

Thank you for reading this book published by The New Press. The New Press is a nonprofit, public interest publisher. New Press books and authors play a crucial role in sparking conversations about the key political and social issues of our day.

We hope you enjoyed this book and that you will stay in touch with The New Press. Here are a few ways to stay up to date with our books, events, and the issues we cover:

- Sign up at www.thenewpress.com/subscribe to receive updates on New Press authors and issues and to be notified about local events
- Like us on Facebook: www.facebook.com/newpressbooks
- Follow us on Twitter: www.twitter.com/thenewpress

Please consider buying New Press books for yourself; for friends and family; or to donate to schools, libraries, community centers, prison libraries, and other organizations involved with the issues our authors write about.

The New Press is a 501(c)(3) nonprofit organization. You can also support our work with a tax-deductible gift by visiting www .thenewpress.com/donate.